T0265083

OPERA, TRAGEDY, AND NEIGHBOURING FORMS FROM
CORNEILLE TO CALZABIGI

Opera, Tragedy, and Neighbouring Forms from Corneille to Calzabigi

EDITED BY BLAIR HOXBY

UNIVERSITY OF TORONTO PRESS
Toronto Buffalo London

ISBN 978-1-4875-0351-2 (cloth)   ISBN 978-1-4875-1809-7 (EPUB)
                                    ISBN 978-1-4875-1808-0 (PDF)

Library and Archives Canada Cataloguing in Publication

Title: Opera, tragedy, and neighbouring forms from Corneille to Calzabigi /
  edited by Blair Hoxby.
Names: Hoxby, Blair, 1966– editor.
Description: Includes bibliographical references and index.
Identifiers: Canadiana (print) 2023052110X | Canadiana (ebook) 20230521223 |
  ISBN 9781487503512 (cloth) | ISBN 9781487518097 (EPUB) |
  ISBN 9781487518080 (PDF)
Subjects: LCSH: Opera – 17th century. | LCSH: Opera – 18th century. |
  LCSH: Tragedy – History and criticism.
Classification: LCC ML1703 .O64 2024 | DDC 782.109/032–dc23

Cover design: EmDash
Cover image: Detail from Corrado Giaquinto, *Medea*, c. 1750–52. National
Trust, Hinton Ampner Place. Credit: National Trust images.

We wish to acknowledge the land on which the University of Toronto Press
operates. This land is the traditional territory of the Wendat, the Anishnaabeg,
the Haudenosaunee, the Métis, and the Mississaugas of the Credit First Nation.

This book has been published with the assistance of the Dean of the
Humanities, Stanford University.

University of Toronto Press acknowledges the financial support of the
Government of Canada, the Canada Council for the Arts, and the Ontario Arts
Council, an agency of the Government of Ontario, for its publishing activities.

Contents

Illustrations

Musical Examples

Figures

Acknowledgments

Mark Thompson demonstrated an interest in and support for this volume from its earliest state as a proposal. The anonymous readers for the press made an abundance of useful suggestions, large and small. Audrey Senior helped to edit the entire volume in its first stages. Melanie Kessinger helped to re-edit it in revised form; she also drew my attention to the painting used as a cover image. Stefanie Tcharos made useful comments on the introduction. Phoebus Alexander Cotsapas corrected and improved some of the French transcriptions and translations in chapters 1 and 2. I am grateful for permission to reprint in revised form portions of "All Passion Spent: The Means and Ends of a *Tragédie en Musique*," which initially appeared in *Comparative Literature* vol. 59, no. 1: 33–62. (Copyright 2007, University of Oregon. All rights reserved. Republished by permission of the copyright holder and the publisher, Duke University Press.) Leah Whittington kindly agreed to take photographs of items in Houghton Library, Harvard College. All the contributors have been patient and generous in their willingness to revise their own chapters and to respond to each other's contributions. Julia Karig Feinberg and Sabrina Yates read the proofs. As usual, I am grateful to my cats for their company. To my wife Caroline:

Le soir qu'Amour vous fist en la sale descender
Pour danser d'artifice un beau ballet d'Amour
Vos yeux, bien qu'il fust nuict, ramenerent le jour,
Tant ils sceurent d'esclairs par la place repandre.

OPERA, TRAGEDY, AND NEIGHBOURING FORMS FROM
CORNEILLE TO CALZABIGI

Introduction: Opera, Tragedy, and Neighbouring Forms in an Age of Quarrels

BLAIR HOXBY

During the period running from the formation of a regular French theatre under Cardinal Richelieu (1637–42) through to the dawn of German Idealism and Romanticism in the closing decades of the eighteenth century, critics almost universally assumed that opera and tragedy should be compared. Such comparisons might privilege one form above the other. They might warn against the dangers of cross-contamination. Or they might suggest how tragedy or opera could be reformed or renewed by transplanting something valuable from the neighbouring terrain. But they almost always assume that opera and tragedy are in dialogue and, at least potentially, in competition.

We can get a sense of the tenor and tone of these critical debates by sampling the views of three of the period's most eloquent and persuasive camps. To refer to these controversialists as belonging to camps may be too schematic since they did not necessarily read each other or identify with established parties, but doing so lets us take the lay of the land.

In the first camp, we might place André Dacier, the perpetual secretary of the Académie française, who insisted in his commentary on the *Poetics* (1692) that although a cursory examination of Aristotle might suggest that music was essential to tragedy, its part in Greek tragedy was, in fact, a cultural accident: "Il faut même avoüer que nous ne comprenons pas bien, comment la musique a pû jamais être considerée, comme faisant en quelque sorte partie de la Tragedie, car s'il y a rien au monde qui paroisse étranger & contraire même à un action Tragique, c'est le chant" (I must confess, I could never well understand, how music came to be considered as making in any respect a part of tragedy; for if there be any thing in the world that appears stranger, and more contrary than another, to tragic action, it

is song).[1] Music and dance, thought Dacier, survived in Greek tragedy as mere artefacts of the superstitious ceremonies from which
tragedy had developed.[2] The concerns of Charles de Saint-Évremond,
reputed to be the most cultured man of his age, ran even deeper. In
his famous letter on the opera (which may have been composed as
early as 1669–70 but was not published until after his death in 1703),
he recalls some of the earliest operas performed in Paris before his
own exile to England. What vexes him most about his contemporaries' fondness for opera, he confesses, is that operas threaten to ruin
one of France and England's greatest treasures, tragedy.[3] The English
critic and dramatist John Dennis – who is perhaps best remembered
as a theorist of the sublime – could not have agreed more. In his 1706
An Essay on the Opera's after the Italian Manner, Dennis predicted that
the English stage was likely to be overthrown by opera. "Thus unless
we use timely Prevention," he warned, "the *British* Muse is like to
meet with the same Fate that *Tithonus* is said to have done of old, who
had no other Fruit of his Immortality, than to see himself depriv'd,
by the length of Days, of all his Strength, his Spirit, and his tow'ring
Thoughts, and eaten and consum'd by the Jaws of Time, till nothing
remain'd of him but an empty Voice." To the mind of Dennis, opera
was a sensationalistic, lascivious, and enervating art form. "Nothing
can be more Gothic than an Opera," he concluded, "since nothing can
be more oppos'd to the ancient Tragedy, than the modern Tragedy in
Musick, because the one is reasonable, the other ridiculous; the one
is artful, the other absurd; the one beneficial, the other pernicious; in
short, the one natural, the other monstrous."[4]

Writing a decade later in 1714, and representing what we might describe as the second camp of controversialists, Pier Jacopo Martello
did not dismiss Dennis's contention that tragedy and opera were quite
different things, but he was far from ready to admit that opera was
pernicious per se. Martello was a librettist, tragedian, and founder of
the Bolognese colony of the Arcadian Academy, which was dedicated

1 Dacier, *La Poetique d'Aristote*, 86. All citations in this introduction refer to the 1733
   edition. The English translations generally follow the anonymous 1705 edition of
   Aristotle's Art of Poetry, which includes "Mr. D'Acier's Notes Translated from the
   French."
2 Dacier, *La Poetique d'Aristote*, 86–7.
3 Saint-Évremond, *Œuvres en prose*, 3: 164, translated in *Works of Monsieur de St.
   Evremond*, 2: 94.
4 Dennis, *Critical Works*, 1: 382, 386, 391–2.

to the renewal and reformation of Italian literature along neoclassical principles after the perceived decadence of the seventeenth century's Mannerist and Baroque styles – styles that Dennis might have lumped under the label of "Gothic." His ingenious and tongue-in-cheek dialogue *Della tragedia antica e moderna* (*Of Ancient and Modern Tragedy*) is set during a visit to Paris, where he exchanges views with an old man who claims to be Aristotle himself, preserved by a life-giving elixir. This setting allows Martello to compare not only ancient and modern but also French and Italian practices. Having heard most of what the pseudo-Aristotle has to say about the duties of a librettist, he exclaims in exasperation, "A quell che ascolto ... egli è più faticoso il far male che bene. Si suda meno a comporre una bouna che una cattiva tragedie, giacché deduco da' tuoi discorsi che il melodrama è po un'imperfetta imitazion de' migliori, e, in consequenza un'imperfetta tragedia ch non può vivere con applause fuor note e del canto" (From what I hear ... it takes less effort to write a good tragedy than a bad one, since, from what you say, I deduce that opera is an imperfect imitation of better dramas, and is hence an imperfect sort of tragedy that cannot win applause unless accompanied by music and singing). To this complaint, the pseudo-Aristotle responds firmly that his interlocutor's mistake is to attend the opera in the belief that poetry should play the chief part; she is a supernumerary of higher rank than painting and lower rank than singing.[5] For Martello, the competition between poet and composer that Saint-Évremond had perceived when he defined opera as "un travail bizarre de Poësie et de Musique, où le Poëte et le Musicien également gênés l'un par l'autre, se donnent bien de la peine à faire un méchant ouvrage" (an odd Medley of Poetry and Musick, wherein the Poet and Musician, equally confined one by the other, take a world of Pains to compose a wretched Performance) had to be resolved in favour of the composer: opera was drama in music.[6] To explain his idea of the proper relationship between music and poetry in an opera, Martello said that if the poetry could be conceived as a substance at all, it must be "come il colore, il quale non è che un sostanza di lume ... accomodata alla superficie a cui serve, dimodoché variamente riflessa, variamente appar colorita" (like color, which is but a luminous substance ... applied to a surface, which, as it reflects light

5 Martello, *Scritti critici*, 291–5, translated in Weiss, "Pier Martello on Opera," 399–401.
6 Saint-Évremond, *Œuvres en prose*, 3: 154, translated in *Works of Monsieur de St. Evremond*, 2: 87.

variously, so it appears variously hued).[7] We might consider Martello the most distinguished exponent of this second critical camp, which insisted that opera was at its most vital, was truest to itself, when it worried least about conforming to the "rules" of declaimed tragedy.

Ranieri Calzabigi and Christoph Willibald Gluck bear witness to a third point of view. These two are famous for their "reform" of opera. In their preface to *Alceste* (1769), likely written by Calzabigi but signed by Gluck, they recall Aristotle's famous comparison of conceiving a tragedy to designing a painting. We find a simple drawing in charcoal more pleasing than the most beautiful colours smeared at random on a white ground, says Aristotle (*Poetics*, 1450a39–b3). With this in mind, Calzabigi and Gluck write that they have restricted music to its true function "servire alla Poesie per l'espressione, e per le situazione della Favola" (of serving the poetry in the expression and situations of the story), considering that its effect should be "qual che sopra un ben corretto, e ben disposto disegno la vivacità de'colori, e il contrasto bene assortito de Lumi e dell'ombre, che servono ed animar le figure senza alterne i contorni" (like those which lively colors and judicious contrasts of light and shades have upon a correct and well-proportioned drawing, serving to animate the figures without altering the outlines).[8] In other words, they too see a potential conflict between poetry and music, tragedy and opera, but they propose to solve the problem by having the music serve the *mythos*, or plot. In their ideal, music, not poetry, provides the colours and the chiaroscuro.

Although these three positions do not capture the full range of contemporary opinion and controversy that swirled around opera from the mid-seventeenth to the early nineteenth centuries, they do stake out three of the most significant points of view taken in these quarrels: (1) that modern opera could prove the ruin of tragedy; (2) that opera and tragedy could only flourish if they staked out separate domains governed by distinct poetics; and (3) that lyric drama, if properly reduced to first principles and shorn of its excesses, represented modernity's best hope of recapturing the legendary power of ancient tragedy.

The first position was advanced by champions of declaimed tragedy from Saint-Évremond through the Italian historian and polymath Ludovico Antonio Muratori to Francesco Scipione, marchese di Maffei,

---

7 Martello, *Scritti critici*, 294, translated in Weiss, "Pier Martello on Opera," 401.
8 Gluck [and Calzabigi], *Alceste* (1769), preface, translated in Weiss, *Opera: A History in Documents*, 119.

author of the most famous Italian tragedy of the century, *Merope* (1713). The second was often maintained by practical men of the theatre, from impresarios to dramatists to librettists. Neither Martello nor Voltaire's disciple Jean-François La Harpe, for example, believed that tragedians should strive for operatic effects or that the opera house, where music reigned, could be expected to stage plots like those found at the theatre. Some version of the third thesis was espoused, with many variations, by a long line of reformers in the eighteenth century, including Apostolo Zeno, Denis Diderot, Pietro Metastasio, Francesco Algarotti, Jean-Jacques Rousseau, and Calzabigi. They wrote not of what opera was as a rule but of what opera could become in their hands. In some cases, they dreamed of an ideal union of French dramatic rules and Italian musical liberties. In others, they yearned for a revival of the pomp, solemnity, and simplicity of Attic theatre. Their beautiful theories were not always implemented in practice.[9] Yet the rapturous reception of Gluck's reform operas *Iphigénie en Aulis* (1773), *Orphée et Eurydice* (1774), *Alceste* (1776), and *Iphigénie en Tauride* (1779) proved that their dreams could be realized by the right genius working in the right conditions.[10] The abbé François Arnaud gushed that Gluck alone had rediscovered the dolour of the ancients.[11] One anonymous pamphleteer enthused, "Ici je me crois véritablement retourné au temps de l'ancienne Tragédie Grecque" (Here I truly believed myself to have returned to the time of ancient Greek tragedy).[12] Another professed, "Toutes les fois que je les entends je me vois rejetéau temps de l'ancienne Athènes, & crois assister aux representations des Tragédies de Sophocle & d'Euripide" (Every time I listen, I feel myself cast back to the days of ancient Athens, and I believe that I am sitting at a production of the tragedies of Sophocles and Euripides).[13]

This collection is titled *Opera, Tragedy, and Neighbouring Forms from Corneille to Calzabigi* on several counts. First, it supposes that the

---

9 The difference between theory and practice is often underlined by Bucciarelli, *Italian Opera and European Theatre.*

10 James Johnson, *Listening in Paris*, ch. 3, argues that Gluck's success was decades in the making, prepared by the development of a culture of sensibility and reconfigurations of the theatre – all of which led to a new culture of attentive listening and intense affective response.

11 Tiersot, "Gluck and the Encyclopedists," 355.

12 *Lettre sur Opéra d'Iphigénie* (1774) in Lesure, *Querelle*, 1: 70.

13 *Problême* (1777), in Lesure, *Querelle*, 1: 245. On Gluck's loss of prestige as an interpreter of Greek tragedy in the early twentieth century, see Goldhill, *Victorian Culture*, ch. 3.

relationship between opera and tragedy during this time span (1641–1784) was a two-way street. For while the era saw incessant calls to reform opera on the model of tragedy, the staged action of operas also inspired tragedians to innovate in declaimed tragedy, expanding the scope for pageantry, spectacle, and performed rituals. The names Corneille and Calzabigi should remind us, in the second place, that the relationship of opera and tragedy was negotiated against a whole series of literary and musical controversies (usually known by the French term *querelles*) that commenced with the *querelle du Cid* (provoked by Corneille's masterful tragedy about Spain's legendary liberator) and ended with the *querelle des Gluckistes and des Piccinnistes* (stirred up by the revolutionary ideas of Gluck and Calzabigi). A brief rehearsal of these controversies may orient readers.

The *querelle du Cid* kicked off when Cardinal Richelieu invited the newly created Académie française to evaluate the merits and demerits of the play. Jean Chapelain spoke for the Académie, a fellow dramatist Georges de Scudéry stuck in his own oar, and Corneille did his best to defend his play. From this controversy emerged many "rules" of French regular tragedy. Although Corneille protested all his life against the inconveniences of respecting the three unities of action, time, and place as well as an over-refined standard of *bienséance* (decorum) – so many beauties sacrificed on the altar of reason! – he nevertheless went on to codify these rules in three of the century's most influential theoretical tracts.[14] These would prove consequential to the reception of both French *tragédie en musique* and Italian opera because they implicitly posed the question of whether these novel forms should respect the rules imposed on French tragedy, should be answerable to a different set of rules, or should be treated as self-legislating products of modern genius.

The *querelle du Cid* was succeeded by the *querelle des Anciens et des Modernes*. In France, this literary controversy is often said to date from 1687 to 1716, but its origins arguably date back several decades earlier to Marin Mersenne's *Questions inouïes ou récréation des savants* (*Unheard of Questions or the Recreation of Scholars*) (1634) and its repercussions

---

14 See Gasté, *La Querelle du Cid*; Dotoli, *Temps de préfaces*; and Civardi, *La querelle du Cid*. Corneille's theoretical tracts are "Discours de l'utilité et des parties du poème dramatique," "Discours de la tragédie et des moyens de la traiter selon le vraisemblable ou le nécessaire," and "Discours des trois unités d'action, de jour, et de lieu," all printed in Corneille, *Théâtre complet*, tom. 1, vol. 1: 51–94. On the emergence of French regular tragedy, see Bray, *Formation*; Lyons, *Kingdom of Disorder*; and Forestier, *Passions Tragique*.

were still being felt in the late eighteenth and nineteenth centuries with the emergence of a philosophy of history. In its first stage, it pit the Moderns, Charles Perrault and Bernard le Bovier de Fontenelle, against the Ancients, Jean Racine and Nicolas Boileau-Despréaux. Perrault's temerity in declaring that Lully and Quinault's *tragédie en musique Alceste* (1674) had excelled its Euripidean model drew Racine into the field. Racine maintained in his preface to *Iphigénie* (1674) that Perrault should be careful not to condemn what he did not understand. The poet was pleased to see, based on the reception of his own tragedy, that the taste of Paris agreed with the taste of Athens and that the same things that moved the tears of the ancients could elicit the tears of modern Frenchmen.[15] In succeeding generations, Jean de La Bruyère, Fénelon, Anne Dacier, Jonathan Swift, Alexander Pope, Montesquieu, Vico, Hume, Voltaire, Diderot, and Rousseau – a who's who of the Enlightenment – all entered the fray, which, in the English context, came to be known as the Battle of the Books. This quarrel turned on many of the great questions of the age. What was the relationship between rules and spontaneity, between conventions and genius? Could the arts progress, or were they destined to decline with the progress of science? What was the proper relationship between words and music, between melody and harmony? Could tragedy or opera teach us something about the origins of language? Were art forms like tragedy and opera naturally inflected as masculine and feminine, free and slavish, virtuous and lascivious?[16]

Yet another series of quarrels set Italian music against French music and Italian librettos against French tragedies and the French equivalent of librettos, *livrets*. The first, waged from 1702 to 1706, pit the abbé Raguenet, a champion of Italian music, against the nobleman Le Cerf de la Viéville, who leapt to the defence of French poetry and music alike.[17] The second, which lasted from 1752 to 1754, is commonly said to have been sparked by a performance of Giovanni Battista Pergolesi's comic intermezzo *La serva padrona* (*The Servant Mistress*) by an Italian troupe that was temporarily allowed to perform at the Opéra, the traditional shrine of *tragédie en musique* as it had been codified by Quinault and Lully. When Friedrich Melchior Grimm published *Le petit prophète de Boehmischbroda*

---

15 Racine, préface to *Iphigénie* in *Œuvres complètes I: Théâtre-Poésie*, 699.
16 Key texts are gathered in Lecoq, *La Querelle des Anciens et des Modernes*. See Fumaroli, "Les abeilles et les araignées"; Buford Norman, "Ancients and Moderns, Tragedy and Opera"; and Larry F. Norman, *Shock of the Ancient*.
17 See Raguenet and LeCerf, *La Première Querelle de la musique italianne*; Naudeix, "Introduction"; and for a broader chronological selection, Fubini, *Music and Culture*, ch. 2.

(*Boehmischbroda's Little Prophet*) a few months later, it elicited twenty-five responses. Jean-Jacques Rousseau's more provocative *Lettre sur la musique française* (*Letter on French Music*) (1753) prompted over thirty replies. Throughout this quarrel, the restrained style of French *tragédie en musique* and the melodically uninhibited style of Italian opera were aligned with a whole series of binary oppositions in which the preferred values of the Encyclopaedists – including personal and political liberty – were often aligned with Italian music.[18] Between 1774 and 1781, a third quarrel erupted between the champions of Niccolò Piccinni and Gluck, with admirers of the Italian composer praising the beauty and grace of his compositions and the champions of Gluck declaring that he had recovered the visceral power of ancient tragedy.[19] The Piccinnist Jean-François Marmontel observed that if the tastes of the Gluckists were right, then Parisians should prefer Shakespeare to Racine, yet they did not.[20] La Harpe grumbled that the principles of the Gluckists would confuse opera and tragedy and thus pervert both theatrical forms.[21] When the title of this book invokes the names of Corneille and Calzabigi, then, it is not just invoking a tragedian and a librettist; it is summoning up representatives of French tragedy and Italian opera, the two most prestigious theatrical traditions in Europe, and it is demarcating the beginning and the end of a great age of literary and musical controversies.

The "neighbouring forms" of our title remind us that the negotiation between opera and tragedy often took part through intermediaries. When Polonius introduces the players visiting Elsinore as "The best actors in the world, either for tragedy, comedy, history, pastoral, pastoral-comical, historical-pastoral, scene individable, or poem unlimited," he is being only a little foolish. Perhaps, if we take "scene individable" to refer to a play that respects the unities of action, time, and place and "poem unlimited" to refer to one that ranges, like most of Shakespeare's and a good many librettists', freely through time and space, he is even being shrewd.[22] To be sure, some humanists were Aristotelean purists who recognized no genres beyond tragedy, comedy, and epic – and these purists often objected to opera as an imperfect imitation of one of these, even as a monstrosity. But others recognized the possibility of far more extensive, complex, and evolving generic systems.

---

18 Key texts are gathered in Launay, *La Querelle des Bouffons*.
19 Lessure, *Querelle des Gluckistes*.
20 Lessure, *Qurelle des Gluckistes*, 1: 180–1; Fubini, *Music and Culture*, 370–1.
21 La Harpe, *Lycée* (1799–1805), 12: 195–8, translated in Fubini, *Music and Culture*, 377–8.
22 Shakespeare, *Hamlet*, 2.2.333–6.

Let us consider a handful of the neighbouring forms that served as ambassadors between tragedy and opera. The first in chronological terms was the fable or pastoral tragicomedy. In their prefaces and prologues to *Euridice* (1600), the first surviving opera, the poet Ottavio Rinuccini and the composers Jacopo Peri and Giulio Caccini, who published rival settings of the libretto, competed for the honour of having been the first to recover the style of singing used by the ancient Greeks when introducing songs into the presentations of their tragedies and other fables. Rinuccini even introduced Tragedy to sing the prologue.[23] Yet a long line of opera historians running through Nino Pirotta and Claude Palisca have insisted that early opera really emerged from more contemporary dramatic forms, such as the Ovidian fable (the key example being Angelo Polizano's 1480 *Orfeo*) or pastoral drama (such as Torquato Tasso's 1573 *Aminta* and Battista Guarini's 1589 *Il Pastor fido* [*The Faithful Shepherd*]).[24] In contemporary generic theory, the pastoral was sometimes considered an intermediate genre between tragedy and comedy and aligned with the satiric or woodland setting described by the Roman architect Vitruvius in his *De architectura* (*Ten Books of Architecture*) and illustrated by the Renaissance architect and scenographer Sebastiano Serlio in 1545.[25] When, as in the case of Guarini's *Pastor Fido*, it was treated not just as a fable but as a tragicomedy, the result could be a "mixed" drama that drew elements from both tragedy and comedy:

> Prende dall'una le persone grandi, non l'azione; la fauola verisimile ma non vera; gli affeti mossi, ma rintuzzati; il diletto non la mestizia; il pericolo non la morte. Dall'altra il riso non dissolute, le piaceuolezza modeste, il nodo finto, il riuolgemento felice, & sopro tutto l'ordine Comico.

---

23 Giulio Caccini, Dedication to *L'Euridice*, in Murata, *Strunk's Source Readings*, 100. Also see Jacopo Peri, Preface to *Le musiche sopra L'Euridice* in Murata, *Strunk's Source Readings*, 151–4; and Ottavio Rinuccini, Dedication to *Euridice* in Strunk, *Source Readings*, 367–8. On the use of prologues as generic signals, see Hanning, *Of Poetry and Music's Power*.

24 On the importance of contemporary dramatic forms to the birth of opera, see Pirotta and Poveledo, *Music and Theatre from Poliziano to Monteverdi*, ch. 1; Pirotta, "Temperaments and Tendencies"; and Palisca, "The Alterati." On the connection between pastoral and music more generally during the period, see Gerbino, *Music and the Myth of Arcadia*. On pastoral drama, see Greg, *Pastoral Poetry and Pastoral Drama*; Chiabò and Doglio, *Origini*; Loewenstein, "Guarini and the Presence of Genre"; Henke, *Pastoral Transformations*; Selmi, *"Classici e Moderni"*; Sampson, *Pastoral Drama*; Schneider, *Pastoral Drama and Healing*.

25 See Hewitt, *The Renaissance Stage*, 18–33.

... it takes from [tragedy] the great persons, but not the action, the plot which is verisimilar but not true, the passions which are aroused but blunted, pleasure but not sadness, danger but not death. From [comedy], laughter which is not dissolute, moderate pleasures, a fictional plot, a happy reversal, and above all the comic order.[26]

The appeal of pastoral as a dramatic foundation for opera is not hard to understand. Because it featured gods, nymphs, and shepherds from the distant past, when music was natural and speech almost poetic, it promised to make song verisimilar. Its indulgence of human passions – and especially of love and love melancholy – was as appealing as its complex, double plots and its *lieto fin*, or happy ending.

For the purposes of this book, what is important to recognize – and what Stefanie Tcharos demonstrates in chapter 4 – is that even eighteenth-century literati like the Arcadians took seriously the idea that a reformed opera might be resettled not only on the foundation of tragedy but also on a reformed version of pastoral. The affiliation between pastoral drama, early opera, and even *opera seria* only seems to be underlined by the fact that the moral censure that was aroused by pastoral drama – Cardinal Bellarmine told Guarini that his play had done as much harm to morals as the heresies of Luther and Calvin had done to religion – attached itself to opera without hesitation. Both forms were accused of sensuality, self-indulgence, and effeminacy.[27] The Arcadians seemed to be aware of the danger and, for that very reason, promoted a chastened version of pastoral drama. Yet, as Tcharos demonstrates, there was often a disjunction between the theoretical aspirations of the academy and the productions of court theatres and public opera houses.

A second neighbouring form, *tragédie en machines*, is the subject of Hélène Visentin's chapter 1. This genre sought to incorporate the impressive stage machines of Italian opera into a dramatic form that would be more palatable to Parisian audiences than were the first, full-blown Italian operas performed in the 1640s. Two of the most famous examples, Corneille's *Androméde* (1650) and *La Conquête de la toison d'or* (1660–1), combine declaimed verse alexandrines in the tradition of French regular tragedy with sung choruses, spectacular machine effects, and changes of scene with each act – thus showing the way for

---

26 Guarini, *Il Verrato* (1588), 19v, translated in Weinberg, *History of Literary Criticism in the Italian Renaissance*, 1080.
27 Gerbino, *Music and the Myth of Arcadia*, 1–2.

tragédie en musique's synthesis of a recitative based on Racinian declamation, modest airs, and spectacles of choral song, dance, and wondrous machine effects.

Dramma giocoso, the subject of Pervinca Rista's chapter 10, can be seen
as an attempt to combine elements of tragedy and comedy much as
Guarini had. Taking the conventions of *opera seria* as his starting point,
Carlo Goldoni involved illustrious character-types (*parti serie*) in plots
that depended for their resolution on the actions of the peasants, servants, buffoons, and other dramatis personae typical of comic opera
(*parti buffe*). He also played against conventional expectations, demonstrating that aristocrats could be buffoons, that servants could be noble at heart, and that humanity shared certain universal values. Early
examples include Goldoni's *Il filosofo di campagna* (*The Country Philosopher*) (set by Galuppi in 1754) and *La buona figliuola* (*The Good Daughter*)
(set by Egidio Duni in 1756 and by Niccolò Piccinni in 1760). Lorenzo
Da Ponte and Wolfgang Amadeus Mozart's *Don Giovanni* (1787) is a late
masterpiece of the genre. *Drammi giocosi per musica* exploit both tragic
and comic conventions in the interest of creating a new realistic drama
suited to a changing society in which class hierarchies could no longer
be taken for granted and were no longer assumed to be immutable.[28]

The prize for the worst-named neighbouring form must surely go
to Vittoria Alfieri, who attempted to introduce the novel and monstrous *tramelogedia*. Alfieri accepted Voltaire's verdict that opera had
killed tragedy for Italians, but he hoped to lead his audiences back to
tragedy gently by way of this hybrid form, which he declared to be
neither tragedy, nor comedy, nor pastoral. Opera-tragedy might be the
plainest name for it, he admitted, but he preferred his own neologism.
Alfieri suggested that the religious cults of the Egyptians, Persians,
Jews, Chaldeans, Arabs, Indians, Celts, Scots, Mexicans, and Peruvians
could furnish the matter for his novel genre because – remote in time
or geography – they were abundantly provided with the marvelous.
Tramelogedia would require the protection of princes, he predicted, because it required two separate acting companies – one expert in tragic
action, another in singing. Alfieri's sole experiment in the form, his
1796 *Abele*, consists of a through-sung first act, a declaimed second act,
two mixed acts, and a declaimed fifth act. Alfieri himself declared that
tramelogedia was inferior to "true" tragedy. But he hoped that it might
serve as an emissary between opera and tragedy: "l'Opera gli animi

---

28 See Heartz, "Goldoni"; Marinelli, *Goldoni as Experimental Librettist*; Emery, *Goldoni as
Librettist*; and Rista's chapter 10 in this volume.

snerva e degrada; la Tragedia gl'innalza, ingrandisce e corrobora. Possa dunque la tramelogedia preparare in parte questo necessario e prezioso cangiamento, per cui gl'Italiani dalla loro effeminatissima Opera alla virile Tragedia salendo, dalla nullità loro politico alla dignità di vera Nazione a un tempo stesso s'innalzino" (Opera debases and enfeebles the mind, while tragedy uplifts, ennobles, and fortifies it. May tramelogedy thus partly pave the way for this necessary and important change, whereby Italians, rising from their effeminate opera to the virility of tragedy, will similarly arise from the nullity of their political condition to the dignity of a true nation).[29] Alfieri's monstrous experiment lies outside the chronological reach of this collection, but the terms the poet employs when describing his aims testify to the continuing vitality of the century's earlier debates about the proper relationship between opera, tragedy, and their neighbouring forms.

Opera, Tragedy, and Neighbouring Forms unfolds as a series of case studies that tell a story. It opens with Hélène Visentin's analysis of two machine plays, Jean Desmarets de Saint-Sorlin's tragicomedy *Mirame* (1641) and Pierre Corneille's *Andromède* (1650). The former was commissioned by Cardinal-Duke de Richelieu, Louis XIII's chief minister (1624–42), as part of his ambitious scheme to reform French theatre and, in so doing, to create an illusion of power that could further the aims of a centralized state. To this end, Richelieu built the first permanent theatre in Paris able to support the deployment of the latest stage machinery from Italy: a proscenium arch, changeable scenes, and central, single-point perspective (known, fittingly, as *l'œil du Prince*, or the eye of the Prince, because only the monarch could see the scene in perfect perspective). In the history of French theatre, Richelieu may be best known for founding the Académie française (1635) and then asking its members to critique Pierre Corneille's *Le Cid* (1637). As we have already noted, the pamphlet war that ensued – known as the *querelle du Cid* – helped to regularize the French ideal of verisimilar theatre.[30] What is less often acknowledged about Richelieu's reform is the importance he attached to stage machinery. With the help of Cardinal Mazarin, his

---

29 Alfieri, *Opere*, 2: 345, translated in Fubini, *Music and Culture*. 264. On Alfieri's engagement with the views of Calzabigi, see Fabrizi, Ghidetti, and Mecatti, *Alfieri e Calzabigi*.

30 Gasté, *La querelle du Cid*; Dotoli, *Temps de préfaces*; Civardi, *La querelle du Cid*.

chief adviser and collaborator at the time, Richelieu recruited a student of Gian Lorenzo Bernini to create an artificial day (by means of a sun that would rise and set during the action of *Mirame*) that could reinforce one of the central tenets of the new, regular French theatre: the unity of time.[31]

When he became first minister to Louis XIII and Louis XIV after the death of Richelieu, Cardinal Mazarin decided to introduce the full splendour of Italian opera to Parisians. He was well qualified to do so, having supervised performances for the Barberini court in Rome.[32] In 1645, he invited a troupe of musicians to perform Sacrati's *La Finta Pazza*, composed in Venice in 1641. Neither the librettist, nor the composer, nor the singers were what held the audience spellbound; the marvelous stage machinery of Giacomo Torelli did.[33] Luigi Rossi's 1647 *Orfeo*, a *comédie à machines* set to music in the style of Italy, dazzled the royal circle but drew criticisms for its reliance on Italian, its generic admixture, and its extravagant expense. Hoping to salvage something from his outlay, Mazarin commissioned Corneille to write a play in the French tradition that could reuse the sets of *Orfeo*. The result was *Andromède* (1650). This play is a landmark in the historical relationship between French declaimed tragedy and Italian opera.[34] As Visentin argues, the subject was natural for a tragedy: it involves noble characters, a conflict between family members (or *philoi*), and a moral dilemma. Yet it was also the perfect vehicle for the deployment of spectacular machines. Its more marvelous episodes, such as Perseus's flight on Pegasus and his battle with the sea monster, seemed to draw the line between what could be accepted in a declaimed tragedy and what could pass at the opera. If we ask ourselves which aspect of Italian opera seemed most useable to Corneille in this project – the spectacle or the music – the resounding answer is the spectacle. Corneille confined the music to short vocal expressions of pathos and to choruses that were meant to mask the sound of the machines when gods appeared.

In chapter 2, I take up a subsequent episode in the emulous rivalry of tragedy and opera: the invention and codification of *tragédie en musique*, a hybrid of French declaimed tragedy, Italian opera, *tragédie en*

---

31   On the artificial day, see Riggs, "Artificial Day"; Lyons, *Kingdom of Disorder*, ch. 4; Hoxby, "Technologies of Performance," 164–70. On Bernini's theatrical activities, see Tamburini, *Bernini e il teatro dell'arte*.

32   Mamczarz, *Le théâtre Barberini*.

33   On Torelli, see Bjurström, *Giacomo Torelli and Baroque Stage Design*; Milesi, *Giacomo Torelli*.

34   See esp. Kintzler, *Poétique de l'opéra français* and *Théâtre et opéra à l'âge classique*.

machines, and *ballet de cour*.[35] The first to envision its potential was
Pierre Perrin. Writing to Cardinal della Rovera in 1659, he reported
that "[a]prés avoir vue plusieurs fois tant en France qu'en Italie la representation des Comedies en Musique Italiennes, lesquelles il a plu aux
compositeurs, & aux executeurs de déguiser du nom *d'Opre*" (having
seen several times, in France as well as Italy, performances of the Italian
dramas in music, which the composers and producers have taken to
calling *Opre*), he had not despaired of creating some very fine ones in
the French tongue, works that would be well received in spite of the
weaknesses of the Italian ones. Perrin believed that the Italian operas
of Giulio Rospigliosi, Luigi Rossi, and Monteverdi's Venetian protégé
Cavalli (all staged in Paris by Mazarin) had been met with only a lukewarm reception in Paris because their Italian recitative was too tedious,
their arias too long and elaborate, their plots too involved, and their
reliance on castrati to play both lovers and ladies too improbable and
distasteful. Yet he believed that opera could be adapted to French taste
because it had the potential to express the passions in a more touching
manner and to impress the imagination and the memory more forcibly than declaimed theatre could.[36] The Académie Royale de Musique,
which Perrin and Robert Cambert directed from 1669 until Louis XIV
revoked their *privilège* in 1672, demonstrated that French opera was not
an impossible monster, but posterity has concurred with Louis de Cahusac that because Perrin and Cambert did not even begin to realize
the full potential of the genre, their successors to the *privilège*, Philippe
Quinault and Jean-Baptiste Lully, really deserve the credit for inventing
tragédie en musique.[37]

Quinault and Lully were intent on differentiating the new genre from
the Italian operas that had been performed in Paris. After commencing
their *tragédies en musique* with an allegorical prologue, they presented
the dramatic action itself in five acts that culminated in *divertissements*:
spectacles of choral song, dance, and spectacular machine effects that
drew on the traditions of both the native *ballet de cour* and the Italian *intermedio*. When selecting subjects, Quinault looked for ones that would
lend themselves to eruptions of the marvelous, magical, or infernal
so that he could integrate these *divertissements* into the action without

---

35 For a brisk review of these earlier forms, see Demuth, *French Opera*, chs. 1–4.
36 Perrin, *Œuvres*, 277–8, translated in Auld, *The "Lyric Art" of Pierre Perrin*, 1: 102–8.
     Auld provides extensive commentary.
37 Cahusac, *La Danse*, 197. All references in the introduction refer to the 2004 edition.

flouting the dramatic laws of necessity, propriety, and verisimilitude. In the eighteenth-century debate on whether myth or history provided the surest foundation for musical tragedy, Quinault's example weighed in favour of myth. Yet to those who were inclined to slight the new art form, Quinault and Lully were all too prone to bowdlerize the classics or to slip into gallantry and romance. For this reason, I focus on one of the most remarkable works to appear after Lully lost his monopoly on French opera, Thomas Corneille and Marc-Antoine Charpentier's *Médée*, which I interpret not only as a complex reading of Euripides's masterpiece but as an experiment in modern audiences' capacity to sit through gloom and horror in the opera house.

Voltaire did not share Racine's suspicion of the success of Quinault and Lully's upstart genre *tragédie en musique*. He believed that if works such as *Armide* or *Atys*, two of their best-known "poems," were recovered from antiquity, they would be idolized.[38] In chapter 3, Downing Thomas resists traditional accounts of French classical tragedy, which depict the eighteenth century as a period of either aesthetic stagnation or adulteration. He also offers an alternative account of Voltaire's drive to introduce more action to French declaimed tragedy. Anglophone critics often attribute this program to Voltaire's exposure to Shakespearean tragedy during his visit to London – and there can be no doubt that the funeral of Julius Caesar and the Ghost of old Hamlet made a powerful impression on him.[39] But Thomas cogently observes that Voltaire's engagement with French *tragédie en musique*, which made far greater use of action and stage spectacle than was permitted according to the rules of regular French tragedy, was intense and lifelong. That he dreamt of producing a *Samson* with his great contemporary Jean-Philippe Rameau – "une tragédie dans le goût de l'antiquité" (a tragedy in the style of antiquity), an "opéra remplie des spectacle, de majesté et de terreur" (an opera filled with spectacle, with majesty and terror) – and did in fact compose seven *livrets*, is well documented.[40] What is revelatory in Thomas's chapter is the consistency with which Voltaire's dream to produce a theatrical experience rooted in scenes of intense distress, acute pain, visible violence, and crowded spectacles was inspired by the example of contemporary opera. These first three chapters trace the relationship between Italian opera, *tragédie en machines,*

---

38 Voltaire, *Siècle de Louis XIV*, in *Œuvres complètes*, vol. 13D, tome 6: 22.
39 See Lounsbury, *Shakespeare and Voltaire.*
40 Voltaire, *Œuvres complètes, Correspondance* 3: 333 (Letter D999, Feb. 2, 1736).

tragédie en musique, and declaimed tragedy from Corneille to its late apogee in Voltaire.

If the French believed they had something to learn from Italian scenographers and composers in the mid-seventeenth century, they felt increasingly confident in the last quarter of the century that they had surpassed Italian letters and even Italian opera. The dismissive judgments that Nicolas Boileau-Despréaux, René Rapin, Dominique Bouhours, and Saint-Évremond passed on Italian tragedy and opera stung literati such as Giovanni Mario Crescimbeni and Lodovico Antonio Muratori.[41] One of the aims of the Arcadian Academy, in which they became thought leaders, was to demonstrate to the French that Italian literature was as capable as any tradition of exhibiting good taste and sound principles. As Stefanie Tcharos acknowledges in chapter 4, that project would eventually lead some Arcadians, such as Apostolo Zeno and Pietro Metastasio, to respect the rules of tragedy, as far as was possible, when composing their librettos. Carlo Goldoni would say that Zeno was the first to understand that tragedies might be represented in lyrical verse without degrading the art form, while Ranieri de' Calzabigi (who would eventually break with Metastasio when explaining his own ideal of tragic opera) declared,

> I nostri drammi dopo che dal celebre Zeno e poi dal nostro Poeta [Metastasio] nella regolar forma in cui oggi si veggono sono stati ridotti, possono chiamarsi una perfetta imitazione della tragedie greche e latine, perché tutte le regole di queste vi sono esattamente osservante, a riserva dell'unità del luogo alla quale la perfezione a cui s' di nostri è giunta l'arte di rapidamente volger le scene, e la necessaria correzione degl'inevitabili difetti che produceva nelle tragedie antiche la troppo ristretta unità, han recato lodevole cambiamento.

> Our operas, after they had been reduced by the illustrious Zeno and later by our own poet [Metastasio] to the regular form in which they are seen today, can be called a perfect imitation of Greek and Latin tragedy – except for the unity of place, for which the perfection attained during our time in the art of scene changing and the necessary correction of the inevitable defects brought about in ancient tragedies by too restrained a unity, have rendered a praiseworthy change.[42]

---

41 See Bucciarelli, *Italian Opera and European Theatre*, ch. 5.

42 Goldoni, *Tutte le opere*, 1: 187; Calzabigi, *Scritti teatrale*, 1: 25, translated in Freeman, *Opera Without Drama*, 61.

Yet in 1690, as Tcharos reminds us, it did not seem inevitable to opera reformers that the libretto must be purified on the model of tragedy. It seemed equally plausible that pastoral drama, especially if it were purged of its most lascivious and erotic elements, could furnish a viable dramatic idiom. No lesser authority than Crescimbeni, the secretary of the Arcadian Academy, championed the merits of pastoral fables in the 1690s and praised Cardinal Pietro Ottoboni's *Adonia* as composed in the best antique taste.[43] Even as late as 1722, Johann Mattheson (singer, composer, music theorist, and close associate of Handel) could point to a Venetian pastoral tragedy of 1695 to maintain that François Raguenet was wrong to assert that French poets such as Quinault had set the standard of excellence for opera librettos.[44] In chapter 4, Tcharos takes as her case study *Gli equivoci in Amore, overo La Rosaura* (*Misunderstandings in Love, or Rosaura*), written by Giovanni Battista Lucini, composed by Alessandro Scarlatti, and sponsored by the same Pietro Ottoboni, now elevated to the papal throne as Alexander VIII. The occasion for the opera was a double wedding that cemented a union between the Ottoboni and three of Italy's most distinguished family lines: the Colonnas, the Zenos, and the Barberini. Tcharos's chapter examines the equivocal generic allegiances of reform opera – often torn between pastoral and tragic models – in this early stage. She argues that the generic ambivalence of the opera is not evidence of an aesthetic failure; it is integral to the social and cultural work that the opera was intended to perform.

Once Zeno retired as the poet laureate of the imperial court of Vienna and Metastasio was named as his successor, contemporaries coalesced around a literary-historical narrative. Zeno had served as a prophet of *opera seria* by establishing its conventions; Metastasio had elevated this imperfect form to the status of true tragedy. Zeno was the Aeschylus of modern *melodramma*, Metastasio its Sophocles and Euripides. Zeno was Italy's Corneille, Metastasio her Racine.[45]

43 Crescimbeni, *Comentarii*, 1: 234, translated in Freeman, *Opera Without Drama*, 21.

44 Mattheson, *Critica musica*, 1: 108, discussed in Freeman, *Opera Without Drama*, 50. Mattheson's comment comes in a lengthy footnote attached to his parallel French-German edition of Raguenet's *Comparison between the French and Italian Musick and Operas*, which appeared in English translation in 1709. For a recent critical edition, see Raguenet and Le Cerf de la Viéville, *La Première Querelle*.

45 Bettinelli, *Opere drammatiche del Sig. Abbate Metastasio*, preface; Giazotto, *Poesia mel-odrammatica*, 94; Napoli-Signorelli, *Storia critica de' teatri antichi e moderni* (1790), 10: 160–70; Arteaga, *Le rivoluzione del teatro musicale italiano*, 2: 67–73; Burney, *Memoirs of the Life and Writings of the Abate Pietro Metastasio*, 3: 326. See Freeman, *Opera Without Drama*, 55–6, 59, 72, 75.

A figure too often elided in these ivory miniatures of opera history is Zeno's pupil and protégé, Luisa Bergalli (1703–79), the first female librettist to write for a public theatre in Italy. (She was preceded in France by Louise-Geneviève de Saintonge (1650–1718), who composed two *livrets* set by the composer Henri Desmarets for the Académie de Musique.) In chapter 5, Francesca Savoia positions Bergalli at the intersection of several momentous cross-currents. Bergalli not only profited from Italy's advanced *conversazioni miste* (or "mixed conversations," the precursors of literary salons), but she also joined the Arcadian Academy while she was in her early twenties. As a controversialist and an editor, she championed the contributions of women to Italian literature. She also sought to reform Italian tragedy and opera according to Arcadian principles and the example of Racine, whom she translated. Her tragic opera, *Agide re di Sparta*, appeared the same year as Metastasio's maiden effort, *Didone abbandanata* (1724). Savoia argues that Bergalli's artistic solutions to the problem of writing an opera libretto – including her strategic use of arias to explore the psychology of her dramatis personae while maintaining the dramatic pace of her fable – owe little to the example of Zeno; instead, Bergalli independently discovers the formulae that Metastasio would eventually turn into conventions. Yet Savoia also argues that Bergalli brings an ethical orientation to her subject matter that is peculiar to her and co-involved with her sex. Bergalli's depiction of the passions, while broadly Cartesian, is gendered: her male dramatis personae display a vulnerability to their passions, while her female characters master their passions by relying on virtues such as patience, forbearance, generosity, and clemency.

Enrico Zucchi revisits the reputation of Bergalli's more famous and prolific contemporary, Metastasio, in chapter 6. Charles Burney's *Memoirs of the Life and Writings of the Abate Pietro Metastasio* (1796) reinforced the judgment of contemporaries that Metastasio was Italy's Sophocles and Euripides, but a critical sea change soon set in. In his *Vita* (*Life*) of 1806, Vittorio Alfieri (1749–1803) dismissed Metastasio as a court servant who entertained the aristocracy with erotic and pastoral idylls rather than exploring the potent political implications of ancient tragedy, with its emphasis on political liberty.[46] In his 1870 *Storia della letteratura italiana* (*History of Italian Literature*), Francesco De Santis undertook a similar, if more personal comparison, observing that whereas Metastasio's adoptive father, Gian Vincenzo Gravina, had written

---

46   Alfieri, *Vita scritta da esso*, 84.

five anti-tyrannical tragedies, the adoptive son had penned scenarios "manca di serietà interior" (lacking in intrinsic gravity).[47] This change of taste, bound up with the larger philosophical developments of German Idealism, Romanticism, and the philology of national literatures, has cast a long shadow, as Zucchi argues.

Metastasio's librettos are, in fact, intensely and earnestly engaged with the political discourse of the day. Zucchi demonstrates that Metastasio never endorses the absolutist doctrine that the king is not bound by the law; indeed, he criticizes the doctrine more frankly than Gravina ever did. Yet neither does Metastasio approve of the idea that the king is ultimately the servant of the people, as the Monarchomachs insisted. Instead, the monarch should exercise free agency while voluntarily submitting to natural law. The distinction between Metastasio's librettos and many of the declaimed tragedies of poets such as Gravina and Alfieri can be seen most clearly in stories centred on dilemmas like those faced by Lucius Junius Brutus, who condemned his sons to death during the Roman Republic in order that the law be strictly applied. This was a celebrated subject of declaimed tragedies in the eighteenth century. But Metastasio prefers scenarios in which a ruler demonstrates his freedom and power by showing clemency. To some Romantic critics, such plot resolutions allowed aristocrats to avert their eyes from the reality that life and politics involve tragic choices and violent collisions. To Metastasio's contemporaries, they were mirrors for princes who might otherwise conduct themselves like despots.

Madame de Staël, who compared Metastasio's librettos unfavourably to Alfieri's tragedies, complained that the colourless passions of his librettos were rooted in neither country nor time.[48] But that very quality may have accounted for their remarkable international success; his librettos were set by composers not only throughout Europe but in Tsarist Russia. Tatiana Korneeva pursues the politics of Metastasian opera in chapter 7 by examining the fortunes of *La Clemenza di Tito* (*The Clemency of Titus*) in two Russian productions, the first performed in Italian in 1742 for the coronation of Tsarina Elizabeth Petrovna, and the second sung in Russian for Tsarina Catherine II in 1778. The subject seemed fitting for Elizabeth because she had ascended the throne thanks to a coup d'état and spared those who opposed her. Nevertheless, because Peter

---

47 De Sanctis, *Opere*, 755.
48 Staël, *Corinne ou l'Italie*, 184. On the early-nineteenth-century reception of Metastasio, see Sozzi, *Da Metastasio a Leopardi*, 1–21.

the Great had said that only those worthy to rule should succeed to the throne, she had to demonstrate that she merited her position, that she was the Titus of Russia. Her production of *La Clemenza* was calculated to affirm symbolically her legitimacy as a ruler and her bona fides as an enlightened reformer.

When, some three decades later, Catherine II commissioned a new version of the opera, which became the first Russian tragedy in music with a chorus and ballets, she was in as much need of legitimation as Elizabeth had been, for she too owed her power to a palace revolt. The poet to whom she turned, Iakov Kniazhnin, had won the reputation of being Russia's Sophocles and Euripides on the strength of his first tragedy, a free adaptation of Metastasio's *Didone abbandonata*. Yet a few years after Catherine's reign began, he found himself condemned to death – officially on the charge of embezzling public funds, but perhaps more likely because of the anti-tyrannical sentiments of his tragedy *Olga* (1770). Korneeva suggests that the price of his pardon may have been his version of *La Clemenza di Tito*. Thus, in *realpolitik* and in the opera house, Catherine discovered the power of manipulating the collective emotions of an audience: she could first arouse fear at the severity of an impending punishment, then transform fear into wonder and gratitude with a display of clemency. In Catherine's reign, the theatre of criminal prosecution, judgment, and sentencing could exhibit the same plot development as a tragedy with a happy ending. In Korneeva's chapter, both Russian versions of *La Clemenza* attempt to resolve what Reinhart Koselleck defines as the great dilemma of the Enlightenment: how to unite moral and political action.[49]

Robert Ketterer takes up Georg Friedrich Handel's *Oreste*, which debuted in London during the critical *opera season* of 1734–5, in chapter 8. Whereas Handel had long enjoyed a virtual monopoly on the production of Italian opera in London, he now faced competition from a rival company, the Opera of the Nobility, under the patronage of Prince Frederick, heir to the throne. With his position as the leading composer in London in peril, Handel produced a remarkable season of revivals, new biblical oratorios, fresh operas based on scenarios drawn from Ariosto, and *Oreste*, a pasticcio opera based on Euripides's tragedy *Iphigenia among the Taurians*.

Ketterer takes a pragmatic approach to this season. Why did it make financial and marketing sense for Handel to propose this program

---

49 Koselleck, *Critique and Crisis*.

of old and new work? And what, in particular, would his audience have recognized and liked about the story of *Oreste*? To answer these questions, Ketterer must first confront our own disdain for pasticcios: because they reuse material, they are generally supposed to lack a genuine source of inspiration or a true unity of form and content. Ketterer maintains that in the case of *Oreste*, which consists entirely of music originally composed by Handel himself, the very familiarity of the score was a selling point – a reminder to London's audiences of all he had already achieved. Ketterer's chapter is also an exercise in classical reception studies. For he argues that most members of the audience would not have approached the scenario through Euripides's famous play but through mediating texts such as Ambrose Philips's 1712 *The Distrest Mother* and Lewis Theobald's 1731 *Orestes*. The very familiarity of the story allowed Handel and his librettist to cut the recitative to the bone, producing a compressed, almost allusive opera. In the context of its original season, *Oreste* formed part of a larger group – comprising *Ariadne in Crete*, *Oreste*, and *Ariodante* – that might be called she-tragedies: in each one, a distressed maiden is victimized by a tyrant reigning on what Ketterer describes as "the wild edges of the world."[50] Such she-tragedies marked a first step on the road toward the sentimental tragedies of the mid-eighteenth century.

Ranieri de' Calzabigi, best known for his collaborations with Christoph Willibald Gluck, revolted against opera's descent into sentimentalism. In chapter 9, Magnus Tessing Schneider examines the mixed reception of his experimental libretto, *Ipermestra o Le Danaidi* (*Hypermnestra or the Danaids*) (1778/1784). Describing it as a work "pieno di squallore, e di spaventosa melanconìa" (full of wretchedness and fearful melancholy) worthy of comparison to a tragedy by Aeschylus (words that might sound like high praise to our ears), critics complained that it marked a return to the barbarity that had ruled the opera house before the Arcadian reform. It presented improbable myth rather than verisimilar history, its scenes of horror and violence were insupportable, and its reliance on dance and stage machinery was excessive.[51] Calzabigi seems to have written the libretto so that it might be set by Gluck during a visit to Naples. But when the visit was cancelled after the death of Empress Maria Theresa, Calzabigi asked the castrato singer Giuseppe

---

50 On the relationship between Greek tragedy and she-tragedy, see Hall and McIntosh, *Greek Tragedy*, ch. 3; Hernandez, "Medaea in Petticoats."
51 Moreschi, "Osservazioni sopra l'*Ipermestra*," 141.

Millico to set it. Gluck, meanwhile, had the libretto adapted for the French stage. The huge cast required for a full production prevented it from ever being realized at the Teatro San Carlo in Naples, but the significance of the composition was not lost on contemporaries. Here was an opera that sought to revive the tradition of Aeschylean tragedy. What's more, it emphasized, not pity, as Metastasian librettos had, but terror as its principal affect. When treating the same myth, Metastasio had omitted Ipermestra's murderous sisters and their bridegrooms; indeed, he had avoided death altogether. To some critics who valued Metastasio for removing every tincture of horror and tragic gloom from the opera house, Calzabigi's libretto marked a step backward in the progress of the arts. We may be more inclined to appreciate it as a tentative step toward the reinterpretation of tragedy that would be undertaken in the nineteenth and twentieth centuries by the likes of Richard Wagner, Friedrich Nietzsche, and Gilbert Murray, a reinterpretation that would emphasize the genre's roots in Dionysian intoxication and the absorption of the scattered individual by the collective.[52]

In the volume's concluding chapter, Pervinca Rista examines the engagement of opera with sentimental tragedy by considering Carlo Goldoni's *drammi giocosi per musica*. Whereas the Arcadian reforms of Zeno and Metastasio had sought to purge *opera seria* of its comic elements, and thus to erect a distinct barrier between tragedy and comedy, Goldoni's quest for a theatre of realism led him to reintroduce comedic elements to his libretto in the quest for a drama of social realism. It did not start that way. He tried and failed to write *opere serie* both as a young man and as an established author; he joined the Arcadian Academy; and he wrote fulsome praises of its most distinguished librettists, such as Metastasio. But a long path of experimentation led Goldoni to write *drammi giocosi per musica*, the precursors of Mozart and Da Ponte collaborations such as *Don Giovanni* (1787). He would eventually complete nearly fifty of them. These operas interweave tragic and comic elements, often distinguishing between the *parti serie* (normally played by aristocrats) and the *parti buffe* (normally played by servants or the middle classes), yet sometimes defying this alignment of social with generic hierarchy and sometimes compressing such distinctions

---

52 For key primary texts, see Wagner, *Art and Revolution* and *The Art-work of the Future* in *Richard Wagner's Prose Works*; Nietzsche, *The Birth of Tragedy*; Murray, "Excursus," in Harrison, *Themis*. For historical context, see Borchmeyer, "Wagner and Nietzsche"; Grey, *Richard Wagner and His World*; Silk and Stern, *Nietzsche on Tragedy*; Ackerman, *The Myth and Ritual School*; Arlen, *The Cambridge Ritualists*; Calder, ed. *The Cambridge Ritualists Reconsidered*; Henrichs, "Loss of Self, Suffering, Violence."

altogether in the *mezzo carattere*, or intermediate character. The results are realistic dramas that are "not in the rigorous and critical sense either tragedies or comedies," as Samuel Johnson observed separately of Shakespeare's plays,

> but compositions of a distinct kind; exhibiting the real state of sublunary nature, which partakes of good and evil, joy and sorrow, mingled with endless variety of proportion and innumerable modes of combination; and expressing the course of the world, in which the loss of one is the gain of another; in which, at the same time, the reveller is hasting to his wine, and the mourner burying his friend, in which the malignity of one is sometimes defeated by the frolick of another; and many mischiefs and many benefits are done and hindered without design.[53]

As should be apparent from this preview of *Opera, Tragedy, and Neighbouring Forms*, many, though by no means all, eighteenth-century critics asserted that opera had originated in the aspiration to recapture the legendary power of ancient tragedy – whether that power was attributed to its poetry, its music, its dance, its effective use of spectacle, or its union of all these arts – and could reach its full potential as an art form only by returning to the example of the ancients or by respecting the canons of French regular tragedy laid down by Corneille and Racine. Yet since the nineteenth century, some of the most influential historians of opera have denied a meaningful connection between the tragedy of the ancients and the efforts of seventeenth- and eighteenth-century composers to arrive at styles of musical text-setting that were intensely dramatic and expressive, styles that we have come to know collectively as the *stile rappresentativo*.[54] The classicist Michele Napolitano speaks for this interpretative tradition when he declares: "[T]hose who have cited the absolute irreducibility of the two cultural phenomena" – tragedy and opera – "must have hit the right mark." For the first operas were

---

53 Johnson, "Preface to Edition of Shakespeare" (1765) in D. Nichol Smith, ed., *Eighteenth Century Essays on Shakespeare*, 109–10.

54 These terms are not used with consistency in the seventeenth century, but G.B. Doni attempts to stabilize them in his *Trattato della musica scenica* (1633–5) and his *Annotazioni sopra il Compendio de' generi e de' modi della musica* (1640); see Carter, "Stile rappresentativo."

pastorals, and even Wagner is a "completely isolated example, the only case of a profound and original rethinking of the legacy of ancient tragedy" before the twentieth century.[55] The spectre of Friedrich Nietzsche lies behind historical narratives like these, which define tragedy and opera as inherently opposed modes of representation. In his 1872 *Die Geburt der Tragödie aus dem Geiste der Musik* (*The Birth of Tragedy*), Nietzsche measures the externalized operatic music of the Florentine Camerata against Schopenhauer's requirement that music be an immediate copy of the will itself and is therefore puzzled how such an imitation of phenomena could be received as a rebirth of true music.[56] Nietzsche maintains that because Renaissance Florentines could not sense the Dionysian depth of music, they turned to a word-and-tone rhetoric of the passions and a voluptuousness of song.[57] Wagner and Nietzsche believed that a similar decadence had occurred in the ancient world. In a note of 1849, Wagner jotted down that tragedy had been born from music with Aeschylus and had decayed with Euripides. Nietzsche went further, observing that whereas her older sister arts had passed away calmly and beautifully at a ripe old age, tragedy died a violent death at the hands of Euripides.[58] As Euripides watched Aeschylus in the theatre, he revolted in his role as thinker against the discordant and incommensurable elements of Aeschylean tragedy. Only one contemporary shared his scruples: Socrates.[59] With the philosopher as his ideal spectator, Euripides began his great struggle against tragedy.[60] He set about to separate the Dionysian element from tragedy and to reconstruct tragedy purely on the basis of an un-Dionysian art. Euripides transferred the entire world of sentiments, passions, and experiences into the souls of his stage-heroes. He founded his new art on *pathos*, not action.[61] Having rehearsed A.W.

---

55   Napolitano, "Greek Tragedy and Opera," 44, 40.

56   Nietzsche, *Birth of Tragedy,* 114.

57   Ibid., 115–16.

58   Borchmeyer, "Wagner and Nietzsche," 330; on the academic orthodoxy of this view by the time Nietzsche was writing, see Henrichs, "The Last of the Detractors," 373.

59   The ancient biographical evidence that links these two contemporaries is shaky at best, as Wilamowitz was prompt to object, but it suits Nietzsche's purpose to make allies of them. U. von Wilamowitz-Moellendorf, *Zukunftsphilogie!*, 48–50; Irwin, "Euripides and Socrates"; Henrichs, "The Last of the Detractors," 386–9.

60   Nietzsche, *Birth of Tragedy,* 76, 81. Kaufmann, *Tragedy and Philosophy,* remarks that "Since World II, Nietzsche's discussion of the death of tragedy has become more influential, and his ideas have become almost a commonplace." Kaufmann tries to show that they are "untenable" (163–6 at 164).

61   Nietzsche, *Birth of Tragedy,* 81, 83, 80, 84.

Schlegel's indictment of Euripides, Nietzsche denies him one of the few merits that Friedrich Schlegel had conceded, his musicality.[62] Euripides was, in fact, so unmusical, says Nietzsche, that he eagerly embraced the innovations of the New Dithyrambic poets, who transformed music into a virtuoso counterfeit of phenomena. Yet nowhere was the un-Dionysian nature of Euripides's plays plainer than in his dénouements, in which the hero, like a gladiator covered with wounds, was occasionally granted his freedom. Accepting F.W. Schelling's contentions that it is inappropriate for anything external to mitigate the bitterness of the hero's fate and that any misfortune that gods can ameliorate is not a genuinely tragic malady, Nietzsche complains that Euripides substitutes the *deus ex machina* for the metaphysical comfort that is proper to tragedy.[63]

Many critics and dramatists writing during our period (1641–1784) did not share Nietzsche's disesteem for Euripides. Indeed, they found in him a model for some of their very practices in the opera house. Let's take two cases in point: Euripides's lost *Andromeda* and his *Iphigenia among the Taurians*. The former was the tragedy that filled the character Dionysus in *The Frogs* with a fierce desire that threatened to consume him unless he could rescue Euripides from Hades (lines 52–4, 58–9). It was also the play that Alexander the Great was said to have recited spontaneously at his last banquet (Athenaeus, *Deipnosophistae* 537d–e). Early moderns would have had to base their idea of the play primarily on the parody of it that, as the ancient scholiasts observed, could be found in Aristophanes's *Women at the Thesmophoria* (lines 1008–132). Just enough could be inferred about the contents of *Andromeda* to be suggestive. It contained the striking spectacle of the forlorn Andromeda chained to the rocks, her flesh as white as a statue's. She lamented to the Night but, until a chorus of Ethiopian maidens arrived to lament in lyric dialogue with her, she was answered only by her voice echoing from the rocks (sung from offstage). She was eventually rescued by Perseus, who made a memorable entrance from the machine.

The importance that the French Jesuit critic René Rapin accords to *Andromeda* is telling. It is no surprise that Rapin should single out *Oedipus the Tyrant* to illustrate the power of carefully prepared recognitions

---

62 On Nietzsche's major debts to A.W. Schlegel, which are acknowledged handsomely in his lectures but suppressed in *Birth of Tragedy*, see Snell, "Aristophanes und die Ästhetik," 116; Henrichs, "The Last of the Detractors."

63 Schelling, *Philosophy of Art*, 89, 258; Nietzsche, *Birth of Tragedy*, 81, 83–4, 107, 109.

and reversals to subject an audience to a revolution of emotions. Yet he has scarcely finished demonstrating the efficacy of such a complex plot before he adduces an instance to prove that stage spectacle and music may grip the imagination just as forcefully: "Ce fût aussi par là que l'*Andromède* d'Euripide ... fit des effets si merveilleux en la ville d'Abdère" (And thus also it was, that the *Andromeda* of *Euripides*...wrought those wonderful Effects in the City of *Abdera*). Referring to a legendary performance of the tragedy by the Hellenistic actor Archelaus, Rapin says that "Les rôles de Persée et d'Andromède, le Malheur de cette princesse exposé au monstre marin, et tout ce qu'il y avait d'affreux et de pitoyable dans cette représentation, fit une impression si forte et si violente sur le people qu'il sortit du théâtre, dit Lucien, possédé, pour ainsi dire, de ce spectacle, et cette possession devint un maladie publique, don't l'imagination des spectateurs fût saisie" (the two Parts of *Perseus* and *Andromeda*, the Misfortunes of this Princess expos'd to the Sea-Monster, and all that mov'd *terrour* and *pity* in this Representation, made so strong and violent an impression on the people, *That they departed*, saith *Lucian, from the Theatre, possess'd (as it were) with the Spectacle, and this became a public Malady, wherewith the Imaginations of the Spectators were seiz'd).*[64]

Such accounts were enough to inspire numerous librettists to write versions of the tale based on what was known of the tragedy and on its retelling in Ovid's *Metamorphoses*. It was staged in Bologna as a "*Tragedia. Da recitarsi in Musica*" (1610); in Mantua, with a lost score by Monteverdi (1620); in Venice, where it was the first work to be staged in a public opera house (1637); in Ferrara, where it gave Francesco Giutti an occasion to employ his impressive stage machinery (1638); in Paris, where, as Visentin explains in chapter 1, it provided the vehicle for Corneille and Torelli's first attempt to adapt Italian opera and Venetian stagecraft to French tastes (1650); in Madrid, when the fourteen-year-old Infanta Maria Teresa, future wife of Louis XIV, commissioned Calderón de la Barca to produce the first fully sung Spanish opera (1653); and in Paris, where Louis XIV himself commended the subject to Philippe Quinault and Jean-Baptiste Lully (1682).[65] The absence of an authoritative original may have been a recommendation to poets

64 Rapin, *Réflexions*, 537, translated by Rymer as *Monsieur Rapin's Reflections*, 115–16.
65 On these operas, see Rosand, *Opera in Seventeenth-Century Venice*, 67–75; Greer, *The Play of Power*, 31–76; Stein, *Songs of Mortals*; and Buford Norman, *Touched by the Graces*, 237–58. More generally, see Bolduc, *Andromède au rocher*.

because it forestalled all direct comparisons. After the controversy between Ancients and Moderns that erupted over their revision of an extant text, *Alceste* (1674), Quinault, Lully, and Lully's occasional librettist Thomas Corneille confined themselves to lost Euripidean tragedies in *Thésée* (1675), *Bellérophon* (1678), *Pérsée* (1682), and *Phaéton* (1683). What's important for us to take away from the popularity of *Andromeda* as an operatic subject is that at least one vein of the tragic tradition seemed to authorize dramas in which love, a lamenting voice, and the spectacular use of machinery all played central roles. They were not mere ornaments or distractions from the tragic theme; they were the very stuff of tragedy.

Euripides's *Iphigenia among the Taurians*, with its doleful anticipations of sacrifice and its joyous recognition between brother and sister, was likewise treated by poets, librettists, and audiences as a touchstone of tragedy. Giovanni di Bernardo Rucellai's *l'Oreste* of 1525 was one of the first regular tragedies of the Renaissance. In the eighteenth century, the treatments of Guymond de la Touche (1757), Gluck (1779), and Goethe (1779) were received with rapture as modern reimaginings of ancient tragedy. Eighteenth-century audiences responded with equal fervour to the numerous attempts to recreate Euripides's lost *Cresphontes* (or *Merope*), another example of tragedy in which a recognition of the "best kind" averts disaster, this time a mother's slaughter of her son. In a letter prefaced to Voltaire's version of the tragedy, M. de la Lindelle (unmasked by Gotthold Ephraim Lessing as none other than Voltaire himself) reports that this averted murder appears to all the literati whom he has consulted in France and Italy to be the most touching and the most truly tragic subject ever in the theatre.[66] By the time Voltaire was writing, the subject had been brought on stage many times, starting in the late sixteenth century.[67] Cardinal Richelieu was the first to bring the subject to Paris (1641), but the next sixty years saw the production of three new versions of the tragedy, including one by Racine's protégé Lagrange de Chancel (1701). In the early eighteenth century, Italian poets recouped the subject. The Venetian librettist Zeno wrote a *Merope* that was set to music by Francesco Gasparini (1711), Ordandini (1717), Predieri (1718), and Giacomelli (1742), with the great castrato Farinelli

---

66 Voltaire, "Lettre de M. de la Lindelle à M. de Voltaire" in *Œuvres complètes*, 17: 235.
67 On the tradition of *Merope* tragedies, see Petrovska, *Merope*. On the Italian *cinquecento* versions, see Herrick, *Tragicomedy*, 101–21; and Ariani, *Tra classicismo e manierismo*, 289–332.

singing the lead. Zeno's libretto inspired his friend Maffei to undertake a declaimed tragedy on the same subject (1713).

Many twentieth- and twenty-first-century readers might object that *Iphigenia among the Taurians* and *Cresphontes* (or *Merope*) are tragicomedies, melodramas, romances, or dramas of reconciliation, not tragedies, and that Aristotle's "final preference" for plays based on such a formula "is the manifestation of a jaded critical palate."[68] But such judgments only serve to emphasize how far our critical categories are from those of the seventeenth and eighteenth centuries. The eighteenth century recognized the tragedy with a happy ending as a legitimate form. The failure of many twentieth-century critics to remember or acknowledge this fact has, arguably, done more to drive a wedge between opera and tragedy than any other misconception. *Opera, Tragedy, and Neighbouring Forms from Corneille to Calzabigi* returns us to a world in which opera and tragedy remained on intimate terms.

---

68 I quote Moles, who, despite offering one of the most insightful expositions of Aristotle's preference for plots like that of *Iphigenia*, cannot suppress his disappointment in the critic or his low estimation of such plays, which he compares to "detective stories, thrillers, and Science Fiction" ("Notes on Aristotle, *Poetics* 13 and 14," 92). Kitto, *Greek tragedy*, devotes chapters to Euripides's "tragicomedies" and "melodramas" and calls *Iphigenia among the Taurians* by turns a "tragi-comedy" and a "romantic melodrama" (327). On the critical history of describing Euripides's tragedies as melodramas, see Michelini, *Euripides and the Tragic Tradition*, 321–3. The "drama of reconciliation" is a term favoured by Hegel but seldom imitated.

1 Machine Plays in France: Between Italian Opera and French Tragedy in Music

HÉLÈNE VISENTIN[1]

The designation of early modern French opera as tragedy in music (*tragédie en musique* or *tragédie lyrique*) speaks for itself. If the first fruitful attempts at operatic forms belonged to the pastoral – *Le Triomphe de l'amour* (1655) by Charles de Bey (librettist) and Michel de la Guerre (composer); *La Pastorale d'Issy* (1659), *Ariane* (1659), and *Pomone* (1671) by Pierre Perrin (librettist) and Robert Cambert (composer); and *Les Peines et les plaisirs de l'amour* (1672) by Gabriel Gilbert (librettist) and Robert Cambert (composer) – tragedy rapidly eclipsed this genre. The first work by Jean-Baptiste Lully and Philippe Quinault produced at the Académie royale de musique in 1673 was titled *Cadmus et Hermione, tragédie mise en musique par Monsieur de Lully.* Thirteen tragedies followed this work between 1674 and 1687, but only two ballets, two masquerades, and one heroic pastoral ensued.[2]

French opera was intentionally created according to the rules of neoclassical tragedy and conceived as a poetic work based on the Aristotelian theory of mimesis, which gives substantial importance to the plot or *mythos* (which Aristotle defined as the "structuring of events" [*Poetics* 1450a5]). Consequently, when Pierre Perrin laid out his vision

---

1 All translations from French into English are from Marie Roche PhD, Fellow at The Arthur F. Kinney Center for Interdisciplinary Renaissance Studies. I also want to thank Marie Roche for her editorial assistance. Phoebus Alexander Cotsapas made additional valuable suggestions on the translations.

2 These dates correspond with Lully's tenure at the Académie royale de musique. In fact, the first performance by Quinault and Lully was *Les Fêtes de l'Amour et de Bacchus* (1672), a pastoral in three acts; however, this play was not a creation, but rather a patchwork of previous comedy-ballets by Molière and Lully, and as such, it was considered an "essay" awaiting the spectacle of *Cadmus et Hermione*.

of French opera, as he explains in his *Letter Written to Monsignor the Archbishop of Turin* (1659), he had in mind spoken tragedy (*la tragédie parlée*), not Italian opera. To this day, scholars consider the letter to be the founding text for the new operatic performances used to display royal power under the reign of Louis XIV.[3]

French opera did not appear all of a sudden. Scholarly works have shown that this genre is the result of a complex combination of a number of dramatic forms, such as the court ballet, pastoral drama, tragicomedy, comedy, comedy ballet, and mythological play, as well as transalpine opera, often called *dramma per musica*.[4] In this chapter, I demonstrate that machine plays were also integral to the emergence and popularity of French opera.[5] More than other dramatic forms, these plays relied on the *merveilleux* and special effects, such as the apparition of gods and other supernatural creatures from above and below the stage, lighting and sound effects, as well as rapid scene changes. More specifically, thanks to Italian stage technology imported into France in the 1640s, machine plays were arguably the most innovative theatre of the time, being first and foremost a visual encounter that aimed to generate surprise, to arouse astonishment, and to foster access to the wondrous.[6]

In contrast to neoclassical tragedy, machine plays by their very nature demonstrate that staged plays do not depend exclusively on a text to achieve their effects.[7] These plays were the product of a collaboration between art specialists, such as machinists, painters, composers, and

---

3 See Bohnert, "La poétique des paroles de musique selon Pierre Perrin," 133–59; Kintzler, *Poétique de l'opéra français*, 181–94.

4 In the bibliography, see selected works by Gros, Prunières, Delmas, Powell, and Louvat-Molozay.

5 For a definition of a "machine" used in various spectacles, see Ménestrier, *Traité des tournois*, 142–3; and Furetière, *Dictionnaire universel*, s.v. "machine."

6 "Tout ce qui se fait par Machines a toujours paru admirable, extraordinaire et surprenant" (Everything that is done by Machines has always seemed marvellous, extraordinary, and surprising) (Ménestrier, *Traité des Tournois*, 141).

7 Based on an Aristotelian conception of theatre in which the spectacle is marginalized, tragedy does not need to be performed on stage to achieve its cathartic effect. The credibility of the plot is the most important element of the process. Following these principles, a large majority of treatises written in the sixteenth and seventeenth centuries focused on the dramatic text, leading to the paradox that playwrights did not have to worry about the audience. L'Abbé d'Aubignac's main advice in his influential *Pratique du Théâtre* (1657) is "[faire] tout comme s'il n'y avoit point de Spectateurs" (Do as if there were no audience) (Livre I, Chap. VI). See the modern edition of the work edited by Baby listed under Aubignac.

playwrights, among others. Machine plays thus provide illuminating examples of the intrinsic tension between performance and text in this type of theatre. They also stretch and challenge the poetic rules (with their respect for the three unities) based on the concept of verisimilitude that d'Aubignac suggests is "le fondement de toutes les pièces du théâtre" (the foundation of all theatrical plays).[8]

Machines captivated audiences with their surprising novelty and aroused astonishment because the secret of how they operated (*ingenium*) remained unexplained.[9] Moreover, visual effects aimed not only to dazzle spectators but also to reveal on stage what neoclassical tragedy sought to hide, thus laying the groundwork for the birth of tragedy in music, a genre that, in contrast to much of the Italian opera considered elsewhere in this collection, was mainly based on plots taken from myths. Laura Naudeix rightly observes, "L'opéra est presque davantage un spectacle de machineries qu'un genre dramatique ou musical" (Opera is almost more a show of machinery than a dramatic or musical genre), as machines could successfully showcase political power.[10] As we shall see, this show of machinery was a French adaptation of Italian opera that was calculated to appeal to French sensibilities and to exalt Louis XIV as *le Roi Soleil* (Sun King). With this in mind, I set machine plays at an important juncture, straddling two forms of power (poetic and political) at a time when Richelieu and Mazarin had institutionalized the theatre as an instrument of royal authority.[11] Fashioned as a French counterpoint to Italian *feste teatrali*, machine plays not only conformed to, but reinforced French dramatic rules, which were more prescriptive and more devoutly respected than they were elsewhere in Europe. Moreover, I demonstrate that *tragédie en machines* played a formative role in both the emergence of regular tragedy and the invention of *tragédie en musique* – the two great achievements of the French classical stage. My analysis focuses on two seminal examples: *Mirame*, a tragicomedy by Jean Desmarets de Saint-Sorlin premiered in January 1641 and commissioned by Cardinal Richelieu, and *Andromède*, a tragedy by Pierre Corneille first performed in January 1650 and staged

---

8 D'Aubignac, *La Pratique du théâtre*, ed. Baby, 123.
9 I refer to the vogue of automatons and *Theatrum Machinarum* literature, which included representational technological treatises or machine books that feature impressive engineering designs and other automatic devices (real or imaginary). See Lefèvre, ed., *Picturing Machines* and Lazardzig, "The Machine as Spectacle."
10 Naudeix, *Dramaturgie de la tragédie en musique*, 121.
11 Blocker, *Instituer un "art."*

under Cardinal Mazarin. These plays were influential because they were both written in response to requests by political authorities. As such, they set the bar high for the design of theatrical stage scenery and machinery according to the dramatic rules of regular theatre – a theatre *"dans les règles."*

Machine Theatre in Context

The historical context out of which the machine plays emerged deserves consideration. If the machine theatre reached its peak in the mid-seventeenth century, the use of machines goes back to the Greco-Roman theatre, with the design of the *deus ex machina* to lower an actor to the stage. Cranes, traps, and other theatrical devices would bring supernatural beings on and off stage. Revolving triangular prisms, called *periaktoi,* could also change the scene. Medieval mystery plays likewise featured specialized machinery, the so-called *feintes,* or *secrets,* to represent, for instance, Paradise and the Hellmouth (as shown in the staging of the renowned Valenciennes mystery play [BnF, Ms. Français 12536]) and various miraculous apparitions. However, during the Renaissance, the conventions of French theatre were re-evaluated in the light of translations of and commentaries on Aristotle's *Poetics* and Horace's *Art of Poetry.* Aristotle demotes *opsis,* or spectacle, to the least important of the parts of tragedy – the story, the construction of the plot, being the most important element – and Horace specifically rejects certain stage effects, such as metamorphoses and bloody murders.[12] As a consequence, the use of machines was called into question. Because tragedy relies on the idea of the representation of the truth, or at least of a believable and credible reality, elements of spectacle such as machines, or *feintes,* were considered false and disruptive and were believed to impede access to truth. As Pierre Laudun d'Aigaliers observes in his *Art poétique français* (1597):

L'argument ne doit point estre feinct, mais vray … Outre la Tragedie, ne reçoit point de personnes feintes, comme Avarice, Republique ny autres, ny mesmes dieux ny deesses comme tesmoigne Horace en son art, *Nec Deus intersit* &c. Et la raison que j'y trouve c'est que si on y introduisoit un Dieu ou deesse, qui sont choses fausses, l'argument aussi seroit faux, &

---

12 "Staging can be emotionally attractive, but is not a matter of art and is not integral to poetry. The power of tragedy can be exercised without actors and without a performance. Staging belongs more to the scene-painter's art than to that of the poets." Aristotle, *Poetics,* translated by Kenny, 25–6.

par consequent ne representeroit pas les faits des hommes illustres selon la verité.[13]

The subject matter must not be fabricated, but authentic ... In addition, tragedy must not use fictive allegorical characters, such as Greed or Republic or others, nor even gods or goddesses, as Horace argues in his work, *Nec Deus intersit* &c. And the reason is that if the play were to introduce a god or goddess, which are false entities, the subject matter would also be false, and therefore would not represent the deeds of illustrious men in a truthful manner.

For this reason, the use of machines in plays in the second half of the sixteenth century and the first third of the seventeenth century was confined to the prologue or dénouement (as a *deus ex machina*) – in other words, to the margins of the spectacle.[14] Most often, spectacular images and special effects were inscribed in the dramatic text as an *ekphrasis*. It was only with the onset of the so-called Quarrel of the Regulars and the Irregulars in the 1630s that an aesthetic of the spectacular began to develop.[15] Jean Chapelain and his followers advocated for a strict respect for the Aristotelian theory by showing the pleasure that is generated by respecting the rules ("le plaisir par la règle," as Georges Forestier puts it), while playwrights such as Georges de Scudéry and I.G. Durval, who claimed to have a modern conception of theatre based on an aesthetic of multiformity (*la diversité du spectacle*), relied on the spectacular potentialities of the dramatic text to reveal the *beaux effets* that would entertain and please the audience, while taking the risk of breaking "la vérité de

---

13 Laudun d'Aigaliers, *Art poétique françois*, 279–80.
14 Laudun d'Aigaliers says: "Toutefois si quelqu'un m'objecte qu'en mes Tragedies, j'ay mis un Dieu Mercure, & une furie, je dis que l'un ne sert que de prologue, et qu'il ne touche en rien de la representation de l'histoire" (However if someone objects that in my tragedies I provide a God Mercury and a Fury, I say that one is only used in the prologue and does not affect the storyline) (*Art poétique françois*, 280). For instance, *L'Amaranthe* (1631), a pastoral by Gombauld, features the appearance of Aurora in the prologue: "L'on faict paraistre l'Aurore dans un char et sur un pivot tirée par des chevaux" (Dawn appears on a chariot and a horse-drawn swivel); *La Filis de Scire* (1631), a comedy pastoral by Pichou, features the allegory of the Night in the prologue as well: "L'on faict paraistre la Nuit dans son char dessus un pivot tiré par des chevaux" (Darkness appears on a chariot and a horse-drawn swivel). These stage directions are quoted from the so-called *Mémoire de Mahelot*, ed. Pasquier, an account of stage sets of plays performed at the Hôtel de Bourgogne.
15 An excellent article that demonstrates that what is actually at stake in this theatrical debate is Forestier, "De la modernité anti-classique au classicisme moderne."

l'action" (the truth of the action), according to d'Aubignac. What may strike some readers as counter-intuitive at first blush is that this period of vigorous debates on poetic rules gave rise to machine plays in France – a theatrical form that already had deep roots in theatrical practice.[16]

Perhaps due to their innovativeness, the nomenclature applied to machine plays is not consistent. Based on my extensive research on the topic, only two plays are explicitly called *tragédies en machines*. These are *Les Amours du Soleil, Tragédie en Machines Représentée sur le Théâtre du Marais* by Jean Donneau de Visé (Paris: Claude Barbin, 1671) and *Le Triomphe de l'Amour Divin de Sainte Reine, vierge et martyre, Tragédie en Machines Dédiée à la Reine* by Alexandre Le Grand (Paris: Charles Gorrens and Jean Gobert, 1671).[17] References to machines can also be found on the title page of *desseins* or *sujets*, which are small programs that provide a detailed account of the performance, explaining the plot in a few words and extensively describing the decors and the machines. These programs often accompanied the performance of major machine plays.[18]

A case in point is the *dessein* of *La Naissance d'Hercule, ou L'Amphitryon* (1649–50), a remake of the comedy *Les Sosies* (1638) by Jean de Rotrou: *Dessein du poème de la grande pièce des machines de la Naissance d'Hercule, dernier ouvrage de Monsieur de Rotrou, représentée sur le Théâtre du Marais, par les Comédiens du Roy* (1649). This title echoes the reprise of *La Descente d'Orphée aux Enfers* (1640) by François de Chapoton – renamed *La Grande Journée des Machines ou Le Mariage d'Orphée et d'Eurydice* and performed at the Théâtre du Marais in 1648 in response to the lavish performance of *Orfeo* at the court. Likewise, *Les Amours de Vénus et d'Adonis* (1670) by Jean Donneau de Visé, named a tragedy in its first edition, is called *tragédie en machines* on the title page of the *sujet*.[19] While playwrights avoided categorizing their plays as *tragédies*

---

16   On the subject of these transformations in the theatrical landscape, see Visentin, "Au cœur d'une mutation socio-politique et esthétique," 509–20; Dominguez, "Les machines du théâtre français."

17   The well-established man of letters, playwright, and journalist Donneau de Visé, founder of the famous gazette *Le Mercure Galant*, wrote the first play. The second play is an isolated case of a religious performance in the provinces, but published in Paris.

18   Publishing a *dessein* of the performance started to be a standard practice when Italian *feste teatrali* were imported by Mazarin in France in the 1640s; for instance, major machine plays performed at the Théâtre du Marais, in the years following the renovations in 1644, were accompanied by a *dessein*. See Visentin, "Le 'dessein' de la pièce à machine."

19   *Sujet des Amours de Vénus et d'Adonis, tragédie en machines, représentée sur le Théâtre Royal du Marais le 2 mars 1670* (Paris: Pierre Promé, 1670).

en machines or even using the word "machines" on the title page, being aware that critics such as Jules de La Mesnardière and l'abbé d'Aubignac were prejudiced against this dramatic form, the performance accounts of these plays highlight the use of machinery. Nonetheless, the use of the term "machines" in the headings of programs underscores the advertising goal of these particular documents, which aimed to attract audiences with the promise of a *grand spectacle*. The fact that the titles of *Les Amours du Soleil* and *Le Triomphe de l'Amour de Sainte Reine*, both published in 1671, precisely stipulate *tragédie en machines* speaks for itself. Not surprisingly, this date (1671) coincides with the emergence of the *tragédie en musique*, and playwrights, as well as theatre companies in Paris, sought to respond to this competition by promoting *tragédies en machines*.

Let us now turn our attention to two prime examples: the tragicomedy *Mirame* (1641) by Jean Desmarets de Saint-Sorlin and the tragedy *Andromède* (1650) by Pierre Corneille. These plays did more than change the history of French theatre and scenography; they advanced France's political agenda, established its credentials as a cultural hegemon, and enhanced the visibility of its dramatic models abroad.

Mirame and the Sun Machinery

The Cardinal-Duke of Richelieu, Louis XIII's chief minister (1624–42), had a profound influence on the theatre: through him, the state and theatre worked in tandem to revive France and shed glory on the monarchy, with the particular goal of making Paris a new Rome by laying the foundations of a reformed theatre.[20] Richelieu achieved this by taking a series of measures to renovate, regulate, and protect dramatic art. As part of his political agenda, the Cardinal commissioned a large theatre capable of hosting about 3,000 spectators. Built in the right wing of his newly constructed Palais-Cardinal, designed by the architect Jacques Lemercier and located next to the Louvre, the so-called Grande Salle de la Comédie was the first building in Paris to be erected with a permanent stage able to accommodate the use of innovative mechanical devices. Recent scholarship highlights the main features of this new theatrical architectural building, of which the Cardinal was particularly proud. It comprised an amphitheatre and two balconies for spectators, a monumental proscenium arch, a system of rapid scenery changes (*scena*

---

20   See Bayard, *Rome-Paris, 1640*.

ductilis) constructed on a central one-point perspective, known as the Prince's eye (*l'œil du Prince*), and state-of-the-art machinery.[21] Cardinal Mazarin, then Richelieu's chief adviser and collaborator, worked with his agent and Secretary Elpidio Benedetti to bring the most talented Roman artists to France to work for the chief minister. Among them was Giovanni Maria Mariani, a pupil of Gian Lorenzo Bernini.[22]

The Grande Salle of the Palais-Cardinal was a novelty in France and a sign of royal greatness and authority. Jean Desmarets de Saint-Sorlin began a dedicatory epistle to Louis XIII by stating, "la France a maintenant un lieu ou j'espere que vostre Majesté triomphera souvent, par les vers & par les beaux spectacles que vostre grand Ministre y fera faire pour célébrer vos conquestes" (France now has a place where I hope your Majesty will often triumph, by the verses and the beautiful spectacles that your great Minister will see performed to celebrate your conquests).[23] For the inauguration of his theatre, Richelieu commissioned a play by Desmarets de Saint-Sorlin, *Mirame*, first performed on 14 January 1641. Desmarets came up with a typical tragicomedy based on a story of a rivalry between Arimant (the secret lover) and Azamor (the official suitor) for the love of Mirame, Princess of Bithynia.

The plot does not involve any supernatural characters, and the dramatic text of the play does not include any particular special effects. However, the performance's highlights were the surprising devices that made possible the representation of sunset and sunrise on stage,

---

21 See Beijer, "Une maquette de décor"; Le Pas de Sécheval, "Le Cardinal de Richelieu"; Tamburini, "Guitti, Buonamici, Mariani, les Vigarani."

22 See Laurain-Portemer, *Études mazarines*, 197–201; and Tamburini, *Due teatri per il Principe*, 247–8. Bernini turned down the invitation to come to Paris to work on Richelieu's theatre, and a string of other artists also declined, including Francesco Guitti and Nicolò Menghini. These refusals led the authorities to hire Mariani, who accepted and came to France.

23 This dedicatory epistle is included in the first in-folio edition of the play *Mirame* (Paris: Henri le Gras, 1641) (BNF Rés. YF-51). In his *Histoire et recherches des antiquités*, Henri Sauval describes the new theatre of Richelieu in these terms: "La maniere de ce Théatre est moderne ... il n'y a personne qui n'avoue que c'est le Theatre de France le plus commode, & le plus Royal" (This type of theatre is modern ... There is no one who does not confess that it is the most practical and Royal French theater) (Paris: Charles Moette and Jacques Chardon, 1724), tome 2, livre septième, 162–3. See Murray, "Richelieu's Theater." As Benoît Bolduc observes, the frontispiece that appears in the luxurious in-folio edition of *Mirame* features an elaborate title (*OUVERTURE du Théâtre DE LA GRANDE SALLE du Palais Cardinal MIRAME Tragicomédie*) that emphasizes the opening of this unique theatre in the capital rather than the play itself. See *La Fête imprimée*, 194–5.

Figure 1.1. *Mirame*: Scene from act 1. The Phrygian king Azamor declares his love for Mirame to her father, the king of Bithynia. Etching by Stefano della Bella, 1641. Credit: Harvard Art Museums/Fogg Museum, Gray Collection of Engravings Fund, by exchange: DeV-M. 937. © President and Fellows of Harvard College.

which allowed for the smooth and unified progress of the plot within a twenty-four-hour period, in adherence with the rule of the unity of time (see Figures 1.1–1.5 and pay particular attention to the backdrop of each stage setting). Having worked on the scenography of the first comic opera *Chi soffre, speri* by Virgilio Mazzocchi (librettist) and Marco Marazzoli (composer), performed at the Palazzo Barberini in Rome in 1639, Mariani knew how to stage the scene to resemble "prospettive di distanza lontanissime illuminate da un sole che col suo giro a poco a poco va a tuffarsi nel mare" (distant perspectives lit by a sun that gradually over time plunged into the sea). Not only did he learn this skill from his master Bernini, but this particular expertise that recommended him to Richelieu.[24] The *Gazette de France*, a new periodical created as a

---

24 Daolmi, "La Drammaturgia al servizio della scenotechnica," 60.

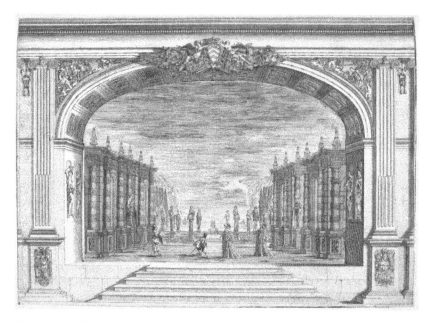

Figure 1.2. *Mirame*: Scene from act 2. Nocturnal meeting between Mirame and her lover, Arimant. Etching by Stefano della Bella, 1641. Credit: Harvard Art Museums/Fogg Museum, Gray Collection of Engravings Fund, by exchange: DeV-M. 938. © President and Fellows of Harvard College.

government mouthpiece, highly praised the special effect of the sun machinery in its review of the performance:

> La nuit sembla arriver en suitte par l'obscurcissement imperceptible tant du jardin que de la mer & du ciel qui se trouva éclairé de la Lune. À cette nuit succéda le jour, qui vint aussi insensiblement avec l'Aurore & le Soleil qui fit son tour d'une si agréable tromperie qu'elle duroit trop peu aux yeux et au jugement d'un chacun.[25]

> Night seemed to arrive incrementally, imperceptibly obscuring the garden, the sea, and the sky, which became illuminated by the moon. Night was followed by day, which came equally imperceptibly with the dawn, and with the sun that made its round with such pleasing deception that the moment was too brief in the eyes and judgment of everyone.

---

25   Quoted in Beijer, "Une maquette de décor," 378.

Figure 1.3. *Mirame*: Scene from act 3. At sunrise, Arimant's farewell to Mirame before being put in prison by Azamor. Etching by Stefano della Bella, 1641. Credit: Harvard Art Museums/Fogg Museum, Gray Collection of Engravings Fund, by exchange: DeV-M. 938. © President and Fellows of Harvard College.

In this way, the sun machine visually emphasized the seamless unity of time. The account published in the *Gazette de France* refers to *Mirame* as "[une] comédie circonscrite par les loix de la poësie dans les bornes de ce jour naturel" (a comedy bound by the rules of poetry and within the confines of a natural day). In addition to the unity of time, the play respected the unity of place. Its front matter specifies this: "La Scene est dans le jardin du Palais Royal d'Heraclée, regardant sur la mer" (The scene is in the garden of the Royal Palace of Heraclea, looking out to sea); and five engravings by Stefano della Bella included in the prestigious in-folio edition of the play underline it (Paris: Henry Le Gras, 1641). (See Figures 1.1–1.5.) Emphasizing the unity of action, each engraving also features the eponymous heroine interacting with the other main characters of the play at the front of the stage and fitting nicely into the perspective scenery. The scenic unity of the Italian stage of the Grande Salle de la Comédie that emerges from this series of engravings underscores the rule of

Figure 1.4. *Mirame*: Scene from act 4. Mirame's madness when she learns of her lover's death. Etching by Stefano della Bella, 1641. Credit: Harvard Art Museums/Fogg Museum, Gray Collection of Engravings Fund, by exchange: DeV-M. 938. © President and Fellows of Harvard College.

the three unities – time, place, and action. In this respect, I agree with Catherine Guillot that,

> On peut supposer que la fable de Desmarets a été conçue et rédigée en fonction du spectacle qu'on voulait faire admirer grâce au dispositif scénique à l'italienne et aux décors voulus par Richelieu.[26]

> Desmarets's tale was presumably conceived and written to serve the spectacle that was meant to be the focus of audience admiration, a spectacle made possible thanks to the Italian-style stage devices and decor desired by Richelieu.

The play's state-of-the-art theatre technologies, I must emphasize, were less important as a means of creating a stage effect than of policing

---

26 "Introduction" to *Mirame, Tragi-comédie*, ed. Guillot and Scherer, 15.

Figure 1.5. *Mirame*: Scene from act 5. The awakening of Mirame who swallowed a false poison. Etching by Stefano della Bella, 1641. Credit: Harvard Art Museums/Fogg Museum, Gray Collection of Engravings Fund, by exchange: DeV-M. 938. © President and Fellows of Harvard College.

the three unities. In other words, the same theatre technologies that the *scena barocca* used to enable surprising and wondrous changes of scene were employed by the stage of the Palais-Cardinal to enforce the newly emerging rules of regular tragedy. While controlling the use of machines, Richelieu made a point of disciplining court entertainments in pursuit of a larger cultural project that could be furthered by the theatre: social and cultural unity.[27] In short, there is no reason to doubt that he intended to sponsor a play that strictly observed the dramatic rules for the inauguration of his theatre. The Cardinal-Duke was an ardent supporter of these poetic conventions, as evidenced by his patronage of the Académie française. In staging *Mirame,* he looked to single-point perspective, the proscenium arch, and stage machinery to reinforce the emerging French doctrine of regular tragedy with its respect for the

27 See Blocker, *Instituer un "art,"* passim.

three unities. In doing so, the Cardinal was clearly following Italian precedents (mainly the Barberini's), and wanted to demonstrate precisely that the technologies of the Italian stage could be adapted to French theatre.[28] In this way, the sun machinery was not just in the vanguard of entertainment but was also a powerful tool put to the service of French cultural and political discourses.

Andromède or the Art of an Integrative Machine Theatre

Following Richelieu's death in 1642, the newly appointed chief minister and the Italian-born Cardinal Mazarin commissioned *feste teatrali* for the French court. The goal was both to enhance the prestige of France abroad and to transform Paris into a leading cultural centre in a political rivalry with Rome.[29] For this purpose, Mazarin invited numerous performers and artists (dancers, singers, actors, composers, etc.). Among them was the renowned Italian stage designer and engineer Giacomo Torelli, who had established his reputation at the Teatro Novissimo in Venice by putting on, among other works, Giulio Strozzi (composer) and Francesco Sacrati's (librettist) *La Finta Pazza* in 1641.[30]

Once in France, Torelli was first asked to redesign the stage and the scenery of the Grande Salle of the Petit-Bourbon (a palace adjacent to the Louvre) to accommodate his most significant machinery innovations for performances of Italian operas on the French stage. The machinery involved a pole and chariot system connected by ropes to a central drum below the stage, thus allowing flat wings to be changed quickly in full view of the spectators. However, despite the spectacular display that had never been seen before in France, *La Finta Pazza* (1645) and, even more so, *Orfeo* (performed in 1647 at the Palais-Royal, the former Palais-Cardinal) by Luigi Rossi (composer) and Francesco Buti (librettist), received mixed reactions. The combinations of different aesthetics (pastoral, burlesque, comedy, and tragedy) in the same play, frequent scene changes, flamboyant music, and lyrics performed in Italian led the audience to think of the performance as excessive and the plot as too intricate to follow. Only the machines really pleased the French audiences, who were more accustomed to regular theatre and the more restrained musical style of French airs. Possibly with this in

---

28   See Hoxby, "Technologies of Performance," 164.
29   See Bayard, ed. *Rome-Paris, 1640,* passim.
30   See Milesi, ed. *Giacomo Torelli,* 147–307.

mind, Mazarin asked Pierre Corneille – newly elected to the Académie française and named official poet of the young King Louis XIV – to create a play in the French dramatic tradition, with the specific request to reuse *Orfeo*'s decors and machines, the cost of which had previously been heavily criticized.[31] Mazarin sought to ease this financial burden during the period of political unrest and successive insurrections known as the Fronde. Corneille's answer to Mazarin's request was *Andromède*, a tragedy in five acts with a prologue based on books four and five of Ovid's *Metamorphoses*.[32]

The mythological story of the rescue of Andromeda by Perseus possesses all the ingredients of a tragic plot: it has noble characters (the royal family of Ethiopia), a conflict between close family members, a dilemma between the duty of a king and his love for his daughter, a rivalry between Perseus (the unsurpassed hero as an image of the young Louis XIV) and Phineus (the anti-hero to whom Andromeda is engaged) for the love of Andromeda, and, last but not least, a heroine who has to confront impending death.[33] And yet the subject seemed ideally suited to using machines to create a *grand spectacle*. In the *Argument* of his play, Corneille states in a somewhat peremptory tone that he found a perfect subject to respond to Cardinal Mazarin's order:

> Pour moi, je confesse ingénument que quelque effort d'imagination que j'aie fait depuis, je n'ai pu découvrir encore un sujet capable de tant d'ornements extérieurs et où les machines pussent être distribuées avec tant de justesse.

---

31 "Car chacun s'acharna sur l'horrible dépense des machines et des musiciens italiens qui étaient venus de Rome et d'ailleurs à grands frais, parce qu'il les fallut payer pour partir, venir et s'entretenir en France" (For everyone harped on about the horrific expense of the machines and of the Italian musicians, who had come from Rome and elsewhere at a high cost, because they had to be paid to leave [Italy], come [to France] and live in France) (Nicolas Goulas, *Mémoires de ce qui s'est passé en France pendant la Régence de la Reine Anne d'Autriche*; quoted by Powell, "Music and Corneille's *Andromède*," 191).

32 Scheduled for the Carnaval of 1648, but postponed because of the sickness of the young King Louis XIV, followed by the disturbance of the Fronde, *Andromède* was finally performed in front of the Court at the end of January 1650 by the Royal troupe on the stage of the Théâtre Royal de Bourbon. The play was well received and was performed abroad. For more details, see the introduction to my critical edition of *Andromède* in Pierre Corneille's *Théâtre*, vol. 4.

33 In his adaptation work, Corneille tightens the dramatic intensity around tragic schemata such as the oppression of an innocent victim and the strife between lovers.

> For my part, I confess candidly that for all the efforts of my imagination since, I have yet to discover a subject so well-suited to so many adornments, and that allows the machines to be used so appropriately.

Choosing to write a play on the myth of Andromeda and Perseus was a way for Corneille to follow in the footsteps of his Italian predecessors.[34] Furthermore, we can assume that it was Torelli who suggested the subject of Perseus and Andromeda to Corneille. After all, Venetian commercial opera began with Francesco Manelli's performance of *Andromeda* at the Teatro San Cassiano in 1637, and Torelli started his career as a stage designer in Venice before his arrival in Paris. In that regard, there are obvious similarities between these *drammi per musica* and the Cornelian *Andromède*, especially regarding the manipulation of the dramatic storyline and the use of an operatic prologue (distinct from the main plot) that praises the heroic values of the Prince. It is also true that Italian opera, with its rich and abundant elements of spectacle, long recitatives, and hybrid genres, distances itself from French theatrical aesthetics (*Orfeo* was termed a *tragicomedia per musica*). As Melpomène, the Muse of Tragedy, states in the prologue of *Andromède*, "Mon Théâtre, Soleil, mérite bien tes yeux, / Tu n'en vis jamais en ces lieux / La pompe plus majestueuse: / J'ai réuni, pour la faire admirer, / Tout ce qu'ont de plus beau la France et l'Italie, / De tous leurs Arts mes sœurs l'ont embellie" (My Theatre, Sun, deserves your eyes, / You never saw in these settings / Pageantry more majestic: / I have gathered together, for your admiration, / All that is most beautiful from France and Italy, / Embellished with all the arts of my sister muses") (Prologue, 2–7). Corneille managed to combine two theatrical traditions, Italian and French, beautifully. He wrote a play that showed the importance of verbal expression through a unified and coherent storyline on the model of the spoken regular tragedy while integrating *avec justesse* nonverbal cues, such as music and machines (Corneille does not include ballet entries).[35] Regarding the music, the playwright states in the *Argument* of his tragedy:

---

34 The Ovidian story of Andromeda and Perseus had been staged in the first half of the seventeenth century, especially in the princely courts in the North of Italy. See Bolduc, *Andromède au rocher*. Also, Mamczarz maintains that Corneille possessed "une connaissance profonde et une assimilation des meilleures conquêtes du drame musical italien" (a profound knowledge and assimilation of the best achievements of the Italian musical drama). ("Quelques aspects de l'interaction dans les théâtres italien, français et polonais," 206.)

35 See Delmas, "L'unité du genre tragique au XVIIe siècle" and Kapp, "Corneille et la dramaturgie du théâtre à machines italien."

Chaque Acte aussi bien que le Prologue a sa décoration particulière, et du moins une machine volante avec un concert de Musique, que je n'ai employée qu'à satisfaire les oreilles des spectateurs, tandis que leurs yeux sont arrêtés à voir descendre ou remonter une machine, ou s'attachent à quelque chose qui leur empêche de prêter attention à ce que pourraient dire les Acteurs, comme fait le combat de Persée contre le Monstre: mais je me suis bien gardé de faire rien chanter qui fût nécessaire à l'intelligence de la Pièce, parce que communément les paroles qui se chantent étant mal entendues des auditeurs, pour la confusion qu'y apporte la diversité des voix qui les prononcent ensemble, elles auraient fait une grande obscurité dans le corps de l'ouvrage, si elles avaient eu à instruire l'Auditeur de quelque chose d'important.

Each act, as well as the prologue, has its own particular decor and deploys at least one flying machine to a musical accompaniment. I have used music only in order to satisfy the ears of the audience while their eyes are transfixed by a machine going up and down, or by something that prevents them from focusing on what the actors might be saying, as in the case of Perseus's fight against the monster. Nevertheless, I have taken great care not to put into song any information that might be crucial to understanding the play. It is common for listeners to misunderstand sung words because of the confusion sown by a multiplicity of voices pronouncing them in unison. If the lyrics conveyed important plot details, the play would be greatly obscured.

The above statement makes it clear that Corneille purposefully chose to limit the musical parts and significantly reduce the importance of the role of music, having in mind the criticisms of Italian opera on the French stage.[36] In total, there are fourteen short vocal parts and musical choruses, six of these musical moments coinciding with the appearances of the gods on stage, and the other eight pieces corresponding to critical lyrical and pathetic scenes. A thorough analysis of the play demonstrates that, in fact, Corneille carefully integrated the use of music in the dramatic text. The singing parts often comment on the plot, echoing the character's lines and highlighting the dramatic intensity of the action.

---

36 It is significant that no musical partitions of *Andromède* have survived. It is also worth mentioning that Corneille chose to work with a French composer, Charles Coypeau dit d'Assoucy, whom he never mentions in the paratexts of his play, in contrast to the machinist Torelli, whose achievements he praises in the *Argument*. For a general discussion on the role of music in *Andromède*, see Sébastiani, "La musique dans l'*Andromède* de Pierre Corneille."

The dramatis persona of Cassiope, Andromède's mother, performs the function of a choir conductor or *coryphaeus*, by dictating the musical moments in the play as a way to draw the attention both of the characters and the spectators toward the gods in the machine. For instance, at the end of act 1, scene 2, when Venus appears in the clouds to pronounce the prophecy that "Andromède ce soir aura l'illustre époux / Qui seul est digne d'elle et dont seule elle est digne" (Andromeda tonight will have the illustrious husband / Who alone is worthy of her and she alone worthy of him) (1.2.358–9), Cassiope commands the choir to start singing: "Ah! Je la reconnais, la Déesse d'Éryce, / C'est elle, c'est Vénus, à mes vœux si propice, / … Peuple, faites des vœux tandis qu'elle descend" (Ah! I recognize her, the goddess of Eryce, / It is she, it is Venus, to my vows so propitious / … People make your wishes while she descends) (1.2.328–31). (See Figure 1.7.) Thus, the music in *Andromède* does not, as the *Argument* states, strictly serve the function of covering the noise of the machinery. Corneille makes sure to incorporate singing parts into the plot via the character of Cassiope.[37]

As with the music, Corneille purposefully limited the number of scene changes during the performance. While Italian productions featured numerous scene changes in full view of the audience within the same act, scene changes in *Andromède* only take place in between the prologue and each of the five acts, for a total of six scene changes. It is of note that the six engravings by François Chauveau included in the beautiful quarto edition (Rouen: Laurens Maurry, 1651; see Figures 1.6–1.11) show how there was both a continuity and contiguity of decors from one scene to another while reinforcing the rules of the unity of place and time.[38] Similarly, the prologue and each following act include one

---

37 See Powell, "Music and Corneille's *Andromède*," 200–1; and Calhoun, "Corneille's *Andromède* and opera," 10–12. On the general role of music in machine theatre, see Louvat-Molozay, *Théâtre et musique*, 365–400.

38 Corneille situates the action in Ethiopia in "La ville capitale du royaume de Céphée" (The capital city of the kingdom of Cepheus). The decor of the prologue shows a seascape in the background, which constitutes the scenery of act 3. The decor of act 1 offers a vista of the public square inside which the audience is shown the palace and the temple respectively represented in close-up in acts 4 and 5. The scenery of the garden in act 2 displays a palace in the background, while the palace decor of act 4 refers to the garden of act 2. Thus, the successive decor suggests a relative unity of place. Also, these sceneries form a narrative whole that underscores traces of temporality. The shadows cast by the characters and buildings, relatively short in acts 1 and 2, lengthen in act 3 and on, suggesting the passage of time as the dramatic action unfolds.

Figure 1.6. *Andromède*: Scene from the prologue. Above a grotto with a view of the sea Melpomène appears in flight while the chariot of the Sun, drawn by four horses, approaches from the right. Engraving by François Chaveau. Houghton Library, Harvard University: GEN (Typ 615.51.299).

machine, except for act 3 when Perseus fights the monster to rescue Andromeda. Besides the elaborate stage machinery of the moving sea with the monster, and the flight of Perseus in the sky, the scene ends with the apparition of Neptune in a chariot, threatening divine vengeance as this god protects Perseus's rival Phineus. In the *Argument*, Corneille minimizes the role of the music in his tragedy, but he amplifies that of the machines: "Il n'en va pas de même des machines qui ne sont pas dans cette Tragédie comme des agréments détachés, elles en font le nœud et le dénouement, et y sont si nécessaires que vous n'en sauriez retrancher aucune, que vous ne fassiez tomber tout l'édifice" (The same cannot be said for the machines, which are not in this tragedy detached embellishments: they accomplish the complication and resolution of the plot; they are so necessary that you would not be able to do away with any of them without toppling the entire edifice). He continues:

J'ai été assez heureux à les inventer et à leur donner place dans la tissure de ce Poème, mais aussi faut-il que J'avoue que le sieur Torelli s'est surmonté

Figure 1.7. *Andromède*: Scene from act 1. Amid a cloud, Venus appears in the public square of Céphée (or Cepheus), king of Ethiopia, to announce the wedding of Andromède (or Andromeda). Engraving by François Chaveau. Houghton Library, Harvard University: GEN (Typ 615.51.299).

lui-même à en exécuter les desseins, et qu'il a eu des inventions admirables pour les faire agir à propos … Il faut en dire autant des autres que j'ai introduites et dont il a inventé l'exécution, qui en a rendu le spectacle si merveilleux, qu'il sera mal aisé d'en faire un plus beau de cette nature.

I was content to invent them and give them a place in the fabric of this poem, but I must admit that Mr. Torelli outperformed himself in realizing these designs, and that he devised ingenious mechanisms to have them operate as intended … The same must be said of the other machines that I proposed and that he made look so marvelous; it would be difficult to imagine more beautiful creations of this kind.

Here, the production of *Andromède* is described as the result of a productive collaboration between the dramatic poet and the scenographer Torelli, even though Corneille underlines the latter's subaltern role: Torelli's *ingenio* is confined to the realization of the playwright's ideas. It is significant to note how much Corneille emphasizes in his *Argument*

Figure 1.8. *Andromède*: Scene from act 2. Eole (or Aeolus) and his eight winds take Andromède (or Andromeda) into the clouds. Engraving by François Chaveau. Houghton Library, Harvard University: GEN (Typ 615.51.299).

that the poetic function of the machines is vital to the structure of the play and its climax: "[E]lles en font le nœud et le dénouement, et y sont si nécessaires que vous n'en sauriez retrancher aucune, que vous ne fassiez tomber tout l'édifice. J'ai été assez heureux à les inventer et à leur donner place dans la tissure de ce Poème" (They accomplish the complication and resolution of the plot; they are so essential that you would not be able to do away with any of them without toppling the entire edifice. I was content to invent them and to give them a place in the fabric of the poem). In fact, within the constraints placed upon him of reusing *Orfeo*'s sets and machines, Corneille managed to integrate those machines into a regular drama that could plausibly claim to be a true tragedy, though one according a limited role to music and spectacle. In other words, he succeeded in creating a coherent and unified storyline while making sure to integrate machines that would suit the plot.

According to the Aristotelian principle of necessity, the structure of the sequence of events frames the story. Moving away from the Ovidian storyline, Corneille invented the oracle of Venus to reinforce the

Figure 1.9. *Andromède*: Scene from act 3. Persée (or Perseus), mounted on
the winged horse Pegasus, is about to save the chained Andromède (or
Andromeda) from a sea monster. Engraving by François Chaveau. Houghton
Library, Harvard University: GEN (Typ 615.51.299).

coherence of the whole plot from the expository act to the dénouement. In his *Argument*, he explains how Venus is the central character
of the play: "[Elle] fait le nœud de cette Tragédie par l'Oracle ingénieux
qu'elle prononce" ([She] ties the knot of this tragedy with the ingenious Oracle she pronounces).[39] Indeed, the Oracle of Venus provides a
new dimension to the dramatic narrative when it foretells, at the end of

---

39 In *Andromède*'s "Examen," a critical examination of his play written in 1660 while
 working on the complete edition of his theatre, Corneille makes changes to this passage devoted to the oracle of Venus: "L'Oracle de Vénus au premier Acte est inventé
 avec assez d'artifice, pour porter les esprits dans un sens contraire à sa vraie intelligence; mais il ne le faut pas prendre pour le vrai nœud de la Pièce: autrement elle
 serait achevée dès le troisième, où l'on en verrait le dénouement. L'action principale
 est le mariage de Persée avec Andromède, son nœud consiste en l'obstacle qui s'y
 rencontre du côté de Phinée à qui elle est promise, et son dénouement en la mort
 de ce malheureux Amant, après laquelle il n'y a plus d'obstacle" (The Oracle of
 Venus, in the first Act, is invented with such artifice as to make the audience think

Figure 1.10. *Andromède*: Scene from act 4. Junon (or Juno), in a chariot drawn by two peacocks, comes to bring her protection to Phinée (or Phineus). Engraving by François Chaveau. Houghton Library, Harvard University: GEN (Typ 615.51.299).

the first act, the union of Andromeda with an *époux parfait* of unknown identity. Venus appears on stage in a magnificent star coming from the sky, a machine created by Torelli "avec tant d'art et de pompe, qu'elle remplit tout le monde d'étonnement et d'admiration" (with so much art and pomp that it fills everyone with astonishment and admiration) (see Figure 1.7).[40] The prediction of finding this perfect spouse leads to

it signifies the opposite of what it truly does; however, this must not be taken to be the crux of the play. Otherwise, the dénouement would occur, and the play would be over as early as the third [act]. The central scene is in fact the wedding of Perseus and Andromeda; the crux of the action lies in the obstacle that exists in the form of Phineas, to whom Andromeda has been promised; and the resolution occurs in the death of this unhappy lover, after which there are no more obstacles). In 1660, when he is in the process of writing a series of "Examens" of his former plays, Corneille speaks more like a theatre theorist than a stage director.

40 See the "Argument" of the play; the engraving of act 1 by Chauveau clearly shows the machine of Venus in the air.

Figure 1.11. *Andromède*: Scene from act 5. The royal family of Ethiopia ascends to heaven alongside Jupiter, Junon (or Juno), and Neptune. Engraving by François Chaveau. Houghton Library, Harvard University: GEN (Typ 615.51.299).

a misunderstanding that stirs the rivalry between Perseus and Phineus (acts 2–3). When Perseus rescues Andromeda in a *coup de théâtre* in act 3 – as he flies through the air on Pegasus – the solution to the Oracle's ambiguous prediction, the reversal of Andromeda's fortune, and the recognition of Perseus as her ideal husband coincide. Finally, once Phineus is out of the way (act 4), after his attempted revenge against Perseus, the dénouement is presented as the realization of the Oracle of Venus, when Jupiter appears on a throne of glory, inviting the family of Ethiopia to celebrate the wedding of Perseus and Andromeda in the sky (see Figure 1.11). Thus, the Oracle of Venus lends coherence to the play's dramatic action, and Venus's appearance on stage underscores the play's founding premise: that the gods take an interest in the fate of mortals. This kind of marvelous effect is normally kept out of sight in declaimed tragedy, but it is put directly before the eyes of the audience in machine plays, much as it is in the Lullian tragedy in music.

Because *Andromède* is a mythological story that involves supernatural elements and thus relies on the marvelous, the challenge for

Corneille was to create a play that could obey the rules of neoclassical tragedy. Among these, respecting the principle of verisimilitude was chief. In fact, for the playwright, the mythological tradition controlled the appearance of the subject to be perceived as real or true, based on conventional wisdom; the spectator attending the performance of a mythological play, such as *Andromède*, knew in advance what to expect:

> Tout ce que la fable nous dit de ses Dieux, et de ses Métamorphoses, est encore impossible, et ne laisse pas d'être croyable par l'opinion commune, et par cette vieille traditive qui nous a accoutumés à en ouïr parler ... L'Auditeur n'est point trompé de son attente, quand le titre du poème le prépare à n'y voir rien que d'impossible en effet; il y trouve tout croyable, et cette première supposition faite qu'il est des Dieux, et qu'ils prennent intérêt et font commerce avec les hommes, à quoi il vient tout résolu, il n'a aucune difficulté à se persuader du reste.[41]

> Everything that the fable tells us of its Gods, and of its Metamorphoses, remains impossible today, and is nevertheless credible by common opinion, and by this old tradition which has accustomed us to hearing about it ... The listener's expectations are not thwarted after the title of the poem prepares him to see in it nothing but impossible things. He finds everything in the poem credible, and after resolutely making the assumption that the Gods exist, and that they take an interest in and involve themselves with men and their affairs, he has no difficulty in persuading himself of the truth of the rest of the story.

Thus, it is not a question of convincing the spectators of the credibility of the mythological subject because it inherently contains a plausibility determined by the currency of the myth.[42] The marvelous in *Andromède* is credible precisely because it belongs to the Ovidian story. And the marvelous dimension of the myth that involves supernatural beings justifies the intervention of machines.

In sum, the performance of *Andromède* in 1650 on the stage of the Petit-Bourbon marks a significant milestone in which Corneille demonstrated how a dramatic text could be seamlessly integrated with nonverbal elements such as machines. Corneille created a regular tragedy

---

41 Corneille, *Discours de la tragédie, et des moyens de la traiter, selon le vraisemblable ou le nécessaire* (1660), in *Trois discours sur le poème dramatique*, 129.

42 On this question of the "merveilleux vraisemblable," see Corneille's *Discours de la tragédie*, passim. See also Naudeix, *Dramaturgie de la tragédie en musique*, 36.

based on a sequence of causal events that could not be realized without the machines of *Orfeo*.

Reading the *Argument*, one can see how much Corneille is fascinated by the machines, as if he is caught up in his own game. For instance, for the flight of Perseus and Pegasus in act 3 (see Figure 1.9), Corneille states, "[Ce vol] donne lieu à une machine tout extraordinaire et merveilleuse" "([this flight] gives rise to an extraordinary and marvelous machine). As John D. Lyons observes, "Corneille locates his authority to debunk and create rules in his ability to test rules through observation of the audience."[43] In this regard, the length of the stage directions as well as the very detailed description of each of the six sets in the 1651 edition of the play – which find an exact correspondence in the six well-executed engravings by Chauveau – testify to his willingness to combine dramatic rules and elements of scenography. Like *Mirame*, *Andromède* underlines how machine theatre played an underappreciated role in the codification of the poetic rules of the three unities and verisimilitude. Corneille showed how a machine play could respect the regularity of French theatre – and thereby uphold the political order envisaged by Richelieu.

To conclude, I would like to broach the question of the translation of technical knowledge related to stage machinery between Italy and France to shed new light on theatre practices of the time that set the stage for the birth of French opera. It is important to stress that the staging of both *Mirame* and *Andromède* were the result of close collaboration between Italian artists and French playwrights and stage directors. Yet Italian aesthetics were bent to the rules of French political power and savoir-faire. This chapter highlights in a unique way both the creative dynamism of such cooperation and the process of appropriation associated with cultural encounter.

The recently rediscovered French artist Georges Buffequin, known as *peintre et artificier ingénieur du Roy*, and *faiseur d'artifices*, worked at the Palais-Cardinal with Giovanni Maria Mariani. His son, Denis Buffequin, worked with Giacomo Torelli on the stage of the Petit-Bourbon and was called *ingénieur décorateur ordinaire du Roy*, and later

43 Lyons, *Kingdom of Disorder*, 21.

appointed *décorateur-machiniste* of the Théâtre du Marais in 1660.[44] While working at the court, both Georges and Denis Buffequin applied their talent to the public theatre at the Hôtel de Bourgogne and the Théâtre du Marais, respectively. Thus, they shared their newly acquired technological knowledge for the benefit of Parisian companies that took advantage of Italian innovations in stage machinery to broaden their repertoire to attract a larger audience.[45]

Moreover, the performances of *Mirame* and *Andromède* can be viewed as *performative* translations. Indeed, French theatre and plays displayed a multiplicity of languages (verbal and visual), all dictated by French convention, political and poetic, including the three unities and verisimilitude. In the introduction of their co-edited book *Translating Knowledge*, Harold J. Cook and Sven Dupré show how cultural translation draws on an influential mechanism of appropriation, adding: "Translation is ... the process by which information and knowledge are transferred from one place to another, often being altered in the process ... Change is not incidental to translation, but it is its very essence, even if unintended."[46] Desmarets de Saint-Sorlin, and, more importantly, Corneille, in their respective collaboration with French and Italian engineers, machinists and various artists, appropriated the aesthetic of Italian operas for a French theatrical tradition, opening the way for a form of theatre based on spectacular effects but subjected to the rules of dramatic composition.[47] *Mirame* and *Andromède* are therefore the first attempts to synthesize the stagecraft of Italian opera with the conventions of neoclassical French tragedy that would serve as a model in the development of French tragedy in music by Quinault/Lully and Charpentier, among others. If Corneille showed how machines could be part of the *tissure* (fabric) of the plot, it would remain for Pierre Perrin to show how music could also be integrated into the fabric of the

---

44 The title of the *dessein* of *Les Amours de Jupiter et de Sémélé* (1666) by Claude Boyer emphasizes the role of Denis Buffequin: *Dessein de la tragédie des Amours de Jupiter et de Sémélé, représentée sur le Théâtre Royal du Marais, inventé par le Sieur Buffequin, Machiniste* (Paris: Pierre Promé, 1666). On Georges Buffequin, see Bayard, "Les faiseurs d'artifice," 151–64 and "Le roi au cœur du théâtre," 199.

45 See Visentin, "Le théâtre à machines: succès majeur pour un genre mineur."

46 "Introduction" in Cook and Dupré, *Translating Knowledge*, 9–10.

47 Kintzler: "l'opéra français se pense contre l'opéra italien et en fonction du système poétique théâtral" (French opera thinks of itself in contrast to Italian opera and in accordance with the theatrical poetic system) (*Poétique de l'Opéra Français*, 185).

operatic text. It is noteworthy that in his *Letter Written to Monsignor the Archbishop of Turin* (1659), Perrin uses the imagery of weaving, a process that suggests the joining of the material of different textures or sources by using a thread.[48] In the domain of the theatre, this reference to weaving and fabric suggests that the playwright's creation may depend on threads spun abroad while at the same time declaring a distinct cultural identity. Machine plays bear the hallmark of seventeenth century France precisely because they merge foreign and native traditions, the ancient with the innovative, the aesthetic with the political.

---

48   Bohnert, "La poétique des paroles de musique selon Pierre Perrin," 137–45.

2 Opera, Tragedy, and *Tragédie en Musique* between Lully and Rameau

BLAIR HOXBY

Writing in the mid-eighteenth century, Louis de Cahusac said that Philippe Quinault "ne fit qu'une faute qu'une modestie mal entendue lui suggéra" (made just one mistake, suggested to him by false modesty) when he devised the genre of *tragédie en musique* in the 1670s – he misnamed it. Had Quinault put "opera" rather than "tragedy" at the head of his *livrets*, Boileau would have judged the form on its own terms, and, "n'aurait plus vu des tragédies autres que les siennes occuper Paris" (no longer forced to see tragedies other than his grab the attention of Paris), Racine "aurait applaudi sans peine *Armide Opéra*" (would have had no difficulty applauding *Armide,* the opera).[1] In Cahusac's view, Quinault took parts from ancient tragedy, Italian opera, and the regular declaimed tragedy of Pierre Corneille "pour former un nouveau qui, sans leur ressembler, pût en réunir toutes les beautés [dans un] ... spectacle français de chant et de danse" (to construct a new genre which, without resembling these, could bring together all their beauties [in a] ... French spectacle of song and dance).[2] Whereas Corneille had drawn his subjects from history, obeyed the unities of action, place, and time, and relied solely on verse and stage action "tirer l'illusion, l'émotion, l'intérêt" (to sustain the illusion, the emotion, and the [dramatic] interest) of his plots, Quinault avoided history, which was already the preserve of declaimed tragedy and instead chose "le merveilleux" (the marvelous) as "la pierre fondamentale de l'édifice" (the foundation stone of his edifice).[3] "La

---

1 Cahusac, *La Danse*, 214–15. All notes in this chapter refer to the 2004 edition. Giroud, *French Opera*, 19, observes that Lully and Quinault's works were simply called "tragedies" most times.

2 Cahusac, *La Danse*, 202. On the many forms of proto-opera that existed before Quinault, see Demuth, *French Opera*, chs. 1–9.

3 Cahusac, *La Danse*, 202–3.

danse la plus composée, les miracles de la peinture, les prodigies de la mécanique, l'harmonie, la perspective, l'optique" (The most complex dance, the miracles of scene painting, the marvels of machinery, harmony, perspective, optical illusion) – all these could form a bearable and even a necessary part of a theatre of enchantment.[4]

Accounts like Cahusac's, most of which date from the eighteenth century, have led Catherine Kintzler to maintain that between Pierre Corneille's first attempt to adapt Italian opera for French tastes in 1650 and Bernard Germain de Lacépède's *La Poetique de la Musique* (1785) – which she cites as the beginning of a new paradigm – *tragédie en musique* developed as a species of dramatic poetry that the French considered modern, distinct from tragedy, yet defensible in terms of Aristotle's *Poetics*. Declaimed tragedy and *tragédie en musique* were mutually constitutive inversions of each other. Both genres were expected to respect the laws of necessity, propriety, and verisimilitude, but the very meaning of those laws changed when the field of action shifted from history to the enchanted world of the opera house. I accept two of Kintzler's most foundational claims: that most critics before 1785 treated livrets as dramatic poems that ought to be answerable to Aristotelean rules and that an increasing number of critics writing after 1785 came to see opera and tragedy as incompatible and almost incommensurable.

Yet this account threatens to underestimate the extent of the territory that tragedy and *tragédie en musique* contested before 1785. Cahusac was scarcely an impartial witness. Having achieved an indifferent success as the author of declaimed tragedies for the Comédie-Française, Cahusac had found his true calling writing on the theory of dance and collaborating with Rameau on innovative lyric dramas and ballets that pursued *le merveilleux* (the marvelous) in lieu of tragic pathos. Cahusac wanted to draw a veil over the most telling moments of contingency and experiment in the history of *tragédie en musique* because they would only provide ammunition for his critics, who complained that his *livrets* lacked tragic intensity.

By the time he was writing in 1754, French declaimed tragedy and *tragédie en musique* had already fought several skirmishes over the legacy of Euripides. It was natural that tragedians should wish to lay claim to the poet whom Aristotle had anointed "the most tragic," yet the fact that Euripides relied so heavily on sung monodies to depict the love and madness of his heroines and that he often concluded his tragedies with the marvelous entrance of deities in machines also recommended him

---

4　Ibid., 203.

to librettists like Quinault, whose *Alceste* sparked a ferocious quarrel in 1674.[5] When Charles Perrault declared it superior to the original, Racine came to the defence of his beloved Euripides and advanced his own claims to be his legitimate heir, and then their allies lined up to support ancients or moderns, declaimed tragedy or *tragédie en musique*.[6]

Quinault withdrew from the field and concentrated, henceforth, on subjects drawn from Ovid and romances, but revivals of his *tragédies en musique* remained popular (and controversial) even after his death in 1686. Knowing full well that his views would "déplaise aux Inventeurs des Tragedies en musique, Poëmes aussi ridicules que nouveux" (displease the inventors of *tragédies en musique*, poems as ridiculous as they are new), André Dacier, the perpetual secretary of the Académie française, insisted in his commentary on the *Poetics* (1692) that although a cursory examination of Aristotle might suggest that music was essential to tragedy, its part in Greek tragedy was, in fact, a cultural accident: "Il faut même avoüer que nous ne comprenons pas bien, comment la musique a pû jamais être considerée, comme faisant en quelque sorte partie de la Tragedie, car s'il y a rien au monde qui paroisse étranger & contraire même à un action Tragique, c'est le chant" (I must confess, I could never well understand, how music came to be considered as making in any respect a part of tragedy; for if there be any thing in the world that appears stranger, and more contrary than another, to tragic action, it is song).[7] Music and dance, thought Dacier, survived in Greek tragedy as mere artifacts of the superstitious ceremonies from which it had developed. They could only have furnished the intermissions (*intermèdes*), not adorned the tragic action itself.[8] As if it were not enough to have the secretary of the Académie dismissing the very premise that had justified the birth of opera in the first place, that Greek tragedy had been sung throughout, Boileau attacked the genre on quite different grounds the next year. In his tenth satire, he censured Quinault and Lully for depicting the loves of Renaud and Roland so seductively that even a virgin from the austere Jansenist convent of Port-Royal who

---

5 Else, *Poetics*, 1453a22–39. Unless otherwise stated, I follow Else's translation of the *Poetics*.

6 Buford Norman, "Ancients and Moderns"; Forestier, "Notice" to *Iphigénie* in Racine, *Œuvres completes*, ed. Forestier, 1: 1555–79; Fumaroli, "Les abeilles et les araignées," 163–78; Larry F. Norman, *The Shock of the Ancient*.

7 Dacier, *La Poetique d'Aristote*, 86. All citations in this chapter refer to the 1733 edition. The English translations generally follow the anonymous 1705 edition of *Aristotle's Art of Poetry*, which includes "Mr. D'Acier's Notes Translated from the French."

8 Dacier, *La Poetique d'Aristote*, 86–7.

happened into the opera house might be expected to model her conduct henceforth on that of the libidinous Angélique or Armide.[9]

Perhaps these attacks goaded the Académie de Musique into mounting a renewed challenge to the domain of declaimed tragedy during the season of 1693, for in no other opera season during the epoch from Lully to Rameau do we find such a concerted attempt to re-imagine the masterpieces of ancient tragedy and to revise some of the foundational works of French classical theatre. Jean-Galbert de Campistron and the composers Louis Lully and Marin Marais opened with *Alcide*, a revision of Sophocles's *The Women of Trachis*, Seneca's *Hercules Oetaeus*, and Jean Rotrou's *Hercule mourant* (1636).[10] Madame Gillot de Sainctonge (the Académie's first female librettist) and the composer Henry Desmarets followed with *Didon*.[11] And Thomas Corneille and Marc-Antoine Charpentier ended the season with *Médée*, the subject with which Thomas's elder brother Pierre had commenced his career as tragedian in 1635.[12] All three *tragédies en musique* dwell on the destructive power of love; they show a fresh interest in presenting the heroic personality in grievous emotional and physical pain; and, for all their respect for generic conventions, they betray dissatisfaction with Quinault and Lully's usual practice of concluding their works with *divertissements*. They prefer uncompromising final tableaux: Hercules in agony, falling on his pyre; Dido in despair, plunging Aeneas's sword into her heart; Médée in triumph, reviewing the destruction she has wrought from her aerial vantage point.

I want to consider the most distinguished of these works, Thomas Corneille and Charpentier's 1693 *Médée*, in conjunction with Hilaire Bernard de Requeleyne, baron de Longpierre's 1694 *Médée*. This pairing undermines some key generalizations of literary and theatrical history. It is often said that while French tragedians were content to arouse pity and fear by working their historical subjects, they left it to librettists and machinists to arouse admiration with their fables based on mythical subjects. The versions of *Médée* that we will encounter in this chapter make it clear that neither declaimed tragedy nor *tragédie en musique* was prepared to cede its claims to the realm of myth, wonder, and the sublime. That said, my focus throughout will be on *tragédie en*

---

9 Boileau-Despréaux, *Satires*, lines 125–48.
10 On the appeal of Rotrou's *Hercule Mourant*, see Cherbuliez, *In the Wake of Medea*, ch. 3. On Marais's work, see Giroud, *French Opera*, 33–4.
11 See Giroud, *French Opera*, 38–41.
12 On Pierre Corneille's *Médée*, see Cherbuliez, *In the Wake of Medea*, ch. 1, with earlier bibliography.

musique. I want to analyze Thomas Corneille and Charpentier's *Médée* in light of some passages in the *Poetics* that adumbrate a tragic ideal that could make use of, rather than be cheapened by, the resources of a fully equipped opera house. I hope to show how the poet, composer, and scenographer all contribute not only to the tying and untying of the plot but to the representation and management of the passions, the common point of convergence and translation for all the art forms in a *tragédie en musique*. Once we recognize that the central concern of a *tragédie en musique* is to lead the psyches of the audience, then even machine effects or dances that might at first appear to be merely ornamental or conventional will be seen to serve a purpose.

Although scholars such as Downing Thomas and Catherine Kintzler and directors such as William Christie and Hervé Niquet have done much to renew interest in the repertoire of *tragédie en musique*, the form continues to deserve more attention outside of specialist circles. It is time we appreciated it as a strongly complex reading of Attic and Roman dramaturgy, one that, unlike "the most able and influential writers and commentators on Greek tragedy in modern times," locates "the essence of tragedy," as the Greeks themselves did, in the passions it represents and stirs up.[13] At the same time, it offers a map of the *grand siècle*'s psycho-corporal geography that is every bit as revealing as that provided by the aristocratic novel.[14] For it charts the way the passions cross the boundary between the mind and body, becoming "thoughts of, or about, the body," translating complex judgments into actions, and engaging theatregoers in a "form of involuntary thinking between people" as they respond viscerally and intellectually to displays of emotion.[15]

Tragédie en Musique: The Invention of a Genre

Writing to Cardinal della Rovera in 1659, Pierre Perrin reported that "Aprés avoir veu plusieurs fois tant en France qu'en Italie la representation des Comedies en Musique Italiennes, lesquelles il a plu aux compositeurs, & aux executeurs de déguiser du nom *d'Opere*" (After having seen several times, in France as well as Italy, performances of the Italian dramas in music, which the composers and producers have taken to calling *Operas*), he had not despaired, as Lully had publicly, of creating "des tres-galantes en nostres langue, & de fort bien recuës en évitant les deffauts des Italiennes"

---

13 Stanford, *Greek Tragedy and the Emotions*, 2.
14 DeJean, *Ancients Against Moderns*, 78–123.
15 James, *Passion and Action*, 86.

(some very fine ones in our tongue – works which would be well received in spite of the weaknesses of the Italian ones), Perrin believed that the Italian operas of Giulio Rospigliosi, Luigi Rossi, and Monteverdi's Venetian protégé Cavalli, all staged in Paris by Cardinal Mazarin, had met with only a lukewarm reception in Paris because their Italian recitative was too tedious, their arias too long and elaborate, their plots too involved, and their reliance on *castrati* to play lovers and ladies too improbable and distasteful. Yet Perrin believed that opera could be adapted to French taste:

> Laquelle avec tous les avantages de la comedie recitée a sur elle celuy d'exprimer les passions du'une maniere plus touchante, parles fléchissements, les élevations, & les cheutes de la voix. Celuy de faire redire agreablement les mesmes choses, & les imprimer plus vivement dans l'imaginations & dans la memoire: celuy de faire dire à plusieurs personnes les mesmes choses, & exprimer les mesmes sentiments en mesmes temps; & representer par des concerts de voix, des concerts d'esprits, de passions, & de pensées, quelquefois mesme en disant les mesmes choses en differents accents, exprimer en mesme temps; des sentiments divers & d'autres beautez iusu'icy peu connuës, mais excellentes, & d'un succés admirable.

> Such a form of theatre has all the advantages of spoken theatre, and the further advantage over it of expressing the passions in a more touching manner by the movement, the rise and fall, of the voice; of having several things repeated in a pleasing way and impressing them more forcibly upon the imagination and the memory; of allowing several persons to say the same thing at the same time, and to express by concerted voices, the unanimity of their spirits, feelings, and thoughts; sometimes even, by saying the same things in different notes, to express at the same time diverse sentiments; and other beauties little known until now but admirably effective.[16]

The Académie Royale de Musique, which Perrin and Robert Cambert directed from 1669 until Louis XIV revoked their *privilège* in 1672, demonstrated that French opera was not an impossible monster, but posterity has concurred with Cahusac that because Perrin "n'effleura pas même le genre" (did not even skim the surface of the genre), their successors to the *privilège*, Quinault and Lully, really deserve the credit for inventing *tragédie en musique*.[17]

---

16 Perrin, *Œuvres*, 277–9. For a translation of the letter, which I follow, see Auld, *Pierre Perrin*, 1: 102–8; Auld provides an extensive commentary on its content.
17 Cahusac, *La Danse*, 197.

Quinault and Lully were intent on differentiating the new genre from the Italian operas that had been performed in Paris.[18] These, they said, offered nothing but a few agreeable devices. They commenced their *tragédies en musique* with an allegorical prologue that glorified Louis XIV, then presented the dramatic action itself in five acts that culminated in *divertissements* – spectacles of choral song, dance, and spectacular machine effects that drew on the traditions of both the native *ballet de cour* and the Italian *intermedio*. When selecting subjects, Quinault looked for ones that would lend themselves to eruptions of the marvelous, magical, or infernal so that he could integrate these *divertissements* into the action without flouting the dramatic laws of necessity, propriety, and verisimilitude.[19]

Whereas Perrin had thought it necessary to exclude "tous les raisonnements graves & mesmes tous l'intrigue" (all serious discourse and even all plot) from his *livrets*, Quinault and Lully advanced the dramatic action in a plain style of recitative that Lully reportedly based on the declamation of the tragic actress Mlle Champmeslé, who was, in turn, said to have been coached by Racine in every detail, even down to the pitch (*ton*) she should use for each syllable.[20] Yet Lully's recitative sometimes exhibits a more deliberate melodic contour and uniform metre. These arioso passages, which are scarce in *Cadmus et Hermione* (1673) but become more abundant in later *tragédies en musique*, lack only the closed form and repetition that we would expect of an air. Lully wanted to let each act evolve in half-tints with no impressive show-pieces for the singers.

The state in which Quinault and Lully left the genre at their deaths is best exemplified by *Armide* (1686), a target of Boileau's tenth satire. Based on an episode from Tasso's epic romance *Gerusalamme Liberata*, *Armide* follows the fortune of a pagan enchantress as she triumphs over a band of crusading knights only to conceive a passion for one of her

18 On Lully and Quinault, see esp. Prunières, *La Vie Illustre*; Anthony, "Jean-Baptiste Lully"; Palisca, *Baroque Music*, 219–30; Kintzler, *Poétique de l'opéra français*; La Gorce, *L'Opéra à Paris* and *Jean-Baptiste Lully*; Beaussant, *Lully*; Couvreur, *Jean-Baptiste Lully*; Wood, *Music and Drama*; Buford Norman, *Touched*; and Thomas, *Aesthetics of Opera*, chaps. 2–3. For an excellent anthology of contemporary documents and comments related to French baroque opera, see Wood and Sadler, *French Baroque Opera*.

19 On the centrality of the marvellous to French *tragédie en musique*, see Perrault, *Parallèle*, 4: 281–4; Brosses, *Lettres familières*, 2: 241; and Cahusac, *La Danse*, 203. These may be found translated in Wood and Sadler, *French Baroque Opera*, 50, 73–4, 44–6. Also see Kintzler, *Poétique de l'opéra français*.

20 Perrin, *Œuvres*, 282; transl. in Auld, *Pierre Perrin*, 1: 105; Rosow, "French Baroque Recitative."

prisoners, Renaud, who is eventually persuaded by his comrades in arms to abandon her to despair. The catastrophe is thus what Aristotle described as two-fold – with virtue rewarded and vice punished. For Rameau and many others, Armide's recitative monologue "Enfin il est en ma puissance" (At last, he is in my power) (2.5) was a high point in the history of French recitative.[21] As Armide beholds the sleeping Renaud with growing rage, she sings each poetic foot on a quarter note, and her vocal lines rise to the prospect of vengeance; as she makes ready to strike, she utters a spasmodic series of contradictory ejaculations and questions; then, as she begins to yield to love, she sings in increasingly subdued tones at half speed.

"Lorsqu'Armide s'anime à poignarder Renaud" (When Armide nerves herself to stab Renaud), Le Cerf de la Viéville reports, "j'ai vu vingt fois tout le monde saisi de frayeur, ne soufflant pas, demeurer immobile, l'âme toute entière dans les oreilles et dans les yeux, jusqu'à ce que l'air de Violon, qui finit la Scène, donnât permission de respire; puis respirant l'à avec un bourdonnement de joie et d'admiration" (I have twenty times seen the entire audience in the grip of fear, neither breathing nor moving, their whole attention in their ears and eyes, until the air for violin which concludes the scene allowed them to breathe again, after which they exhaled with a murmur of pleasure and admiration).[22] Such exhibitions of competing passions are even more common in act 3, which commences with Armide asking herself in a monologue, "Ah! si la liberté me doit être ravie, / Est-ce à toi d'être mon vainqueur?" (Ah! If of liberty I must be bereft, / Is it you who must be my conqueror?) and ends with her summoning Hate to root Love out of her heart – only to dismiss him and remain Love's captive. Yet the subject also gives Quinault and the scenographer Jean Berain ample opportunities to introduce spectacles that seem required by the plot. In act 1, Armide's victory over the captured knights of the Crusades is celebrated in a pompous triumph that belies her own vulnerability to her prisoner Renaud; in act 2, Armide's magical powers provide the pretext for a *divertissement* in which demons in the shape of nymphs, shepherds, and shepherdesses cast a spell of sleep over Renaud; in act 4, the sensual pleasures of Renaud's dalliance with Armide are represented in dance; and in act 5, her private devastation is externalized when she orders her demons to destroy her enchanted palace in a spectacle of fiery destruction (see Figure 2.1). The conclusion of the tragedy is not as shattering as it might have been, however, because Lully's bright,

---

21   Rameau, *Observations*, 70–122; Dill, "Rameau."
22   Raguenet and Le Cerf, *La Première*, 649.

Figure 2.1. In Quinault and Lully's *Armide*, demons destroy Armide's enchanted palace, and she herself exits in a flying chariot. Berain revived this spectacular finale for *Médée* (1693). Archives nationales (France), COTE 0/1/3238, fN 57.

dance-like music is neither purgative nor cruelly ironic. As Claude Palisca observes, the close of *Armide* must have fallen short of the "fury" imagined by Quinault, for "its melodizing sequences and refrains, its worn triadic clichés, and its persistent anapests lay bare the limitations of Lully's idiom."[23] The conclusion of *Armide* must have suggested to Thomas Corneille and Charpentier just what force such a spectacle might have if only it were supported by a *livret* and a score that could reinforce its power to terrify and purge.

In Search of Tragedy

In the legend of Medea's infanticide in Corinth, Thomas Corneille found a subject that was perfectly suited to the resources of the Académie de Musique. In antiquity, Medea's infanticide had furnished the matter for tragedies by Euripides, Ovid, and Seneca – though Ovid's tragedy had been lost. Since then, it had been dramatized by Jean de La Péruse

---

23   Palisca, *Baroque Music*, 228.

(1554) and Thomas's elder brother Pierre (1634) at key moments in the development of declaimed tragedy in France. But, while Medea herself had appeared as a character in *ballets de cour* and in Quinault and Lully's *Thésée*, her abandonment and revenge had not yet furnished the matter for a *tragédie en musique*.[24]

Euripides's *Medea* exploits the dramatic potential of Medea's spiritual, as opposed to physical, suffering. It charts the turmoil of Medea's passions and the wavering of her aims. It turns song, and particularly the monodies that Medea sings behind the *skene*, into a metaphor of revelation. And it employs machinery to stage the ancient repertoire's most spectacular *coup de théâtre* – Medea's escape in a chariot of the sun, a conclusion that Aristotle and Dacier alike condemned.[25]

If, as Bernard Knox has argued, Euripides's Medea begins by speaking the language of Sophocles's Ajax and ends by speaking like a goddess from the machine, Seneca's starts out with all the hauteur of a goddess. His Medea is never prostrate. Despite having been deprived of all other means of support, she is confident that she can fall back on herself: "Medea superest – – hic mare et terras vies / ferrumque et ignes et deos et fulmina" (Medea is left – in her thou beholdest sea and land, and sword and fire and gods and thunderbolts) (lines 166–7).[26] "Medea," the Nurse begins, only to be answered, "Fiam" (I will be) (line 171). It is the gradual revelation of Medea's character that drives the play to its brilliant conclusion, when, having killed his children, Medea finally confronts Jason with the rhetorical question, "congugem agnoscis tuam?" (Dost recognize thy wife?) (line 1021).

I believe that when Thomas Corneille thought about how to combine and transform these plays into a *tragédie en musique* that would respect the conventions established by Quinault and Lully even as it aspired to the power of classical tragedy, he bore in mind Aristotle's confusing but suggestive assertion that "there are four species of tragedy, for that is also the number of 'parts' that have been discussed": the complex, the pathetic, the ethical, and an unnamed fourth species exemplified by *"The Daughters of Phorcys* and also the *Prometheus* and all the actions in Hades." Some commentators believed that Aristotle must be describing different species of plot: the first was marked by recognitions and reversals; the second by the hero's change of fortune for the worse; the third

---

24 Jaffee, *Medea among the Ancients and Moderns.* On some near-contemporary treatments of Medea, see Giroud, *French Opera*, 28.
25 Aristotle, *Poetics*, 1454a36–b2; Dacier, *La Poetique d'Aristote*, 253, 255–6.
26 All quotations are from Seneca, *Tragedies*, cited parenthetically. Translations are by Frank Justus Miller in the same edition.

by his change of fortune for the better; and the fourth by no change of fortune at all (on the theory that the fortunes of those in Hades do not change). But others concluded that the types should correspond to four of the six parts of tragedy discussed elsewhere in the *Poetics*: fable, manners, sentiment, diction, music, and spectacle. They furthermore inferred that the types should not be mutually exclusive if, as Aristotle says, "one should try to have all (the 'parts') or at least the most important ones and as many of them as possible" (*Poetics*, 1455b32–56a5).[27] *Médée*, I would argue, is an imaginative response to the latter line of interpretation: it answers the invitation implicit in the proposition that the finest tragedy will present a plot that is punctuated by reversals and recognitions, will stage scenes of physical or spiritual suffering, will present an action that seems inextricably tied to the manners of its

27 Commentators on the *Poetics* translate the first three species as (1) *complicata, perplexa*, or *piegata*, (2) *pathetica, passionevole*, or *affetuosa*, and (3) *morata* or *costu-mata*. Most leave the fourth species unnamed but speculate on its nature. See, for example, Robortello, *In librum Aristotelis De Arte Poetica Explicationes*, 210; Vettori, *In primvum librvm Aristotelis de arte poetarum*, 176; Piccolomini, *Annotationi Di M. Allesandro Piccolomini, nel libro della poetica d'Aristotele*, 255. As Castelvetro observed, the puzzle was that the first species seemed to be derived from Aristotle's two-fold division of plots into complex and simple plots, while the second and third species seemed to be derived from two of the six qualitative parts of a tragedy. Was the fourth derived from one of these two other divisions? Castelvetro concluded that it was probably the simple tragedy because the fortune of characters in Hades could not be reversed (Castelvetro, *Poetica d'Aristotele*, 1: 506–7). Nicolò Rossi attests, however, to the widespread opinion that the fourth species of tragedy concerned events that transpire in an inferno (Rossi, *Discorsi intorno alla tragedia*, 117). Daniel Heinsius, who had considerable authority in France, believed that the last three species were all forms of simple tragedy, with the fourth being the "legendary, as if someone should compose a play from Virgil's sixth book, Homer's eleventh, as well as what takes place in the underworld" (Heinsius, *Tragoediae contitutione*, 62). In his copy of Heinsius, Racine named the first three types *implexa, pathetica*, and *morata* (Racine, *Œuvres de J. Racine*, 6: 290). Dacier, describing the passage as "peut-être le plus difficile de toute la Poëtique" (perhaps the most difficult in all of the *Poetics*) (*La Poetique d'Aristote*, 326), ingeniously suggested that the passage might mean that tragedies could be either complex or simple. These were the two principle sorts of tragedy, which might, in turn, be divided into pathetic tragedies (involving deaths, torments, and wounds) and moral tragedies (representing the happiness of persons commendable for their virtue) (*La Poetique d'Aristote*, 312–13). In the twentieth century, Bywater's translation of the fourth type as a form of tragedy featuring "spectacle" has been accepted by several editors and translators (Bywater, *Aristotle*, 53, 248–50), as Else notes (Else, *Poetics*, 525), but Else, favouring an interpretation closer to Castelvetro's, describes the four species as complex, fatal, moral, and episodic (Else, *Poetics*, 523–40). Both Bywater and Else propose emendations to the text.

hero and heroine and is in that sense "ethical," and will make full use of spectacle, as Greek tragedies featuring the Furies or set in Hades did, to arouse the passions of pity and fear in the audience.

Like most *tragédies en musique*, Médée commences with a Prologue glorifying Louis XIV.[28] To the sound of music, the palace of Victory descends from the clouds, revealing Glory, Victory, and Bellone, the goddess of war, all of whom indulge in double-speak that turns the king's wars into bids for peace. They set up *gloire* (glory), a term that Jason and Créon will soon turn into a dirty word, as the highest virtue. They take an interest in the supplication of mortals. And they countenance the advice of a male shepherd who, like the Jason of the tragedy, favours variety in love. The main action then exhausts these pieties and gallantries before destroying their very foundations. That at least some of Louis XIV's subjects would have been perfectly ready to perceive the ironic relationship between the Prologue and tragedy proper is suggested by a remonstrance that Fénelon addressed to the king in December of 1693: "Cette gloire, qui endurcit votre cœur, vous est plus chère que la justice, que votre proper repos, que la conservation de vos peuples qui périssent tous les jours des maladies causées par la famine, enfin que votre salut external, incompatible avec cette idole de gloire" (This glory, which hardens your heart, is dearer to you than justice, than your own peace of soul, than the preservation of your peoples who are dying every day of sicknesses caused by the famine, and even than your eternal salvation, incompatible with this idol, glory).[29]

Whereas Euripides's Medea has already been abandoned by Jason when she sings her opening lament from within her house, Thomas Corneille delays Médée's discovery of Jason's secret plans to marry Créuse until the third act, when recognition and reversal coincide. In keeping with the practices of French classical theatre, he supplies his protagonists with confidantes and creates a liaison between scenes by always retaining at least one character on stage from one scene to the next. Realizing that Aristotle had faulted the appearance of Aegeus in Corinth

---

28   The most complete and detailed reading of the score of *Médée* is Duron, "Commentaire." Cessac, *Charpentier*, chap. 14, also offers an insightful reading. Hitchcock, *Charpentier*, chap. 5, focuses on Charpentier's characterization of Médée. Jaffee, *Medea among the Ancients and Moderns*, analyzes selected scenes in great detail and in the context of other representations of Medea. Thomas, *Aesthetics of Opera*, chap. 4, argues that the Charpentier's compositional practice exceeds the expected function of illustrating a libretto. A recording is available from Les Arts Florissants. A DVD recording of a performance that is not fully staged is available from Le Concert Spirituel.

29   Fénelon, *Correspondance*, 2: 277.

as insufficiently prepared by Euripides, he instead invents another suitor for Créuse named Orontes. He is thus able to establish two overlapping love triangles in which Jason and Créuse are both the objects of emulous desire and Médée and Orontes are both deceived and rejected. Rather than let Créon die embracing his daughter in her poisoned dress, he has Médée drive Créon insane with the sight of a Fury so that the maddened king may assassinate Orontes and then commit suicide. That leaves Créuse free to die, lamenting, before the eyes of Jason. As in Euripides's tragedy, Médée then kills her children, taunts Jason with the deed, and escapes through the air in a chariot drawn by dragons.

The work's *divertissements* intrude on the action like apparitions from a dream world. At the end of act 1, Corinthians and Argives put on a display of wrestling and dancing as they sing in close harmony that love has no weakness when glory upholds it – a position that is promptly proven untenable in the next act when a duet between Créon and Médée sets *amour* and *gloire* at odds. At the end of act 2, Orontes presents a masque of Cupid in which a chorus informs us solemnly that the homage of a lover who wishes to please is sincere and constant – a profession that has already been disproved by Jason. In act 4, phantoms disguised as beautiful women with sweet voices (a seventeenth-century version of "fembots") lure Créon's guards away from him. These *divertissements* seem to vaunt the transfigured world of the stage, to proclaim their allegiance to Apollo boldly so that we may enjoy their negation in the play's concluding spectacle of destruction.

Aristotle, Plutarch, and their commentators stressed that one of the reasons that audiences enjoyed tragedies – despite the distasteful events they depicted – was that they were imitations whose accuracy and artistry afforded pleasure, just as the skillful painting of a cadavre provoked spectators to wonder and delight.[30] "L'invention, l'ordonnance, le dessein, la proportion des parties qui le composent, l'arrangement général des matières" (The *invention*, the *contrivance*, the *design*, the *proportion* and *symmetry* of parts, the *general disposition* of matters) of a dramatic poem were especially capable of generating the pleasure produced by sheer artistry, said René Rapin.[31] As if in response, the poet, composer, and scenographer of *Médée* all emphasize the way in which the characters are brought together and the plot is tied and untied with a respect for symmetry worthy of a geometrician.[32] This symmetry is to

---

30 Aristotle, *Poetics*, 1448b9–12; Plutarch, "How to Study Poetry," in *Moralia* 18.
31 Rapin, *Réflexions*, 390–1 (Pt. 1, ch. 18); Rapin, *Réflexions*, trans. Rymer, 25.
32 For a suggestive analysis of the motives for and functions of symmetry in French classical theatre, see Greenberg, *Corneille*.

be taken as evidence that the play's foundations are solid and its pretensions to being a "complex" tragedy valid.

Thomas Corneille and Charpentier make particularly effective use of recitative dialogues and air-like duets to chart the characters' shifting alliances and their ebbs and flows of power over each other. In act 1, scene 2, Médée and Jason sing a love duet in which Médée is already nostalgic and Jason already disingenuous. Parallel double-duets in act 2, scene 5, and act 3, scene 1, the first sung plaintively in a minor mode and the second more aggressively in a major mode, then underline the fact that Jason and Créuse have cemented their relationship and that the spurned and abused Médée and Orontes have formed a temporary alliance to foil their plans. The characters' reversals of fortune are also underlined by these interviews and duets. In act 2, scene 2, Médée begs Créuse to take pity on her children in an air that is often painfully chromatic – a plea that Créuse silently disdains. In act 5, scene 2, the situation is neatly reversed when Créuse begs Médée slowly in what Charpentier characterized as the "dark and sad" mode of C minor for the pity that she withheld from Médée, a plea that Médée answers with stern demands delivered in the "gay and warlike" mode of C major.[33] For now it is she who possesses the power of a king and father.

It is Jason and Créuse's duets that chart their reversal of fortune most clearly. Finding themselves alone at last in act 2, scene 5, they wish in the "tender and plaintive" key of A minor that sweet repose might be displaced by the pleasurable agitation of love: "Doux repos, quittez-moi, ne revenez jamais" (Sweet repose, leave me, never come back). This is an audacious wish, for, in seventeenth-century usage, "le repos" was a cardinal virtue and a desirable state of happiness.[34] Pierre Corneille's Infante in *Le Cid* prays for it in the first sense: "Assure mon repos, assure mon honneur" (Secure my peace of mind, secure my honour).[35] In one of her most famous airs, the Médée of *Thésée* regrets her loss of "doux repos" in the second sense: "Doux repos, innocente paix, / Heureux, heureux un coeur que ne vous perd jamais" (Sweet repose, innocent peace, / Happy, happy a heart that never loses you).[36] And in

---

33 Charpentier wrote in terms of modes rather than keys, and I follow Ranum in respecting his practice. For a complete list of the *énergies* that Charpentier attributed to various modes, see Cessac, *Charpentier*, Appendix 2; these are also discussed and compared to similar lists compiled by other composers and theorists in Ranum, *The Harmonic Orator*, 318–46.
34 Stanton, "The Ideal of 'Repos.'"
35 Corneille, *Théâtre complet, Le Cid*, 1.3.143.
36 Jaffee, *Medea among the Ancients and Moderns*, 260–70.

Racine's *Phèdre*, the heroine recalls the moment before her fatal passion in the same terms: "mon repos, mon bonheur semblait être affermi" (my repose, my happiness seemed to be secure) (1.3.271).[37] For Créuse blithely to wish away such a state makes her seem wanton rather than vulnerable to the sway of her own passion like the young Médée or Phèdre. As Créuse introduces the idea and its musical figure, Jason takes her up on it. Their staggered entrances express all the fresh excitement of the chase, while the tentative nature of their relationship is suggested right up to the close of the duet when they seem to bring their song to a close with a deceptive cadence at "jamais" (never) – only to have the accompaniment follow with a vi chord on the downbeat of the measure so that they may arrive at a perfect authentic cadence by reiterating their wish that repose never return.

In act 5, scene 6, their wish is answered with tragic irony. Médée touches Créuse with her wand and enjoins her laconically, "Connoissez tout ce que je suis" (Learn everything of what I am). Créuse's bodily agony is a figure of inner knowledge: now she understands what Médée is through and through. But it is also Médée's idea of poetic justice. The princess wanted the agitation of love, the flame of passion? Well then, let her tremble and burn! As Créuse's alarm degenerates into pure suffering, her decline is figured by descending sevenths. When Jason enters, Créuse finds herself begging him, in terms reminiscent of Médée's, not to abandon her. As she consoles herself with the thought that she will at least die before Jason's eyes, she seems to anticipate her own death with her descending scale, which ends on the tonic at "yeux" (eyes) – the same note that will soon mark her demise. She has settled into the "dark and plaintive" mode of F minor. Jason recognizes the scene for what it is, a terrible "spectacle" that Médée has staged to break his heart. But Créuse transcends Jason's harsh recitative with her lament, "Helas! prests d'estre unis par les plus douces chaînes, / Faut-il nous voir separer à jamais?" (Alas! Ready as we are to be united in the sweetest bonds, / Are we now to be separated forever?). Much as he had in their happy love duet of act 2, "Doux repos, quittez-moi," Jason joins her, singing in canonic imitation. Kay Jaffee observes that the music, with its brief passages of homophonic declamation, two interwoven voices, and the bass playing in counterpoint, sounds like one of Charpentier's *leçons de ténèbres*.[38] We should be put in mind of the desolate book of Lamentations (from which the *leçons* are drawn) and the emotional career of

---

37 Racine, *Œuvres Complètes. Phèdre*, 1.3.271.
38 Jaffee, *Medea among the Ancients and Moderns*, 268.

Holy Week (during which they are performed), for the music seems determined to register absolute loss even as it strives to rise above that loss. It is typical of late-seventeenth-century tragedy, whether declaimed or sung, to spare no efforts to generate pathos at the death of even a deeply flawed character: for a moment, the perturbations of the character's soul are everything. Throughout Créuse's final lyrical flowering, harmonic changes have been sounding like a death knell at regular intervals: her end cannot be deferred forever. Finally, the bassline, with its descending scale, seems to pull her down to earth, and we return to the reality of her suffering. In recitative, she announces, "Je perds la voix, mes forces s'affoiblissent, / C'en est fait, j'expire, je meurs" (I lose my voice, my strength weakens. / It is done, I breathe my last, I die) (5.6). As Créuse sings "je meurs," she descends to the tonic, the same note on which she anticipated her death before Jason's eyes, but the orchestra follows with a diminished third, the same painful interval that marked Médée's separation from Jason. It then prolongs the dominant before finally settling on the tonic. The effect is to dilate the moment of her death. This is the tragic conclusion of Jason and Créuse's heedless wishes in act 2.

Berain's scenes also underline the essential order of the *livret*.[39] Whereas Berain normally reserved the spectacular effect of having an entire palace descend from heaven to earth for the *deus ex machina* of the fifth act, he employs it in the Prologue of *Médée* to translate Gloire, Victoire, and Bellone from the heavens to underline how different will be the trajectory of this tragedy: the only one in a machine in act 5 will be Médée herself – proof, wherever she flies, that there are no gods (see Figure 2.2). Act 1 transpires in a public square with statues and trophies set up on pedestals and a triumphal arch (see Figure 2.3). As Médée and her confidante Nérine stand before this setting in the opening scene, the tableau immediately establishes a potential conflict between the public and the private, the masculine and the feminine, *gloire* and *amour*, the power of rulers and the devices of women, the sacred aura of majesty and the profane charisma of actresses who, as surely as kings, inhabit two bodies, their own and their role's. In act 3, when Médée never leaves the stage, the gloomy interior setting begins to figure her inner self (see Figure 2.4). And in act 5, when Médée's palace occupies the backdrop, the scene underlines the fact that her palace, and not the triumphal arches and trophies associated with all legitimate, male authority, is now the locus of power, making good Médée's boast that Créuse must now look to her to find the power of a king and father. At the conclusion of the play, Berain's staging of

---

39   On Berain in general, see especially La Gorce, *Berain*.

Figure 2.2. The Prologue of *Médée* is set in the countryside. The Palace of Victory appears in the clouds, moves forward, and fills the stage. We can imagine the scene by referring to Giacomo Torelli's earlier scene from *La Venere Gelosa*, act 1, scenes 2-6 (Venice, 1643, Teatro Novissimo), in which the Palace of Venus descends from the clouds. Engraving by Marco Boschin. By permission of the Theater Collection, Harvard University. Torelli brought Venetian stagecraft to Paris. Vigarani and Berain more often reserved this effect for the ends of Quinault and Lully's *tragédies en musique*. The Palace of Venus appears in a *gloire*, for instance, for the finale of *Persée*.

Corinth's destruction by flame makes good the *livret*'s insistent descriptions of love and passion as flames, flames that Médée has all along been bent on literalizing – first with the poisons that burnt Créuse, now with the flames that threaten to engulf Jason (see Figure 2.1). But it is important to bear in mind that Berain was not striving to shake the audience's sense of safety as some stage engineers such as Gian Lorenzo Bernini had done earlier in the century when they set the stage on fire or threatened to inundate the audience with a diverted river. By 1693, even such spectacular machine effects as the palace that descended from the clouds, the

Figure 2.3. Jean Berain, a Public Square. *Médée*, act 1 (Paris, 1693, Académie Royale de Musique). Berain's scene suggests the kingly majesty of Créon and the martial heroism of Jason, both of which are set against the feminine passions and power of Médée. Archives nationales (France), COTE 0/1/3242, fN 17.

chariot that flew through the air, or the city that burst into flame were an established part of the repertoire of master stage engineers (see Figures 2.5 and 2.6).[40] Berain would not have had it any other way. For by the late seventeenth century, Descartes's stress on the need for audiences to feel secure in the theatre before they could take a pleasurable excitement in the passions stirred up there had won wide acceptance. Berain's scenes were intended to arouse a perturbation in the souls of the audience that, while forceful, would fall short of being truly alarming.

The personality of Médée, originally sung by Le Rochois, the highly regarded creator of Lully's Armide, dominates the entire work. In this sense, *Médée* is a tragedy of *ethos,* a word that Aristotle's commentators usually translated as *mores, mœurs, manners, customs,* or (by the eighteenth century) *character. Ethos,* said Aristotle, was one of the natural causes of the action that a plot imitates (*Poetics* 1450a1–11). Dryden

40   Bjurström, *Giacomo Torelli*, 196–211; Hoxby, "Technologies."

Figure 2.4. Jean Berain, a place intended for Médée's invocation. *Médée*, act 3 (Paris, 1693, Académie Royale de Musique). Demons bring poisons and the dress of Créusé. A chorus of monsters is born. Archives nationales (France), COTE 0/1/3242, fN 67.

explained that this was so because "the manners in a Poem, are understood to be those inclinations, whether natural or acquir'd, which move and carry us to actions, good, bad, or indifferent in a Play; or which incline the persons to such, or such actions."[41] Medea is vengeful, Rapin says by way of illustrating this point, and her actions must be seen to follow from her *mœurs*.[42]

Charpentier's score answers the charge by providing Médée with a signature theme, a passage of throbbing sixteenth notes played by the strings. We hear it in the first scene when Médée predicts that she will show "Ce qu'est Médée & son pouvoir" (Who Medea is and what is her power). The theme recurs whenever Médée settles on a course

41 Dryden, "The Grounds of Criticism in Tragedy," in *Works*, 13: 234.
42 Rapin, *Réflexions*, 420–1 (Pt. 1, ch. 25); Rapin, *Réflexions*, trans. Rymer, 38.

Figure 2.5. Stage design by Francesco Guitti. Engraving by Giovonni Battista Torre. From *La Contesa Torneo fatto in Ferrara per le nozze dell'illustrissimo signor Gio. Francesco Sacchetti coll'illustrissima signora D. Beatrice Estense Tassona* (Ferrara: Francesco Zuzzi, 1632). By permission of the Victoria and Albert Museum (London). Guitti seems to have been the first scenographer to introduce an airborne temple, but he was soon followed by Giacomo Torelli, Carlo Vigarani, and Jean Berain, all of whom used the device multiple times. By the time *Médée* was staged, it was a "theatregram."

of action, and because it is precisely such decisions that, according to Aristotle, define a hero's character or manners (*Poetics* 1450b7–9), it becomes a musical figure of her character. At the mid-point of the tragedy, it becomes associated with the infernal powers that Médée summons up. In act 5, when her deliberative reason and her fury, her actions and her character, finally converge on the terrible resolution to kill her children, her speech itself falls into the pattern of sixteenth notes found in her theme. As it recurs with a tragic inevitability, the theme implies that Médée's personality drives the action of the play. But it also suggests that we can truly understand her, truly understand the significance of the theme first sounded in this scene, only after all the events of the drama have unfolded. It functions like the gnomic utterances of Seneca's Medea, which lead inexorably from "Medea/ Will I be" to "Dost recognize thy wife?" But in the case of Charpentier's tragedy, Médée

Figure 2.6. Set design by Alfonso Parigi. Engraving by Stefano della Bella. From *Le nozze degli dei: favola dell ab' Gio. Carlo Coppola; rappresentata in musica in Firenze nelle reali nozze de serenis.mi gran duchi de Toshana Ferdinando II. e Vittoria principessa d'Vrbino* (Florence: Amadore Massi and Lorenzo Landi, 1637). By permission of the Houghton Library, Harvard University. Such burning ruins had become a standard image of Hell in Florence, but it is easy enough to see how they could suggest to Berain the spectacle of a burning palace with Médée in her flying chariot and demons raining down a hail of fire on Corinth.

doesn't even have to ask the rhetorical question: the violins ask it for her as she appears in the sky above Jason.

Aristotle's mention of Sophocles's *Ajax* as an example of the "pathetic" species of tragedy persuaded many of his commentators that a pathetic tragedy should prominently display the physical or spiritual suffering of the hero. The *Ajax* repeatedly asserts that the madness and mental anguish of its hero are worse than the physical pain he endures when he falls on his own sword. The play therefore reinforced the belief of commentators that when Aristotle named the pathos of a tragedy its one essential plot element, he was referring to a suffering that might be physical or spiritual. As Castelvetro explained,

> Prima la passione si considera o come dolorosa o come angosciosa. Io domando passione dolorosa come è l'essere ucciso come fu Laio, e l'essere fedito come fu Filottete, o l'essere legato nella mala maniera che fu legato

Prometeo nel monte Caucaso, o l'esser fatta forza come fu fatta a Tamar, e simili cose. E domando passione angosciosa come fu quella che sostenne Teseo, credendo che Ippolito suo figluolo avesse fatta forza alla matrigna, e come quella che sostenne Eolo quando riseppe lo scelerato congiugnimento di Macareo e di Canace suoi figliuoli.[43]

The pathos may be of two kinds, physical or spiritual. Physical pathos consists of being killed like Laius; or being wounded like Philoctetes; or being cruelly bound as was Prometheus on Mt. Caucasus; or being raped as was Tamar; and similar things. Spiritual pathos is the kind experienced by Theseus, when he believed that his son Hippolytus had violated his stepmother, and by Aeolus when he learned that his children Canace and Macareus had engaged in wicked intercourse.

The assumption that the pathos of a tragedy might be both physical and spiritual – or indeed, only the latter – was reinforced by the range of words commentators used to translate the term: *affectus, perturbatio, passio, passione*. All these could denote the spiritual disturbances that we would call the passions.[44] We have already seen that *Médée* presents scenes of physical suffering such as the deaths of Orontes, Créuse, and Médée's children and, in this sense, qualifies as a "pathetic" tragedy. It remains to consider now how the play imitates the spiritual suffering of its characters.

Throughout the seventeenth century, greater and greater importance was attached to the passions. Because they might be sources of either good or ill, happiness or pleasure, and because they were felt in the soul and were in that sense indubitable, they were, at least from the human perspective, the measure of all things. Actions, and particularly changes of fortune, assumed significance only as they were felt.[45] "Wise poets," wrote Sir William Davenant while he was in exile in Paris in 1650, "think it more worthy to seeke out truth in the passions, then to record the truth of actions."[46] The abbé d'Aubignac observed that "il ne se faut pas contenter d'émouvoir une passion par un Incident notable ... mais il la faut conduire jusqu'au point de sa plénitude. Ce ne'est pas assez d'avoir énbranlé l'esprit des Spectateurs, mail il [les] <le> faut enlever" (it is not enough to raise a passion upon a good incident ... but it must be carried to the point of fullness. It is not enough to have shaken the mind of the spectators, you must ravish it).[47] He conceived of these

---

43   Castelvetro, *Poetica d'Aristotele*, 1: 300–1.
44   Heinsius, *Tragoediae contitutione*, ch. 8.
45   Mace, "Dryden's Dialogue," 91.
46   Davenant, "The Authors Preface," in *Gondibert*, 5.
47   Aubignac, *La Pratique*, 467.

affecting exhibitions as part of a sequence in which a dramatist like Pierre Corneille could produce "by degrees" what his English translator described memorably as a gallery of "monuments" to the passions.[48] The passions were closely related to, and sometimes treated as synonymous with, the affections, and they overlapped with what we would term the emotions.[49] Indeed, in his *Treatise of the Passions*, Descartes said that he would prefer to speak of the "émotions de l'âme" (emotions of the soul) because "de tout les sortes de pensées qu'elle peut avoir, il n'y en a point d'autres qui l'agitent et l'énbranlent si fort que font ses passions" (among all the sorts of thought it can have, there are no others which agitate [the soul] and shake it so strongly as these passions do).[50] Most sixteenth- and seventeenth-century writers, following in the tracks of Cicero and Augustine, held that virtually all the passions could be described as forms of appetite or aversion. For instance, in a lecture on catharsis delivered in 1586, the Florentine critic Lorenzo Giacomini defined an affection as a spiritual movement or operation of the mind in which it is attracted or repelled by an object it has come to know. It was a result, he said, of an imbalance in the animal spirits and vapours that flowed through the body. Either internal or external sensations could stimulate the body to alter the state of its spirits.[51] Like Aristotle, Giacomini conceived of the passions as discrete states – "anger, pity, fear, and all similar emotions and their contraries" (Aristotle, *Rhetoric* 1378a) – in which the body and mind tended to remain fixed until a subsequent sensation stimulated another alteration of the vapours.[52] Most theorists held that there were a limited number of basic or primitive passions – perhaps as few as four or as many as eleven. The passions were seen to be such a fundamental part of what it was to be human – for it was they that translated

---

48 Aubignac, *Whole Art*, 3: 47.
49 For general discussions of the passions, see especially Levy, *French Moralists*; James, *Passion and Action*; and Newbold, introduction to Wright, *The Passions of the Mind in General*. On the importance of the passions to seventeenth-century theories of tragedy, also see Mace, "Dryden's Dialogue" and Wasserman, "Pleasures of Tragedy." On their musical expression, see Ranum, *The Harmonic Orator*, chap. 11. On the shifting lexicon of the human heart in late seventeenth-century French literature, see DeJean, *Ancients Against Moderns*, 78–94.
50 Descartes, *Œuvre philosophique*, 3: 974; translated in *Passions*, art. 28. For recent accounts of Descartes's theory of the passions, see Rorty, "Descartes on Thinking with the Body"; Kambouchner, "Descartes and the Passions"; and Williston and Gombay, *Passion and Virtue in Descartes*, all with earlier bibliography.
51 Giacomini, *Orationi e Discorsi*, 38. The discourse is reprinted in Weinberg, *Trattati*, 3: 345–71.
52 Hathaway, *Age of Criticism*, 351–60; Palisca, "Alterati," 24–9. The translation of Aristotle's *Rhetoric* is by J.H. Freese.

complex judgments into actions and negotiated the vexed relationship between the soul and the body, the self and its environment – that writers such as Jean-Pierre Camus, Nicholas Coeffeteau, Marin Cureau de la Chambre, René Descartes, Nicholas Malebranche, and Guillaume Lamy devoted entire treatises or sections of treatises to naming and describing them. Poetic metres, rhetorical figures, facial expressions, gestures, tempos, and modes were all duly studied with the ambition of arriving at a universal rhetoric of the passions.[53]

Theorists of *tragédie en musique* generally agreed that if it was to imitate and move the passions successfully, its verse must be different from a declaimed tragedy's. Whereas the spoken word appealed most forcefully to the reason and will, song was particularly well equipped to touch the passions. In deference to this view, Thomas Corneille eschews difficult arguments and flights of poetic imagery in favour of clear, direct expressions of feeling. He writes in short, irregular lines using a strictly confined vocabulary. His discipline leaves Charpentier ample opportunity to translate the movement of characters' souls into a musical equivalent expressed in terms of vocal inflection, tempo, pauses, and modes.[54] When setting recitative, Charpentier lets the verse dictate the note values and cadences, but by having a singer deliver a line at the top or bottom of her range, in an ascending or descending melodic line, quickly or slowly, he can determine whether the speech is heard as public or private, triumphant or despairing, furious or pathetic. The very restraint of Charpentier's text setting means that when he does indulge in a madrigalism – when Médée's surcharged passion finds a release at the phrase "je sens couler mes larmes" (I feel my tears flow), and her vocal line descends in a graceful melisma that paints her tears (3.3) – it can be remarkably affecting.

Charpentier was interested in the extent to which any given mode, characterized by a distinctive major or minor triad, could be said to embody, and thus lead the psyche toward, a particular passion, and he therefore

---

53 For the relationship of various forms of expression to the passions, see, for example, Mesnardiere, *La Poétique*, 399–409, on metrical forms; Arnaud, *Art of Speaking*, on tropes and figures; Bulwer, *Chirologia*, on hand gestures; Le Brun, *Conférence sur l'expression*, and Montagu, *Expression of the Passions*, on facial expressions and postures; Roach, *Player's Passion*, chaps. 1–2, and Barnett, *Art of Gesture*, on stage actions; Mersenne, *Harmonie universelle*, Duncan, "Persuading," and Ranum, *The Harmonic Orator*, on musical rhetoric.
54 The idea that monodic music should be a heightened representation of natural speech or expressions of emotion, such as sighs, is widespread. See, for example, Galilei, *Dialogo*, in Strunk, *Source Readings*, 318–19; Dubos, *Réflexions*, 1: 386–7; Saint-Mard, *Réflexions sur l'Opéra*, 10–11.

compiled the list of "*énergies des modes,*" sometimes translated as "key feelings," from which I have drawn my characterizations of the various modes as "soft and plaintive," "gay and warlike," and the like. It seems likely, as Patricia Ranum has argued, that he used the word *énergie* to suggest both the Greek *energeia,* or the force of soul that propels the rhetorical act of persuading, and the similar *enargeia,* or pictorial vividness, so that he associated each mode with both a "persuasive tone of voice and a colorful theatricality."[55] Charpentier is willing to switch modes each time a character expresses a distinct sentiment. Thus, when Médée first enters the stage, she sings in the "furious and quick tempered" mode of F major, but as she claims that her powers could still be at Jason's disposal if only he would remain faithful, she modulates through the "grave and pious" mode of D minor: "La fuite, l'exil, la mort même, / Tout est doux avec ce qu'on aime" (Flight, exile, death even, / Everything is delight with the being one loves) (1.1). When he wants to underline the fact that characters talking to each other are feeling contrasting sentiments, Charpentier will even have them sing over or past each other in different modes.

The way all the musical and visual resources of an opera house can be co-ordinated to create a gallery of monuments to the passions is best illustrated by the central scene complex of *Médée.* When Jason takes leave of his wife in act 3, Médée remains alone on stage to lament in the "grave and pious" mode of D minor that he is insensitive to the tenderest fire that ever burnt in a heart (3.3). The troubled wanderings of her thought and the perplexities of her soul are beautifully suggested by Berain's scene, with its mysterious corridors receding at oblique angles, its barred doors, and its half-hidden oculus (see Figure 2.4), and they are enacted, too, in the form of Charpentier's *rondeau,* with its suspensions, unexpected shifts of colour, and insistent refrain, "Quel prix de mon amour, quel fruit de mes forfaits!" (Such is the price of my love, such is the fruit of my sins!) (3.3). The key words of this refrain – "prix," "amour," "fruit" – are accented harmonically to create a sense of expanding dissonance. Médée's sentiments change rapidly. As she thinks about the fact that she forced a hundred monsters to yield to Jason, her pulse quickens, her ire flashes, and the violins play for a moment without mutes; but then, as she recalls the tranquillity that once reigned in her heart, she sings slowly in 3/2 metre and in an elegiac mood, mourning the loss not only of her innocence but of her natural feelings – including, we realize with a mixture of horror and sorrow, her maternal affections. A string accompaniment, written in a low register with expressive counterpoint,

---

55 Ranum, *The Harmonic Orator,* 322.

figures her inchoate passions. Contemporary physiological theory predicted a delay between felt emotion and speech, a delay figured here, I
think, by the relationship between score and text: the strings, representing Médée's felt emotion, anticipate her vocal line.[56] As words finally fail
her and she stands alone on stage, the strings extend the melodic line of
her air to suggest that she retains a residue of passion.

When Nérine enters to warn Médée of the secret marriage that is
afoot, the strings play a prelude of throbbing sixteenth notes like those
we heard at the beginning of the drama, when Médée predicted darkly
that, if Jason proved untrue, he would learn "Who Medea is, and what
is her power." Suddenly, as she sings in the "magnificent and joyous"
key of B-flat major, her voice rises above the strings to announce one of
the crucial choices that will, in Aristotle's terms, establish her character.
She determines that if there is nothing in her despair to frighten him,
she'll let crime separate them, just as crime united them (3.4).

Having dismissed Nérine, Médée stands alone on stage for the first time
since lamenting, "Quel prix de mon amour." Singing low in her range, she
calls upon the Black daughters of Styx (3.5). As they play a disconcerting
rhythmic figure of held notes tied by a slur to a rapid-fire series of sixteenth
notes, the strings represent the powers of hell being slowly roused into
motion. We should not permit the conventional aspects of this scene to de-
tract from its significance. For it is a means of preserving and staging one of
the central ambiguities of Attic tragedy, which, it has been said, instantiates
the reversibility of Heraclitus's saying: "[I]t is the character of man that one
calls *daimōn*"; or conversely, "what one calls character in man is in fact a
daimōn." All that a Greek hero says and does on the stage may be consistent
with his character, yet Attic tragedies suggest that his words and actions
could also be the expression of some external spiritual force, a *daimōn* op-
erating through him.[57] Euripides's *Medea* maintains both possibilities. For
all any external observer can tell, it is some god who overpowered Medea
with love and throws suffering on her in waves of despair (lines 527–31,
362–3). When she tells her Tutor why she looks so sad, she maintains the
same ambiguity: "I have every reason, old man. The gods, and I in my
madness, have contrived it so" (lines 1013–14).

However alien this idea may seem to us, it is a paradox that the seventeenth century was prepared to accept. Sermons and spiritual autobiog-
raphies provide ample evidence that men and women experienced their
selves not as bounded egos but as voids open to spiritual influences. In the

---

56 Golding, *Classicist Acting*, 97.
57 Vernant and Vidal-Nacquet, *Myth and Tragedy*, 37.

colourful imagery of Lancelot Andrewes, "a house will not stand empty long. One spirit or other, holy or unholy, will enter and take it up." To be yourself, then, was to be inhabited by something other than yourself.[58] In *Médée*, the heroine's inner chamber, which has served as a figure of the self for the entire act, is now occupied by hell's denizens: Vengeance, Jealousy, and a chorus of demons (see Figures 2.4–2.7). These may be the most perfect expression of her character, but, then again, what we have been perceiving as her character and her passions may all along have been the expression of some demonic influence. In the declaimed tragedy of Racine, that paradox might be suggested subtly by a word like *furie*, which is enough to pose the question, Is the Hermione of *Andromaque* merely in the grip of a passion, or is she possessed? At the Académie de Musíque, it could be expressed using all the marvels of operatic staging and the expressiveness of music. Charpentier underlines this ambiguity by employing the theme that has thus far been associated with Médée's character to figure hell itself.

I have written thus far of the imitation of the passions, but it is important to bear in mind that to stage the passions meant to *induce* them. The writings of Aristotle, Cicero, Horace, and Quintilian on the arts of rhetoric and oratory all affirmed that the surest way to arouse an affection was to *represent* it in the pitch, rhythms, and gestures appropriate to it.[59] For Giacomini and his followers, who understood that the word *catharsis* had a medical sense in ancient Greek, the natural sympathy that existed between humans meant that when a hero displayed his passions on stage, the sight and sound agitated the souls of the audience and attracted their passions – so that the actor's display functioned like a cure, drawing out and purifying the passions of the audience. Other writers, including Descartes, Rapin, Dryden, and the abbé Dubos, stressed that entering into the passions of characters on stage was, in and of itself, one of the chief pleasures afforded by the theatre.[60] The soul preferred being agitated even by seemingly painful emotions like pity and terror rather than being left in its naturally sluggish state.

If a passion or affection was a spiritual movement or operation of the mind in which it is attracted or repelled by an object it has come to know, and if one tended to remain fixed in such a state until dislodged

---

58 On the "pneumatic" self, see Shuger, *Habits of Thought*, 97–105, esp. 100, where she quotes *The Works of Lancelot Andrewes*, 11 vols. (Oxford: OUP, 1854), 3: 191.

59 Else, *Poetics*, 1455a; Euripides, *Suppliant Women*, lines 180–3; Cicero, *De Oratore*, 2.45–6; Horace, *Ars Poetica*, lines 99–108; Quintilian, 6.2.

60 Descartes, *Passions*, art. 94; Rapin, *Réflexions*, 361–3 (Pt. 1, ch. 7), 427–30 (Pt. 1, ch. 26), 532–8 (Pt. 2 , chs. 18–19); Dryden, referring to Rapin, in "The Grounds of Criticism in Tragedy," in *Works*, 13: 232; Dubos, *Réflexions*, 1:1–8.

Figure 2.7. Jean Berain, demon. Musée du Louvre, Collection Rothschild, Paris, 1721 DR. Photo: Réunion des Musées Nationaux / Art Resource, NY.

from it by a new object or thought, it made sense that a dramaturgy that was bent on agitating the soul would present a continuous variety of passions on stage, so that love might be followed by hate, or joy by despair. Because writers thought the passions were associated with derangements of the body's humours and spirits, they resorted naturally enough to tidal metaphors. The music theorist Marin Mersenne explained that the heart expanded when joyful and sent up vital spirits to the face, thus turning it rosy, whereas

> quand la tristesse est excessive, les mesmes esprits se retirent au cœur en trop grande multitude, & l'étouffent, parce qu'il ne peut plus se mouvoir, ny s'ouvrir: de sorte que des ces deux passions sont semblables au flux & reflux de la mer, car la ioye est semblable au flux. ... Mais la crainte & l douleur sont semblables au reflux qui retire ce qu'il avoit amené: car la crainte & l'effroy rendent le visage pasle, & la contenance morne & hideuse, en retirant le sang & les esprits, & font que la melancholie corrumpt le peu de sang qui reste dans les veines.

> when sadness is excessive, the same spirits return to the heart in too great a multitude and stifle it, because it can no longer move, nor open; so these two passions are like the flux and reflux of the sea because joy is like the flux. ... but fear and sadness are like the reflux, which takes away what it had previously brought in, because fear and terror render the face pale and make the countenance mournful and hideous as the blood and spirits leave and melancholy corrupts the little blood that remains in the veins.[61]

Mersenne's vivid physiological description makes it clear that when Dryden writes of "The Passions rais'd and calm'd by just Degrees, / As Tides are swell'd and then retire to the Seas," he is pointing to a style of dramaturgy whose ambition is to subject the audience to a sea change of emotions that will be felt vividly in the body (*Aureng-Zebe*, Epilogue, lines 7–8). I have argued that the *divertissements* of *Médée* recur throughout the tragedy like manifestations from the dream world of Apollo so that they may be negated at the conclusion of the tragedy. The imagery of Mersenne and Dryden points to another function: they provide the high tides of joy that are necessary if the low ebbs of fear, terror, and melancholy are to be deeply felt.

Although Dacier declared it absurd that "les ingenieurs & les ouvriers" (engineers and workmen) should be thought able to regulate our

---

61 Mersenne, *Harmonie universelle*, 368; Duncan, "Persuading the Affections," 160.

passions and therefore be given "tout l'honneur des passions que nous sentirions en voiant une Tragedie" (all the honour of those passions that we feel when watching a tragedy),[62] Berain's scenes do in fact play on the heart-strings – as they should in a tragedy that aspires to comprise all the species of tragedy, including the fourth, which, according to one line of interpretation, used spectacle to stir the tragic emotions. Berain's scenes establish a rhythm in which the audience is persuaded to identify deeply with the pathos of the characters on stage and then, because "the Passions ... suffer violence when they are perpetually maintain'd at the same height," is offered the relief of a novel scene.[63] The excess of spirits generated by this new object of wonderment should, in turn, make the audience more responsive to the imitations of the passions that will follow. Thus, Berain's engineering could be said to put the audience through passionate gymnastics and turn them into emotional athletes primed for all the exhilaration that a theatre of the passions could afford.

Many seventeenth-century critics believed firmly that tragedies could end happily, not only because so many of Euripides's tragedies did but because the prospect of an impending evil could arouse the passions of pity and terror almost as effectively as the sight of actual suffering without running the risk of freezing the audience with horror.[64] With this justification, the vast majority of seventeenth-century operas and *tragédies en musique* and a good number of declaimed tragedies were resolved with a *lieto fine*, or happy ending. Yet some critics argued just as stoutly that happy endings interfered with tragedy's end of accomplishing a catharsis by pity and fear.[65] Just what Aristotle meant when he referred to tragedy's cathartic function remained a subject of speculation, but by the end of the seventeenth century, commentators had examined most of the ways in which the word was used by the ancients. In a commentary that received a wide readership in France, Paolo Beni observed how often the ancients – from Euripides to Hermes Trismegistus – spoke of fire and water as cathartic agents that purified even as they destroyed.[66] Like the other *tragédies en musique* presented in 1693, *Médée* makes the unusual choice to deny its audience the relief of a *lieto fine*. It instead stages a spectacle of purgative destruction. When Médée appears in the sky in a chariot drawn by dragons (see Figures 2.8 and

---

62 Dacier, *La Poétique d'Aristote*, 225.
63 Dryden, "The Grounds of Criticism in Tragedy," in *Works*, 13: 242.
64 Hoxby, *What Was Tragedy?*, ch. 4. On the political implications of this theory of theatrical affective experiences, see Korneeva's chapter in this collection.
65 Summo, *Discorsi poetici*, 34–5.
66 Beni, *In Aristotelis poeticam commentarii*, 194–212; Hathaway, *Age of Criticism*, 285–6.

Figure 2.8. Jean Berain, Médée in her chariot. This drawing may survive from a reprise of *Thésée* rather than the first performance of *Médée*. The same actress played Médée in both *Thésée* and *Médée*, 1543 DR. Musée du Louvre, Collection Rothschild, Paris. Photo: Réunion des Musées Nationaux/ Art Resource, NY.

2.9), Jason can utter no more than a few impotent lines before she has the last word: "Voyant Corinthe en feu, ses Palais embrasez, / Pleure à jamais les maux que ta flame a causez" (Seeing Corinth in flames, its palaces burnt down, / Weep forever over the ills that your passion has caused) (5.8). As Médée exits the stage, Charpentier's music collapses into a frenzied rush of strings, the palace and its statues break asunder, demons enter from all sides with torches, night falls on the ruins, and a hail of fire falls from the sky (see Figure 2.1). This is the sort of purgation by fire and water – Médée's flames and Jason's tears – that *Armide* could only anticipate weakly. This is the gauntlet that the Académie de Musique threw down for the Comédie-Française in 1693.

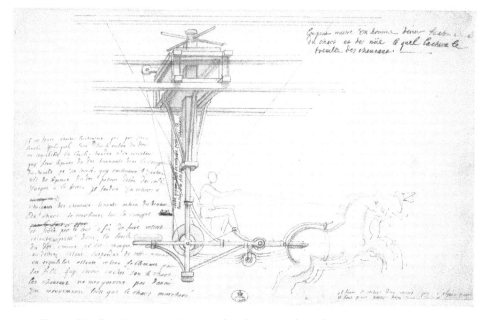

Figure 2.9. Berain's annotations on his drawings for a flying chariot, which appears in the finale of Quinault and Lully's *Phaéton* (1683), give some sense of the mechanical difficulties that had to be surmounted in order to create the spectacular illusions of the French baroque stage. Archives nationales (France), COTE 0/1/3241, fN 37.

Médée at the Comédie-Française

Hilaire Bernard de Requeleyne, baron de Longpierre, took up the gauntlet in the following year. Longpierre remains best remembered for his translations of Anacreon, Sappho, and Theocritus and for his attack on Charles Perrault and the Modern party in the Quarrel of the Ancients and Moderns. His general reputation is aptly summed up by the title of a recent introduction to his life and works, "Plus érudite que grand poète, hélas!" (Erudite, rather than a great poet, alas!).[67] Yet his *Médée* of 1694 does make for an interesting comparison to Thomas

---

67 Minel, "Introduction" to Longepierre, *Médée*. This edition also contains Longpierre's *Parallèle de Monsieur Corneille et de Monsieur Racine* (1986) and the abbé Pellegrin's *Dissertation sur le tragédie de Médée* (1729). It does not, however, supersede T. Tobari's edition of 1967.

Corneille and Charpentier's *tragédie en musique*. For while it achieved only a slight success at its debut, it became a standard of the repertoire after its revival in 1728 and a vehicle for some of the century's most distinguished actresses, including Mlle Dusmesnil, Mlle Clairon, and Mlle Raucourt. It was performed almost as frequently as Corneille's classic *Le Cid* (134 times versus 186).

In his preface, Longepierre explains that it was the very simplicity of the subject, so different from the taste of his own age, that attracted him to the fable: he wanted to give to the public something written in the antique taste. In *Médée* he found "une action grande, tragique et merveilleuse" (an action grand, tragic, and full of wonder). What's more, writing in the wake of Boileau's influential translation of Longinus's *On the Sublime*, he found a prooftext of the sublime, which could demonstrate how simplicity, grandeur, and force could unite to produce an overwhelming effect on viewers – not despite, but because of the work's disregard for the rules. Longepierre's *Médée* contains sensational scenes of sorcery (drawn chiefly from Seneca), the death of Créuse on stage, and, most remarkable of all, Médée's final escape in a chariot pulled by dragons. When we remember that both Aristotle and Dacier had faulted this resolution, Longepierre's stubborn retention of it is striking.[68] In his preface to *Iphigénie*, in which Racine introduces a second, unrecognized Iphigénie to avoid having the goddess Diana appear from a machine and substitute a hind on the altar, Racine had asked, "Et quelle apparence encore de dénouer ma tragédie par le secours d'une déesse et d'une machine, et par une métamorphose, qui pouvait bien trouver quelque créance du temps d'Euripide, mais qui serait trop absurde et trop incroyable parmi nous?" (How could I have possibly succeeded in bringing my tragedy to an end with the help of a goddess and stage machinery, and by a metamorphosis which might have found some credence in Euripides's days but which would be too absurd and too incredible in ours?).[69] Longepierre, who in many respects considered himself a custodian of Racine's legacy, rejects this emphasis on verisimilitude and plausibility in favour of the sublimity and almost brutal simplicity of the antique. This was common ground that neither the Académie de Musique nor the Comédie-Française was willing to yield without a contest at the end of the seventeenth century.

---

68 Aristotle, *Poetics*, 1454a36–b2; Dacier, *La Poétique d'Aristote*, 258–9.
69 Racine, *Œuvres completes*, ed. Forestier, 1: 698; Racine, *Iphigenia/Phaedra/Athaliah*, trans. Cairncross, 50.

3 Tragedy in Flux

DOWNING A. THOMAS

Eighteenth-century France witnessed a gradual mutation of tragedy as it was embodied in the works of Pierre Corneille and Jean Racine and was reflected, digested, and codified in contemporaneous treatises and commentary on theatre and poetics. The tragedies of Corneille and Racine functioned as the gold standard for writers and reformers throughout the eighteenth century and across the continent. Their works inspired the poetic reforms of the Arcadian Academy in Rome; they served as benchmarks in Johann Christoph Gottsched's *Deutsche Schaubühne* (*The German Stage*) (1741–5), fueling his efforts to transform German theatre; and, to take a specific theatrical example, Racine was an unavoidable model for Christoph Willibald Gluck and his librettist François-Louis Gand Leblanc du Roullet in their push to reimagine French opera, starting with *Iphigénie en Aulide* in 1774.

Simplified versions of literary history have bequeathed to us a high point of theatrical practice in seventeenth-century France, objectified as French neoclassical theatre, with the eighteenth century generally seen as a period of aesthetic doldrums or adulteration. Literary and cultural historians have spoken of the deterioration or the decline of tragedy, as eighteenth-century playwrights attempted unsuccessfully to recapture the summits reached by seventeenth-century authors.[1] Briefly touching on the tragedies of Voltaire, Prosper Jolyot de Crébillon, and Antoine

---

1 See Brewer, "Stages of the Enlightened Sublime," 5–18. High points of literary achievement are always and only seen, of course, in retrospect. As Charles Dill reminds us in "Pellegrin, Opera and Tragedy," Racine himself was chastised at the time by René Rapin for having given too much berth to "des tendresses frivoles" (frivolous affections). Thanks go to John Iverson for help with identifying Voltaire's correspondents.

Houdar de La Motte, Fernand Brunetière laments the contamination of tragedy by what he characterizes as novelistic procedures, such as recognition scenes.[2] André Lagarde and Laurent Michard, in their influential literary primer, quickly pass over Crébillon's attempts to jolt audiences through horror and note that Voltaire's weakness as a playwright stemmed from his inability to get out from under the sway of seventeenth-century models, notably that of Racine.[3] Similarly dismissing eighteenth-century tragedy, Lytton Strachey offers a colourful comparison between Racine and Voltaire: "Racine's work resembled one of those elaborate paper transparencies which delighted our grandmothers, illuminated from within so as to present a charming tinted picture with varying degrees of shadow and of light. Voltaire was able to make the transparency, but he never could light the candle; and the only result of his efforts was some sticky pieces of paper, cut into curious shapes, and roughly daubed with color."[4] For twentieth-century commentators, as Cécile Dudouyt has remarked, "only the empty shell of classical tragedy survives in Voltaire's plays."[5] As a result of characterizations like these, the eighteenth century has often been viewed as a mostly negligible period in the history of tragedy, the ebb between the flows of Shakespeare, Corneille, and Racine, on the one hand, and of the Schlegels and Schiller, on the other.

The lived theatrical landscape of eighteenth-century France, in contrast to the story we have inherited from literary history, was extremely active and constantly shifting, with influences from abroad creating new opportunities and challenges for theatrical practice, newer genres such as the opera putting pressure on traditional forms, and new aesthetic expectations from audiences, all of which opened theatre to intense experimentation and new directions.[6] Denis Diderot, for example, imagined different forms of spoken and sung theatre, and theorized a new *genre sérieux*, rupturing and merging generic boundaries. Indeed, the two genres Diderot believed held the most promise for a theatre of the future were the *genre sérieux* and the lyric theatre, both of which

---

2 Brunetière, *Manuel de l'histoire*, 287, 299.
3 Lagarde and Michard, *XVIIIe Siècle*, 185.
4 Strachey, *Books and Characters*, 158.
5 Dudouyt, "Voltaire's Subliminal Enlightenment," 157.
6 For an excellent summary of the active and evolving theatrical scene and the many questions it raises about our scholarly approaches to it, see Darlow, "Eighteenth-Century French Musical Theatre," 68–77. For a more recent attempt to rehabilitate eighteenth-century tragedy, see Hoxby, *Shadows of the Enlightenment*.

highlighted great passions and were "more likely to attract, arrest, and enthrall audiences."[7] La Motte, for his part, focused his dramaturgy on forcefully engaging the spectator through staged action rather than verbosity: "[T]oute la Tragedie doit être action" (The entirety of the tragedy should be action), as he wrote in the preface to his tragedy, *Romulus*.[8] On the practical side, emerging theatrical and commercial entities competed with the established theatres, prompting both creative but conservative-minded theatrical regulations, and aggressive new entrepreneurial moves. Although not all of these new directions proved popular or lasting, they do point to a theatrical culture that continued to be influenced by past successes while it was at the same time pushing to reinvent itself.

One of these areas of theatrical experimentation and challenge was opera. Opera in France developed alongside neoclassical tragedy beginning in the 1670s as *tragédie en musique*, initially conceived as an alternate form of tragedy. From the seventeenth century to today, critics have variously argued that *tragédie en musique* destroyed the beauty of Attic tragedy, thrived as an inverted form of neoclassical tragedy (where what was sublimated or hidden in spoken tragedy was made manifest and deliberately staged in opera), or in fact came closer to ancient tragedy than contemporary spoken tragedy was able to do.[9] Writing in the mid-eighteenth century, Charles Batteux remarked that in *tragédies en musique*, "ce qui intéresse le plus n'est pas le fonds même de l'action; mais les sentimens qui sortent des situations amenées par l'action" (what engages [audiences] the most is not the plot itself, but the sentiments that emerge from the circumstances put in place by the plot).[10] In an article focused on the aims of the theatrical experience, Blair Hoxby has remarked that *tragédie en musique* constitutes "a complex reading of Attic dramaturgy, one that ... locates 'the essence of tragedy,' as the Greeks themselves did, in the passions it both represents on stage and

---

7   Hoxby, *What Was Tragedy?*, 147.
8   La Motte, "Second discours," 4: 155–6.
9   Adrien Baillet claimed that Pierre Quinault's and Jean-Baptiste Lully's *Alceste*, had ruined Euripides's tragedy, *Alcestis* (*Jugemens des sçavans sur les principaux ouvrages des auteurs*, 4 (pt. 5): 323–4). Catherine Kintzler has argued that French opera is an inverted or displaced form of spoken tragedy, which nonetheless operates according to the same playbook (*Théâtre et opéra à l'âge classique*, 18). Elsewhere, I have suggested that *Médée*, the opera by Thomas Corneille and Marc-Antoine Charpentier, was more closely aligned to Euripides's tragedy than was Pierre Corneille's spoken tragedy of the same name (Thomas, *Aesthetics of Opera in the Ancien Régime*, 129–53).
10   Batteux, *Les Beaux arts*, 344–5. Unless otherwise noted, all translations are my own.

stirs in its audience."[11] In addition to this focus on sentiment, opera also modified the nobility and grandeur of the hero as Corneille had drawn him, as I have remarked elsewhere, shaping a hero who is less vain, impetuous, and cruel – traits to which moderns such as La Motte objected in spoken tragedy.[12] It is possible to understand changes in spoken tragedy during this period as accommodations of, or reactions to, opera within the range of theatrical options that were available to the eighteenth-century public. In what follows, focusing on Voltaire, I will highlight the influence of opera on his understanding of tragedy in particular and on theatrical expression in general, and the promise opera held to further Voltaire's own theatrical aesthetic and sensibilities. I suggest that Voltaire's complex and sometimes fraught attraction to opera and to what opera can accomplish as theatre, together with his failure to deliver any sustained contribution in the genre, is transformed into an effort to shape spoken tragedy with lessons from *tragédie en musique*.[13]

As one of the most prolific playwrights of the eighteenth century, Voltaire struggled throughout his career with audiences, actors, commentators, and himself over how to improve or reinvent tragedy and how best to present these innovations to audiences. Voltaire was the author of fifty plays, from his *Oedipe* in 1718 to his final tragedy, *Irène*, performed at the Comédie-Française in March, 1778, just two months before his death. Though he is known to us primarily as a philosopher, as Russell Goulbourne has remarked, "for him, and for his contemporaries, his theatre was his most significant literary monument," beginning first and foremost with his tragedies.[14] Voltaire opened up tragedy to new subject matter, including French history and medieval settings, and wrote eighteen comedies. As the author of seven libretti, Voltaire also knew something of the appeal of musical theatre.

---

11 Hoxby, "All Passion Spent," 35.
12 See Thomas, "Lyric Heroes," 65–85.
13 Here, I build on Guyon-Lecoq's insight: "On soulignera, d'ailleurs, que Voltaire qui parle volontiers d'opéra devient, curieusement, aussi muet qu'une tombe, dès qu'il entretient ses correspondants ou ses lecteurs d'une 'nouveauté' qu'il prétend introduire su la scène tragique, et dont tout spectateur avait fait cent fois l'expérience en allant à l'opéra" (It is worth underscoring that Voltaire, who speaks readily of opera, curiously becomes mute as a tomb as soon as he discusses with his correspondents or readers a 'novelty' that he claims to introduce to tragedy and which any spectator would have seen a hundred times at the opera) (*La Vertu des passions*, 198).
14 Goulbourne, "Voltaire's Masks," 94 ; also see Dudouyt, "Voltaire's Subliminal Enlightenment."

Gioachino Rossini's early-nineteenth-century adaptation of Voltaire's *Tancrède* for the Teatro La Fenice in Venice may be seen as a latter-day justification of Voltaire's intuition and of his attempts to develop a form of tragedy that could build on the emotional power the lyric theatre could wield.

Voltaire was decidedly interested in the effect that opera had on spectators. He clearly admired Philippe Quinault, who created the first French operas in the 1670s and 1680s with composer Jean-Baptiste Lully. Referring to two of their most famous *tragédies en musique*, Voltaire writes: "On sait par coeur des scènes entières de Quinault; c'est un avantage qu'aucun opéra d'Italie ne pourrait obtenir. ... Si on trouvait dans l'antiquité un poème comme *Armide* ou comme *Atys*, avec quelle idolâtrie il serait reçu!" (Everyone knows entire scenes of Quinault by heart, an advantage that no Italian opera could obtain. ... If one could find a poem like *Armide* or *Atys* in Antiquity, with what idolatry it would be received!).[15] Voltaire wrote glowingly about Lully's recitative in 1767 to Michel-Paul Guy de Chabanon, an influential theorist and commentator: "La déclamation de Lully est une mélopée si parfaitte que je déclame tout son récitatif en suivant ses nottes et en adoucissant seulement les intonations; je fais alors un très grand effet sur les auditeurs, et il n'y a personne qui ne soit ému" (Lully's declamation is so perfect that I can declaim all of his recitative, following the musical tones but merely softening the intonations. Thus, I can create a very significant effect on the listeners, and no one is left unmoved).[16] Here, as in many other of Voltaire's letters and publications, the emphasis is on the effect of operatic declamation on the audience, and in particular on the emotion generated in the listener; and these topics were perennial interests, obsessions even, of Voltaire's in the theatre. Despite his failure to get his opera *Pandore* staged, the work occupied him on and off from 1740, when he finished it, to 1774, when Gluck's *Iphigénie en Aulide* took up all the attention of the opera world, making it impossible for him to move forward with the version of *Pandore* that was finally completed with Jean-Benjamin de la Borde.[17] Voltaire's correspondence reveals that he was preoccupied with what opera could accomplish for theatre and with his own efforts in the genre.

---

15 Voltaire, *Siècle de Louis XIV*, ed. Diego Venturino, *Oeuvres complètes*, vol. 13D, tome 6, 22.
16 Voltaire, *Correspondence*, 32: 489.
17 On the history of *Pandore*, see Trousson, "Introduction," 331–48. Laborde took over the project after the death of Joseph-Nicolas-Pancrace Royer.

Modern commentators have focused primarily on Voltaire's operatic failures. *Samson* was rejected twice by the censors and was never performed. *Pandore*, too, never saw the light of day. The two operatic works performed during his lifetime – both performed at court in 1745 in a theatre constructed in the Grande Écurie at Versailles, and both collaborations with Jean-Philippe Rameau – have been marginalized for the most part as works of circumstance. The first, *La Princesse de Navarre*, was composed for the wedding of the dauphin with the infanta Maria Teresa of Spain. The second, *Le Temple de la gloire*, celebrated the French military success over the Dutch, British, and Hanoverian forces at the Battle of Fontenoy. The former was revived in Bordeaux in 1763 and again, at court, in 1769, before disappearing from the stage until 1977. The latter was revived at the Paris Opéra a handful of times in 1746 until its very recent revival.[18]

It is clear that Voltaire's appreciation of opera was qualified, both because he recognized the strengths and the limitations in the genre and because at times he expressed doubt about his own ability to write effective libretti.[19] In a letter to his associate Berger, referring to *Samson*, Voltaire's *tragédie en musique*, which was written to be performed with music by Jean-Philippe Rameau, Voltaire comments: "J'ai fait une grande sottise de composer un opéra; mais l'envie de travailler pour un homme comme M. Rameau, m'avait emporté. Je ne songeais qu'à son génie & je ne m'apercevais pas que le mien (si tant est que j'en aie un) n'est point fait du tout pour le genre lyrique" (I was very foolish to compose an opera; but I got carried away by the desire to work with a man like Mr Rameau. I was thinking only of his genius and did not understand that my own [insofar as I have any] is not at all made for the lyric theatre).[20] While he appears to repent having participated in the project at all in the above letter to Berger, a few years later, writing to Nicolas-Claude Thieriot after seeing Rameau's *Castor et Pollux* in 1737, his thoughts return to "l'enfant mort-né de Samson" (the still-born child, Samson), as he referred to the opera in a subsequent letter: "Je ne songe point à sa musique [Rameau's] que je n'aie de tendres retours pour Samson" (Every time I think of his music [Rameau's] I feel nostalgic

---

18 See Goulbourne's introductions in Voltaire, *Oeuvres complètes*, 28A: 109–25, 284–92. The original 1745 version of *Le Temple de la gloire* was staged in 2017 and subsequently issued in an audio recording by the Philharmonia Baroque Orchestra & Chorale under the direction of Nicholas McGegan.

19 See Ridgway, "Voltaire's Operas," 119–51.

20 Voltaire, *Correspondence*, 2: 451.

about Samson).[21] Overall, as Camille Guyon-Lecoq has remarked, "le jugement de Voltaire est, dans l'ensemble, singulièrement favourable à certains aspects de la tragédie lyrique et invite à lire avec précaution certains propos de condamnation qu'il a pu tenir de loin en loin et que des événements et des intérêts particuliers et transitoires inspirent manifestement" (Voltaire's judgment is singularly favourable to certain aspects of the lyric theatre, and invites us to read skeptically certain pronouncements he made here and there against it, and that specific, passing events and interests clearly inspired).[22] From the very beginning of his theatrical career, Voltaire focused much of his craft and commentary on the effects of theatrical representation on the spectator. He inherited an understanding of tragedy as dramatic poetry, first and foremost. However, in many comments on his published plays and in his correspondence where he focused on his vision for representing tragedy, he emphasized emotion and spectacle. As Isabelle Degauque has argued:

l'écriture dramatique de Voltaire est animée par le désir d'émouvoir le public, de créer des effets saisissants propres à lui faire verser des larmes. Ne négligeant pas le plaisir visuel que le spectateur cherche de plus en plus au théâtre, Voltaire rêve d'un théâtre qui autoriserait la représentation de scènes de grande violence, de douleurs aiguës et d'intense détresse, scènes propres à ébranler profondément l'assistance.

Voltaire's dramatic writing is animated by the desire to move the spectator, to create striking effects designed to elicit tears. By not neglecting the visual pleasure that the spectator increasingly seeks in the theatre, Voltaire dreams of a theatre that would authorize the representation of scenes of great violence, acute pain and intense distress, scenes that are apt to profoundly disturb the audience.[23]

It is this underlying desire to refocus tragedy on the immediate impact (or *force de frappe*) and the secondary effect, or cognitive and emotional response, that, in part, led Voltaire to try his hand at opera and, more broadly, to explore what tragedy could learn from opera.

In his "Discours sur la tragédie à Milord Bolingbroke," published as a preface to *Brutus*, after referring to the defects of English theatre (notably, the fact that it generally does not observe the strict unities of

---

21 Voltaire, *Correspondence*, 6: 451; and Voltaire, *Correspondence*, 4: 412.
22 Guyon-Lecoq, *La Vertu des passions*, 190.
23 Degauque, *Les tragédies de Voltaire*, 273.

time, place, and action that served as a theoretical guard rail for French playwrights), Voltaire points out to the Englishman that "vos pièces les plus irrégulières ont un grand mérite, c'est celui de l'action" (your most irregular plays have a great merit, which is that of action).[24] While dramatic poetry remained the core of tragedy, discourse itself was not the primary mover of theatrical effect for Voltaire: staged action was what had the most profound effect on audiences. Despite his objection to slipshod English attention to dramatic unities, what he saw as the beneficial theatrical emphasis on action across the Channel allowed Voltaire to criticize the French over-reliance on discourse: "Notre délicatesse excessive nous force quelquefois à mettre en récit ce que nous voudrions exposer aux yeux" (Our excessive delicacy forces us sometimes to put into words what we would like to reveal to the eyes).[25] Staging actions and events that could not be represented as such on stage according to the strictures of spoken tragedy was precisely what opera was able to do, even obliged to do, as a genre. Supernatural appearances and acts, dream states, physical violence, large gatherings, hallucinations all proliferate in *tragédie en musique*.[26] Voltaire argues in the prefatory material to *Sémiramis* that opera has many faults; he remarks, in particular, the ways in which maxims and songs serve as vehicles for unnecessary, secondary love interests, distracting from the primary action. Nevertheless, he remarks, in the end "l'enchantement qui résulte de ce mélange heureux de scènes, de choeurs, de danses, de symphonie, et de cette variété de décorations, subjugue jusqu'au critique même" (the magic that results from this fortunate mixture of scenes, choruses, dances, instrumental music, and the variety of the decors, subjugates even the critic).[27] Voltaire is clear that there is no place in tragedy for action for action's sake or action devoid of poetic backbone. As he writes in the preface to *Les Scythes*, spectacle can go too far: "[I]l ne faut pas pousser le terrible jusqu'à l'horrible"; "[Q]uatre beaux vers de sentiments valent mieux que quarante belles attitudes" ([O]ne must not push terror until it becomes horror"; "[F]our beautiful sentimental verses are worth more than forty beautiful postures).[28] Yet,

---

24 Voltaire, "Discours sur la tragédie à Milord Bolingbroke," *Oeuvres complètes*, 5: 164.
25 Ibid.
26 Kintzler, *Théâtre et opéra à l'âge classique*, 9.
27 Voltaire, "Dissertation sur la tragédie ancienne et moderne," *Sémiramis*, ed. Robert Niklaus, *Oeuvres complètes*, 30A: 148.
28 Voltaire, "Préface de l'édition de Paris," *Les Scythes*, ed. Robert Niklaus and Thomas Wynn, *Oeuvres complètes*, 61B: 353.

Voltaire's theatre pushes the envelope of spoken tragedy by trying to capture for spoken tragedy the strong effect that opera had on audiences, while avoiding the shortcomings of the *tragédie en musique*.

Even aside from opera, theatrical practices within the Comédie-Française fought against the focus on action that Voltaire sought in his tragedies. In the preface to *Brutus*, he complains about the French practice of seating spectators on the stage: "Les bancs qui sont sur le théâtre destinés aux spectateurs, rétrécissent la scène, et rendent toute action presque impraticable" (The seats for spectators that are located on the stage narrow the space for acting, making any action almost impracticable).[29] Voltaire complains that in comparison to the English, who go too far in some respects, the French censor themselves excessively. Why, Voltaire asks, is it permitted to commit suicide on stage, as Athalie does in Racine's tragedy and Jocaste does in Voltaire's *Oedipe*, while at the same time *bienséances* (what is and is not acceptable to stage) do not allow for murder to be represented on stage?[30] In imagining that his opera *Samson* would be staged at some point (though in the end it never was), Voltaire reiterates his desire for spectacle, action, effect: "Un beau spectacle bien varié, des fêtes brillantes, beaucoup d'airs, peu de récitatif, des actes courts, c'est là ce qui me plaît" (A beautiful, varied spectacle, brilliant celebrations, many airs, little recitative, short acts, that's what pleases me). He contrasts his aims for the opera with the practices of the Comédie-Française, which he characterizes as the place for sentimentality. Voltaire wants to set a different dramatic tone and pace with *Samson*: "Je veux que le Samson soit dans un goût nouveau, rien qu'une scène de récitatif à chaque acte, point de confident, point de verbiage" (I want Samson to be done in a new style, with nothing but one scene of recitative in each act, no confidant, no wordiness).[31]

While Voltaire characterizes opera in the 1730 preface to *Oedipe* as "un spectacle aussi bizarre que magnifique" (a spectacle as bizarre as it is magnificent), going on to list a few of the nonsensical things that can happen on the operatic stage, he also borrows from the lyric theatre elements of spectacle that often made opera more attractive to audiences and more successful than spoken tragedy at the

---

29   Voltaire, "Discours sur la tragédie à Milord Bolingbroke," *Oeuvres complètes*, 5: 165. John Renwick notes here that the Comédie-Française eliminated these seats on the stage in 1759, thanks to the liberality of the comte de Lauraguais (165 n. 18).

30   Ibid., 172–3.

31   Voltaire, *Correspondence*, 3: 294.

box office.[32] A number of structural elements of *tragédie en musique* as a genre resulted in large gatherings on stage, principally the obligatory dance numbers and the choruses.[33] Voltaire sought to bring some of this monumentality, and, above all, the effect it could create on audiences, into his spoken theatre. While Corneille had not done so in his *Oedipe*, Voltaire added a silent chorus of Thebans to his version of the tragedy, verbally represented by two individual spokesmen. Roman senators gather in front of the Capitol at the opening of *Brutus*, arranged in a semi-circle around Brutus and Valerius Poblicola to create an effect of grandeur, something like a chorus from ancient tragedy, albeit a silent one.[34] As Cécile Dudouyt remarks, "When the performing space was freed of spectators in 1759, Voltaire immediately wrote a play to exploit the potential of the new arena open to him. In *Tancrède* he had no less than eighty supernumeraries present on stage."[35] In the penultimate scene of *Mérope* (5.7), Voltaire brings an entire crowd on the stage. Dudouyt argues, too, that Voltaire injects a novel use of space into his plays. The spaces of tragedy are no longer the antechambers and vestibules of Racine, but the public spaces of temples, palaces, and tombs: "Voltaire thus draws the action outside, and effectively puts it under the public eye (as well as the eye of his audience)."[36]

Voltaire's tragedies highlight the impact on audiences of witnessing striking dramatic images and actions. In *Mérope*, the crowd Voltaire summons sees the body of Polifonte at the rear of the stage covered in a blood-stained cloth and then witnesses Égiste arrive in the middle of the scene with a bloody hatchet in his hands. As Voltaire notes in his preface to *Les Scythes*, he wanted to push beyond the verbal:

> On ne savait guère auparavant que réciter proprement des couplets, comme nos maîtres de musique apprenaient à chanter proprement. ...

---

32 Voltaire, "Preface to the 1730 Edition," *Oedipe*, ed. David Jory, *Oeuvres complètes*, 1A: 272. In a letter to Pierre Robert Le Cornier de Cideville (15 November 1732), Voltaire notes that much effort is required to "attirer le monde à la comédie, et je voi presque toujours que le plus grand succez d'une bonne tragédie n'aproche pas celuy d'un opera mediocre" (draw people to the theatre, and I see almost always that the greatest success of a good tragedy cannot match that of a mediocre opera) (Voltaire, *Correspondence*, 2: 250).

33 Dance was incorporated into every act of every French opera up until the Revolution. See Harris-Warrick, *Dance and Drama*, 1.

34 Voltaire, *Brutus*, ed. Robert Niklaus and John Renwick, *Œuvres Complètes*, 5: 185.

35 Dudouyt, "Phantom Chorus," 222.

36 Ibid.

Qui aurait osé, comme M. Le Kain, sortir les bras ensanglantés du tombeau de Ninus, tandis que l'admirable actrice qui représentait Sémiramis [Marie Anne Françoise Dumesnil] se traînait mourante sur les marches du tombeau même? ... C'est là en effet la véritable action théâtrale. Le reste était une conversation quelquefois passionnée.

Previously, we barely knew anything except how to recite couplets properly, just as our music teachers taught us to sing properly. ... Who would have dared, as Mr. Le Kain did, to emerge from Ninus's tomb with bloody arms while the admirable actress representing Sémiramis [Marie Anne Françoise Dumesnil] lay dying on the steps of the very same temple? ... That is the effect of true theatrical action. The rest was a sometimes passionate conversation.[37]

The final scene of *Oedipe* brings an opera-like intrusion of *le merveilleux* in the form of thunder and lightning; and, as previously mentioned, Jocaste takes her own life on stage. Voltaire demonstrates an ambivalent attitude toward stage effects. On the one hand, as Manuel Couvreur remarks, he became angry when the famous actress La Clairon requested that a scaffold be erected on stage in *Tancrède* (an effect Voltaire would have dismissed as too brazen, too English). Yet, only two years later, he staged "Olympie se précipitant vivante dans le bûcher où se consume le cadavre da sa mère" (Olympie throwing herself alive into the fire where her mother's body was being consumed).[38] Voltaire sought to use strong dramatic moments and vigorous staging to elicit reactions in the spectators, whether reactions of fear, shock (as with *Olympie*), or tears of despair. He often praised performances that had such an effect on audiences that they were brought to tears. Following the 1748 performance of *Mérope* at the court of Stanislas Leszczynski in Lunéville, he makes a particular point of noting that "on y a pleuré tout comme à Paris" (we cried there just as in Paris).[39] Tears are the sign of an effective tragedy for Voltaire, one that comes from the use of the right poetic elements together with a judicious application of dramatic and stage effects. Voltaire's interest in eliciting strong emotions in the spectator points to a shift in theatrical aesthetic and is echoed in Diderot's similar push for stronger emotional impact, notably by focusing on mother-daughter or father-son relationships.

---

37 Voltaire, "Préface de l'édition de Paris," *Les Scythes*, ed. Robert Niklaus and Thomas Wynn, *Oeuvres complètes*, 61B: 352.
38 Trousson and Vercruysse, *Dictionnaire général de Voltaire*, 93, s.v. "Art Dramatique."
39 Voltaire, *Correspondence,* 10: 209.

La Motte's commentaries on theatre provide an opportunity to compare his attempted revitalization of theatre and tragedy to that of Voltaire. La Motte was primarily a librettist, poet, and author of comedies before he tried his hand at spoken tragedy. Though Voltaire condemned the prescriptive approach to theatre his older contemporary outlined in his literary criticism, there are nonetheless important areas of at least tacit agreement. First, both La Motte and Voltaire used recognition scenes as a vehicle for creating an emotional impact on the spectator, creating opportunities to wrap up scenes or acts with moments of elation, not unlike the eighteenth-century operatic practice of placing duets as emotionally laden musical and dramatic events at the end of acts.[40] In particular, the effect of mother-child recognition scenes is one on which Voltaire depends in a number of his tragedies, including *Mérope*, *Ériphile*, *Sémiramis*, *Olympie*, and *Oreste*. While nineteenth-century literary historians such as Ferdinand Brunetière decried recognition scenes because they saw them as facile effects, threatening the supposed purity of the aesthetic summits attained by Racine and Corneille, it is worth noting that recognition scenes are an indelible feature of both Attic tragedy and early opera. As Terence Cave has forcefully argued, anagnorisis is at once a trivial contrivance (he compares it to a cuckoo clock) and an effective mechanism to generate shock and emotion in audiences: "The emblem of this trivial aspect of recognition is of course the birthmark, the scar, the casket, the handbag. ... The other face of recognition as a scandal is the one that takes us directly to what is most crucial to our sense of the literary, to the capacity of fictions to astonish us, upset us, change our perceptions."[41] Eighteenth-century reformers felt that by incorporating such scenes they could draw on classical practice and, at the same time, and most importantly, have greater emotional impact on audiences.

Second, both authors underscore the importance of action and condemn verbiage. La Motte borrowed a focus on spectacle from his operatic experience. "La plupart de nos pièces ne sont que des dialogues et des récits" (Most of our plays are nothing but dialogues and narratives), he writes disparagingly.[42] Similarly, Voltaire remarks disdainfully that

---

40 "*Ah ma mère! ah mon fils! ah mon frère! ah ma soeur!* Ces exclamations seules sont presque sûres de nos larmes" (*Oh, my mother! Oh, my brother! Oh, my sister!* Only these exclamations are almost sure to move us to tears) (La Motte, "Second discours," 595).
41 Cave, *Recognitions*, 2. See his treatment of Voltaire's uneasy relationship with recognition, 121–6.
42 La Motte, "Second discours," 607.

"nous avons en France des tragédies estimées, qui sont plutôt des conversations qu'elles ne sont la représentation d'un événement" (in France, we have esteemed tragedies that are more like conversations than they are representations of an event).[43] La Motte echoes Voltaire's condemnation: "Combien d'actions importantes que le spectateur voudrait voir, et qu'on lui dérobe sous prétexte de règle, pour ne les remplacer que par des récits insipides en comparaison des actions mêmes!" (How many important actions that the spectator would like to see are hidden from him on the pretext of rules, only to be replaced with narratives that are insipid in comparison with the actions themselves!).[44] Voltaire remarks on the excesses of both French and English theatrical practice. While the French keep many actions that would have the potential to create an indelible impression on the spectator out of sight, in the wings, the English represent all sorts of actions on stage, too many in Voltaire's view. Throughout his career, he sought to rebalance French tragic drama by offering up more spectacle to his audience.

Finally, like other commentators from the period, both Voltaire and La Motte express reservations over the preponderance of love in tragedy. La Motte lamented the omnipresence of "l'amour qu'on trouve trop dominant dans nos tragédies" (love, which is too dominant in our tragedies).[45] In the prefatory discourse to *Eriphyle*, Voltaire exclaims:

Mais ne vous plairez-vous qu'aux fureurs des amants,
A leur pleurs, à leur joie, à leurs emportements?
N'est-il point d'autres coups pour ébranler une âme?
Sans les flambeaux d'amour, il est des traits de flamme;
Il est des sentiments, des vertus, des malheurs
Qui d'un coeur élevé savent tirer des pleurs.

Will you only seek to please the madness of lovers,
their tears, their joy, their passions?
Are there no other effects that can move the soul?
Without the flames of love, there are sparks;
There are sentiments, virtues, misfortunes
That can draw tears from a noble heart.[46]

---

43 Voltaire, "Discours sur la tragédie à Milord Bolingbroke," *Oeuvres complètes*, 5: 164.
44 La Motte, "Second discours," 608.
45 La Motte, "Discours préliminaire," 532.
46 Voltaire, "Discours," *Eriphyle*, ed. Robert Niklaus, *Oeuvres complètes*, 5: 394.

Voltaire tirelessly sought to imagine what these "other effects" might be – for example, the mother-child recognition scenes he preferred – and to incorporate them into his dramaturgy. True passion is acceptable for Voltaire as long as it is the primary mover of the tragedy. Love is "la passion la plus théâtrale de toutes, la plus fertile en sentiments, la plus variée: elle doit être l'âme d'un ouvrage de théâtre, ou en être entièrement bannie" (the most theatrical of all passions, the most fertile in feelings, the most varied: love must be the heart of a play or be banished from it entirely). What draws his ire is, above all, the affectation of *galanterie*: the theatre is "presque toujours défiguré par ces amours de commande, par ces intrigues galantes" (almost always disfigured by these loves on command, these gallant intrigues).[47] Markers of *galanterie* for Voltaire in opera were the maxims shaped into exportable airs by Quinault and Lully. Voltaire constantly denounced this "baroque" practice, "[cette] infinité d'airs détachés" ([this] plethora of detached airs). He gives the example of an air from Quinault's and Lully's *Thésée* – "Le plus sage / s'enflamme et s'engage, / Sans savoir comment" (The wisest / is aroused and engaged, / Without knowing how) – which occurs discordantly, as Voltaire recalls it, precisely at the point where Theseus is about to be poisoned, before his father recognizes him by the sword he gave him as a child.[48] Voltaire misremembered the structure of the final act since in actuality the air closes the opera after the king has already recognized his son and Medea has fled, destroying everything in her wake. The point he sought to make, however, is that detachable airs like this one – sung here, moreover, by secondary characters – are flawed because they distract the audience from the dramatic core of the tragedy.

In his commentary on Thomas Corneille's *Ariane*, Voltaire pursues the same line of reasoning. Voltaire condemns the dramatist's use of maxims, citing the air "On se livre à l'amour sans qu'on sache pourquoi" (One gives oneself to love without knowing why) from act 1, scene 1, along with examples from other plays. "Redisons toujours," Voltaire writes, "que ces vers d'idylle, ces petites maximes d'amour conviennent peu au dialogue de la tragédie; que toute maxime doit

47 Voltaire, "Lettre à Monsieur le Marquis Scipion Maffei," *Mérope*, ed. Jack R. Vrooman and Janet Godden, *Oeuvres complètes*, 17: 220.
48 Voltaire, "Dissertation sur la tragédie ancienne et moderne," *Sémiramis*, ed. Robert Niklaus, *Oeuvres complètes*, 30A: 147. The term "baroque" is mine: see Thomas, "Baroque Opera."

échapper au sentiment du personnage, qu'il peut par les expressions de son amour dire rapidement un mot qui devienne maxime, mais non pas être un parleur d'amour" (Let's reiterate that these idyllic verses, these little maxims of love hardly fit with tragic dialogue; that any maxim must come out of the character's feeling, that the character can say a word rapidly that becomes a maxim, but not be a wordsmith of love).[49] He again cites lines from *Ariane* (I.1), where King Oenarus muses on the spontaneity of love: "Non, ce n'est point par choix, ni par raison d'aimer, / Qu'en voyant ce qui plaît, on se laisse enflammer" (No, it is not by choice, nor through reason, / That in seeing someone pleasing, one falls in love). Voltaire rejects these verses because they create an extradiegetic distance that, one might argue, serves no function other than to provide courtiers with lines they can recite to their lovers outside the opera house. He contrasts these lines from *Ariane* with one of the most striking and cited scenes from the entire French baroque operatic repertory: the moment when Armide threatens the sleeping Renaud with a dagger in Quinault and Lully's *tragédie en musique* of 1686: "Achevons – je frémis – vengeons-nous – je soupire" (Let's do it – I shudder – let's take revenge – I sigh). Here, Voltaire argues, "l'amour parle en elle, et elle n'est point parleuse d'amour" (love speaks through her; she does not babble on about love).[50] In other words, Voltaire argues that Armide embodies the passion through action, in this instance through the hesitation she encounters as she points a dagger at Renaud, rather than merely talking about it.

In seeking to create a similar effect on his audience in *Sémiramis*, Voltaire emulates Quinault in act 5, scene 2, when Azéma implores Sémiramis to help her save Arzace from Assur's intrigues. Sémiramis has just learned that Arzace is her son. At the moment when Azéma reminds her that she is to marry him, the danger of the predicament hits her: "Arzace! il est … parlez; je frissone; achevez: / Quels dangers? … hâtez-vous …" (Arzace! he is … speak; I shudder; finish: / What dangers? … make haste. …).[51] The incoherence of the utterance is designed to reveal the love that speaks in her, albeit this time (unlike in *Armide*) it is the purified love to which Voltaire returned time and again: maternal love. The ellipses also signal, without explicitly articulating, the terror of what might have transpired had Sémiramis been unaware that

---

49   Voltaire, "Remarques sur *Ariane*, tragédie," *Commentaires sur Corneille*, ed. David Williams, *Oeuvres complètes*, 55: 982.
50   Ibid., 983.
51   Voltaire, *Sémiramis*, ed. Robert Niklaus, *Oeuvres complètes*, 30A: 242.

Arzace was her son. It is not an extradiegetic utterance that comes from reflection and mastery of the situation, as is the case with Oenarus's maxim. Sémiramis's words are intended to be the expression of an unbridled emotion, words that form no complete sentence or any coherent thought. And they are designed, too, to invoke that feeling in the spectator. This is the stuff of tragedy as Voltaire understood it, and of which he found an example in Quinault and Lully's final opera. The inability to complete sentences and fully formed thoughts – which Voltaire admired in Quinault and Lully, and which he adopted in *Sémiramis* – functions as both the marker of emotion that goes beyond words in the staged tragedy and the trigger of intense emotion in the spectator.

Voltaire's own operas also reveal attempts to reconcile the contested place of love in theatre. *Le Temple de la gloire* was written with Rameau and first performed at court in 1745 in celebration of Louis XV's victory in battle at Fontenoy. The libretto begins with the story of two failed attempts to enter the Temple. In the end, only Trajan is admitted; and, as soon as he is admitted, he transforms the exclusive Temple of Glory into the Temple of Happiness, which he proclaims open to all. While Bélus is denied entry into the Temple in act 1 on account of his bellicose ways, and Bacchus receives the same treatment in act 2 for his lack of virtue, Trajan is welcomed into the Temple because the glory he achieves through victory in battle is coupled with magnanimity when he frees those whose rebellion he had quashed. The chorus proclaims: "Toi que la victoire / Couronne en ce jour, / Ta plus belle gloire / Vient du tendre Amour" (You whom victory / Crowns today, / Your most beautiful achievement / Comes from tender Love). In the conclusion to his *Temple de la gloire*, Voltaire attempts a reconciliation of love and glory, two core dramatic motivations that had traditionally been placed in opposition to each other as antonymous choices for heroes. Furthermore, the love that is proclaimed victorious is not romantic passion, but rather the ruler's pure love for his people: "O peuples de héros qui m'aimez et que j'aime, / Vous faites mes grandeurs; / Je veux régner sur vos coeurs" (O heroic people who love me and whom I love, / You make my greatness; / I want to reign over your hearts).[52] Celebrating Louis XV's victory over the combined enemy forces at Fontenoy on the stage constructed in the Versailles stables, Voltaire miraculously resolved the conflict between glory and love. Louis XV appears not to have been particularly impressed by the philosophical lesson the

---

52   Voltaire, *Le Temple de l'amour*, ed. Russell Goulbourne, *Oeuvres complètes*, 28A: 369.

librettist hoped to convey. When Voltaire asked the king, addressing him as Trajan – "Trajan est-il content?" (Trajan, is he happy?) – Louis XV is reported simply to have glared at him icily.

A similar attempt to create an opera that would offer a moral spectacle is articulated in the manuscript prologue that Voltaire wrote for *Samson*. Set in the opera house, the prologue stages a mise-en-abyme, so that the mythological characters on stage represent themselves, playing for the audience of the Opéra. La Volupté is surrounded by les Plaisirs and les Amours. La Volupté, holding nothing back, encourages her entourage to work their magic on the spectators, to do what they do best and what the audience expects of them: "Répandez vos douces erreurs; / Versez dans tous les coeurs / Votre charmante ivresse; / Régnez, répandez mes faveurs" (Spread your sweet errors; / Spread to all hearts / Your charming intoxication; / Reign, spread my favours).[53] However, the message is transformed at the end of the short prologue when Virtue arrives and joins the festivities: "Je viens m'unir à toi pour mieux régner sur eux [mortels] / Sans moi, de tes plaisirs l'erreur est passagère: / Sans toi, l'on ne m'écoute pas: / Il faut que mon flambeau t'éclaire, / Mais j'ai besoin de tes appas. / Je veux instruire et je dois plaire" (I come to join you in order to better reign over them [mortals] / Without me, the error of your pleasures is fleeting: / Without you, no one listens to me: / My flame must illuminate you, / But I need your attractions. / I wish to instruct and I must please).[54] Just as Voltaire had reconciled love and duty at the conclusion of *Le Temple de la gloire*, in the prologue to *Samson*, appropriately for a biblical opera, he is able to unite love and virtue.

Voltaire's most notable adoption of operatic effects is in *Sémiramis*. The tomb of Ninus is the setting that dominates both the beginning and the end of the tragedy. Arzace, the son of Queen Sémiramis, having been secretly taken away as a child after the ambitious Assur murdered his father, has returned to Babylon. For his safety, he has been kept unaware of his identity. Alone in act 1, scene 2, he hears the complaints of Ninus's ghost: "Du fond de cette tombe, un cri lugubre, affreux, / Sur mon front pâlissant fait dresser mes cheveux; / De Ninus, m'a-t-on dit, l'ombre en ces lieux habite" (From the bowels of this tomb, a lugubrious, horrible cry, / Makes my brow turn pale and my hair stand on end / The ghost of Ninus, I am told, haunts this place).[55] The

---

53   Voltaire, *Samson*, ed. Russell Goulbourne, in *Oeuvres complètes*, 18C: 319.
54   Ibid., 322.
55   Ibid., lines 119–21, 174.

stage directions here indicate that "on entend des gémissements sortir du fond du tombeau" (moans are heard coming from the bowels of the tomb). Voltaire's commentary on this scene shows his desire to make the intrusion of *le merveilleux* into something necessary and, he argues, with a degree of speciousness, even natural: "J'ose affirmer, que lorsqu'un tel prodige [l'ombre] est annoncé dans le commencement d'une tragédie, quand il est préparé, quand on est parvenu enfin jusqu'au point de le rendre nécessaire, de la faire désirer par les spectateurs, il se place alors au rang des choses naturelles" (I dare to claim that when such a marvel [the ghost] is announced at the beginning of a tragedy, when it is prepared, when one has managed to make it necessary and desired by the spectators, it falls under the category of natural things).[56] He suggests the necessity of the appearance of Ninus's ghost, even its foundational quality, by arguing that "on voit dès la première scène, que tout doit se faire par le ministère céleste; tout roule, d'acte en acte, sur cette idée" (one sees from the very first scene that everything must be accomplished by supernatural means; everything moves forward, from act to act, based on this idea).[57] Instead of seeing a ghost in her dreams, as Athalie does in act 2, scene 5, of Racine's *Athalie*, Sémiramis, "éperdue" (overcome) with emotion as the stage directions indicate, believes that she actually sees Ninus's ghost before her in act 1, scene 5. Voltaire describes the ghost of Ninus in his correspondence as appearing "toute blanche, portant cuirasse dorée, sceptre à la main et couronne en tête" (all white, wearing a golden breastplate, sceptre in hand and a crown on his head).[58] Voltaire lauds *Athalie* repeatedly; and in *Sémiramis*, it is as if he had determined to make the dreamed ghost of Racine's play materialize in the theatre.

Sémiramis in particular allows us to see how Voltaire attempted to channel the poetic summits of neoclassical tragedy while at the same time adapting audience-centred techniques perfected by the upstart *tragédie en musique*. It is worth underscoring, by way of conclusion, that Voltaire's dramaturgy of strong emotion is in no way antithetical to his lifelong insistence on the moral imperatives of tragedy. Instead, the strong feeling Voltaire sought to elicit in the spectator through tactics borrowed from opera served ideally to heighten the effect of the civic and personal virtues his tragedies displayed. As Logan J. Connors

---

56 Voltaire, "Discours sur la tragédie à Milord Bolingbroke," *Oeuvres complètes*, 5: 162.
57 Ibid., 163.
58 Voltaire, *Correspondence*, 10: 292.

writes, this type of dramaturgy "confounds the traditional binary of reason against passion."[59] By attempting to bring into tragedy something of the effect that opera had on audiences, it is as if Voltaire imagined, however fleetingly, that he might be remembered as the Metastasio of the French theatre. Metastasio's operas were focused on royal sovereignty, featuring "human subjects before whom the sovereign assumes responsibility in the name of a public trust … [adapting] eighteenth-century norms of sovereignty to new enlightenment ideals."[60] If Voltaire did indeed project himself into Metastasio's creations, it was less because of their connection to absolutist rule than because his operas were brilliant dramaturgical creations, deftly engaging the audience in the work and focused in many cases on Enlightenment ideals. The French Metastasio would similarly deliver a form of theatre that could attract audiences through the representation and incitement of strong feeling while at the same time offering an upstanding spectacle that would deliver moral lessons. Indeed, Voltaire imagined that a new emphasis on action and feeling would serve as an ideal vehicle for this content. The glimpses of operatic influence we can perceive in his theatrical output provide an opportunity to see how Voltaire sought to create newer forms of tragedy that would have even more powerful effects on his audience.

---

59 Connors, "'Sentiments raisonnables,'" 74. Though Connors is describing La Motte's vision of tragedy, in this respect his remarks are entirely consonant with Voltaire's aims here.

60 Feldman, *Opera and Sovereignty*, 242. For a discussion of Metastasio that re-evaluates the political content of his dramaturgy, see Zucchi's contribution to this volume.

4 Temptations of Love: Negotiating Tragic and Pastoral Inheritances at the Crossroads of Opera's Early Modern History

STEFANIE TCHAROS

Conventional histories of eighteenth-century opera often define the relationship between tragedy and the developing *dramma per musica* as one set early in the century by the likes of Apostolo Zeno and Pietro Metastasio, who looked to tragedy for their model of a well-made libretto. This historical reduction is supported by (and likely originates from) contemporary critical writings that credit Zeno for single-handedly creating a modern tragedy in music.[1] It is a history that conveniently narrows in on generic features and the authority of recognized figures as a means of accounting for change. More recent historical studies have taken a broader view of the effect that French models of tragedy had on theatrical reform. This work has placed opera within a larger context of production and has probed the social and political ramifications of French and Italian theatre in this period.[2] Yet, even this valuable line of historical research may stress a trajectory pointed toward an eventual stabilization of *dramma per musica*, when practitioners perceived tragedy as the ideal costume with which opera could announce a change of identity. In this chapter, I wish to unsettle this sense of steady progress toward a stable category by returning to an earlier phase of opera when the model of tragedy had not yet solidified. Tragedy, though rich in

---

1 See Muratori's letter to Zeno from 20 May 1699, published by Biagi, "Lettere inedite di Lodovico Antonio Muratori ad Apostolo Zeno." For an English translation, see Freeman, *Opera Without Drama*, 23; also see the translation and discussion of this letter in Bucciarelli, *Italian Opera and European Theatre*, 114.
2 The kind of analysis presented by Bucciarelli in *Italian Opera and European Theatre* is a key example that builds on the important work of Piero Weiss and Reinhard Strohm in their focus on the formative role French theatre had on the developing *dramma per musica*. See especially Weiss, "Teorie drammatiche a 'infranciosamento'"; and Strohm, *Dramma per musica*.

historical importance, was sometimes juxtaposed and even entwined with other poetic forms, especially pastoral models, which were also foundational to opera's earliest history. My aim is to explore such critical points of intersection between tragedy and pastoral as a history that informs opera's transition into *dramma per musica*.

Opera has always displayed an orientation toward the past, with its earliest narratives focused on the stories of Apollo and Dafne, Orpheus, and the abandoned Ariadne. Furthermore, its inventors appealed to the example of ancient tragedy to justify their own experiments with sung drama even if the relationship with ancient theatre was largely fabricated.[3] In fact, late-Renaissance humanists realized that in practical terms, opera's more viable model was contemporary pastoral theatre. As an invented form (pastoral theatre did not exist in classical antiquity), the pastoral could fluidly move between allusions to a quintessential classical heritage and the diverse literary and dramatic approaches of its modern practice. This conjoined relationship with the pastoral endowed early opera with a flexibility not as easily found in tragedy but necessary for the genre's initial experiments and ongoing alterations.

That said, in this nexus of creativity and invention, tragic elements were not fully replaced. Rather, they were transformed to fit a humanist system of values. Giuseppe Gerbino contends that in late sixteenth-century theatre what was classical tragic sorrow (intended to produce a cathartic effect) was actually replaced by a dramatization of "love suffering" as influenced by pastoral poetry. The acts themselves were not tragically calamitous but evoked situations that were full of "tragic potency" in their simulation of sorrow or pain caused by love's cruelty. Pleasure was thus achieved through a spectator's emotional response to such suffering. The dramatic act of tragedy was updated to suit the needs of a new early modern disposition.[4]

---

3   In the Epilogue to his book, Giuseppe Gerbino reveals how Ottavio Rinuccini (1562–1621), among the leading poets who sought to revive musical aspects of ancient tragedy, avoided public expression of his skepticism about the classicist intentions discussed and developed in the Florentine academies. Gerbino writes: "Rinuccini would have probably agreed that while his idea of tragedy was ancient in origin, the contents were not" (*Music and the Myth of Arcadia in Renaissance Italy*, 379).

4   Gerbino summarizes his argument in the following passage: "The reflection on the need to update the notion of tragic revolved around an *ambiguous point of intersection between tragedy and pastoral* [...] it is more important to comprehend and enjoy the tragic-pastoral ambiguity within which the ideas of a modern existential condition and of a modern tragic sensitivity were debated, tested, and offered to aristocratic audiences as mirror-images of their own perception of themselves" (emphasis mine). *Music and the Myth of Arcadia in Renaissance Italy*, 396.

As we know from opera's seventeenth-century history, music and staged drama offered a powerful platform for telling complex narratives and representing affect. But opera also became an irresistible commercial commodity, which in turn initiated new pressures on its practices, ones that became more variegated through a host of producers and practitioners involved in opera's multimedia business. As Wendy Heller has argued, the tether between ancients and moderns was further compromised by opera's ongoing dynamic transformation as a form of public entertainment.[5] Scholars have written amply about the onset of opera's late seventeenth-century critical turn, when a concern over opera's commercialism and its corruption of literary ideals and social morals fed into a larger spirit of reform that penetrated early modern culture in broad and encompassing ways. Tragedy figured prominently in this reform movement because it served as a formal model with an honoured reputation. It coincided, however, with other examples that preferred the poetic and dramatic legacy of the *favola pastorale* as a model that could also legitimize *dramma per musica*.[6]

For the purposes of this chapter, I wish to stress a sense of flux that characterizes the run-up to a more stable *dramma per musica*. During this transitional period, librettists invoked specific dramatic models and expressive forms and, in doing so, often invested them with new meaning. While their choices may have been informed by ongoing debates about the past and reformed future of opera, they were also influenced by the political aims of their patrons and the expectations of their audiences. It is with these considerations in mind that I examine how early practitioners of *dramma per musica* drew on pastoral and tragic models of poetry and drama. In past scholarship, authors have noted a similar overlap between pastoral and tragic

---

5 "[As] both vocal and instrumental virtuosity became a tool of musical expression, and stagecraft became an increasingly valued component in musical theatre, it is not surprising that some of the reverence toward the ancients began to erode" (Heller, "Opera Between the Ancients and the Moderns," 278).

6 Bucciarelli traces the influence of French tragedy on *dramma per musica* back to libretti produced in Venice in the 1680s, which appear in conjunction with the first Italian prose translations of French tragic dramas. She also highlights the dramatic writing of the Roman poet, Carlo Sigismondo Capece, as an example of a librettist whose experiments range from pastoral to tragedy. His early librettos from the 1680s document this predilection toward pastoral models and "anticipate the orientation and taste of the soon-to-be-established *Accademia dell'Arcadia*" (113). But, by 1697, he produces *La Clemenza d'Augusto*, modelled after Pierre Cornellie's *Cinna*, which was several years before Corneille's tragedy was translated into Italian prose in 1701. See *Italian Opera and European Theatre*, 81–9, 111–17.

orientations, a kind of hybridity in a small number of operas from this era of reform.[7] More recently, Ayana Smith has carefully analyzed the importance of the Arcadian librettist Alessandro Guidi as critical for uniting pastoral and heroic qualities and exemplifying reformist elements of the new Arcadian pastoral genre. She underscores the importance of Giovanni Maria Crescimbeni (the Academy of Arcadians' first administrator and scribe) for endorsing Guidi's stylistic novelty and using it to document his own definition of the "heroic pastoral," which incorporated tragic features into the pastoral genre to create a more serious orientation.[8] In this chapter, my focus is less oriented toward establishing the onset of a pastoral and tragic hybridity as debated in the reform literature. Nor is my discussion aimed at identifying a body of works that evoke these elements or tracing when tragic features became a dominant approach. Rather, I dwell on the ambiguity and view the quality of admixture as symptomatic of this transitional phase of opera, in which we find a range of experiments that may call on a number of historical influences and reflect different points of intersection between tragedy and pastoral in *dramma per musica*. I am most interested in uncovering these relationships within the larger complex of operatic production, for which the importance of event, representation of power and patronage, and even commercialism affected how different agents mediated tragic and pastoral inheritances at the crossroads of opera's early modern history.

---

7 Strohm recognizes such hybrids (such as the *pastorale eroica per musica*, or the *melodramma eroico pastorale*) as a kind of sub-genre of *dramma per musica*, which is befitting of a pastoral orientation because of its setting or presence of non-royal characters despite the occasional introduction of heroic themes. See *Dramma per musica*, 2–3. Susan M. Dixon offers a somewhat different take on hybridity, one that was quickly abandoned when "melancholic aspects of love in pastoral dramas were replaced by the seriousness of tragic action." See *Between the Real and Ideal*, 32. I, too, have recognized such hybrid tendencies in Roman opera from these very decades; see Tcharos, *Opera's Orbit*, 41.

8 Ayana Smith, *Dreaming with Open Eyes*, 39–74. For his definition of the "heroic pastoral," see Crescimbeni, "Dialogo Quinto," *La bellezza della volgar poesia*, 186. Guidi's *L'Endimione* and Crescimbeni's discussion in *La bellezza* of his own *favola pastorale*, *L'Elvio*, are dramas highlighted for their importance to poetic invention and to Arcadian ideology. Though critical to the reform literature, none of these pastoral dramas was ever set to music, as Crescimbeni himself regarded music as a destructive element, perhaps not in theory, but at least in practice. In this sense, these examples do remain somewhat exceptional and are different from the focus of this chapter.

I begin with a sequence of events that took place in Rome in the fall of 1690 as a means to situate this chapter's larger discussion in the granular details of production surrounding an individual work: the opera, *Gli equivoci in Amore, overo La Rosaura*, with libretto by the abbot Giovanni Battista Lucini and music by Alessandro Scarlatti. There were three known printed libretti for this work between 1690 and 1692, suggesting the opera's staying power and attraction for different audiences.[9] Yet it is an opera that could be, and has been, easily forgotten for a number of reasons. In the first place, its libretto is not authored by someone we recognize as a well-known poet. Lucini was not a name frequently cited or heralded in the critical literature for his libretto's innovative success, and it seems his work was not part of a larger canon.[10]

Entitled a *dramma per musica*, *La Rosaura*'s label does not immediately advertise a pastoral orientation, yet its narrative is not strictly serious or fully oriented toward tragedy either, lending the opera a somewhat amorphous generic status. The opera tells the story of two sets of lovers about to be betrothed (Rosaura and Celindo; and Elmiro and Climene), intentionally mirroring the real-life occasion for which the opera was initially written: the wedding of two aristocratic couples conjoined under the auspices of papal politics and shifting governmental dynasties in late seventeenth-century Rome.[11] In the opera, the main protagonists are royal and noble, and the story is set in the ancient kingdom of Cyprus, with few major scene changes (a garden, a forest, the sea), all of which could evoke the intimacy and natural simplicity of the pastoral, even if the narrative's main characters are

---

9 *Gli equivoci in amore overo La Rosaura, Dramma in musica* in 3 acts; A-Wn, D-WD, F-Pc (Acts 1 and 2), GB-Lbl; facsimiles of Acts 1 and 2 edited by Eitner, *Publikation älterer praktischer und theorestischer Musik-Werke*, Bd. 15 *Die Oper von ihren ersten Anfängen bis zur Mitte des 18. Jahrhunderts*, 1–222.

10 In concordance with Tim Carter's argument, it seems that Lucini may suffer the effects of "canon chauvinism," and he is overshadowed by other names that "percolate to the surface." See "Mask and illusion," 246. According to Saverio Franchi, Giovanni Battista Lucini was born in Ancona (1639) and died in Rome (26 March 1709). He was a cleric and a lawyer and was later made judge for the Campidoglio. He was a dramatic author and librettist and appears to have been engaged with the robust intellectual life of Rome, belonging to the Accademia degli Umoristi, Accademia dei Disuniti, and later the Arcadians under the pastoral alias *Iola Creteo*. *Drammaturgia Romana*, 1: 866. Also see Maylender, *Storie delle Accademie D'Italia*, 213, for mention of Lucini's name among the Disuniti.

11 Details of the patronage and individuals involved in the double nuptial are detailed below.

not actual shepherds. And, like a bucolic tale, *La Rosaura* follows a typical trajectory that depicts characters in and out of love, with the necessary entanglements that involve deception, misunderstanding, and personal suffering, and inspires a continuous flow of emotive performances engineered not only to move and entertain audiences but also to convey a more substantive message.

The focus of this work is on its title character, Rosaura, who stands apart from the rest of the cast due to her circumstances and her actions. Though ostensibly betrayed by her lover and confronted by other amorous temptations, Rosaura sets the moral course for this opera by rebuking the frivolity of passion and insisting on a love full of valour, truth, and constancy. Love is therefore a central theme,[12] and it is likely that these notions of rational love would have resonated with Roman literary reformers who, as Smith discusses, argued in favour of improving pastoral drama by incorporating such moralizing elements.[13] As a *dramma per musica*, however, *La Rosaura* also bore a resemblance to other 1690s productions that endorsed an ideal of virtuous honour.[14] Thus, in keeping with the period's intellectual attraction to tragic models, especially French classical tragedy, *La Rosaura*'s authors may have indeed

---

12 Love is prefaced in the work's short prologue, which describes a chaotic storm created by Venus's son, Amore. Venus recognizes that Love's piercing intrusions are full of pride, scorn, and jealousy, but she implores her listeners to leave things to her because opposed to Cupid's fatal blows are Virtue and Constancy, whose countenance will settle the storm. I-Rn 34.1.G.10, *Gli equivoci in amore overo La Rosaura*, 13–14.

13 Smith connects the kinds of dramatic features she identifies in Guidi's *L'Endimione* to the influence of Queen Christina's philosophical rationalism and interest in the ideal of a pure love developed in Petrarchan Neoplatonism. These intellectual and emotional commitments were in turn recontextualized in the emerging Arcadian Academy in Rome. See *Dreaming with Open Eyes*, 47. As much as Arcadian literati saw the new developments in pastoral dramas as a departure from the libertinism of Renaissance pastoralism, the female prototype of a pure and chaste love was also found in pastoral poetry, as noted by Gerbino. He argues for the centrality of women who play key roles in poems from the early sixteenth century and who were divided into categories of nymphs and shepherdesses, with each embodying different social and sexual traits. Shepherdesses were lascivious, but nymphs represented "a high model of femininity, combining beauty, chastity, and nobility." *Music and Myth of Arcadia in Renaissance Italy*, 86.

14 In the same year of *La Rosaura*'s production, Roman audiences were also treated to *La Statira* (1690) at the city's major public theatre, the Teatro Tordinona. This opera was also composed by Alessandro Scarlatti, with its libretto by Cardinal Pietro Ottoboni, and conveyed messages of virtuous honour and morality. See Carter's discussion of the opera in "Mask and Illusion," 270–7, and Smith's broader analysis in *Dreaming with Open Eyes*, 126–72.

understood that even if a narrative was not directed to incite pity or fear, the appeal of an "unjustly persecuted heroine" is what involved audiences emotionally in the work and encouraged their responsiveness and empathy.[15]

As a protagonist, Rosaura displays the qualities of other major characters from opera and spoken drama, qualities that are conveyed not only through her actions but through the sententiae of the libretto upholding virtue, morality, and even female chastity. In this respect, it is important to recognize that La Rosaura should not be essentialized as an ideal case. A different opera example from this same juncture might point to somewhat similar or different conclusions, but this potential for exception and variability is precisely the point. La Rosaura helps us take a snapshot of this ambiguous point of intersection where legacies held much weight, but where transformation and continuity intermixed. Using this opera as an exploratory case, my analysis considers how tragedy presents a site for negotiating different and competing histories, some of which are operatic and evoke a range of aesthetic trends, others of which are cultural, literary, and dramatic, and find their roots in both Renaissance models, but also in later seventeenth-century reformists ideals about pastoral and tragic forms. We must understand, however, that La Rosaura was an opera reproduced across several years and was immersed in both the particulars of context and the dynamics of operatic representation. Opera, more than any other cultural form of its generation, was a powerful and unique assemblage that could harbour a complex historical dialogic and still bring conditions of the immediate performance or event into focus.

Two Weddings, Opera, and the Potential for Tragedy

In September 1690, a Roman diarist and local news chronicler, Carlo Cartari, reported a notable celebration that he titled *Matrimonium inter Magnates*, which announced a set of upcoming magisterial weddings.[16]

---

15 Using Pierre Corneille's discussion of his *parties intégrantes*, Bucciarelli explains his recognition of "the difficulty in defining that particular type of pleasure that comes from witnessing the vicissitudes of two unfortunate lovers or of an unjustly persecuted heroine. But it was precisely this type of pleasure, the pleasure of being moved to tears, that brought large audiences to the theatre." *Italian Opera and European Theatre*, 6.

16 *Matrimonium inter Magnates*: "Martedi sera 26 di Settembre furono sottoscritti li Capitoli di Matrimonio ha il Sigs/Prencipe Marco Ottoboni, Nipote di S. Sta' Generale dell Galere Pontifice, e fratello del Sigs. Prencipe Antonio Ottoboni Generale di Santa Chiesa, e Castellano di questo Castello Sto. Angelo: e la Sig.ra Donna

Conjugal unions between noble families had long inscribed the most fundamental relationships between family, property, social status, and power.[17] In this instance, the arranged union was not just one, but a *double* nuptial, which was particularly opportune considering the recent installation of Pietro Ottoboni as Pope Alexander VIII in 1689. One of the unions involved Prince Marco Ottoboni, nephew to the pope, who was betrothed to a bride of significant social status in Rome: Tarquinia Colonna. The second marriage concerned Donna Cornelia Zeno, whose father, Francesco, formed part of the distinguished Zeno family from Venice, and whose mother, Chiara Ottoboni, was Pope Alexander VIII's niece. Donna Cornelia was betrothed to Urbano Barberini, Prince of Palestrina, the last male heir of the Barberini line, a family of great noble and papal prominence in Rome throughout much of the seventeenth century.[18] It is critical to observe how the expected cultural function of conjugal unions was manoeuvred here quite strategically. Key alliances with local dynasties forged through marriage were essential for decisively linking the new Ottoboni papacy, whose family was from Venice, to Roman households with deep historical lineage.[19]

Tarquinia Colonna sorella del Prencipe di Carbognano; La detta sera di mercordi furono sottoscritti li Capitoli di Matrimonio ha il Sig.S Principe di Palestrina Maffeo Barberini, e la Sig.ra Donna Cornelia Zeni Pronipoti di S.Stà cioè nipote delli Sig. Prencipi Antonio, e Marco Ottoboni nipoti del Papa." I-Ras, *Archivio Cartari-Febei*, Busta 102, fol. 255r–v. The dates of the given weddings from Cartari appear to be Tuesday, 26 September for Marco Ottoboni, and Wednesday, 27 September for Donna Cornelia Zeno.

17 These fundamental relationships are what John A. Marino terms the *casa*. See his "Introduction: On the Grand Tour," 2.

18 Cartari spends several pages of his reported news for 1690 on events and activities related to these nuptials, stressing the dynastic and geographic symbolism by including a list of presents given to Tarquinia Ottoboni (née Colonna), and making particular note of Marco Ottoboni's new housing location at the illustrious Palazzo Ludovisi on the Via del Corso. See entries for I-Ras, *Archivio Cartari-Febei*, Busta 102, esp. 327r: "Il Sig. Don Marco Ottoboni; e sua Consorti Colonnesi si prepararanno andare ad habitare nel Palazzo al Corso; et il Sig. Don Antonio con la Consorti [riterranno] ad habitare nel Palazzo della Cancelleria." As connected to these nuptials, consider that Pope Ottoboni showed little restraint in providing his family with favours, property, and positions of power. On the Ottoboni dynasty, issues of nepotism, and the powers of patronage, see Olszewski's *Cardinal Pietro Ottoboni (1667–1740)*, esp. 11–79.

19 The importance of papal sovereignty and its relationship with lay aristocracy in late seventeenth-century Rome has been explored in detail by Ago, "Hegemony," 229–46. Ago argues that a shift in emphasis of governance with Innocent XI's "anti-festive rigour," and disengagement from local social politics during this period, is

It should come as no surprise that the celebration of such unions was therefore a major symbolic event, timed carefully to confirm the emergence of papal sovereignty in this important transitional moment. In what ways, then, was theatre (specifically opera) used to accomplish this social undertaking? What historical role could tragedy play at this political juncture?

We learn from newsletters of the period that major steps had been taken by November 1690 to support a series of entertainments, including the composition of several operas marking the double nuptials of the Ottoboni family.[20] Of particular political importance was *Gli equivoci in Amore, overo La Rosaura*, whose title page from the 1690 libretto was explicitly dedicated to the double nuptials, announcing the opera's performance at the very happy weddings of the celebrated couples, spelling out clearly the familial alliances (Ottoboni and Colonna; Ottoboni and Barberini), and dedicating the libretto to the princesses of the Ottoboni family.[21]

For the specifics of this commission, the thematic of love and *La Rosaura*'s pastoral elements would have been in keeping with ceremonial traditions of matrimonial events. Stemming from Renaissance practices, pastoral plays were sometimes staged for wedding celebrations, as they often ended with a requisite happy conclusion when convoluted love intrigues resolved into the proper realignment of paired couples

---

what added to the growth and prestige of the remaining old feudal families, like the Orsini and Colonna. Alexander VIII, by contrast, actively confronted social politics using his own family contacts and influence to help eliminate members of other families from centralized positions of prominence (240–1).

20 Marco's brother, Antonio Ottoboni (who was made General of the Church), and Antonio's son, Pietro (who had been made Cardinal and given the position of vice-chancellor), were behind the patronage, organization, and in some cases, the authorship of the festivities, which included the composition of several operas. Of particular use for charting this history have been the collected documents from the *Avvisi Marescotti*, published and referenced by Staffieri in *Colligite fragmenta*. For discussion of the critical importance of the year 1690 for the Ottoboni dynasty and its ancillary effect on the history of culture and music in Rome during this period, see Carter, "Mask and illusion," 270–7; and Tcharos, *Opera's Orbit*, 20–3. In the documents published in his Appendix C of Olszewski's *Cardinal Pietro Ottoboni*, the double nuptials are noted (309), as are other descriptions of great Venetian splendor now brought to the Roman capital (316).

21 "*GLI EQUIVOCI / IN AMORE, / OVERO / LA ROSAURA / Drama per musica. / DA RAPPRESENTARSI / Nelle felicissime Nozze / Dell'Eccellentissima Signora la Signora Donna Tarquinia / Colonna, con l'Eccellentissimo Sig. D. Marco Ottoboni / Duca di Fiano, e Generale de Mare / di Nostro Signore &c. / E dell'Eccellentissima Signora Donna Cornelia*

through marriage.[22] Yet we must also consider that some of *La Rosaura*'s features and themes were also resonant with a broader reform ethos that emanated from a key intellectual circle whose influence dominated the cultural landscape and whose mission was to adopt ambitious reform programs for literature and drama.

If 1690 was already an important turning point for papal and social politics in Rome, it was likewise a landmark year for arts, letters, and culture with the official inauguration of the Accademia degli Arcadi, a powerful literary and intellectual movement critical for engaging arguments on artistic taste and the reform of literature, philosophy, and religion.[23] The group's pioneering members had established this more formal academy to honour the deceased Queen Christina of Sweden (1626–89), whose private gatherings were known as the Accademia Reale.[24] This

---

/ Ottoboni, con l'Eccellentissimo Signor / D. Urbano Barberini, Principe / di Palestrina &c. / Dedicato alle Eccellentiss. Signore Principesse / D. MARIA, D. TARQUINIA / E D. CORNELIA / OTTOBONI." I-Rn 34.1.G.10, *Gli equivoci in amore overo La Rosaura*, 3. The opera, *Amore e Gratitudine*, with libretto penned by Cardinal Pietro Ottoboni, and music composed by Flavio Carlo Lanciani, was also produced in fall 1690 with possible connections to the same set of events, themes, and context for which *La Rosaura* was composed, but was not designated a *dramma per musica* and instead entitled a *dramma pastorale*. See Franchi, *Drammaturgia Romana*, I, 635–6.

22 Cox and Sampson explain this convention as part of a longer debate over a woman's virtue and the concern for female chastity. In pastoral narratives, the female nymph is forced to abandon a lifestyle of independence and instead is "tamed and socialized in preparation for the vital institution of marriage." See "Volume Editors' Introduction," in Campiglia's *Flori, A Pastoral Drama*, 20.

23 The Raguananza degli Arcadi also had their first official gathering in fall, in October of 1690, as initiated by the lawyer and poet Vincenzo Leonio and the prelate Giovanni Mario Crescimbeni. There were fourteen founding members at this original meeting. For a description of the origins and institutionalization of the *Arcadi*, see Crescimbeni, *La bellezza della volgar poesia*, 217–30. For an overview of these first years of the academy, see Santovetti, "Arcadia a Roma Anno Domini 1690," 21–37.

24 Christina, the only surviving legitimate heir of King Gustav II Adolf of Sweden, converted to Catholicism, abdicated her throne, and had arrived in Rome by 1655. On the establishment of Christina's academies, see Maylender, *Storia delle Accademie d'Italia*, Vol. I, 255–9; and Stephen, "A Note on Christina and her Academies," in *Queen Christina of Sweden*, 365–71; and more recently, Åkerman, *Queen Christina of Sweden and Her Circle*. The Arcadian Academy has been written about thoroughly in literary, art historical, and musicological scholarly writing. See my book, *Opera's Orbit*, for an exploration of the Academy's influence over the range of debates and discourses over opera's early modern reform, esp. 21–45. Also see Minor, *The Death of the Baroque and the Rhetoric of Good Taste*, esp. chapter 5, "A Short History of the Academy of Arcadians," 115–26, and Smith, *Dreaming with Open Eyes*, esp. chapter 1, "Founding Arcadia: The Aesthetics of Verisimilitude and *Buon Gusto*," 17–38.

accademia, comprised of nobles, intellectuals, clerics, and students attending the Roman colleges, formed a critical intellectual and artistic nexus in Rome. Alexander VIII was a member of Christina's early academy, and his nephews, especially Cardinal Ottoboni, played an active role, writing poetry and opera libretti for Arcadian-oriented events.

Paramount for the Arcadians was a cultivation and re-establishment of good taste (*buon gusto*), which was largely motivated by a perceived sense of decline in Italian literature that the Arcadians linked to broader cultural decay. That said, not everyone involved in the first phase of the society agreed upon the means to achieve this reform. If there was some common rallying point, even well before *gli Arcadi* were made official, it was a general desire to eradicate the seventeenth-century literary style and theatrical modes predicated on the extravagant, vivid wordplay associated with *marinismo* (the poetic imitators of Giambattista Marino, 1569–1625).[25] In the face of what they perceived as literary decadence, reformers sought the naturalism and verisimilitude of earlier literary models, especially from those sourced in pastoral poetry, but also the gravity and solemnity offered by tragic drama. The debates over models for the future of Italy's *buon gusto* were often fraught, at times conflicting, and sourced from diverse influences. *La Rosaura* serves as an interesting document to reflect and complicate these multiple visions of reform.

One source for *La Rosaura's* possible resonance with Arcadian-oriented themes is found in visual references revealed in the frontispiece of the opera's 1690 libretto (see Figure 4.1). The image presents the Ottoboni coat of arms, which adorns the top of the page, yet the drawing below the opera's announced title conveys the libretto's main subject: Love – personified as Cupid, or Amore – standing among rustic ruins with a dramatic mask strewn at his feet, perhaps a symbol of the theatrical event itself. Also curious is the backdrop, which includes some trees, an ancient pyramid to the left of Amore, and farther off a faint depiction of some structures, possibly a tower and cupola-dotted vista of a more modern Rome, or at the very least an urban centre that would be distantly connected to this otherwise Arcadian scene. Representations of Arcadia in artistic pastoral landscapes and in poetry of the period often encompassed multiple temporalities and settings, highlighting the binary of old and new to make vivid the

---

25 On the revival of humanist ideals of good taste within the context of Arcadian Rome, see Minor's study of the rise of *buon gusto*, *The Death of the Baroque*, 26–60.

Figure 4.1. *Gli equivoci in Amore, overo La Rosaura*, I-Rn (34.1.G.10/4), frontispiece.
Biblioteca Nazionale Centrale di Roma.

contrast between ancient and modern.[26] Using this frontispiece for *La Rosaura*, the patrons appear to have carefully situated their orientation no longer toward their Venetian provenance alone but to a new cultural milieu evocatively associated with "Arcadian" Rome. This opera is a starting point to reveal the calculated process of social penetration pursued by the Ottoboni dynasty. In the case of *La Rosaura*, it was an event to mark and celebrate the given arranged marriages to stress new connections with local families of significant social prominence. The nuptial celebrations also coincided with appointing family members to key administrative or ecclesiastical offices, and raising their profile in cultural and intellectual societies through patronage and active participation, as we might imagine from these Arcadian references. This opera, then, may have intentionally endorsed themes of virtuous love and constancy, not only to complement a wedding celebration but also to declare an affiliation with leading cultural movements and their social circles.

La Rosaura was thus engaged in a relational network in which a musical drama written to mark a double wedding became a point of intersection between (on the one hand) fragile papal and dynastic politics and (on the other hand) the cultural legacy of opera and the impetus to reform contemporary Italian culture. Making sense of how these forces intersect is no easy matter, yet it is essential to our task as close readers and historians of opera and theatre. We must do justice to the force of musico-poetic developments (which yielded new configurations of expression), but also to the contingencies of the occasion. In what follows, I analyze selections from *La Rosaura* in light of opera's pastoral heritage and tragic aspirations – both of which were inflected by contextual politics and the longer-lived discourses that marked this particular intersection of opera's early modern history.

---

26 Crescimbeni imaginatively described many of the Academy's activities as erasing temporal and spatial boundaries, as if happening in a distant past, but also occurring in the very presentness of early modern Rome. See Crescimbeni's *L'Arcadia del Canonico Gio. Mario Crescimbeni*, in his Introduction, "L'autore a chi legge." Pyramids seem to have figured in other Arcadian events with some symbolic importance. Dixon describes a 1705 Arcadian Olympiad for which a temporary amphitheatre had been built in the garden of Prince Vincenzo Giustiniani (outside what is now the Porta del Popolo). Making up part of the amphitheatre was a circle of nine ancient pyramids, each built of wood and covered with flowers, serving as display mounts for *lapidi di memoria*, plaques with epitaphs, or honorifics of deceased Arcadians. See *Between the Real and Ideal*, 57–61.

A Model of Virtue

The first scene of *La Rosaura*'s act 1 opens within the domestic space of an antechamber. This is not the natural setting expected of a *bosco pastorale*, and there are no immediate indications to suggest the pastoral archetype. Instead, we enter in the middle of an animated conversation between two friends, Elmiro and Celindo, who are revealed as the main male protagonists of the opera. The libretto's subtle pastoral thematic, however, is suggested when Elmiro explains to Celindo that upon arrival in Cyprus he had been unexpectedly struck by love when he noticed a beautiful nymph unknown to him. This vision now deeply moves him, stirring his soul desperately with intense emotion and inspiring his first brief aria, "Non è più mia quest'alma" (This soul is no longer mine).[27] His sentiments signal distress over his disorienting surrender to a power he feels is not his own.

Meanwhile, Elmiro's absorbed emotionality is countered by Celindo, who expresses (in recitative only) a much more measured response, reminding Elmiro of his arranged marriage to the beautiful Climene. Celindo does not mince words and implores Elmiro to remove his amorous thoughts, preserve his honour, and avert temptation.[28] He appears as the reasoned opposite to Elmiro's love-struck delusion, yet he is also a loyal friend whose sympathy is begged by Elmiro's agony and desperation. This implicates Celindo in Elmiro's precarious plan to have him feign affections for Climene to distract her while Elmiro attempts to woo his new beloved. It is soon made known, however, that Elmiro's anonymous nymph is none other than Rosaura, Celindo's betrothed. Thus, both female characters are unwittingly embroiled in the set-up and become innocent victims in this plot of deception. When Rosaura

---

27   "Non è più mia quest'alma, / Hò già perduto il cor; / Sparì dal sen la calma, / Fugò novo desio, l'antico amor" (This soul is no longer mine, I have already lost my heart; calmness has disappeared from the breast, a new desire chased away the old love) (I-Rn 34.1.G.10, *Gli equivoci in amore overo La Rosaura*, 15). All translations are mine unless otherwise indicated. I am grateful to Giovanni Zanovello for his helpful translation insights.

28   "Sovvengati, che in Cipro, / Oggi sei giunto, Elmiro, / Per celebrar le nozze / Con la vaga Climene, / Or come in un istante, / D'altra bellezza, amante, / Hai l'onore, e la fè posto, in oblio?" (Remember Elmiro, that today you are in Cyprus to celebrate [your] wedding with the beautiful Climene? Since you [are] now in love with another beauty, have you instantly placed in oblivion [your] honour and [your] faithfulness?); "Fuggi dunque il periglio" (Therefore, escape the danger) (I-Rn 34.1.G.10, *Gli equivoci in amore overo La Rosaura*, 15–16).

realizes Celindo's actions (through a fabricated love letter he writes to Climene), she is deeply wounded by what she perceives as a devious and cruel betrayal. The bundle of errors and confusion among the four lovers sets the stage for the opera, and is described by the work's librettist, Lucini, as a knot of emotions "which poetry uses to perform its marvel."[29]

The centre of the opera focuses on the title character, Rosaura. Her first major solo in act 1, scene 4, is momentous and self-defining as she considers the depth of Celindo's deception. Rosaura begins this scene with a brief recitative, "Qual mia colpa, ò sventura?" (What fault of mine, or misfortune?), which is followed by two contrasting arias that more fully introduce Rosaura and display the range of her character. The first, "Se delitto è l'adorarti" (If adoring you is a crime) continues her self-reflection as she contemplates what has happened to her. If there was any guilt on her part, she claims, it was only that she loved Celindo (see Example 4.1).[30] Scarlatti sets this simple aria in ternary form with a steady largo tempo that remains nobly restrained throughout. Hovering over D minor, the setting of the aria's first two lines creates rhetorical drama by heightening Rosaura's poignant answer to her self-inquiry with an upward leap of an octave in measure 7, placing stress on her rejoinder: "Io son rea d'un grand error" (*I am* guilty of a grand mistake) [emphasis added]. With a reflective simplicity, this aria elegantly underscores Rosaura's regret for her miscalculation and delusion.[31]

In what follows, the reality of Celindo's deeds becomes clear, and self-query and confusion are replaced by the resolution of action.

---

29 From the *La Rosaura*'s Argomento: "Al che essendosi Celindo imprudentemente introdotto, sorpreso nell'essecuzione di questa finzione da Rosaura, fa nascere quell'errore, che con aprire la sorgente degli affetti, suol tessere l'avvolgimento, et il nodo, di cui si serve a fare il suo mirabile la Poesia" (Having Celindo unwisely agree [to pretend to court Climene], only to be caught by Rosaura in the execution of that fiction, provokes the misunderstanding which, by opening the source of affections, weaves the winding and tying of the knot, which poetry uses to perform its marvel) (I-Rn 34.1.G.10, *Gli equivoci in amore overo La Rosaura*, 5r).

30 "Se delitto è l'adorarti, / Io son rea d'un grand error; / Tu Signor de miei voleri, / E Tiranno de pensieri. / Altra colpa che l'amarti, / Non ritrovo nel mio core" (If adoring you is a crime, I am guilty of a great mistake; you, master of my desires, and tyrant of my thoughts. Other than loving you, I can't find a fault in my heart) (I-Rn 34.1.G.10, *Gli equivoci in amore overo La Rosaura*, 19).

31 All three examples in this essay are based on Eitner's edition. See *Die Oper von ihren ersten Anfängen bis zur Mitte des 18. Jahrhunderts*, 135–40; 145–8.

Example 4.1. Alessandro Scarlatti, *La Rosaura*, act 1, scene 4, "Se delitto è l'adorarti" (Rosaura).

In the second aria of this scene, "Per vostro onore, un fulmine" (For your honour, a thunderbolt) unleashes a very different emotional profile of Rosaura, one full of anger and intensity, yet focused and commanding.[32] This da capo al segno aria opens with a spirited C minor ritornello that contains a rousing scalar motif supported by the busy part work of Scarlatti's dense contrapuntal setting. As the soprano enters, Rosaura acquires a new authoritative energy, using rapid descending scalar runs (on the line: "Vibrate ò Dei, sì sì" [Quiver, oh Gods, yes, yes]) to evoke the image of her remonstrance. The swift dynamism of her musical statement beseeches her listeners' attention. She calls on the Heavens to strike down Celindo for betraying her dignity, underscoring the central tenet of honour represented so forcibly in this opera. (See Example 4.2.) This bold and assertive dimension of Rosaura's character is not simply effective for creating a captivating musical moment,

---

32 "Per vostro onore, un fulmine / Vibrate ò Dei, sì sì; / A che ferir i tempi, / E preservar poi gli empi? / Piagate, / Fulminate, / Colui che mi tradì" (For your honour, a thunderbolt quiver, oh Gods, yes yes; Why wreck the temples and then protect the wicked? Slash, strike down, he who has betrayed me) (I-Rn 34.1.G.10, *Gli equivoci in amore overo La Rosaura*, 20).

but as we will see, it symbolically emphasizes her commitment to virtue as the fundamental message central to this opera.

In the subsequent scene (act 1, scene 5), Elmiro confronts Rosaura to profess his affections and request her love. For Rosaura, however, his effusive display is an affront, and their exchange throughout this scene helps reveal the opera's most critical juxtaposition of pastoral and tragedy as symbolized through pastoral love and virtuous honour. When Elmiro pleads for mercy and compassion, Rosaura bluntly retorts that for the women of Cyprus, it is foolish and vain to speak of love.[33] She uses this tenet to fuel her next aria, "Saprò ben'io difendere, del core la libertà" (I know well how to defend the freedom of my heart), a rousing bravura-like aria that asserts how she knows better than to capitulate to an erotic love predicated on all things physical for mere attraction.[34] Instead, with great confidence, she thwarts Elmiro and insists the heart must be kept free from such destruction to the soul.

Elmiro is left devastated. He uses the scene's last aria, "Chi diede, ahi lasso" (Who gave, ah misery), for a pained, introspective musing on the doubled-edged mystery of love, where the joy of beauty is coupled with the sting of suffering that inevitably results from unrequited affection. His misery is compounded by his miscalculated desire for someone with a "heart of rock" who disguises her "hate and spite" with a physical beauty equalled only by the wonders of nature.[35]

In terms of its musical setting, Elmiro's lament decisively forms the climax of this exchange. Set in a C minor mode Scarlatti chose this closing da capo aria for his most elaborate musical setting of the scene, using the obbligato string parts to shadow Elmiro's thoughts. Like a tragic chorus, they enhance the poignancy of Elmiro's interrogatory last

---

33 "Ch'alle Dame di Cipro, / È follia, vanità, parlar d'amore" (And for the women of Cyprus, it is madness, and vain to speak of love) (I-Rn 34.1.G.10, *Gli equivoci in amore overo La Rosaura*, 21).

34 "Saprò ben'io difendere, / Del core la libertà, / Né un crine, un ciglio, un labro, / Che di rovine è fabro, / Quest'alma ferirà" (I know well how to defend the freedom of my heart. Neither a hair, eyelash, nor lip, which are makers of ruins, will hurt this soul) (I-Rn 34.1.G.10, *Gli equivoci in amore overo La Rosaura*, 21).

35 "Chi diede, ahi lasso, / A un sen di neve / Un cor di sasso? / Chi ti compose / Di gigli, e rose, / D'ostro, e cinabro / Le guance, e il labro, / E poi nascose / Nel cor, nel petto, / Odio, e dispetto, / Che prende solo, / Del mio grand duolo, / Piacere, e spasso?" (Who gave, ah misery, to a breast of snow, a heart of rock? Who composed your cheeks and lip from lilies and roses, from royal purple, and cinnabar, but then concealed in [your] heart, in [your] breast hate and spite, [a breast] which only takes pleasure and delight from my great sadness?) (I-Rn 34.1.G.10, *Gli equivoci in amore overo La Rosaura*, 22).

Example 4.2. Alessandro Scarlatti, *La Rosaura,* act 1, scene 4, "Per vostro onore, un fulmine" (Rosaura).

line, "Che prende solo, del mio grand duolo, piacere, e spasso?" (Which only takes pleasure and delight from my great sadness?), asking why a nymph so beautiful could find delight in Elmiro's unrequited love. Scarlatti complicates the rendering of the word "delight" (spasso) by using the musical setting to underscore the irony of the moment. (See Example 4.3.) In this passage, he traps the vocal line on "spasso" by creating a hypnotic but vocally limited sequence that hovers repeatedly over a cadential pattern (before the aria's return to its original key of C minor). The effect diminishes the vocal line through this obsessive iteration, especially when set against the more dramatic and rhetorically emotive solo violin (mm. 26–27), whose repeated drooping gesture punctures this moment with more urgency and clarity than Elmiro's voice can convey.

Despite this suffering, and amid further confusion and occasional bouts of humour, Elmiro remains persistent and repeatedly pursues Rosaura throughout much of this opera. On all accounts, Rosaura remains resolute in her virtue. Her reasoned constancy ultimately wins and conclusively pulls everyone else along: forcing Celindo to recognize his mistake, obliging Elmiro to the fidelity and love of Climene, and securing a happy ending with a profound moral: love can be honoured, but only when dishonesty is punished, and constancy reigns higher than any other quality of beauty.[36]

Historical Conjunctures

As the opera's critical focal points, how then do Rosaura and the thematics of virtue resonate with certain dramatic or poetic inheritances? In fundamental ways, Rosaura participates in a long lineage of female archetypes that predate Arcadian reform models. She could harken back, for instance, to a Petrarchist Laura, distant and inaccessible. Rosaura may also evoke the nymphs who populate sixteenth-century poetry, who embody beauty but also chastity, and who often send their lovers (like Elmiro) into desperate delusion.[37] More specifically, we might also see Rosaura's virtuous character modelled after a kind of

---

36 See my brief discussion of this opera in *Opera's Orbit*, 41.
37 Cox and Sampson explain how the model of chaste nymphs (as symbolic alternatives to sexual love) were "in embryo in the Italian lyric tradition from the time of Dante and Petrarch," and had "become codified, in a classicizing Neoplatonic form, in the theoretical love literature of the fifteenth and sixteenth centuries, where it performed a valuable role in reconciling the courtly cult of love with the ascetic traditions of Christianity." See "Volume Editors's Introduction," 21.

Example 4.3. Alessandro Scarlatti, *La Rosaura*, act 1, scene 5, "Chi diede, ahi lasso," (Elmiro).

heroism embraced in late-Renaissance tragedy, a genre readapted to emphasize humanist notions of virtue that could outweigh society's baser instincts and surrender to pleasure. The role of women in these dramas is extremely important; especially striking is the number of Renaissance tragedies with titles alluding to strong female characters valued for their depictions of honour and constancy. Yet, like Rosaura, these female protagonists also ran the risk of appearing inhuman to their lovers because of their rigidity and harshness.[38] We could also contextualize this interest in female virtue as part of Counter-Reformation spiritual movements, which aimed to persuade congregants toward religious renewal and focused devotion. Biblical heroines, especially those who rejected erotic love, had become role models for a redemption they provided by overcoming the sins of the flesh, and their didactic acts of morality were critical to the Church's re-establishment of a conception of chaste love predicated on honour and virtue.[39] An interest in female virtue and its overlap with tragedy was not new, but Rosaura certainly kept company with other virtuous heroines populating devotional forms, tragic drama, and more recent operas centred on morality tales.[40]

Still, no matter how critical the thematic of virtue is to this opera, Rosaura's honour requires a necessary tension to stress its constancy and fortitude. Her nobility of character is further accentuated by Elmiro's languishing lovesick condition: a contrast necessary to fuel the opera's expressive motor. Love as an element in tragedy was fraught

---

38 Andrews suggests that three-quarters of Italian Renaissance tragedies bore the titles of female heroines, giving them more stature and prominence than in other theatrical genres, but at the risk of making the women cruel and "suffering bloody outrage before the end of the play." See "The Cinquecento Theatre," in *The Cambridge History of Italian Literature*, 291.

39 In *The Devout Hand*, Rocco examines the relationship between women, religion, and the visual arts by centring her analysis on Counter-Reformation ideologies. These discourses reveal critical links between the Church's concern about women and their lack of virtue, and artistic practices, both high and low, whose aims were meant to be didactic and transformative. In his "Discorso intorni a gli'oratorii" published in *Oratorii, overo Melodrammi sacri*, Vol I, Arcangelo Spagna, a cleric and librettist of oratorios (a sacred musical genre that borrowed from operatic forms), strongly recommended authors avoid erotic heroines and instead find religious models of penitence and virtue (Herczog edition, 9).

40 In less than a decade after *La Rosaura*, themes of female innocence and virtue began to appear in operas at the turn of the eighteenth century, as documented by titles such as *La forza della virtù* and *La forza dell'innocenza*. See Bucciarelli's discussion in *Italian Opera and European Theatre*, 6.

with debate. For some, the inclusion of passions, and the role of love in tragedy, was a key argument *against* the model of seventeenth-century French tragedy. Melania Bucciarelli documents how Muratori argued for tragic settings based on passions other than love and how Gravina viewed the subject of love as compromising theatre's didactic objective because of its association with the stylistic excesses of a poetic language that reformers were aggressively trying to reject.[41]

When hosted in opera, however, love could offer a critical link to help broker pastoral and tragic inheritances that were uniquely apposed in this musico-dramatic landscape. Let us return to the discussion of Elmiro's aria, "Chi diede, ahi lasso," in act 1, scene 5 of *La Rosaura* (see Example 4.3). Elmiro's monologue is psychologically absorbing, both in terms of the scene's rhetorical pacing and because of Scarlatti's musical setting. This moment immerses listeners into the depth of Elmiro's misery through the emotional concision of an operatic aria. We might even admit that the musical setting, with its drooping, lamenting gestures, helps generate a temporary emotional empathy with Elmiro, even if undeserving. His aria, in all the ways that it functions, reflects a longer history that originates in opera's Renaissance models. As Gerbino argues in his exploration of the myth of Arcadia, pastoralism was created and preserved *by music*. Music was the sonic intervention that offered its many poetic shepherds and nymphs the necessary salve to soothe the pains of love, just as it serves Elmiro (and listeners) at this juncture.[42] And yet, what is most telling is that the very persistence of love as the catalyst for musical expressivity is used as a necessary contradistinction to Rosaura's virtuous rationalism (inspired by tragic models). In fact, we might argue that Rosaura's heroism depends upon such love-sickness as the very source of emotional weakness and sensual temptation to overcome. If a pastoral love was once inescapably desired but destructive, in the new reformist landscape, passion was to be socially managed and transformed into a new conception. As a narrative and expressive element, love was useful in its function as both counter and essence of virtue.

As central protagonists, Elmiro and Rosaura thus represent an iconic incongruity that reflects this pastoral-tragic juxtaposition: Elmiro as the sentimental shepherd, who in spite of his agony holds desperately

---

41 Bucciarelli, *Italian Opera and European Theatre*, 85.
42 "If it is true, as Augustine and Petrarch believed, that language begins with desire, and that desire generated language, the Renaissance obsession with love poetry becomes a gigantic monument to the inadequacy of language to soothe desire." Gerbino, *Music and the Myth of Arcadia in Renaissance Italy*, 9.

to love; and Rosaura as the consummate noble heroine who firmly resists temptation. This fundamental opposition of reason versus emotion was to be maintained in tension for all of the didactic lessons and creative potential it could inspire. In *dramma per musica*, the reasoned decision to resolve one's moral dilemma was merely the end point of a longer tangled process, what Martha Feldman describes as "a labyrinth of passions" that ranged from the extremes of affliction and sorrow (love suffering) to redemption and heroism (tragic virtue).[43] We can't underestimate the structural, conventional, and performative influence this range of emotions provided opera at this juncture, allowing each work the possibility for a fluid process of production and re-production. This workshop of sensibilities is what made opera wondrous and largely formed the source from which audiences derived their pleasure in ways unique from spoken drama and written poetry.

To understand *La Rosaura* involves appreciating it as an opera production – in dialogue with large-scale historical configurations, yet also mired in the pressures of its local needs and realities. We might speculate that Rosaura's virtue and chaste constancy were strategically chosen as an ennobling message for the dual couples being celebrated. But there are some curious features about the opera's production history: it was not limited to a one-time-only dynastic event but appears to have been subsequently performed for the public stage as well.[44] In these consecutive performances, the poet Lucini was thus commissioned to create a more broadly engaging entertainment, likely reminiscent of Venetian models (perhaps a nod to the regional heritage of his patrons).[45] With the opera's different iteration for a commercial performance, Lucini included an obligatory comic character to provide contrast to the spare cast of noble characters, using the witty servant to break from the drama and address the audience with wry commentary about love's foolishness

---

43 Feldman, *Opera and Sovereignty*, 8.
44 There are three known printed libretti for this opera: 1690 I-Rn 34.1.G.10; 1691 I-Rn 34.1.F.37; 1692 I-Rn 34.2.A.30. The first 1690 libretto does not mention Lucini, but the 1691 publication states his full name; the third from 1692 gives his initial (G.B.L.) only.
45 We must recognize that Roman entertainment in these decades comprised a varied mix of Venetian operatic reproductions for the larger public theatres, operas with reformist influences (pastoral and tragic, and often, but not exclusively, produced for private theatres), and didactic-oriented dramas done at the Jesuit colleges. See Tcharos, *Opera's Orbit*, 20–45.

in contradistinction to his more serious counterpart, his patroness Rosaura.[46]

The 1690 double nuptials of the Ottoboni family may have originally launched *La Rosaura*, but the opera was not limited to the politically motivated matrices of this synchronic event. Instead, it draws upon multiple orientations, including the problems of erotic love set within a lingering context of a post-Tridentine morality. It also exhibits the aesthetic transformations of post-Marinist poetry, however mired in conflicting cultural and literary viewpoints. Above all, *La Rosaura* had the objective to convey a sense of entertainment as motivated by the realities of noble patronage and commercial publicity, even when such a process was conjointly influenced by the acts and decisions made by the artists themselves. This cluster of influences forms a crucial nexus that helps reveal the complexities of pressures and interplay of different forces that coalesce at this historical juncture. In histories of opera, we have too often reduced such a complex interval to simple steps of subtraction or addition: opera stopped doing *that*, and started doing *this*. But in truth, opera was doing cultural work far too complex for such transitions to be that smooth.

As we have seen, the relationship between tragedy and *dramma per musica* is more than surface definitions of form and style used in routinized descriptions. Tragedy may have been useful for ideologues as a lauded touchstone of literary excellence, but in practice, it offered opera a platform to examine human emotion, reframed and recontextualized by modern conditions of culture. *La Rosaura* thus exposes how cultural forms are not only informed by pragmatic considerations of place, politics, and occasion but influenced by elusive notions of taste and affect and embedded in complex, overlapping historical developments – whether literary, musical, cultural, or political. Writing a convincing history of opera and tragedy very much depends on our ability to resuture these complex temporal legacies.

---

46 We know from *La Rosaura*'s 1692 production that the comic character of Lesbo was likely successful, enough to have Lucini (or another poet) augment this feature by having a further comic character added – Lisetta, Lesbo's lover.

5 Claiming Women's Moral Agency: Luisa Bergalli as Poet Librettist

FRANCESCA SAVOIA

The in-depth analysis of an early eighteenth-century and virtually unknown Italian opera libretto would make too small a contribution to the present volume were it not for the rich cultural context and special concurrence of factors and circumstances surrounding its creation, which this essay also explores as relevant features of the intertwined histories of opera and tragedy in Italy. Let us enumerate them. First, although the author – Venetian-born poet, playwright, and translator Luisa Bergalli (1703–79) – was not the first woman ever to write dramatic texts for music, she deserves an honoured place in history as the first woman ever to write opera librettos for the public theatre.[1] Second, she lived

---

1 In France, Luoise-Geneviève Gillot de Saintonge (1650–1718) penned two full-length *tragédies en musique*, *Didon* and *Circé*, which were set to music by Henry Desmarets and first performed at the Théâtre du Palais-Royal in 1693 and 1694, respectively. See Hoxby's essay in this volume. In Italy, Francesca Caccini (1587– after June 1641), who served the Medici court for twenty years as a music teacher, composer, and singer, provided that court with numerous musical entertainments: the only surviving opera, whose text and music she composed, is a comedy fashioned after an episode of Ariosto's famous poem (*La liberazione di Ruggiero dall'isola d'Alcina*), and was performed on 3 February 1625 at the Villa Poggio Imperiale in honour of the Polish Prince Władisław's visit for carnival. Other women performers and composers of dramatic works for music who lived before Bergalli (Barbara Strozzi, Élisabeth Jacquet de la Guerre, Maria Anna von Raschenau, Caterina Benedetta Gratianini, and Camilla de Rossi) or were her contemporaries (Elisabetta De Gambarini) appear to have availed themselves of texts by male poets; as per Margherita Grimani, active in the first decade of the eighteenth century, the names of the librettists of her two oratorios and one *componimento dramatico* for the court of Vienna remain unknown to this day. To my knowledge, no woman besides Bergalli wrote opera librettos for the public theatre until the German playwright Helmina von Chézy (1783–1856) provided Weber with the text for his romantic-heroic opera *Euryanthe* (first performed in Vienna at the Theater am Kärntnertor on 25 October 1823).

and operated in Venice, which was not only the theatrical and musical capital of Europe at the time but also the home to a flourishing community of women writers and artists.[2] Third, Bergalli studied under Apostolo Zeno, a highly regarded and well-connected scholar and antiquarian, who preceded Pietro Metastasio as the Poet Laureate to the imperial court of Vienna and was himself a prolific librettist, known for his efforts in restoring good taste to Italian poetry and returning decorum to operatic plots and characters. And finally, as a work produced in the same year as Metastasio's dramatic debut, *Didone abbandonata*, Bergalli's earliest dramatic work, *Agide re di Sparta*, allows us to view some of the most important theatrical controversies and intellectual debates of the day – including their underlying aesthetic, socio-political, and national motivations – through the eyes of an Italian woman of letters.

Luisa Bergalli at the Cross-currents

The founding of the literary academy of Arcadia in 1690 and the subsequent proliferation of its colonies throughout Italy, as well as the spread of the so-called *conversazioni miste* (forerunners of the salons), enabled an increasing number of Italian women to participate in cultural transactions and production, and this, in turn, gave rise to a new phase of the *querelle des femmes* in the form of a lively debate on women's education and their role in society. One of the earliest public discussions of this subject was sponsored in 1723 by the academy of the Ricovrati (Recovered) of Padua, in the Venetian state. Nowhere in Europe did such debate start earlier and more earnestly than in Italy, and nowhere in Italy did women of middle or even lower classes find an environment more propitious to their studies and their intellectual, social, and professional advancement than in the Republic of Venice.[3]

At the same time, stimulated by the new currents of thought coming from France, and goaded by the harshly unfavourable opinions that French critics had expressed about Italian literature (starting with Bouhours in his 1687 *La Manière de bien penser dans les ouvrages d'esprit*, sometimes loosely translated as *The Art of Criticism*), early eighteenth-century Italian intellectuals were also undertaking the

---

2 See Cox, *The Prodigious Muse*.
3 A well-publicized debate on the subject of women's education was sponsored by the academy of the Ricovrati of Padua in 1723. See Messbarger, "The Italian Enlightened Reform." On women's networks of personal and professional support in eighteenth-century Venice, see Sama, "'On Canvas and on the Page.'"

monumental task of rethinking and rationalizing their entire national literary output. Indeed, the very concept of a national literature had to be established, issues of form and genre readdressed, and a canon redrawn to respond to a new, slowly rising civic consciousness. Working at this project of reclamation and re-edification, Italian literati found that the place that should have been occupied by tragedy – recognized by most as the highest literary genre in terms of style and moral function – was sadly vacant, and the majority of them placed the blame for this unfortunate predicament on the extravagant makeup and continuous popularity of the *dramma per musica*. Mario Crescimbeni and Vincenzo Gravina, founders of Arcadia, and Ludovico Antonio Muratori, the leading Italian scholar of this age, were among the first to indict contemporary opera, which was culpable, in their view, for good dramatic poetry and true tragedy being absent from the Italian stage.[4] The year his friend Antonio Vallisneri, member of the academy of the Ricovrati (The Recovered) and professor of medicine at the University of Padua presided at the above-mentioned debate on women's learning, the erudite marquis Scipione Maffei happened to publish, in Verona, the first of three volumes of his *Teatro Italiano* (*Italian Theatre*), a collection of early modern Italian tragedies.[5] In the preface, Maffei reminded his readers how Western culture was in debt to Italy, and more specifically to the Veneto region, for reviving the tradition of Greek and Roman drama, which had been all but forgotten during the Middle Ages.[6] With his collection, Maffei clearly intended to provide impetus for the creation of a new Italian tragic repertoire, to which he had already personally contributed by writing *Merope* (1713), a tragedy that had been very successfully performed in Modena, Verona, and Venice, and soon after translated into several languages. Like the criticism of musical drama initiated by Crescimbeni, Maffei's exhortation

---

4 While all three writers held a negative opinion of contemporary opera, they expressed their criticism in very different terms in their respective poetics tracts: Crescimbeni, *La bellezza*; Muratori, *Della perfetta poesia italiana*; Gravina, *Della ragione poetica*; and Gravina, *Della tragedia libri uno*. For an overview of their different stands on opera, see de Benedetto, "Poetics and Polemics," 17–21.

5 Maffei, *Teatro*.

6 Maffei, *Teatro*, 1.2. The passage referred specifically to an early humanist from Padua, Alberto Mussato, author of *Ecerinis* (c. 1314), a Latin verse tragedy modelled after Seneca's *Thyestes*, and to the better-known Renaissance dramatist and grammarian, Gian Giorgio Trissino, author of *Sofonisba* (published in 1525 but written much earlier), one of the first tragedies to show complete deference to classic, Aristotelian rules.

to resume the fatally interrupted Italian Renaissance dramatic tradition was part of the original Arcadian plan to restore sobriety, simplicity, and dignity to Italian poetry. While neither the tracts of Crescimbeni, Gravina, and Muratori, nor Maffei's *Teatro*, could stop or slow operatic production, they did encourage a robust debate regarding the general reform of Italian theatre, and they did lend momentum to the efforts undertaken by Italian librettists such as the Venetian Apostolo Zeno to curb opera's most outlandish qualities by supplying composers, singers, and impresarios with more regular texts.

Zeno was a man of parts. He was a dedicated historian and antiquarian, a friend and correspondent of Muratori, and a co-founder, with Vallisneri and Maffei, of *Il giornale dei letterati d'Italia* (*The Journal of Italian Literati*) (1710), which quickly became an essential point of reference for Italian intellectuals of the pre-Enlightenment period. He was also an intensely active poet librettist who worked not only for the commercial theatres of Venice and other Italian cities but also (later) for the court theatre of Vienna. The influence that French rationalism and French classical theatre had upon him, and the range of interests and breadth of knowledge that he brought to this kind of work, made his librettos quite different from (and far superior to) most. However, he wrote opera librettos more to finance his scholarly research and his book and coin collections than to obey a genuine expressive, poetic impulse. The specific qualities of his contribution, as a poet dramatist, to the reform of *melodramma* have not always been easy to determine, perhaps because of the chronological proximity of Metastasio, "the true poet" who provided the body of work that was to be the main source for composers, and the uncontested model for librettists, almost until the end of the century.[7] Nevertheless, there is no doubt that Zeno's librettos already displayed some of the dramatic characteristics of classic *opera seria*.

The life and work of Luisa Bergalli can be situated precisely at the confluence of the phenomena that have been here described, and should be interpreted in light of both the *querelle des femmes* and the debate on Italian literary and theatrical reform. She took full advantage of the gender-neutral practices of Italian academies (joining Arcadia in her early twenties) and benefited from the social and professional

---

7   British music historian Charles Burney wrote that "no author had penetrated into the refinements of the art [of poetry] as Metastasio" (Burney, *Memoirs of the Life and Writings of the Abate Metastasio*, 3:299).

"miscegenation" that characterized the Venetian cultural community. Although poor and a commoner, she received a first-rate liberal arts education: she learned French at a very early age from her Piedmontese father, was tutored in philosophy by Antonio Alberghetti (of the charitable order of the Somaschi Fathers, who had long been educating and forming youth in Venice), studied Latin and Italian with Antonio Sforza, dramatic literature with the already mentioned Zeno, and drawing with the portraitist Rosalba Carriera, a very successful woman artist. Bergalli must have also had some access to the rich libraries that her mentors and friends (such as Zeno and Jacopo Soranzo) owned personally or (like Sforza) cared for on behalf of affluent patricians.[8]

Bergalli was one of the earliest and most indefatigable eighteenth-century promoters of the intellectual abilities, moral discernment, and emotional intelligence of her sex. In 1726 – when the proceedings of the aforementioned 1723 Paduan debate had yet to appear in print – she published a two-volume anthology containing poems by more than two hundred and fifty Italian women writers from the medieval period to her time. The writings of these women had been, for the most part, entirely ignored or, once published, relegated to obscurity.[9] With this collection, Bergalli aimed at providing sufficient evidence of female literary talent not just to uphold the right of women to an education but, above all, to claim for them (and for herself) the kind of institutional recognition and authority that was routinely granted to far less accomplished male members of the Republic of Letters.

Among eighteenth-century Italian learned women, Bergalli also holds a special place as the very first woman to write opera librettos for the public theatre. Indeed, by authoring two original *drammi per musica*, one oratorio, two tragedies, one comedy, and countless translations and stage adaptations, besides co-directing and co-managing the Teatro Sant'Angelo for one year with her husband Gasparo Gozzi,

---

8 Jacopo Soranzo (1686–1757), a Venetian senator and wealthy collector and patron, was a passionate bibliophile and assembled, in his lifetime, a great number of precious manuscripts and printed books. The copy of the first and only edition of Bergalli's 1728 tragedy, *Teba*, found in the collection of the Houghton Library at Harvard (one of the very few copies extant today), bears the handwritten name of this patrician, indicating that Soranzo was presumably its original owner; Antonio Sforza worked as a librarian for Jacopo Soranzo. The catalogue of Soranzo's library, *Catalogus librorum here venales erunt Patavii*, was published in 1780 (also in Italian and French). See Mitchell, "Trevisan and Soranzo"; Zorzi, "La stampa."
9 Bergalli, *Componimenti poetici*. On this work: Chemello, "Luisa Bergalli," 49–88; Curran, "Recollecting the Renaissance," 263–86.

Bergalli ventured into theatrical fields almost entirely untried by Italian women writers.[10] Scholars have long known that in Bergalli's time, in addition to several occasional private and public performance venues, Venice counted at least seven active public theatres (five of which were opera houses), and four *Ospedali*, specializing in the rigorous musical training of the most promising among the orphaned girls in their care, who set up and offered regular musical recitals. The city generated locally, or attracted from other Italian cultural centres (such as Naples) and from abroad, a wealth of professional theatre and opera artists who staged public theatrical performances from November to *mardi gras*, and then again during a shorter season around the Ascension. The *Serenissima* offered, in other words, a most diverse, rich, and accessible musical and theatrical life. It was fertile ground for "cross-breeding," development, and innovation in those areas. Bergalli's lifelong interest in both operas and stage plays must be understood in this context. Aiming at revealing what "pulpit" *opera seria* specifically provided to this young, cultivated Venetian woman, this essay will now focus on the play that inaugurated the first and most satisfying phase of Bergalli's career, when she had not yet married Count Gasparo Gozzi, had not yet begun to bear his children and the brunt of seemingly endless family troubles, and was not yet the

10 Bergalli authored and published two tragedies, *Teba* (1728) and *Elettra* (1743), the comedy *Le avventure del poeta* (1730), two *drammi per musica*, *Agide re di Sparta* (1725) and *Elenia* (1730), and the oratorio *Eleazaro* (1739). Bergalli's very first biographer, Mazzuchelli, mentioned five other opera librettos by her, presumably written between *Agide* and *Elenia*: *Placida*, *Alcibiade*, *Agrippina*, and *Andromaca* (*Gli scrittori d'Italia*, 2 (pt. 2): 926–9). *Placida* is indeed briefly discussed in one of Zeno's letters to Bergalli, along with an *Arianna* (*Lettere di Apostolo Zeno*, 4: 63–4); but no text nor record of publication exist of any of them. From Latin, Bergalli translated Terence's plays: *L'Adria* in 1727, *L'eunuco* and *L'affannatore* in 1728, *I due fratelli* in 1729, *Il Formione* in 1730, and *L'Ecira* in 1731. These comedies were then collected in *Le commedie di Terenzio, tradotte in verso sciolto da Luisa Bergalli*. From French, she translated six tragedies (*Andromaca, Mitridate, Berenice, Ifigenia, Britannico*, and *Bajazed*) and one comedy (*I litiganti*) by Racine, collected and published in two volumes as *Opere di Racine tradotte*; one comedy by Molière (*Il misantropo*, in 1745); two tragedies by Duché (*Il Gionata* and *L'Assalonne*) and one by la Motte (*I Macabei*), published together in the second volume of *Teatro ebraico ovvero Scelta di tragedie tratte d'argomenti ebraici*; and one tragedy by Mme. Du Boccage (*Le amazzoni*, in 1756). See Ferrari, *Le traduzioni italiane*; Santangelo and Vinti, *Le traduzioni italiane*. Gasparo Gozzi and Luisa Bergalli introduced at the Sant'Angelo a repertoire that included their own translations and adaptations of French plays and at least one original *azione scenica* written by Bergalli (difficult to say if in collaboration with her husband or not) entitled *Bradamante*. See Selfridge-Field, *A New Chronology*, 576.

favourite target of her brother-in-law playwright Carlo Gozzi's misogynistic gibes.[11]

Between Zeno and Metastasio: The Making of a Libretto

Right when Metastasio was making his own real debut as a dramatist with *Didone abbandonata* (set to music by Domenico Sarro for the February 1724 premiere in Naples, and by Tomaso Albinoni for the first Venetian production in late December), Zeno encouraged Bergalli, not quite twenty-two years of age, to launch her literary career by writing a libretto.[12] Her first drama, *Agide re di Sparta*, was dedicated to Count Rambaldo of Collalto (frequent patron of Venetian operas and well-regarded member of the Austrian imperial court), and was performed in Venice at the Teatro San Moisè, after the traditional Christmas *novena*, on 26 December, 1724, with the music of Giovanni Porta (c. 1677–1755).[13]

The play testifies to Bergalli's familiarity with Venetian musical theatre and with the general guidelines followed by her mentor in drafting his own librettos (at least thirteen of which he co-authored with fellow librettist Pietro Pariati, who took care of versification). With *Lucio Vero*, at the very dawn of the century, Zeno had made his first attempt at a new and more restrained style of *melodramma*. One important step he took in this direction was to relinquish, in large measure, mythological and pastoral subjects in favour of historical ones, which he felt could lend opera some intrinsic realism. He also eliminated erotic and comic scenes, managed to reduce in part the elaborate spectacle that had accompanied more fanciful subject matters, and achieved, in many cases, more unity and coherence of action. Above all, he strove for more

---

11 For further biographical information on Luisa Bergalli see Mutini, "Bergalli, Luisa"; Stewart, "Luisa Bergalli"; Savoia, "Una storia tutta da raccontare," 109–22.

12 See Selfridge-Field, *A New Chronology*, 377. Metastasio had already written two *azioni teatrali* (*Endimione* in 1720, and *La Galatea* in 1722), but *Didone* was his first full *dramma per musica*.

13 The title page of *Agide*'s libretto is dated 1725, but the opera premiered at the very end of December 1724. See Selfridge-Field, *A New Chronology*, 377–8. Porta was a pupil of Francesco Gasparini, who had set to music several of Zeno's *drammi* (*Antioco* in 1705, *Ambleto* and *Statira* in 1706, *L'amor generoso* and *Anfitrione* in 1707, and *Merope* in 1711, to mention just the ones for which he provided the first, original score). Porta himself would join the many opera composers who reset to music many of Zeno's texts: *Venceslao* (as *La Lucinda Fedele*) and *Flavio Anicio Olibrio* (as *Il trionfo di Flavio Olibrio*) in 1726, *Lucio Papirio dittatore* and *Gianguir* in 1732, and *Ifigenia in Aulide* in 1738. For a complete list of Zeno's and Porta's works, see Sala di Felice, "Zeno, Apostolo," and Tiedge, "Porta, Giovanni."

dramatic congruity and an elevated tone that could give opera at least a semblance of classical and moral correctness. *Agide* appears to comply with these principles, while also responding to the interests and personality of Bergalli and forging beyond Zeno's solution to opera.

As the *Argomento* discloses, the subject of *Agide* was inspired by (rather than drawn from) a contemporary historical source, Pier Antonio Foresti's *Mappamondo Istorico* (*Historical Map of the World*) and a sixteenth-century fictional one, Giambattista Giraldi's *Gli Ecatommiti* (*The Hecatommites*), each containing a version of a particular episode of ancient Greek history that, as will be made clear, attracted Bergalli's attention for specific, personal reasons.[14] The play consists of three lean acts, requiring two set changes each and the kind of scenery suited to a story of *talamo e trono* (nuptial bed and throne), such as the stage of the San Moisè could easily accommodate.[15] While many operas ended with a chorus (joining or replacing the principal singers on stage for the final song), and fewer operas called for a chorus to open and close just one of its acts (for example, Zeno's *Ormisda re di Persia*, staged in Vienna in 1721, with music by Antonio Caldara), Bergalli's *Agide* both begins and ends with short choruses. The first one functions as both background and prelude, celebrating the end of the siege of Sparta by the Macedonians, and giving thanks to the city's saviour, Antianira, the woman-warrior who killed the enemy king (*Agide* 1.1.9), while the second and final chorus tells the proverbial moral of the story, proclaiming that "Il soffrir d'anime oneste / Suole pace alfin trovar. / Anche dopo

---

14 In the front matter of *Agide*, acknowledging the sources that inspired her choice of subject matter, Bergalli wrote: "Da Cintio Giraldi, e dal P. Foresti s'ebbe la prima idea, onde il Dramma fu composto" (The idea that first occasioned the composition of this drama came from Cinthio Giraldi and P. Foresti) (*Agide*, 7).

15 In the Italian poetical tradition, *talamo*, or the nuptial bed, and *trono*, or a sovereign's seat, have functioned as symbols of marital status and power, respectively. We find the two terms frequently used in Italian operatic texts of Bergalli's time, whose plots almost inevitably involved love and power struggles and the use of marriage as a political instrument. Multiple *mutazioni di scene* (set changes) in each act were common in such *drammi per musica*, requiring that they be staged in large and well-equipped opera houses. Among Zeno's plays performed at the San Cassiano, *Antioco* (music by Gasperini, 1705) and *Merope* (music by Gasparini, 1712) required eight different settings, and *Teuzzone* (music by Lotti, 1707) nine; *Alessandro Severo*, performed at the San Giovanni Grisostomo (music by Lotti, 1717), called for eight. Observing the unity of place was not contemplated even by reformers like Zeno, who managed to do so only in his *Temistocle*, a simpler *azione scenica*, with just one setting (an army camp by the Persian city of Susa), performed in Vienna in 1701 with the music of Antonio Ziani, on the occasion of Leopold I's birthday.

le tempeste / Spunta il sol più lieto in mar" (Just as the sun shines more joyfully on the sea after a storm, the suffering of honest souls is usually met by a peaceful ending) (*Agide* 3.11.57).[16]

As Zeno would have wanted, the plot of *Agide* is well guided: in the course of the first act, the multiple, tangled root causes of the conflict emerge, while, in the second, the dramatic arc reaches its apex, and in the third, impending catastrophe is evaded, and the traditional happy resolution attained. However, the count of the scenes per act (respectively, thirteen, fourteen, and eleven) and the relative count of *a solo* recitative and aria numbers and recitative solo scenes, suggest that Bergalli strove for more economy than her mentor ever did: most of Zeno's librettos easily count five to ten scenes more than *Agide*, and consequently more arias and more *a solo* scenes per act, as well as longer dialogues and monologues in recitative style (some exceeding one hundred verses).[17]

Accepting as an inevitability that a three-act opera format would impose a quicker pace on the dramatic action than a five-act declaimed play would, Bergalli preferred to focus on the dramatic potential of the arias. In this way, Bergalli's approach is closer to Metastasio's than Zeno's. The latter had declared "il dover cantarsi da capo a piede le ariette musicali" (having to sing the musical arias twice, from head to foot) to be one of the most serious challenges that opera posed to *vraisemblance*, and he firmly believed that to this and other "simili inconvenienti, non è possibile che si dia riparo" (to such hindrances, remedy cannot be found). Zeno thought that the best a librettist could do was to maintain the unity of action, introduce characters well suited to perform that

---

16 All parenthetical references to *Agide* refer to act, scene, and page number.

17 Act 2, scene 1 of Zeno's *Merope* (32–6), as well as act 2, scene 12 and act 3, scene 8 of his *Alessandro Severo* (37–9 and 51–5) contain good examples of long dialogues in recitative form. Particularly notable is the number of *a solo* recitative and aria scenes in the Bolognese version of *Merope* (three in each act) and, again, in *Alessandro Severo* (four in the first act and two in each of the following). Zeno's *Ifigenia in Aulide*, which premiered in Vienna in 1718 with the music of Caldara, also contained a good number of *a solo* scenes (two each in the first and second act, and three in the third act). Thinking of the *a solo* recitative and aria scenes of musical drama as the operatic equivalent of monologues in spoken tragedy, it should perhaps be noted that, unlike Corneille, who abandoned the use of soliloquies in his later plays, Racine – the French dramatist most admired by Zeno – never dispensed with them. See the table detailing the number of soliloquies and their length in nine of the eleven tragedies by Racine in Pocock, *Problems of Tragic Forms*, 192. Racine's *Iphigénie*, which is the tragedy closely imitated by Zeno in drafting his homonymous *dramma per musica*, contained four soliloquies.

action (or plot), respect decorum, and cultivate the moral sensibilities of the audience.[18]

Agide's arias reveal Bergalli as a thoughtful and skilled lyricist, if not a particularly elegant one: the arias average six or eight verses in length, and most consist of two isometric stanzas, each ending with a cadential *verso tronco* (truncated verse), which would confirm the traditional *da capo* structure of the songs.[19] As for the recitatives, none of which counts more than sixty lines of dialogue or twenty lines of soliloquy, they all comprise blank verses and do not present any kind of strophic organization. Prosodic data and analysis of scene construction tell us, in sum, that in this relatively economical play arias are quite conspicuous. Bergalli's attention to and reliance on arias in *Agide* stands out not so much because they grace over sixty percent of the scenes, but rather because they are all carefully conceived to bring those scenes to their close, and none is interpolated in the recitatives.

More specifically, as the sample analyzed later in this essay will show, Bergalli's arias are designed and positioned to fulfill the function of distilling and presenting the characters' often contrasting attitudes and / or responses to what has transpired in the recitatives (which remain the main vehicle of dialogue and action). They tend to be less abstractly conceived than many of the arias found in Zeno's plays and more dramatically active, by either answering directly to the situation represented in the scenes in which they occur, or by helping to delineate the characters and their development in a typologically varied succession throughout the play.[20] There is no doubt that Bergalli paid serious attention to the distribution and quantitative relation between recitatives and arias in

18 Zeno's quoted reflections on the poetics of musical drama – prompted by Muratori's *Della perfetta poesia* – can be found in a famous letter he addressed to the marquis Giuseppe Gravisi on 3 November 1730: *Lettere di Apostolo Zeno*, 4: 278.
19 Although the only print edition of *Agide*'s libretto is pretty shabby, and the lines of the text of all arias do not appear typographically organized in separate stanzas, the *da capo* structure – a form that dominated Italian arias for almost three-quarters of the eighteenth century – is confirmed by the presence of cadential *versi tronchi* as well as by the clear indication that a repetition of the first stanza followed at the end of the second.
20 *Statira*, a drama written by Zeno in collaboration with Pariati (originally set to music by Gasparini in 1705, and then reset by Albinoni in 1726), featuring two important female characters, a *travesti* part, a love "quadrilateral," plus an odd man out like that found in Bergalli's play, makes for a good comparison. In spite of Zeno's strong reservations to set-piece songs, this opera is packed to the brim with arias (thirty-eight in all), most of which are too formalized and formulaic to help us identify the characters' personalities and tell them apart. Zeno, *Statira*.

her drama. In doing so, she was fully aware of the conventions that had gradually emerged in the past seventy years of opera history and that Metastasio would eventually sort out and codify.

In the absence of the original score (of which no extant copy is known), it is, of course, impossible to determine what kind of relationship Bergalli's text and Porta's music maintained, or how effectively the two conveyed together the ebb and flow of dramatic tension and emotions.[21] Too little can be deduced, moreover, from the scant information we have about the interpreters and the circumstances of the performance to get a sense of how clearly drawn and convincing the characters might have appeared on stage in the end.[22] Nevertheless, much can be inferred from a comparative analysis of the libretto to help us better understand Bergalli's position in operatic tradition and/or innovation. Furthermore, by studying specifically her handling of characters and plot in *Agide* and in her only tragedy, *Teba*, it is possible to recognize how her choices were inflected, in both, by her feminist stance and commitment.

Aesthetic and Ethical Underpinnings of Bergalli's Playwriting

An examination of *Agide*'s plot and character development reveals the underlying motives of Bergalli's work. Besides its namesake, King Agide, and the principal heroine, Antianira, the play counts four other characters: captive princess Timocla, daughter of the defunct king of the Macedonians; Agide's son, Prince Damida; Antianira's suitor, Prince Filoastro; and the leader of Agide's army, Gilippo. They are all characters who are noble by birth or, in Antianira's case, by merit. Notwithstanding the epic-heroic premises of the story, there are no real *scene di popolo* (crowd scenes), as can be found in more grandiose operas, except

---

21 Almost half of the scores of Porta's thirty operas are completely lost to us; of the rest, often only fragments remain.

22 Angelo Maria Cantelli, a *virtuoso* in the service of the prince of Modena, who played the title role of Agide, and his daughter Stella Fortunata Cantelli, who played the role of Antianira, came into conflict with the impresario of the San Moisè, Antonio Gaspari, who played the role of Damida, because they were unprepared for both the autumn and carnival seasons of 1724–5. The productions most affected were apparently those of *Laodice* (text by Angelo Schietti, music by Tomaso Albinoni, performed on 14 October 1724) and *Il nemico amante* (text by Giuseppe Maria Buini, music by Fortunato Chelleri, performed on 9 December 1724), which became the subject of the litigation brought by Gaspari. It is not clear whether the production of *Agide* suffered as well. See Selfridge-Field, *A New Chronology*, 373, 375, and 380.

that Antianira comes on stage, as the text reads, "seguita da molta parte dell'esercito" (followed by a great part of the army) (*Agide*, 1.1.9); and, in one climactic instance at the end of the second act, the presence of some extras is required: they play Gilippo's hired hands, paid to fake a coup that he can claim to have averted, and accuse Damida of having plotted against his father. Gilippo's elaborate sham, reluctantly supported by Filoastro, and his well-delivered, timely lies succeed in convincing Agide of his son's guilt, thus landing Damida in prison to await execution. The sinister malice of Gilippo sets off quite effectively Agide's flaws as a father and a ruler who easily misplaces his trust; even more so, it sets off the generous nature of the play's "honest souls," namely the female characters, Antianira and Timocla. Gilippo's treacherousness functions well with both the morally instructive aim of the play and its operatic demands for situations charged with readily perceivable affects that music could support and interpret. Of course, those demands had always appeared to opera practitioners to be best served by resorting to love intrigues, and *Agide* complies by featuring – in a court setting – two couples of mismatched young lovers, plus a villainous odd man out.

Before the end of the first act, it is clear that Timocla, in spite of herself, has fallen in love with Damida, the Spartan prince who, unbeknownst to his father, has declared himself to her. Agide, without consulting his son, has promised him in marriage to Sparta's saviour, Antianira, encouraging the heroine's own feelings for Damida, and prompting her to sever the relationship with Filoastro, thus making him an ally in Gilippo's vengeful scheme. Like Idaspe in Zeno's *Statira*, Gilippo appears from the start to be pursuing a sort of private vendetta against Damida, strongly resenting him for the power the prince has simply inherited, and for having won the affection of Timocla, the woman he wanted for himself. The villain's hand is forced by circumstances that he himself helps to create and over which he finally loses control: this manages perhaps to give his actions, and the play, a faintly tragic sense of inevitability. More to the point, the rather complicated chain of misplaced loves and loyalties forming the basis of *Agide*'s plot, and ending in Gilippo's exposure and death, allows Bergalli to address the need for both morally instructive and lyrically expressible content. She does so while setting off the female character as the kind of ethical agent who, through the supreme Cartesian virtue of generosity, manages to control her own desires and emotions and restore the order that other characters' passions have upset. Indeed, if Bergalli had a philosophical system in mind upon which to base her dramatic playwriting, it was Cartesian in essence. Although Descartes did not concern himself with the aesthetic nature and merits of dramatic art, he reflected upon tragic theatre from a moral perspective, and he considered it a useful means of experiencing passions without falling victim to the disruptive effects that they have in real life. Bergalli appears to have subscribed to the principles – hailing from Cartesian doctrine, and endorsed by many early eighteenth-century theorists, first and foremost René Rapin – that absence of affective motion is disagreeable in theatre, that spectators crave to be moved, and that any drama failing to stir emotions is dull and falls short of its intended goals: her use of arias in *Agide* confirms this.[23] She also showed great regard for the moral content of all her dramatic works, and clearly considered tragic theatre as an instrument of moral instruction. However, she appraised and treated the ethical, didactic, and entertaining potential of different genres as distinct, and approached all of them from her stance as an advocate of women's rights who wished to deepen the audience's engagement with her female dramatis personae.

In her tragedy *Teba,* written a few years after *Agide,* the protagonist has been forced to marry the usurper of her elder brother's throne, the tyrant Alessandro. The latter has taken a fancy to another woman of the court, the fair Ismene, and could repudiate Teba (or worse, sentence her to death on trumped-up charges) that he might remarry. Yet the heroine appears firm in her belief that, as Alessandro's wife, she could never betray him and support the revenge scheme of her surviving younger brother. Like Maffei's *Merope,* whose plot shares elements with that of Bergalli's tragedy, *Teba* ends happily: the impending evil of the protagonist's trial, wrongful conviction, and death is averted by the tyrant's own demise. Unlike Merope, however, Bergalli's heroine does not and cannot even contemplate taking revenge: if, on the one hand, she dismisses her old father's appeals to place her trust in God, on the other hand, she does not actively work to extract herself from danger. She simply accepts herself being an ill-used woman and spurned wife as fated: the fortitude and dignity with which Teba bears such a common womanly plight is what Bergalli intended to mark her character as tragic.

The ideological conservatism of Bergalli's tragedy may say more about her deference to classical French tragedy than it does about the values of contemporary Venetian society. Teba's father Jasone, with his firm belief in the unfailing help of the heavens, is the character staged

---

23 See Wasserman, *The Pleasures of Tragedy*, 288.

by Bergalli to exemplify such conservatism: not only does he oppose regicide as intrinsically abhorrent, but he also disapproves of any act of rebellion, even against the tyrannical king who keeps him captive, caused the death of his elder son, and cruelly abuses his daughter. Thus, while the hateful nature of Alessandro is on full display throughout the tragedy, his final assassination at the hands of Teba's younger brother is reported in the end as happening almost by transcendental intervention (*Teba* 5.7.68), in partial validation – it would appear – of Jasone's sole reliance on divine justice. However, it is Teba's situation that Bergalli's audience was meant to find most unjust and repellent; it was this woman's condition that the playwright intended to excite fear and pity; it was her resistance to exacting retribution, and her virtue in distress that Bergalli intended the public to admire.

Agide emphasizes moral concerns as well, albeit that the ethical workings of an *opera seria* could not be those of tragedy, nor could absolutist tropes, common to the genre at the time, satisfy this Venetian woman librettist. What her *dramma per musica* puts on display from the very beginning is, in fact, the irreparably compromised authority of a king who owes his military victory over the enemy to the brave exploit (part of the play's backstory referenced in the first act) of a woman warrior. This female warrior subsequently saves him from his own inability to see through the lies and deceptions plaguing his court, from committing the atrocious injustice of condemning his own son on fabricated evidence of treason, and from having him summarily executed.

The recourse to the figure of the woman warrior – which, from a medieval jumble of mythology, biblical stories, popular legends, and history, had resurfaced so powerfully in sixteenth-century Italian epic poetry in response to the very first secular discussion of women and humanistic debate on the relative merits of the sexes – betrays Bergalli's interest in pursuing, first of all, a feminist and obliquely autobiographical agenda. Unlike the most illustrious Renaissance lady-knight, Bradamante, Antianira is a commoner, like Bergalli. While Ariosto, by casting his noble heroine as the ancestor of the Este dynasty, inevitably destined her to relinquish the role of warrior and accept that of obedient wife and good mother, Bergalli relegates the military skills and strategic abilities of her heroine to the background of the play, not with a view of her embracing an idealized, womanly, domestic role, but rather to foreground other qualities. Cognitive-emotional intelligence and deep-rooted moral sense make Antianira mistress of her own fate and qualify her to act more effectively than her male counterparts in private as well as in public circumstances.

In *Agide*'s story, the male characters offer the spectator negative exempla of the power of passions when neither reason nor inner virtue can be called upon to keep them in check: they act irrationally, uncharitably, in a cowardly manner, or downright wickedly. Patience, forbearance, and generosity, as well as clarity, maturity of judgment, a sense of justice, and clemency, are all behaviours displayed almost exclusively by the play's heroines. To be sure, many of the *drammi per musica* penned by Zeno, before initiating Bergalli into the genre, had featured exemplary virtuous characters. But with the notable exception of Griselda (the female protagonist of one of the few plays that he adapted from narrative fiction and from an Italian source), Zeno had consistently chosen his champions of righteous behaviour among the great male leading figures of ancient and medieval history. On the contrary, Bergalli, whose play is named after a legendary Spartan king, very early on divests him of any exemplarity. It is Antianira who dispenses lessons in tolerance and compassion to Agide, even though she is increasingly convinced that Damida loves Timocla and that her hopes to marry the prince are, therefore, null and void.

The Use of Female Character Arias in *Agide*

Confounded by his son's reaction to the announcement of the marriage he has arranged for him, King Agide is embarrassed and angered by the possibility that Damida might refuse Antianira, and the very idea of his heir loving a Macedonian princess positively outrages him. While Antianira refused to listen to what Gilippo had to say about Damida's disregard for her, and the almost reluctant applause with which he welcomed the victory that she had secured (*Agide* 1.3.12), the king is quick to give credit to the villain's slightest innuendos, and ready to interpret his son's secretly cultivated affection for Timocla as a personal challenge to his parental and sovereign authority. "Se il figlio ama colei" (If my son loves her), he tells Antianira, "Donna, lo giuro / Ambi saprò punir; ed a Timocla / la morte" (I swear to you, woman, / that I shall punish them both; / and Timocla with death) (*Agide* 1.11.21).

A horrified Antianira interrupts the king, begging him to defer any such decision, implying that his judgment is premature, to say the least, and suggesting that alternative solutions can and must be found to the brutal one of killing the object of his son's affection. Although humiliated and pained, Antianira reasons that Damida should not be blamed, much less condemned, for loving Timocla, as love cannot be helped.

Far from being resentful, the heroine's second recitative and aria, following this exchange with Agide, show great empathy:

ADIANIRA: Deh! Per poco
Almen l'ire sospendi; al figlio tuo
Tolga l'amato oggetto
   Ogn'altro tuo comando.
Fuor, che il funesto, e atroce
Della morte di lei.

AGIDE: Tu di temprar suo mal cercar non dei.

ADIANIRA: M'è ingrato è ver, ma l'amo
         E bramo al caro sposo
         Le pene di allentar.
      E sin coi mali miei
         Io gli darei conforto,
         Che basta il suo riposo
         Quest'alma a consolar.

ADIANIRA: Ah! Restrain your anger
At least for a while: if you wish
To take away from your son
The object of his affection
   Do it by issuing any other order
But the dreadful and grievous one
That would send her to her death.

AGIDE: You must not try to mitigate his offence.

ADIANIRA: I love him, though ungrateful.
         And long to lessen
            The pains of my betrothed.
      If with my very woes
         His comfort I secure,
         My soul shall find
         Some solace in his repose. (*Agide* 1.11.20–1)

When previously forced to confront Filoastro in her first recitative and aria number, Antianira had employed quite a different tone. By addressing the heroine with the casual familiarity to which he still believed himself entitled, and assuring her that, should she decide to return to him, he would take her back, Filoastro had prompted the harsh response that he subsequently bemoaned in his *a solo* scene, calling Antianira unfaithful, thankless, and yet fatally irresistible

(*Agide* 1.5.14).[24] In their exchange, Antianira had rejected Filoastro's veiled accusations and grievances, firmly staking her claim of independence and denying that he ever had any right over her:

ANTIANIRA: Prence t'intendo;
              Vuoi dir, che se una volta
              Ti amai pretendi ancora
              Ch'io t'ami?
FILOASTRO: È vero.
ANTIANIRA: Or, s'egli è vero ascolta
              Tu degno oggetto
                  Dell'alto affetto mio non fosti mai:
                  Né ingiusta or sono,
                  Se ti abbandono;
                  Grata fui troppo allor, quando t'amai.

ANTIANIRA: Prince, I understand your meaning.
              Because I loved you once,
              You claim that I should love you still?
FILOASTRO: Just so.
ANTIANIRA: Then listen to me:
              You have never been
                  The worthy object of my deepest affection:
                  I am not being unfair
                  By leaving you now;
                  I was once too obliging in granting you any love.
              (*Agide* 1.4.13)

These lines of recitative and aria are matter-of-fact, curt, and combative, as perhaps is fitting, since Antianira is, after all, the "alta guerriera, / che l'altera, a noi funesta / empia testa, fè cader" (the brave woman-warrior who made the wicked head of the ominous enemy roll) (*Agide* 1.1.9). Nonetheless, it is fair to assume that in this instance, while scoring a point for women's right to self-determination against men's sense of entitlement and ownership, Bergalli did not let her heroine

---

24 It is worth noting that the role of Filoastro was played by a woman, the mezzo-soprano Anna Tessieri (nicknamed *la Girò*), who had made her Venetian debut in Albinoni's *Laodice* the previous October, and was then aged fourteen. She was from Mantua and had gone to Venice in 1722 to study singing. In her teen years, she sang many *travesti* roles, such as this one in *Agide*. See Talbot, "Girò [Tessieri], Anna."

garner much sympathy from her audience. In the space of five scenes, however, this commanding stance gives way to the atoning, plaintive mood and inflection of the second, already quoted aria (more regular, and much longer), signalling that Antianira has developed greater compassion and is, in turn, worthier of public sympathy.

Later, in the second act, when she finds herself finally face to face with a tearful Damida, his despondency and cowardly, indecisive behaviour provoke Antianira, and the heroine ends up acting rather impatiently, much as she had with Filoastro, to whom, in fact, she alludes in her recitative lines:

ANTIANIRA: Ma, che? Sì vile io sono
Di pregar d'amor chi me non ama,
E in tempo, che d'amore altri me prega?
Taci; più non ti ascolto;
Che quale dal tuo labbro uscire io n'oda
Rifiuto, o pentimento,
L'uno previene il mio, l'altro nol voglio.
Rimanti a tuoi disprezzi,
E diverrà mia pace il tuo cordoglio.
      Ti lascio alle tue lagrime:
         Vorrei vederti l'anima
         Nel pianto tuo dissolversi
         Senza provar pietà.
      Il dolce amore, e tenero,
         Che il sen tutto accendevami
         Tosto vedrai rivolgersi
         In giusta crudeltà.

ANTIANIRA: But, what? Should I demean myself
By begging love from someone who does not love me,
When another begs me for love?
Be silent: I no longer listen to you;
Let me hear not, from your lip,
Rejection or repentance,
One preempts mine, the other I don't want.
Continue to be scornful,
And your grief shall bring me peace.
      I leave you to your tears:
         I would like to see your soul
         Dissolve in them
         Without feeling pity.

> The sweet and tender love
> That set my heart ablaze
> Soon you shall see
> Turning into just cruelty. (*Agide* 2.9.34–5)[25]

All this suggests that Antianira is as emotionally and painfully involved in the love bind of the play as the other characters, yet she is also capable of learning from it and moving on. Her unselfishness and steadfastness allow her to endure her suffering better. Her pain does not cloud her judgment, but rather translates into solicitude and clairvoyance, making her – and not Agide – the protagonist who can see the drama through to its conclusion.

At the beginning of act 2, Agide discloses to Antianira what he believes to be the "evil plots of an ungrateful son": their dialogue recitative reveals how Bergalli wanted the character of a woman without rank or title to appear much more cogent and judicious than that of the high-born, older man in power. Agide does not understand how Antianira can defend Damida, and she calmly observes that it is not right or wise to take at face value the accusations made against him by a known rival (Gilippo). "Più che all'accusa," replies Agide, "io presto fede al reo / pallor, che lo sorprese / nell'incontrarsi in me" (More than any accusation, I sooner believe in the guilty pallor that he [Amida] displayed in meeting me); and Antianira underscores the weakness of the clues that the king is bringing forth to condemn his own son of treason (*Agide* 2.1.24–5). Still unaware of Gilippo's true colours, and having long before promised to help the latter win Timocla's hand, Antianira tries now to assuage Agide's wrath by suggesting that he marry the captive princess to the army leader. She gives this recommendation not with self-serving intentions, but rather because it is the sensible thing to do at this time, and because she holds out a reasonable hope of saving both Damida and

---

25 It is interesting to note that Giovanni Porta, who left Venice in 1737 to accept a position as *Hofkapellmeister* at the Bavarian court of the Elector Karl Albrecht, when staging a version of his 1731 *Farnace*, nine years later in Munich, replaced the original librettist Antonio Maria Lucchini's text for Berenice's aria in act 1, scene 14 with Bergalli's text for the above-quoted aria of Antianira. This is, therefore, the only portion of Bergalli's libretto for which a score exists. *Farnace. Dramma per musica da rappresentarsi nel teatro di S.A.S.E di Baviera nel Carnevale del'anno 1740*, 22–3. Porta's score for this opera is part of the collection of The International Music Score Library Project (IMSLP), also known as the Petrucci Music Library, accessible online at https://imslp.org.

Timocla from a far worse outcome than that of not being able to join in marriage.

Damida has been summoned, and Antianira must interrupt her counselling and leave, having no heart to be present at the king's confrontation with his son. The torture of witnessing a loved one's suffering is, quite appropriately, the theme of her exit aria:

Mira quell'usignolo
Cui sta periglio inante;
Si lagna, e la pietosa
Sua fida, dolce amante
Piange pel caro ben.
E doglia tal ne sente,
Che pria, che al di lui duolo
Restarsene presente,
Mesta spiegare il volo
Altrove le conviene.

When a nightingale in danger
Sings his plaintive mournful song
His sweet and faithful lover
Feels pity and cries for him.
And her grief is so profound,
That rather than remaining
And be present at his pain,
She sadly flies away. (*Agide* 2.1.25)

The motif of songbirds' faithfulness and enduring love was traditional, and this aria features a nightingale, the creature that had become the symbol of poetic and lyric creativity itself. In an operatic text, the image of a nightingale was also often used to give vocal ornamentation a raison d'être and to justify the expressive indulgences of particular singers.[26] Bergalli's verses do not especially appear to lend themselves

---

26 One such "nightingale" aria was "Usignuoli che piangete," one of the twelve songs now remaining of *La Candace o siano Li veri amici*, an opera by Vivaldi (on a 1712 libretto by Francesco Silvani probably revised by Domenico Lalli), first performed in Mantua in 1720. Martha Feldman reminds us that "Singers were expected to listen closely to the actual song of birds ... and many, like castrato Filippo Balatri (1682–1756), prided themselves on their adeptness in imitating them." She mentions another famous "nightingale" aria, "Quell'usignolo che innamorato," sung "with

to vocal virtuosity, nor do they echo the conceit of the nightingale's song in its traditional form. Rather, they adapt the metaphor to the circumstances in which the heroine happens to find herself at this point in the plot.

The prominence Bergalli clearly intended to give to her female characters – as I have shown so far by focusing on Antianira – is assured above all by the number and nature of the arias assigned to their roles: while Filoastro has only two arias, Gilippo three, and Agide and Damida four each, Antianira has a total of six arias, two per act, securing her presence and influence throughout the play. She also displays a wider range of prosodic and lyrical expression.[27] As for Timocla, although she is second to Antianira and sings fewer arias (two in the first act, and one in each of the following), all four of her numbers are absolutely essential in creating and sustaining pathos in the play.[28] While Antianira's

---

no less than eleven cadenzas" by Carlo Broschi in the role of Epidite in Geminiano Giacomelli's *Merope*. See Feldman, *Opera and Sovereignty*, 94. The text of this aria was provided by Lalli for the 1734 Venetian production of Giacomelli's opera, as an alternative to the one Zeno had originally thought for act 2, scene 6 of his 1711 libretto for Gasparini; however, the original text contained one significant aria also featuring an avian simile: Merope's "Vedrassi nel suo nido / la casta tortorella" (1.7). This aria was maintained in the 1717 production of the opera in Bologna, where Licisco's original aria (1.6) was instead replaced by one containing yet again bird imagery (L'augellin, che si nasconde). *La Merope*, 20–2. Doves, swallows, and various other birds would make their appearance in Metastasio's librettos as well.

27 We know of no other productions of Bergalli's *Agide* besides the one of the 1724–25 carnival season, and, of course, the number of arias assigned to any role in an opera would often change from one cast and/or musical setting to another. Zeno's *Merope*, which after Gasparini's original one had at least twenty-eight new musical settings over the next sixty-five years, was considered by the author one of his best dramas, perhaps also because large portions of the original recitative text survived the revision process of subsequent productions. See Paul Cauthen, "Merope." As far as the arias were concerned, however, Zeno complained of the alterations made to his text since the opera's debut and did not want his name published on the frontispiece of the libretto's first edition. In the January 1712 production, the title role was played by soprano Maria Landini, the highest-paid musician in Vienna at that time, and counted eight arias and one duet; in the Bologna 1717 production, with the music of Orlandini, the role of Merope was instead played by contralto Giovanna Albertini, nicknamed *la Reggiana*, and had six arias, one duet and an ensemble. The role of princess Argia, which counted only one aria in Gasparini's version of the opera, was played in Bologna, in Orlandini's setting, by soprano Francesca Cuzzoni (also known as *la Parmigiana*, then prima donna in the service of the court of Tuscany) and had three arias, one per act.

28 The soprano Chiara Orlandi (*la Mantovanina*), active in Venice since 1717, played the role of Timocla. See Timms, "Orlandi, Chiara."

sense of justice and reasonableness allow the happy conclusion – in which she begs for and obtains Agide's forgiveness of Filoastro (for his involvement in Gilippo's plot) and agrees to marry him, thus leaving Damida free to marry Timocla – it is this princess's *onesta dissimulazione* (honest deceit) that provides more appreciable emotional complexity, if not dramatic suspense, to the play.

In the first act, at the news of Agide's decision that Damida should marry Antianira, Timocla is overcome by jealousy. When Gilippo then tests her by offering – should she wish it – not only to "troncar l'alte speranze" (dash the high hopes) of the commoner Antianira but to "dispose" of Damida, Timocla hurriedly says that taking revenge on her father's killer would be enough. The aria that follows is a riddle that Gilippo and the audience can all too easily solve:

È vero, che di duolo
Di sdegno, e di furore,
Crudeli, infausti oggetti,
Voi tutti siete a me:
Perché poi contro un solo
Il misero mio core
Oggi così si affretti
Dirlo non voglio a te.

In truth you're all
Cruel and ominous
Objects of my grief,
My anger and my fury:
Why then against one only
my miserable heart
today persists
I do not want to say. (*Agide* 1.8.17)

When Timocla reappears in act 2, it is to hear the end of the dramatic dialogue recitative between Agide and his son, when the king reveals that he knows her to be the reason why Damida refuses Antianira's hand, and threatens him with imprisonment (*Agide* 2.2.26). The princess intervenes, and because her coming to the prince's defence would make him even guiltier in his father's eyes, she resorts to reverse psychology, advocating for his swift arrest and death (*Agide* 2.3.28). Her stratagem backfires, however, when Agide promises to condemn his son to certain death if Timocla does not consent to marry Gilippo that very day. In the following *a solo* scene, she debates within herself what to do and finally plans – much as Racine's Andromaque does in response to Pyrrus's ultimatum – to kill herself "tosto / sciolta la disperata, alta promessa" (as soon as the desperate and arduous promise [of marrying Gilippo] is fulfilled) (*Agide* 2.5.31).

When the villain next confronts her, for extra dramatic effect Timocla is made to swear that she will be his wife right when Prince Damida (not yet under arrest) happens by. The prince's pained confusion and his remonstrations prompt Timocla's third aria, a farewell exit aria of enigmatic quality (at least in its textual brevity, if not in what might have been an arousing musical and vocal setting):

> Che dir poss'io?
> Vivi, se m'ami, e lieto vivi. Addio.
> Addio per sempre, addio,
> Caro nemico mio
> Ricordati di me.
> Ma cessi il tuo tormento,
> Che in quello, ch'io già sento
> Mi dolgo anche per te.

> What can I say?
> Live, if you love me, live content. Farewell.
> Farewell, forever farewell,
> My dearest enemy,
> Remember me.
> Do not torment yourself,
> The pain I feel already
> Is enough for you as well. (*Agide* 2.8.33)

At the beginning of the last act, only partially satisfied with having obtained his rival's arrest and death sentence, Gilippo must taunt Timocla, and the excessive appetite for vengeance he displays in his last recitative dialogue and aria (*Agide* 3.2.44) is witnessed by Antianira, and signals the beginning of the end. Neither woman believes Damida capable of the crime of which he stands accused, and the growing conviction that Gilippo is, in fact, the architect of the prince's fall and impending death becomes the basis of their alliance. Should she ascertain that Damida is completely innocent, Antianira promises Timocla to rush to his defence, thus prompting the princess to sing her gratitude: her last aria aptly features a pastoral simile involving a lost nymph, lightning that flashes suddenly in the darkening sky, scaring her but also showing her a possible way out of the woods ("Qual di notte ninfa al bosco" [Like a nymph in the wood at night], *Agide* 3.3.46).

In the following scene, Filoastro confesses to having been Gilippo's accomplice, discloses the details of the plot, and is dispatched by Antianira to atone for his misdeed by attempting to free Damida. When the heroine, hardly able to conceal her anger, confronts Gilippo with the treachery she has just uncovered, the villain resorts to one last lie, and successfully convinces her that Damida has already died, thus buying himself time – he believes – to complete his revenge and flee. Although unavoidable and expected, the happy ending is thus delayed for another four scenes, and the drama engages briefly – beyond the ultimately averted, but at this point still possible, death of Damida – with a more general and broader tragic sense of death.[29]

The delayed positive resolution makes room for Antianira's last two, very sombre arias: in one, she evokes "l'orrido, e cieco abisso" (the horrid, and blind abyss) of Hell (*Agide* 3.5.49), where Gilippo belongs, and in the last one she imagines Damida already dwelling "negli Elisi" (in the Elysian Fields) (*Agide* 3.8.51). In the penultimate scene, desperate Timocla and remorseful Agide are united by their common grief in a piteous duet (the opera's only one), at the end of which Antianira returns with the news that Gilippo, caught right when he was about to kill Damida in his cell, has taken his own life instead. The innocent prince reappears in the last scene, where, among general jubilation, the two young couples and the king make their peace.

Bergalli's Ultimate Agenda

With *Agide*, Bergalli demonstrated her ability, as a female poet, to negotiate the many difficulties of a dramatic genre that had been practised exclusively by male writers; but the scope of the play went beyond a display of skills. Although articulated along with other literary and dramatic principles, the true aim of the opera reform attempted by Zeno and undertaken by Metastasio was a Cartesian and moral one that Bergalli fully embraced. By creating male characters mostly incapable of keeping their human passions in check, while endowing her heroines with rational and spiritual faculties that allowed them to control the actions incited by such passions, Bergalli wanted to claim moral agency and authority for herself and women in general. When considering

---

29 This is in line with what happened in "tragedie di fin lieto" or tragedies with a happy ending (including Bergalli's own *Teba*), in which, according to Giraldi, "Events should come about in such a way that the spectators are suspended between horror and pity until the end" (Giraldi, *Discorsi di m. Giovanbattista Giraldi Cinzio*, 220–1). The English translation is the one found in Hoxby, *What is Tragedy?*, 13.

more closely the fictional source from which she drew inspiration, and the amplification of the story that she deemed necessary to perform, further and conclusive evidence of her intention can be found.

The theme of the last portion of Giraldi's *Gli Ecatommiti*, containing the story of Antianira, is "atti di cavalleria" (acts of chivalry); the appointed narrator of the novella is, like Bergalli, an unmarried young woman, who begins by stating that such a topic would be more suited to young men who are knowledgeable about knightly pursuits, or even to a woman married to such a man.[30] The figure of this narrator, Giulia, must have attracted Bergalli as much as the character of Antianira, whom the storyteller depicts as a damsel of low condition but very generous heart, endowed with "animo virile" (a manly soul) though she belongs to the "infermo sesso" (weak sex). While she apologizes for her age and inexperience in her introduction (as Bergalli does in the dedication of her *Agide*), Giulia is emphatic in her recognition of the emblematic quality of the story that she is telling, which demonstrates "che è maraviglioso lo ingegno delle donne, quando applicano l'animo intentamente a spedire qualche cosa d'importanza" (that women's wisdom is marvelous, when they apply their minds singlehandedly to accomplish something of importance).[31] What is particularly noteworthy, however, is that the character of Timocla – completely absent from Giraldi's novella – is Bergalli's original creation. Certainly, the traditional opera requirement for at least two female singing roles – preferably in conflict with one another – could not be better satisfied than by introducing this Macedonian princess into the plot; nevertheless, we have seen what a significant contribution Timocla makes to *Agide*, and how she displays the kind of penchant for well-intentioned concealment and simulation that appears to distinguish many of Bergalli's female characters from their male counterparts, including *Teba*'s Ismene, and both heroines in her other opera libretto, *Elenia*.[32] Unlike Selene, whom Metastasio introduces in his version of *Dido and Aeneas*, Timocla complements Antianira without falling into the traditional pattern of feminine victimhood, thus adding nuance to the play's depiction of womanhood.

No eighteenth-century-opera dramatist's body of work would come close to garnering the fame of Metastasio's twenty-seven *opera seria*

---

30   I consulted and quoted from a nineteenth-century edition of Giraldi's work: *Raccolta di novellieri italiani*, 3: 220.

31   Ibid., 3: 222.

32   See Stewart, "Eroine della dissimulazione."

librettos: besides eliciting hundreds of musical settings, his dramas would run to innumerable editions, becoming well known across Europe and beyond. It is all the more remarkable, therefore, that a young woman librettist, at her first attempt, should arrive at some of the same solutions that Metastasio adopted throughout his career. Like most Metastasian *drammi per musica* – and without turning into an allegory of enlightened male leadership, as many of those did – *Agide* is based upon characters engaged in moral action: agents who are either wholly self-absorbed and focused on personal survival, well-being and gain, or concerned for the needs and interests of others, and generally capable of pursuing what reason recommends. The positive or negative outcomes of their deeds are predicated on the special fusion of Aristotelian poetics and Cartesian ethics that both Bergalli and Metastasio espoused and that this essay illustrates. Like Metastasio, Bergalli also appears to have grasped how important a strategic use of arias was to the psychological delineation and dramatic development of characters. She likewise recognized how a balanced distribution of arias and recitative lent crucial support to the successful production of an opera. Bergalli's Venetian-acquired flair for what would work on the operatic stage, combined with her solid trust in the strength of a woman's mind, and, therefore, in the unique potential of female characters, allowed her to achieve impressive results in a genre besieged by the demands of its multiple artistic mediums and practitioners, while furthering her overall feminist agenda.

6 Metastasio's Theatre and Early Modern Political Philosophy: Tyrannicide, Clemency, Natural Law

ENRICO ZUCCHI

During the nineteenth century, dramatists and literary scholars represented Pietro Metastasio as a frivolous author whose theatre did not include any sort of political content. In his autobiography *Vita*, published posthumously in 1806, Vittorio Alfieri contributed to the creation of this long-lasting image of Metastasio with a portrait of the author genuflecting to Queen Maria Theresa, as was customary at that time. The depiction of Metastasio kneeling to the empress with an adulatory attitude marks Alfieri's strong condemnation of poetry that aimed to celebrate sovereigns. Metastasio's theatre, in his opinion, was as servile as its author, meant only to dwell on erotic and pastoral matters, something very far from the political subject of his own *Tragedie*.[1]

Underplaying the relevance of Metastasio's theatre is not peculiar to Italians; Alfieri's judgment is repeated by several other European critics. First, they emphasize the fact that opera, by definition, cannot be tragedy. In her *Corinne, ou l'Italie* (1807), Madame de Staël reinforces the notion that a distinct gap separates the political tragedy of Alfieri from the lyrical operas of Metastasio, which could not even represent the passions, because they received "dans tous les pays, dans toutes les situations, la même couleur" (the same colouring in all countries and situations).[2] A.W. Schlegel endorses this belief, acknowledging, once again, the otherness of Metastasio's plays compared to the genre of tragedy: his operas are defined contemptuously as "tragischen Miniaturen"

---

1 Alfieri, *Vita scritta da esso*, 84. For an interesting comparison between Metastasio's and Alfieri's dramatic works, see Perdichizzi, "Metastasio e Alfieri."
2 Staël, *Corinne ou l'Italie*, 184. If not explicitly mentioned, all translations in this chapter are mine. On the early nineteenth-century reception of Metastasio, see also Sozzi, *Da Metastasio a Leopardi*, 1–21.

(tragic miniatures).[3] Moreover, these critics believe that Metastasio's plays, which they judge as mere evasions of politics, cannot forge the conscience of a nation. Francesco de Sanctis confirms this prejudice. In his *Storia della letteratura italiana* (*History of Italian Literature*) (1870), he insists on the idyllic and elegiac nature of Metastasio's theatre, which was very different from the politic output of the works of his master, Gian Vincenzo Gravina (1664–1718), the author of five anti-tyrannical tragedies.[4] According to de Sanctis, Metastasio aimed to amaze his audience with a theatre "che manca di serietà interiore" (lacking in intrinsic gravity),[5] which often resorted to comic episodes and, in general, to a degradation of the heroic quality of the characters he was portraying. Within his theatre, Metastasio playfully portrayed even the magnificent Caesar, while "sonava il violin e faceva all'amore" (playing the violin and making love).[6]

It is not surprising that this opinion, expressed by such important authors, has had a long-term influence on scholarship on Metastasio: although some critical essays in the last two decades have tried to correct this bias, and to reconsider his operas afresh, we can still find works nowadays underlining the frivolousness and superficiality of Metastasio's operas.[7] The purpose of this chapter is to highlight the political content of Metastasio's plays, which often contain allusions to the most recent political theories, and which seem to be more alive to contemporary political discussion than has been previously thought.

Indeed, if Romantic criticism denied the political implications and the "tragic" status of Metastasio's plays, several eighteenth-century authors recognized the fact that his *drammi per musica* were full of remarkable political sentences. According to Aurelio de' Giorgi Bertola (1753–98),

---

3 Schlegel, *Vorlesungen über dramatische Kunst und Literatur*, 355. On Schlegel's reception of Metastasio's theatre, see Goldin Folena, "Le 'tragiche miniature' di Metastasio," in *Il melodramma di Pietro Metastasio*, 47–72.
4 On the often unexplored connection between Gravina's and Metastasio's plays, see Beniscelli, *Felicità sognate*, 9–16; Luciani, "Aporie del modello tragico," in *Sacro e/o profane nel teatro fra Rinascimento ed età dei Lumi*, 375–85. The influence of Gravina's tragedies on Alfieri's plays has been more often examined in the footsteps of Robuschi, "Il Gravina tra Tito Livio e Vittorio Alfieri."
5 De Sanctis, *Opere*, 755.
6 Ibid.
7 Among the works that underline the political content of Metastasio's works, see Messineo, "I finali dei drammi metastasiani"; Cristiani, "L'idea di impero," *La Rassegna della letteratura italiana*, 93–105; and Cohen, *The Politics of Opera*, 225–43. For a general re-evaluation of the political contents of seventeenth- and eighteenth-century opera, see Korneeva, *Le voci arcane*.

Metastasio often offered insights within his works into the political culture of the time.[8] Andrea Rubbi (1738–1817) highlighted the congruence of Metastasio's maxims with civic honesty, far from the political unscrupulousness prescribed by the Reason-of-State.[9] A volume of maxims drawn from his plays accompanied the Genoese edition of his works.[10]

Moreover, several people did not think that tragedy and opera were incompatible, nor did they accept the proposition that opera could not aspire to the dignity of tragedy. Ranieri de' Calzabigi (1714–95) considered Metastasio a tragic poet whose works were admired not only by people caught by the beauty of the music, but also by their readers.[11] Several well-known European scholars took Metastasio seriously as a tragic playwright, such as Voltaire (1694–1778), who believed that Metastasio was "le seul qui ait su joindre aux agrémens de l'opéra les grands mouvements de la tragédie" (the only one who was able to match the pleasantness of opera with the solemn tragic passions of tragedy).[12] Voltaire also wrote that two tragic scenes of Metastasio's *Clemenza* were "comparable à tout ce que la Grèce a eu de plus beau, si elles ne sont pas supérieurs" (comparable, or maybe better than the best Greek ones).[13] Metastasio himself refers to his plays as tragedies and seeks to demonstrate in his apologetic theoretical dissertation, *L'Estratto dell'Arte Poetica* (1773), that the musicality of these works, so often considered the element that detracted from the tragic nature of his *drammi*, was characteristic of Greek tragedy, which was entirely sung.[14]

If it is true that Metastasio's attitude differs from that of Gravina, writing plays that were extremely dissimilar to the anti-tyrannical tragedies of his teacher, it is equally true that political content is not absent from his *opera seria*. The purpose of this chapter is not to revive the eighteenth-century critical tradition, assuming that Metastasio wrote political tragedies, but actually to prove that, although he was

---

8 Bertola de' Giorgi, *Osservazioni sopra Metastasio*, 50.
9 Rubbi, *Elogio di Pietro Metastasio*, 58.
10 Metastasio, *Massime, similitudine e descrizioni*.
11 Calzabigi, "Dissertazione su le Poesie Drammatiche del Signore Abate Pietro Metastasio," 85.
12 The quotation is drawn from a letter written by Voltaire to Charlotte Sophia von Aldenburg on 9 March 1756: Voltaire, *Correspondance. Janvier 1749–Décembre 1757*, 99.
13 Voltaire, *Sémiramis*, 9.
14 This idea, already supported by Gravina in his *Della tragedia*, published in 1715 – see Gravina, *Scritti critici e teorici*, 555 – is drawn on by Metastasio in his later dissertation on Greek tragedy: Metastasio, *Estratto dell'arte poetica d'Aristotile*, 114–15. On the diffusion of this idea within the Italian eighteenth-century theatrical debate, see Zucchi, "Metastasio e Calzabigi all'origine dei cori alfieriani," 84–7.

celebrating the Habsburg sovereigns and did not often deal with the anti-tyrannical ideas of Gravina, his theatre was even more "political" than that of his master. In fact, Metastasio expanded the spectrum of the political theories mentioned within his works, representing and discussing from time to time several different philosophical positions, neglected by many other dramatists. In his mind, he entertained competing discourses – to borrow an expression from J.G.A. Pocock's works – that he put in the mouths of the various characters, not only to create a theatric dialectic but also to support his own political theory.[15]

"Princeps Legibus Solutus": Is the Prince Bound by the Law?

Metastasio is often considered to be, if not a completely unengaged dramatist, a committed supporter of Habsburg absolutism and a court poet who intended to praise the monarch in all his plays. Certainly, his works, commissioned by Charles VI or Maria Theresa, often contain celebratory elements meant to honour the king and queen, mainly in the paratexts that introduce the plays' imprints. Nevertheless, in Metastasio's theatre we will not find any clear or hidden allusion to one central issue of early modern absolutist theory: the idea that the prince is above the law. The principle that "princeps legibus solutus" (the king is not bound by the law) had been a key statement within political absolutism since the Roman Empire. Originally enunciated in Ulpianus's *Lex regia*, this adage (*Princeps legibus solutus*) was rehearsed constantly by theorists of absolutism during the medieval and early modern ages.[16] Jean Bodin structures the seventeenth-century notion of absolutism on this basis, recalling Ulpianus's statement. In the chapter dedicated to supreme authority within his *Six livres de la République* (1576), he asserts that the prince is not bound by any law, that he can freely promulgate new rules and cancel the old ones, and that he is not even subject to the laws that he creates.[17]

---

15 Pocock, *Political Thought and History*.
16 Ulpianus's sentence is included in *Digesta* 1:3, 31, and was later drawn on by Thomas Aquinas (*Summa theologiae* quaestio 96, art. 5). On the relevance of this adage within the early modern discussion of sovereignty, see Wyduckel, *Princeps legibus solutus*; Pennington, *The Prince and the Law 1200–1600*; Van Nifterik, "Lex princeps legibus solutus abrogata"; and Maffi, *Princeps legibus solutus*.
17 According to Bodin, "La souveraineté donnée à un Prince sous charges et conditions, n'est pas proprement souveraineté, ni puissance absolue: si ce n'est que les conditions apposées en la creation du Prince soyent de la Loy de Dieu ou de nature" (the sovereignty given to a Prince under charges and conditions is not properly sovereignty, nor absolute power, unless the conditions affixed in the creation of the prince are God and natural law) (Bodin, *Les six livres de la République*, 128).

Of course, these lawyers and political writers, while describing the supreme authority of a prince not bound by any law, also tried to imagine some restraints to the exercise of this apparently limitless power. Seneca the Younger, in his *Consolatio ad Polybium* (VII), invented a formula that is often echoed in sixteenth- and seventeenth-century political treatises, and by Bodin himself: "Caesari quoque ipsi, cui omnia licent, propter hoc ipsum multa non licet" (Caesar has less in his power upon this very account, that everything is in his power).[18] Along with several authors of his time, Bodin states that the limits to absolute sovereignty are laws of God and nature. But the possibility of a prince who does not respect these sacred bonds is not even considered within these treatises; Bodin has a total confidence in the king's goodness. Another limit given to supreme authority in seventeenth-century political writings is the prince's wisdom. In his dissertation *De la sagesse* (1601), Pierre Charron (1541–1603) describes the features that distinguish a prince from a tyrant. According to Charron, the prince respects and safeguards God's and nature's laws, whereas the tyrant abuses his power to contravene these rules. Moreover, while the prince is concerned with public happiness, the tyrant thinks only of his personal benefit.[19]

Thus, in early modern absolutist theory, the only limit that restrains the exercise of supreme authority is the prince himself; his goodness and his wisdom are the only bonds that can prevent him from abusing his power and becoming a tyrant. This conception of a limitless power, supported by Roman law, was a cause of embarrassment for men such as Gravina, who combined a fervent respect for the Roman juridical system with an antipathy to absolutism. Gravina's solution is to try to demonstrate that Ulpianus's adage has only a narrow application: it should not be understood as a general principle, but as a gloss on a particular nuptial law to which every other citizen was subjected.[20] This original juridical interpretation allows us to understand how Gravina

---

18 Translated by Stackhouse in *The English Particles rendered into Classical Latin*, 42. The passage is mentioned in Bodin, *Les six livres de la République*, 150.

19 According to Charron, "Les conditions d'un bon Prince et d'un tyran sont toutes notoirement dissemblables, et aisées à distinguer. Elles reviennent toutes à ces deux points: l'un garder les loix de Dieu, et de nature, ou les fouler aux pieds. L'autre, faire tour pour le bien public et profit des subiets, ou faire tout servir à son profit et plaisir particulier" (The conditions of a good Prince and of a tyrant are notoriously dissimilar, and easy to distinguish. They all return to these two points: one respects the laws of God, and of nature, the other violates them. Secondly, the prince does everything in his power for the public good and for his subjects' profit, whereas the tyrant make everything serve for his benefit and particular pleasure) (*De la sagesse*, 524).

20 Gravina, *De ortu et progressu juris civilis*, 510–12. On Gravina's interpretation, see Addante, *Repubblica e controrivoluzione*, 63.

was striving to reconcile his confidence in the Roman juridical system, which he considered perfect, with his anti-absolutist political beliefs.

We should now consider how Metastasio represents this supreme authority. If he was a really committed supporter of absolutist theory, we would find within his theatre several allusions to Ulpianus's adage, and the legitimation of the fact that the prince is not bound by the law. On the contrary, his plays seem to reflect a very different position. One of his first and maybe most "tragic" *drammi*, *La Didone abbandonata*, performed in Naples in 1724, already deals with absolutist theory: both Dido and Iarba, the king of the Moors, are rulers who pretend not to be bound by any law. During the first act, Iarba, who appears at the court of Carthage under the guise of the ambassador Arbace, reproaches Dido for her relationship with Enea, which began when she was already engaged to Iarba. Dido replies that she does not have to justify herself: because she is queen, she is the only one who can impose laws on herself, and nobody else can claim authority over her heart or her decisions:

> Son regina, e sono amante
> E l'impero io sola voglio
> Del mio soglio e del mio cor.
> Darmi legge in van pretende
> Chi l'arbitrio a me contende
> Della gloria e dell'amor. (1.5)[21]

> I am queen and I am a lover, and I alone want to rule the empire of my throne and of my heart. Those who pretend that I cannot freely decide who I have to love and what I have to do in order to be a glorious sovereign, claim in vain to give commands to me.

Iarba upholds absolutist theory in yet stronger terms, for he considers, in a later monologue, that the sovereign can do anything he wants. Even the worst actions committed by the prince turn out to be fair and just only because someone who is beyond the law does them:

> È sol virtù quel che diletta e giova.
> Fra lo splendor del trono
> belle le colpe sono,
> perde l'orror l'inganno,
> tutto si fa virtù. (1.7)[22]

---

21 Metastasio, *Tutte le opere*, 11.
22 Ibid., 13.

The only thing that delights and benefits is virtue.
Under the splendour of the throne,
even faults are beautiful
and deception loses its awfulness,
because everything becomes virtue.

The only character who proves to have a different conception of sovereignty within this play is also the only one depicted positively, Enea. He is ready to renounce his private benefit to follow his destiny and reach a more honourable goal. When Dido threatens to kill Iarba for talking to her in a disrespectful way, Enea tries to discourage her from such a cruel action and invites her to be clement. But she responds that she does not accept any counsel because she is queen, and a queen promulgates laws without any guidance, depending only on her will.[23] Dido is of course the representative of a distorted absolutism, and Metastasio seems to condemn her actions. It is not surprising that, after Enea's departure, the elegiac plot quickly turns into tragedy; since he has been refused and humiliated by Dido, Iarba takes revenge on his beloved by setting fire to the royal palace, and the queen commits suicide. Therefore, this deformation of supreme authority only seems to have negative effects on the state's life: the fire destroys Carthage and nobody benefits from this situation.

Perhaps a more suitable dramatization of the possible weaknesses of absolutist theory can be found in *Demofoonte*, first staged in 1734 in Vienna and dedicated to Charles VI. Here, there exists a strong discrepancy between the subjects, who always have to respect the law, and the king, Demofoonte, who is not bound by the law. This incongruity is made clear in the opera's backstory: every year in Thrace, the citizens must sacrifice a virgin girl to gain Apollo's benevolence. Therefore, annually, the name of each Trachian girl is put into a ballot box and randomly selected. Yet the year of the story, King Demofoonte commands that the name of his daughter be left out of the box, enraging Matusio, father of Dircea, who demands an equal treatment. In the dialogue between Dircea and Matusio in the opening scene of the play, the daughter reminds her father of absolutist theory, according to which "a' sovrani è

---

23 Dido says: "Consigli or non desio: / tu provvedi a' tuoi regni, io penso al mio. / Senza di te finor legge dettai; / sorger senza di te Cartago io vidi. / Felice me; se mai / tu non giugnevi, ingrato, a questi lidi!" (I don't want your advice: you have to take care of your kingdom, I will think of mine. Without you until now I have dictated laws, raised Carthage without your help. I would have been happier if you had never come to these shores, ingrate!) (Metastasio, *Tutte le opere*, 27).

suddita la legge" (the law is subjected to the sovereign):[24] the king can break the law whenever he desires. On the contrary, Matusio, who is asking for equality before the law, complains about the king's discriminatory behaviour; indeed, Demofoonte seems to apply the rules rigidly when his judgment addresses other people, but when he or his family are concerned, he always bypasses the law.[25] In the following scenes, Demofoonte forbids his son Timante, who is in love with Dircea, from marrying her, because she is of humble origins, and an ancient law prescribes that a prince can only marry a princess. Demofoonte, who claims to be faultless, according to another major issue of absolutist theory, clearly judges in an arbitrary way, using the law only to accomplish his desires, because he considers himself beyond any rule.[26] Again in this case, Metastasio strongly condemns this kind of distorted absolutism: in the final *Licenza*, he draws a parallel between Demofoonte – unjust, dishonest, and so intemperate that he is ready to sentence his innocent son to death – and Charles VI, celebrated as the model of the perfect absolutist sovereign, who is mild, clement, and himself respectful of the law.[27]

In contrast with some seventeenth-century absolutist treatises, Metastasio is not willing to stake all on the sovereign's natural goodness. He looks to other guards on the prince's potential excesses. For example, in his *Adriano in Siria* (1732), he stages the story of an emperor, Hadrian, who almost turns out to be a tyrant when he puts his personal gain ahead of public wealth, abusing the law to trade the Syrian reign for Emirena, to whom he is attracted, although he is already engaged to Osroa. What prevents Hadrian from becoming a tyrant is not his own wisdom, but the virtuous example of Emirena and Osroa, who are both eager to renounce their private happiness to achieve a wider good.[28]

Metastasio does not celebrate early modern absolutism. Rather, he seems to criticize it even more frankly than Gravina did: a prince who

---

24 Ibid., 639.
25 Referring to Demofoonte's behaviour, Matusio says, "Ei che si mostra / delle leggi divine / sì rigido custode, agli altri insegni / con l'esempio la costanza" (He who presents himself as such a rigid guardian of the divine laws has to teach others constancy by his example) (Metastasio, *Tutte le opere*, 639).
26 According to Demofoonte, "il re non erra" (the sovereign is never in error) (Metastasio, *Tutte le opere*, 660).
27 Metastasio, *Tutte le opere*, 690–1.
28 For a deeper analysis of Metastasio's *Adriano in Siria*, see Zucchi, "Sovrani temperanti e tiranni lascivi."

does not consider himself bound by the law can often turn into a despot. Moreover, he suggests a correction to this limitless power, which can easily degenerate into tyranny because it is not bound by the law, demonstrating how subjects, by dint of their own virtue, can teach the prince how he himself can be virtuous.

The Idea of a "Rex Servus" and the Banned Regicide

Another example of significant early modern political theory to which Metastasio seems to allude is that of the Monarchomachs. They were originally French Protestant political theorists who, in the late sixteenth century, criticized absolute monarchy and religious persecutions, arguing that the people have the right to kill their king if he turns out to be a tyrant. According to the Monarchomachs, the aim of the state is the people's happiness. Sovereignty originally resided with the citizens, who decided to cede it to a king with the aim of achieving this objective. In their opinion, the prince, far from being unfettered by the law, is bound by the uninterrupted judgment of the people; he is only an officer of the commonwealth. Indeed, the citizens keep the power to revoke the authority granted to the king, and they can remove him at any time from his office. While absolutist theory declared the king's body to be sacred and untouchable, the Monarchomachs claimed the right of rebellion and justified the assassination of sovereigns who behaved as tyrants. This conceptual framework, described most clearly in the *Vindiciae contra tyrannos* (1579), whose author was probably Philippe du Plessis de Mornay (1549–1623), was later supported by several leading political philosophers, both Protestants and Catholics, such as George Buchanan, Johannes Althusius, Juan de Mariana, Francisco Suárez, and John Milton.[29]

Metastasio alludes to this line of argument within his plays, always condemning the position of the Monarchomachs. Although he does not enthusiastically support the idea of an absolutist authority not bound by the law, neither does he authorize any right or act of rebellion against the king. Once we have this context in mind, *Ezio*, performed in Rome in 1728, presents itself as a theatrical work meant to

---

29 The *Vindiciae* were published under the Latin pseudonym of Stephanus Junius Brutus, but are commonly attributed to Philippe du Plessis de Mornay. On the Monarchomachs' political theory and its legitimation of the tyrannicide, see Jouanna, *I monarcomachi protestanti francesi e il dovere di rivolta*, 499–521; Turchetti, *Tyrannie et tyrannicide de l'Antiquité à nos jours*, 333–970; Lee, *Popular Sovereignty in Early Modern Constitutional Thought*, 121–58; Skinner, "The Origins of the Calvinist Theory of Revolution," 309–30; and Dzelzainis, "The Ciceronian Theory of Tyrannicide."

forbid regicide in any circumstances. In the play, the emperor Valentinian III is in love with Fulvia, who is already engaged to Captain Aetius.
Valentinian tries to force the girl to marry him while her fiancé is far
from Rome, fighting for the empire. When Aetius comes back after the
triumphal campaign against Attila and the Huns, he is informed by
Flavia's father, Massimo, that Valentinian is trying to marry his beloved. Since he is a committed supporter of the Roman Empire, and he
has full confidence in his emperor, Aetius thinks that maybe Valentinian does not know that he and Flavia are already engaged. The interesting dialogue between Massimo and Aetius shows two opposing
perspectives; on the one hand, that of the Monarchomachs, supported
by Massimo, according to which a bad king can righteously be killed;
on the other hand, the absolutist one, maintained by Aetius, who affirms that the sovereign's body is sacred, and that subjects should always remain loyal to the king:

> MASSIMO: All'amor tuo tradito
>   dovresti una vendetta. Al fin tu sai
>   che non si svena al Cielo
>   vittima più gradita
>   d'un empio re.
> EZIO: Che dici mai! L'affanno
>   vince la tua virtù. Giudice ingiusto
>   delle cose è il dolor. Sono i monarchi
>   arbitri della terra;
>   di loro è il Cielo. Ogni altra via si tenti,
>   ma non l'infedeltade.[30] (1.3)

> MASSIMO: You should take revenge on your betrayed love. You know well
>   that one does not kill a more pleasing victim in Heaven than a wicked king.
> EZIO: What are you saying! The concern defeats your virtue; sorrow is
>   an unjust judge. The monarchs are judges over the earth, and the Heaven
>   is their house. You can try every other way, but not betrayal.

Of course, Metastasio supports Aetius's position: the captain is represented as the perfect warrior, always loyal to his king and so honourable that he risks being sentenced to death so as not to betray his fiancé's
father. On the contrary, Massimo appears a mean and contemptible

---

30 Metastasio, *Tutte le opere*, 200.

character: he engages in a conspiracy against Valentinian, does not exculpate Aetius when falsely accused of the plot by the king, and repeatedly invokes Machiavelli's views in support of a depraved philosophy of realpolitik. In the end, Massimo is even ready to exploit Aetius's apparent death to lead a popular conspiracy. He is about to kill the emperor when Aetius stops him, once again displaying his virtue and exercising clemency. Although mistreated and unfairly condemned by the prince, Aetius never justifies the sacrilegious act of regicide. This represents Metastasio's settled opinion even before he moved to Vienna to become the poet to the Habsburgs in Vienna.[31]

Another fitting example of Metastasio's criticism of the Monarchomachs' ideas is suggested in his *Demetrio*, a play staged in 1731, in which, after the death of King Alexandros, the Syrian princess Cleonice is asked to choose a husband who will become sovereign. The princess is in doubt about whether to marry Olinto, a Syrian nobleman striving to be king, or to follow her heart, opting for the humble shepherd Alceste, who in the end turns out to be the usurped prince Demetrio. Understanding that she should prefer Olinto for political reasons, Cleonice tries to take more time, but the Syrian prince tells her to decide quickly, saying that otherwise, without a king, the people will cause political turmoil. The opera begins with the princess complaining about being hurried. She affirms that women can be legitimate sovereigns and that sovereign kings are not servants of the people:

> Fra pochi istanti
> al destinato loco
> il popolo inquieto
> comparir mi vedrà. Chiede ch'io scelga
> lo sposo, il re? Si sceglierà lo sposo,
> il re si sceglierà. Solo un momento
> chiedo a pensar. Che intolleranza è questa,
> importuna, indiscreta? I miei vassalli

---

31 The supporters of this thought did not only conceive of the Monarchomach theory as abstract philosophical thought; the allusion to this kind of writing during the early modern age often implied concrete action. The conspiracies that led to the murders of Henry IV, king of France (1601), and the English sovereign Charles I (1649) were also justified through some of the Monarchomachs' treatises, such as Juan de Mariana's *De rege et regis institutione* (1594) and John Milton's *Tenure of Kings and Magistrates* (1649). On this point, see Herrero Sánchez, "El padre Mariana y el tiranicidio"; Oporto, "Suárez, Mariana y el tiranicidio."

sì poco han di rispetto? A farmi serva
m'innalzaste sul trono, o v'arrossite
di soggiacere a un femminile impero? (1.1)[32]

In a few moments, the restless people will see me in the square. Do they
ask me to choose the groom, the king? The groom will be chosen, as well
as the king. I ask you just for a moment to think. What intolerance is this,
annoying, indiscreet? My vassals have so little respect for me? Did you
raise me to the throne to be your servant? Or do you just feel embarrassed
because your sovereign is a woman?

Later, Cleonice reaffirms this statement, blatantly renouncing the throne
because, due to the nobles' pressure, she is not free to decide whether to
marry Olinto or Demetrio: "E ben su questo trono / regni chi vuole. Io
d'un servile impero / non voglio il peso" (Well, leave this throne empty
for those who want to reign. I do not want the weight of a servile empire) (1.8).[33] The notion that the king is the people's servant is one key
issue of the Monarchomachs' theory, based on the idea of a *rex servus*
or a *rex subiectus*. As shown by Quentin Skinner, the contract through
which the citizens cede their power to the king appears to be, for the
Monarchomachs, a kind of concession that the people can revoke at
any time, due to the fact that the people are superior to the king "as a
universitas or corporate body."[34] According to Metastasio, the sovereign
should be considered neither a mere state official nor the people's re-
tainer. The monarch should be allowed to govern independently and
without external pressure. This autonomy is not just a prerogative of
monarchs; it is a condition of good government. Only when the people
are left free to choose can they choose for the best. Cleonice demonstrates this principle when she freely opts for the best solution for her
subjects, even though she must sacrifice her own passions.[35]

Natural Law: Hobbes and Inviolable Rights

If we return to the *Tragedie cinque* written by Metastasio's master, we
can gather that Gravina is skeptical about the theory of early modern

---

32   Metastasio, *Tutte le opere*, 419.
33   Ibid., 434.
34   Skinner, *From Humanism to Hobbes*, 39.
35   The plot is centred on the choice of the king who has to marry Cleonice. The queen,
     although in love with the shepherd Alceste, sacrifices her love and opts to marry
     Olinto due to her political responsibilities. However, in the end Alceste turns out to
     be Demetrio, the son of the usurped king and the rightful heir to the throne.

natural law. He fully agrees with the fact that some natural inviolable rights exist, but he is alarmed by the theorization of an unlimited absolute power, as described in Thomas Hobbes's *Leviathan*.[36] The theory of natural law, which had deep roots in Roman jurisprudence and medieval Scholasticism, was an important font of ideas for early modern political theorists such as Hugo Grotius, Thomas Hobbes, and Samuel Pufendorf; it maintained that a natural legal system existed before positive law and could not be overthrown by national rules: all people have some natural, fundamental rights as human beings, which should be respected by legislators and governors. Metastasio seems to draw on the same opinion of Gravina about the political theory of natural law: in his plays, he still considers natural rights to be a brake that can somehow limit the sovereign's power.

Metastasio does not even mention some elements of the theory of natural law. For example, nowhere does he invoke Hobbes's contractual account of sovereign power in which humans living independently in a state of nature cede their natural powers to a sovereign to escape a state of perpetual war and enter into a civil society.[37] Other ideas are invoked, but not enthusiastically endorsed. For instance, in the first scene of *Demofoonte*, Matusio makes a statement that is typical of natural law: the principle according to which all men are born with the same rights and nothing immutable distinguishes the king from the subject. Dircea's father complains that the king left the names of his daughters out of the ballot box of the girls to be sacrificed; indeed, even if he is subjected, he is a father just like Demofoonte, so he claims the same right to protect his children.[38]

However, Metastasio seems not to favour the idea of social and juridical equality. Matusio's opinion is not considered fair; his character is only pathetic, not reliable on this political issue. This key concept of the theory of modern natural law was also condemned by Gravina, who thought, on the contrary, that men were born with different physical and intellectual faculties, arguing that the smartest and wisest people (*sapientes*) should rule over the uncultivated (*rudes*) according to the ancient theory of *ius sapientiorum* (the rule of the wise).[39]

---

36 On the reception of Hobbes's work in Gravina's tragedies and in his juridical works, which often aimed to condemn *Leviathan* and its ideas, see: Zucchi, "Tirannide e stato di natura," in *Prima e dopo il Leviatano*, 193–226.

37 On early modern contractualism see Duso, *Il contratto sociale*.

38 "Io forse / perché suddito nacqui, / son men padre del re?" (Am I less of a father than the king because I was born as a subject?) (Metastasio, *Tutte le opere*, 639).

39 On the juridical and political reasons why some Italian men of letters in the eighteenth century supported the theory of *ius sapientiorum*, see Ajello, *Arcana Juris*, 160–72; Lomonaco, "Diritto naturale e storia."

What Metastasio finds more interesting about the theory of natural law is the fact that the king must always respect natural rights if he wants to be a good sovereign. In his *Siroe*, first staged in Venice in 1726, he tackles a typical matter concerning the theory of natural law: the right of primogeniture. In his *Leviathan*, Hobbes considered the right of primogeniture the fourteenth of the inviolable natural laws, so this allusion is very precise.[40] Within the play, we once again find a strong opposition between two models of sovereigns. On the one hand, the Persian king Cosroe proves to be a tyrant because he prefers his younger son Medarse, who always flatters him, to his older son, Siroe, who is a great soldier, beloved by the Persian people. When Cosroe decides to bequeath his kingdom to Medarse, Siroe accuses him of putting his personal feelings above the good of the state and natural laws:

> Appaga pure, appaga
> quel cieco amor che a me ti rende ingiusto.
> Sconvolgi per Medarse
> gli ordini di natura. (1.1)[41]

> Please satisfy the blind love that makes you unfair to me. Disrupt even nature's orders in favour of Medarse.

On the other hand, Siroe is the model of the perfect sovereign, who always respects natural rights. Indeed, when his beloved Elmira asks him to help her in taking revenge against Cosroe, who killed her father some years before, Siroe refuses to be an accessory to the king's murder, even if he too has been mistreated. In his speech, Siroe alludes to the theory of natural law when he explains to Elmira that he must protect his father even if he has been cruel:

> ELMIRA: Io confonder non so Cosroe col figlio.
>   Odio quello, amo te; vendico estinto
>   il proprio genitore.
> SIROE: E il mio, che vive,
>   per legge di natura anch'io difendo. (2.2)[42]

---

40   Hobbes, *Leviathan*, 236. On the list of natural rights introduced by Hobbes in *Leviathan*, see Dyzenhaus, "Hobbes and the Legitimacy of Law."
41   Metastasio, *Tutte le opere*, 73.
42   Metastasio, *Tutte le opere*, 93.

ELMIRA: I cannot confuse Cosroe with his son. I hate him, but I love you.
I just want to take revenge for my parent's death.
SIROE: And mine, who lives, by nature's law, I also defend.

In the end, Siroe is falsely accused by Medarse of hatching a plot to kill his father, and Cosroe decides to sentence his son to death, transgressing natural laws once again, as Elmira reminds him.[43] But Cosroe's sentence is not carried out: the Persian people rise up against the vicious king, and only Siroe manages to quell the rebellion, saving his father's life. Here Metastasio does not support the possibility of the subjected people revolting against a bad sovereign, but he passionately states that a good king always respects natural rights and forgets the personal wrong he has endured to benefit the state.

Enlightened Absolutism: The Clement King

The previous sections have shown how Metastasio often opposes two different models of sovereignty: one defends personal privileges, and the other, supported by Metastasio and embodied by the Habsburg kings, aims to bring happiness to people, though sometimes at great personal sacrifice. This kind of juxtaposition is evident in his *Didone abbandonata*, in which the author compares the conflicting characters of Dido and Aeneas, or even in his *Demofoonte*, built on the contrast between the humble and wise Aetius and the biased protagonist. Sometimes, as in *Adriano in Siria*, these opposed positions coexist in the same character: the emperor Hadrian is initially unfair and only interested in satisfying his own desires, but then, looking at the positive example of other characters, he turns into a good sovereign, abandoning his personal ambitions. In other cases, such as in his *Alessandro nell'Indie* (1729), the king is the figure of the perfect sovereign from the beginning, resulting in a very weak plot, since all the characters are positive and there is no evolution or change during the play.

Within *Il re pastore* (1751), Metastasio defines his idea of sovereignty in a vibrant way, as we can gather from the dialogue between the wise Agenore and the shepherd Aminta, who unexpectedly turns out to become king. Agenore warns Aminta that he cannot use his power to earn some profit; on the contrary, the kingdom has to benefit from the

---

43 "Ah, se ti scordi / le leggi di natura / un fatto sol tutti i tuoi pregi oscura" (If you forget the laws of Nature, one bad deed overshadows all your qualities) (Metastasio, *Tutte le opere*, 113).

actions of the sovereign, who must only seek the public's happiness. The king's personal gain coincides with the subjects' happiness:

> Il regno a te non giova,
> tu giovar devi a lui. Te dona al regno
> il Ciel, non quello a te. L'eccelsa mente,
> l'alma sublime, il regio cor, di cui
> largo ei ti fu, la pubblica dovranno
> felicità produrre; e solo in questa
> tu dei cercar la tua. (2.3)[44]

The kingdom does not benefit you, whereas you must benefit it. Heaven gives you to the kingdom, not the kingdom to you. The excellent mind, the sublime soul, the royal heart that you were given so generously, will have to produce public happiness. Only in this may you look for your personal happiness.

From his first plays, Metastasio praises the idea of a martyr king who seeks the public's happiness over his own ambition. This key concept in his political theatre, present in the 1720s and throughout his career, persists alongside the celebration of the sovereign's clemency.

One of the most popular eighteenth-century political theories was enlightened absolutism. Its proponents expressed full confidence in the goodness of the sovereign, who always strove for the happiness of his subjects and could best be compared to a good shepherd concerned for his flock or a loving father attentive to the best interest of his children. Of course, Metastasio's plays, especially those written in Vienna, enthusiastically support this theory, particularly as far as the legal conduct of the sovereign is concerned. We have already assumed that Metastasio believes that the king is bound by the law, contrary to early modern absolutist political dissertations. On the contrary, our exploration of Metastasio's reflection on different political theories leads me to conclude that in his view, the king's murder – or more generally the people's revolt against the sovereign – was not an option. Yet at the same time, Metastasio held just as sincerely that the prince must always respect natural laws.

Theorists of enlightened absolutism underline the fact that the prince is himself bound by the law, and that he has to respect all natural rights. Lodovico Antonio Muratori (1672–1750) in his treatise *Della pubblica*

---

44 Metastasio, *Tutte le opere*, 1133.

felicità (1749), one of the most relevant eighteenth-century books on the subject of sovereignty, insists that "molto più poi s'hanno a ricordare i principi, che s'essi comandano al popolo, anche le leggi debbono comandare al principe" (sovereigns must remember that the prince should obey the law, just as the subjected people obey the prince).[45] According to Muratori, the sovereign must always respect natural law, whereas he can often deviate from civil and criminal rules when he has good reason to do so. Because the aim of his reign is to make his subjects happy, the prince can mitigate the full force of the law by being clement in some cases. Although it would be unfair not to punish people who have been found guilty of murder, the prince should be clement with those people who commit lesser crimes during a moment of anger or without malice.[46]

The prince, then, is subordinated to the law. But he should not apply the rules through the strict enforcement of legislation because he punishes only in his capacity as father. Still, Muratori's theory is far from seventeenth-century paternalism, as seen, for example, in Robert Filmer's *Patriarcha* (1680), in which the author states that the subjects have the political obligation to observe the sovereign's law, just as sons have the moral duty to obey their fathers. Muratori's main interest is not in justifying political authority in all cases; his prince is not properly a father but a smart and compassionate man who can judge wisely – sometimes punishing, sometimes forgiving.

While Muratori stresses the importance of the ethical actions of the prince, who is morally bound to pursue the public good, Montesquieu (1689–1755), in his *L'esprit des lois* (*Spirit of the Laws*), published one year before Muratori's treatise, offers a more secular and even cynical perspective on eighteenth-century politics. For instance, in his opinion the monarchy is based not on the virtue of the people, as it is in a republic, but on their desire to preserve honour and reputation. However, Montesquieu agrees with Muratori on the fact that the prince should be a clement judge and that his actions should inspire mercy and pity. In the chapter devoted to the prince's clemency, Montesquieu asserts that "la clémence est la qualité distinctive des monarques" (clemency is the distinctive quality of sovereigns) who are adored by their subjects because of the exercise of their mercy.[47] In a few decades, legal and political

---

45 Muratori, *Della pubblica felicità*, 64.
46 Ibid., 64–5.
47 Montesquieu, *De l'esprit des lois*, 104. On the notion of a clement king in French opera, see Bloechl, *Opera and the Political Imaginary in Old Regime France*.

theory would develop in a different direction from that charted by Muratori and Montesquieu: Cesare Beccaria (1738–94) considers outdated the concept of clemency in his 1764 *Dei delitti e delle pene* (On Crimes and Punishments), stating that everyone has to respect every rule without any kind of derogation, since people are equal before the law.

However, as far as the subject is concerned, we have to observe that Metastasio's theatre between 1730 and 1740 already formulates an image of the sovereign who is subject to the law but in the meantime is able to judge fairly and even to depart from the rules when it is necessary through the exercise of his clemency. This happens a decade before the publication of Muratori's and Montesquieu's works, so Metastasio's operas are not just mirrors of the times, they are doing real cultural work.

The most important play devoted to this idea is indubitably *La clemenza di Tito* (*The Clemency of Titus*), first staged in 1734 for Charles VI and based on Suetonius's *De vita Caesarum* (*Life of the Caesars*) but also inflected by Pierre Corneille's *Cinna, ou la clémence d'Auguste* (*Cinna, or the Clemency of Augustus Caesar*) (1634).[48] The plot is very simple: although everyone recognizes the goodness and generosity of the emperor Tito, a group of Roman patricians conspires against the sovereign's life. Sesto, a great friend of Tito, numbers among the plotters because he wishes to please his beloved Vitellia. When the conspiracy is brought to light, the senate, applying the rules of Roman law, sentences the conspirators to death, but Tito, exercising his clemency, pardons the conspirators.

Tito's thoughts on the Roman juridical system are very significant. In the first act, while talking to the prefect Publio, he asserts that if the law were strictly applied, nobody would be safe from its rigour, because all men are in some sense guilty:

> Se la giustizia usasse
> di tutto il suo rigor, sarebbe presto
> un deserto la terra. Ove si trova
> chi una colpa non abbia, o grande o lieve?
> Noi stessi esaminiam. Credimi, è raro
> un giudice innocente
> dell'error che punisce. (1.8)[49]

---

48   On the connection between Corneille's *Cinna* and Metastasio's *La clemenza di Tito* see Sannia Nowé, "Epifanie e metamorfosi della clemenza," in *La cultura fra Sei e Settecento*, ed. Sala Di Felice and Sannia Nowé, 171–96.

49   Metastasio, *Tutte le opere*, 709.

If justice used all its rigour, our world would soon be deserted. Where can you find someone who has not a fault, big or slight? Let us examine ourselves. Believe me; it is rare to find a judge who is innocent of the error that he is going to punish.[50]

Here, of course, Metastasio is overlaying Roman law with Christian law and crime with sin, and there is a clear allusion to the gospel story of the woman caught in adultery and condemned to being stoned (*John* 8: 1–11). Just like Jesus, Tito seems to invite the one who is without sin to cast the first stone; the judges are probably as guilty as the sentenced. The only juridical solution to this impasse is clemency, as Tito states a few lines later, when Metastasio seems to allude directly to the *Codex Theodosianus* (*Theodosian Code*) (9.7):

Se il mosse
leggerezza, nol curo;
se follia, lo compiango;
se ragion, gli son grato; e se in lui sono
impeti di malizia, io gli perdono. (1.8)[51]

If he was moved by lightness, I do not care; if by madness, I feel sorry for him; if by reason, I am grateful to him. And if by a malicious instinct in him, I forgive him.

In the third act, when he is asked to sentence his friend Sesto to death, Tito wavers. He tries to embody the memory of the example of Brutus, who condemned his sons in order to strictly apply the law. However, in his opinion, this model of rigour, typical of Rome's republican government, cannot be resuscitated in a monarchical system, where clemency must reign. Consequently, he decides to exculpate Sesto, saying that "se accusarmi il mondo / vuol pur di qualche errore, / m'accusi di pietà, non di rigore" (if the world aims to accuse me of some mistake, I prefer to be charged with pity, and not strictness).[52] When he alludes to the history of Brutus, a very popular subject for the eighteenth-century

---

50 Metastasio's statement here is very close to that of Shakespeare's Hamlet: "God's bodykins, man, much better: use every man / after his desert, and who should 'scape whipping? / Use them after your own honour and dignity: the less / they deserve, the more merit is in your bounty. / Take them in" (*Hamlet*, 2.2.413–17).
51 Ibid. Bruno Brunelli underlines the allusion to the *Codex Theodosianum* in his commentary to the edition of Metastasio's plays (ivi, 1500).
52 Metastasio, *Tutte le opere*, 743.

plays meant to endorse the idea of a strict application of the law, Metastasio is clearly marking the stylistic and ideological opposition of his operas to declaimed tragedies.[53]

The Sovereign and the Law in Metastasio's Poetics

Even though Metastasio does not often deal with Gravina's antityrannical ideas, political content is not left out of his later *opera seria*. On the contrary, he seems to draw on a peculiar element of his teacher's tragedies, namely the attention to the connection between the sovereign and the law, reviewing several early modern theories dealing with this issue. If Gravina, who was also a famous jurist, represents some sovereigns committing crimes because they consider themselves above the law, Metastasio portrays several kings who are enabled to moderate their desires and administer justice in the interest of their subjects, refusing personal benefit, despite the difficulties that this renunciation implies. Metastasio displays the weaknesses of Bodin's theory, according to which the king is not bound by the law, while also rejecting the Monarchomachs' theory, which allows the subjected people to retain the right of rebellion. In preference to both, he underlines the sacredness of natural law. His *drammi per musica* are so fully in line with the theory of enlightened absolutism that he anticipates ideas not fully and clearly articulated by legal and political treatises until the second half of the century. In his plays, Metastasio prepares the ground for the positions of Muratori and Montesquieu, who held that the sovereign should be a clement shepherd and not an abuser of his absolute power. Assuming that the king must always respect the natural law, but that, at the same time, he can suspend even positive laws by exercising his clemency in the interest of the people's happiness, Metastasio actively contributes to the contemporary political and juridical debate. His theatre, in which this reflection on the king and the law is so fundamental, cannot be defined as unengaged at all.

Metastasio's theory of political sovereignty was soon overshadowed by the French Revolution. Poets and political theorists no longer began to think in terms of kingdoms or empires, but in terms of nations. Theatre itself was considered the perfect instrument to

---

53 For a juridical and political interpretation of the subject of Brutus in eighteenth-century Italian theatre, see Zucchi, "Suddito o giudice?", 355–62. For the French theatre, with particular attention to the tragedy of Charles Porée and to the Jesuit plays, see Tilg, "Jesuit Tragedy," 202–6.

create a national spirit, as is proven by Friedrich Schiller's 1785 *Die Schaubühne als eine moralische Anstalt betrachtet* (*The Theatre Considered as a Moral Institution*):

> Unmöglich kann ich hier den großen Einfluß übergehen, den eine gute stehende Bühne auf den Geist der Nation haben würde. Nationalgeist eines Volks nenne ich die Aehnlichkeit und Uebereinstimmung seiner Meinungen und Neigungen bei Gegenständen, worüber eine andere Nation anders meint und empfindet. Nur der Schaubühne ist es möglich, diese Uebereinstimmung in einem hohen Grad zu bewirken.

> I cannot possibly neglect to mention the great influence that a fine standing theatre would have upon the spirit of our nation. I define a people's national spirit as the similarity and agreement of its opinions and inclinations concerning matters in which another nation thinks and feels differently. Only the stage is capable of eliciting a high degree of such agreement.[54]

Whereas Alfieri tried to forge the conscience of a nation through his tragedies, Metastasio, who conceived his theatre as a mirror for both princes and subjects, was striving to build within his operas the supranational conscience of the European court.

---

54 Schiller, *Werke*, 20: 99; translated in Schiller, *Theatre Considered as a Moral Institution*, in *Friedrich Schiller*, 217.

7 Game of Thrones in the Russian Empire: Metastasio Revisited for St Petersburg

TATIANA KORNEEVA

If Italian opera, since its origins in seventeenth-century Florence, was conceived as a genre charged with political valences and allusions, the situation was no different when the form was imported into the Russian empire thanks to the extraordinary "brain drain" of Italian composers, librettists, actors, and musicians. From the first decades of the eighteenth century, Italian theatre and its artists became vital to the Russian empresses, who championed opera and theatre as patrons, critics, and spectators, and who used Italian opera as a sounding board to glorify and mythologize their victories as well as their close ties to European modernity and Slavic identity. Italian musico-theatrical repertoires performed at the courts of three Russian tsarinas – Anna Ioannovna (r. 1730–40), Elizabeth Petrovna (r. 1741–61), and Catherine the Great (r. 1762–96) – held a crucial position in the Russian spectacle of absolutism, providing scripts for theatrical re-enactments of sovereignty.

In this context, the *drammi per musica* of Pietro Metastasio (1698–1782), which enjoyed wide popularity at all European courts, were performed in Russia on the occasion of solemn events such as name days, birthdays, coronation anniversaries, or the weddings of hereditary princes. They represented a significant phenomenon within the cultural life of the country.[1] Despite the importance of Metastasian theatre for Russian

---

1 Metastasio's popularity in eighteenth-century Russia has been documented since the reign of Empress Anna Ioannovna, the tsarina who imported Italian theatre, opera, and chamber music to the Russian court and was well aware of the socio-political importance of the performing arts. Under her patronage, the comic interlude *L'impresario delle Canarie* was performed in 1733, while *Il finto Nino, ovvero La Semiramide riconosciuta* and *Artaserse* were performed in 1737 and 1738 in honour of the tsarina's birthday, both to music of Francesco Araja (1709–ca. 1770). For the

musical and literary culture, critical investigations into the reception of the imperial poet's *opere serie* remain scarce.[2] This chapter attempts to fill this gap by examining two Russian adaptations of *La Clemenza di Tito*, a Metastasian work of most extraordinary and enduring success. The first of these adaptations is the *opera seria Miloserdie Titovo* (*The Clemency of Titus*) with music by Johann Adolf Hasse and a libretto adapted by Johann Stählin, performed in 1742 to mark the coronation of Elizabeth Petrovna. The second adaptation is the first Russian musical tragedy *Titovo miloserdie* (*The Clemency of Titus*), written in 1778 by Iakov B. Kniazhnin (1740–91) on the commission of Catherine II. This chapter seeks first to delineate the recontextualization of the Metastasian libretto and the way its function changes during the reigns of Elizabeth and Catherine. Considering that both Russian versions were artistic productions by the court and for the court, I inquire into the motives that influenced the choice of the Metastasian *Clemenza* as the opera performed for very specific court festivities. Focusing on the significance of the works within the historical-political context through which the original libretto came to be transformed, I endeavour to shed light on the complexity of the manipulation of the libretto and the factors that influenced the "re-writers" of the Caesarian poet.

Cultural Transfers between Vienna, Dresden, and Moscow

Metastasio's *La Clemenza*, performed to the music of Antonio Caldara (1670–1736) on 4 November 1734 to celebrate the name day of Emperor Charles VI (r. 1711–40), depicts an episode from the life of the Roman

---

coronation of Elizabeth Petrovna, *La Clemenza di Tito* was performed in 1742. At a celebration of the tsarina's birthday in 1755, *Alessandro nell'Indie* was performed in a setting by Araja, while the opera was revived in 1757 at the Oranienbaum Theatre with music by Vincenzo Manfredini (1737–99). In 1760, the last Metastasian opera during the reign of Elizabeth was performed: the *Siroe*, set to music by Hermann Friedrich Raupach (1728–88). In 1762, *L'Olimpiade*, with music by Manfredini, was premiered on the occasion of the coronation of Catherine II, and returned to the stage in 1765 to celebrate the empress's birthday. In 1766, *Didone abbandonata* and *Il re pastore* were performed, both set to music by Baldassare Galuppi (1706–85). Galuppi's successor, Tommaso Traetta (1727–79), staged *L'isola disabitata* and *L'Olimpiade* in 1769, and the following year, for the anniversary of the coronation, he produced the *Antigono*. In St Petersburg, Giovanni Paisiello (1740–1816) composed seven works based on libretti by Metastasio: *Nineta* (1776), *Achille in Sciro* (1778), *Alcide al bivio* (1780), *Didone abbandonata* (1796), *Zenobia* (1797), and *Alessandro nell'Indie* (1799).

2 On Metastasio's libretti in Russia, see Garzonio, "Metastasio e la poesia russa tra classicismo e romanticismo." On the presence of Metastasio during the 1770s, the

emperor Titus Vespasian. Its simple plot can be summarized succinctly. Vitellia, daughter of the late emperor Vitellius and jilted lover of Titus, is desperate to regain the throne that had belonged to her father before he was ousted by Titus. For this reason, the woman convinces the patrician Sextus, a friend of Titus who is in love with her, to instigate a plot against the emperor. Upon discovering the conspiracy, Titus nevertheless forgives the traitors for the good of Rome.

The opera was composed during a period of great political-military strife for the Habsburgs, due to the War of the Polish Succession (1734–8). Clemency, the main virtue on which Metastasio constructs the figure of the prince, was therefore meant to be both a central virtue for the public image of Charles VI and a message of support for his subjects, who felt a strong need for reassuring images in the face of defeats.[3] Indeed, the ideological and political values represented in the opera aimed to organize a social consensus for imperial power, while inviting the sovereign to align his decisions with those of the dramatis personae of the plot.[4]

As a result of the moral imperative to show the qualities of the ideal sovereign and to hold up a dramatized mirror for princes, the Metastasian *Clemenza* became a great success throughout the European courts and was performed over fifty times. Contrary to what one might suspect, the most popular and most performed production of the *Clemenza* in the eighteenth century was not the last *opera seria* by W.A. Mozart (1791), but rather the opera by Johann Adolph Hasse (1699–1783), kapellmeister at the Saxon-Polish court of Prince Frederick Augustus II (r. 1694–1733).[5] Due to the good relations between the reigning Saxon family and the Russian imperial court, news of the success of Hasse's version, which was performed in Dresden in 1738 on the third anniversary of the coronation of Frederick Augustus as king of Poland, also reached Russia. In Moscow, the opera was the centrepiece of the celebrations for the coronation of Tsarina Elizabeth Petrovna, which took place on 29 May 1742. The libretto and score used for this production arrived in Russia because of contacts between the city of Dresden and the opera's director, Jacob von Stählin (1709–85), a key figure in the history of the cultural transfer of Italian opera.

---

most salient period of his reception in Russia, see Russo, "'Nitteti' e 'Demetrio' alla corte di Caterina II."

3 Joly, "Metastasio e l'ideologia del sovrano virtuoso."

4 See Enrico Zucchi's chapter in this volume and his discussion of Metastasio's preference for tragic plots centred on the ruler's clemency.

5 On the biography of Hasse, see Mellace, *Johann Adolph Hasse*, 27–151.

During the fifty years he spent in Russia, Stählin was a professor of eloquence and permanent secretary of the Academy of Sciences, founder and director of the Academy of Fine Arts, editor in chief of the German edition of the newspaper *Petersburgskaia gazeta* (*The St Petersburg Gazette*), as well as the author of articles for *Primechaniia na Sanktpetersburgskie vedomosti* (*Notes on the News of St Petersburg*), in which he sought to familiarize Russian readers with the opera. These various appointments allowed Stählin to become a privileged observer of Russian cultural life and the first historiographer of Russian musical theatre and ballet.[6] Stählin, however, was not only an academic and scholar, but also a shrewd courtier and diplomat who, thanks to a network of contacts skillfully constructed over decades, managed to remain in service at the court of four different emperors: Anna, Elizabeth, Peter III, and Catherine II.

The libretto of the Moscow production exists today in Italian and Russian, by way of a translation by Ivan Merkur'ev (?–1748), translator and secretary to the Ministry of Foreign Affairs.[7] This translation respects the dramaturgical structure and the narrative plot of the opera while also implementing substantial changes: in the first act there are only two scenes from the Metastasian libretto; the sixteen scenes from the second act are reduced to eleven, and the thirteen scenes of the third act have become eleven. The concluding *Licenza*, which had made clear the mirror relationship between the opera and its dedicatee-commissioner Charles VI, is also removed. Indeed, the reference to the new dedicatee is expressed in the prologue "Россия по печали паки обрадованная" (Russia rejoicing again after sorrow) written by Stählin specifically for the Moscovite production, initially in Italian and then translated into Russian, German, and French.[8]

Hasse's music was used for less than half of the Moscow variant, as the first half of the opera was set to music by Domenico Dall'Oglio (1700–64), while the second half was composed by Luigi Madonis (1690–ca. 1770).[9] While the cuts and changes highlight the need to adapt the score to the expressive resources of the local opera company, the addition of Stählin's prologue and the reduction of recitatives and arias reveal the desire to go beyond the mere importation of a finished

---

6 Cf. Malinovskii, *Zapiski Jakoba Shtelina ob iziashchnykh iskusstvakh v Rossii*, 1: 7–26; Liechtenhan, "Jacob von Stählin, académicien et courtesan."
7 [Metastasio, Stählin, and Merkur'ev], *Miloserdie Titovo*; hereafter cited parenthetically. Unless otherwise noted, English translations are mine.
8 Stählin, "Rossiia po pechali paki obradovannaia." Prologue to the opera *Miloserdie Titovo*, in [Metastasio, Stählin, and Merkur'ev], *Miloserdie Titovo*, n.p.
9 Lutsker and Susidko, "'Miloserdie Tita' v Rossii."

product.[10] Opera scholars who are aware of how often Metastasio's *La Clemenza* was adapted and reset may nevertheless be surprised by the daring revisionism of Stählin's and Kniazhnin's versions. Despite the fact that Merkur'ev's clumsy, line-for-line translation was intended for reading purposes only, the Moscow production of the *Clemenza* represents the first step in acquiring an identity for the Russian opera that stands apart from the European models, and it is responsible for having influenced the literary and aesthetic tastes of Russian culture.[11]

The *Clemency* of Elizabeth

Stählin's prologue is a rich source of information about the meaning of the opera in the context of its time. At first glance, the main function of the *Clemenza*, performed in the new opera house before an audience of five thousand, resembled that of Metastasio's original libretto for Charles VI: the opera was offered to Elizabeth as the noblest form of praise. In fact, Stählin claims that the Metastasian libretto constituted the ideal subject to portray "жизнерадостный нрав и высокие душевные качества императрицы" (the joyful nature and the sublime spiritual qualities of the empress).[12] Its prologue in two acts, likely translated by Mikhail Lomonosov (1711–65), introduces two main characters: Rutenia, the personification of Russia, and Astrea, who stands for Justice. In the first act, Rutenia laments her fate in the empty darkness and comforts her weeping sons (the Russian people) by telling them that Peter the Great lives on in his daughter Elizabeth, who will soon be able to return Russia to its former glory.[13] In the second act, Astrea descends from heaven to announce to Rutenia the ascension of the new empress and to paint a bright future for the Russian empire. It is no coincidence that the goddess has bestowed upon Elizabeth the virtues of justice, valour, humanity, generosity and clemency, qualities personified by characters in the allegorical ballet accompanying Astrea. Of course, primary

---

10 The part of Titus was sung by the contralto Caterina Giorgi (fl. 1729–56, d. 1756), while the role of Annius was performed by her husband, tenor Filippo Giorgi (d. 1775); Publius was sung by soprano Caterina Masani, and Servilia by Geronima Madonis, wife of Luigi Madonis. The part of the prima donna, Vitellia, was performed by Rosa Ruvinetti Bon (fl. 1730–62), wife of the painter Girolamo Bon (ca. 1700–60), while the primo uomo, Sextus, was played by the castrato Pietro Morigi (fl. 1729–68). The scenery was created by the set designer, Girolamo Bon.
11 On the development of Italian opera into an important component of Russian court culture and celebratory ceremonies, see Korndorf, *Dvortsy Khimery*, 22–3.
12 Stählin, "Izvestiia o muzyke v Rossii."
13 Stählin, "Rossiia po pechali paki obradovannaia," act 1.

emphasis is placed on the last quality in the list: clemency. Elizabeth had ascended the throne thanks to a coup d'état on 25 November 1741 (allegorized by the rising of the sun and the joyful choir of singers), but she did indeed show clemency toward her enemies, suspending the death penalty for Count Andrei Ostermann (1686–1747), Field Marshal Burkhard Christoph von Münnich (1683–1767), and the ousted Tsarina Anna Leopol'dovna in January 1742. The connection between this historical fact and the performances of the opera, occurring in May of the same year, is evident.[14]

Stählin's prologue, therefore, contextualized the dramatic situation for the Russian public, while at the same time broadening its horizons. By demonstrating the empress's indulgence, the prologue linked the opera's subject to a political context and a celebratory occasion that are quite different from that of the opera's premiere in 1734. If, on the one hand, the prologue underscores the appropriateness of the opera's subject for a performance on the occasion of the coronation, on the other hand, it proves that the reasons for selecting the *La clemenza* are not limited to the encomiastic character of the libretto. Nor can the reasons for choosing this theme for the Moscow production be attributed to material conditions, such as the absence of the court composer Francesco Araja, who had been sent to Italy to enlarge the Italian opera company. In fact, Stählin's prologue went beyond articulating the equivalence between Elizabeth and the Roman emperor; Astrea's aria in the second act of the prologue emphasizes the fact that it is Peter's daughter who obtained the Russian throne and who would restore his image as the promoter of modern Russia.

The reference to Peter I (r. 1721–25) is essential to understanding the reasons for the choice of subject matter and the function of the opera within its Russian context. As Richard Wortman and Cynthia Whittaker have shown, Peter the Great, who had pioneered the creation of modern political culture, was responsible for the many innovations that affected the law of succession to the throne.[15] Convinced that his eldest son, the Tsarevich Alexei, was unfit to advance the project of his reforms to modernize Russia, Peter I abrogated the principle of birthright: with a law issued on 5 February 1722, he abolished the dynastic transition of power, giving the current monarch the right to appoint his own

---

14 On the fact that Russian court theatre, and the *opera seria* in particular, were performances filled with political allusions and designed for a specific monarch, see Ogarkova, *Tseremonii, prazdnestva, musyka russkogo dvora*.

15 Wortman, "The Representation of Dynasty and 'Fundamental Laws' in the Evolution of Russian Monarchy"; Whittaker, "Chosen by 'All the Russian People.'"

successor and decreeing that naming someone "worthy" of reigning was the only legal criterion for succession to the throne.[16] Since Peter died before appointing his successor or leaving any male descendants (Alexei died in prison while awaiting execution on the charge of conspiring to overthrow the emperor), his decree made the entire process of succession unstable and arbitrary, ushering in the era of palace revolutions. In post-Petrine Russia, there was no law governing succession to the throne, and manifestos published after coups d'état legitimized the ruler's right to legal succession by invoking four criteria: appointment by the previous monarch, the dynastic principle, personal merit, and election by the people. No eighteenth-century monarch could boast possession of all four criteria for the right to the throne, but some possessed at least two of these requirements.[17] After Peter I, the only basis of legitimacy was the appointment by the previous ruler, but this solution *de jure* was often criticized by public opinion. At the same time, the tradition of hereditary succession stood strong, and anyone who did not belong to the Romanov dynasty, at least by marriage, dared not lay claim to the throne. Even birthright, despite having been abolished by Peter I's law, was invoked whenever it was deemed expedient.

Thus, Stählin's prologue incorporated the opera into the official program of every eighteenth-century Russian monarch, defending their rights of succession in the public arena by creating as complete a list as possible of the criteria of their legitimacy. While retaining some of the functions of the original libretto – the celebratory elements and the aspects intended to hold up a mirror to the ruler and reassure her subjects – the function of the prologue was primarily to recontextualize the dramatic events for a particular ruler and the Russian public. In fact, at the end of the prologue, a monument is erected on stage with an inscription marking the presence of all the principles of Elizabeth's legitimate succession. As the heiress of Peter I and a reformer like him, the empress was deemed worthy to govern the country and was elected by popular consensus: "Да здравствует благополучно / Елизавета / достойнейшая, вожделенная, коронованная / императрица / всероссийская, / мать отечества / увеселение человеческаго рода / Тит времен наших" (Long live / Elizabeth / the most worthy, the most desirable, and crowned / All-Russian / Empress / Mother of the Fatherland / delight of the human race / Titus of our times).[18]

---

16 Whittaker, "Chosen by 'All the Russian People,'" 3.
17 Kiselev, "'By the Rights of the Whole World.'"
18 Stählin, "Rossiia po pechali paki obradovannaia," act 2.

The Metastasian libretto is strongly recontextualized for the specific occasion of Elizabeth's coronation to make explicit the comparison between the new merciful empress and Titus, employ the language of clemency for the shaping of her own imperial persona, demonstrate to the tsarina's political allies and opponents that there was no inconsistency between her legal policies and their symbolic representation, and provide an authoritative model of absolutist kinship. For these reasons, it is interesting to examine what specific meaning the libretto acquired in the Russian political context and what image of sovereignty it sought to convey. From this perspective, it would be appropriate to investigate the significance of the analogy outlined at the end of the prologue between Elizabeth as "Mother of the Fatherland," and Titus as "Father of the Fatherland," along with the political significance of the domestic world depicted in the opera.

From the very first lines, the libretto emphasizes that the virtue that makes Titus an exemplary sovereign is his role as father of the Roman people. Indeed, when Sextus tries to convince Vitellia to abandon the idea of a coup, he says that Titus is considered "красота миру всему, отец Риму чтится / Другом себя кажет нам" (the joy of the whole world, father of Rome / friend of us) (1.1, p. 2). Titus's role as father to his subjects is confirmed as the virtue necessary for the exercise of power in the meeting of the senate, which confers on Titus the title "Father of the Fatherland" (1.3 p. 6). If, in the Metastasian original, identification between the state and the family functioned as an intermediary between the ruler and his fellow citizens, in the Russian version the reference to the close kinship between Titus – i.e., Elizabeth – and his people served to emphasize the existence of a charismatic basis on which to found her power.

Moreover, the rhetoric of family in the opera was that of representing the ruler's power as a form of government that allows the sovereign to reign in the name of the public benefit. The role of the father and the office of the sovereign are closely intertwined in the figure of Titus, as is evident in the account of the measures taken by the emperor upon discovering the conspiracy. These measures metaphorically allude to the actions of Elizabeth during the coup d'état:

О ежелиб ты знала! Каким он разводом,
Видя поправляет, все меж своим народом,
Смелых удерживает, тихих ободряет,
Хвалы, грозы, обеты, как делать всем знает,
Вкупе Рима защитник, страшный полководец
И друг, вкупе и Монарх, гражданин и отец. (2.4, p. 20)

If only you knew! How he
Oversees and governs his people,
He holds back the audacious, encourages the shy,
He praises, threatens, promises, he knows what everyone must do,
He is a protector of Rome, an outstanding military leader
A friend, a monarch, and a father all in one.

Titus's effort to unite public rule and private conscience in his character can be read in light of *Critique and Crisis: Enlightenment and the
Pathogenesis of Modern Society*, in which Reinhart Koselleck identifies a
characteristic feature of the Enlightenment in the radical revision of the
relationship between morality and politics.[19] The libretto thus reflects
the paradigm shift in eighteenth-century political thought described
by Koselleck, which moves from reasons of state and the clear separation between moral and political action toward public happiness and
the vision of the ruler's function in securing the common good. This
rejection of the model based on the duality of politics and morality is
reflected in the libretto's frequent references to the figures of Brutus
and Manlius Torquatus. In the moment when Titus is faced with the
decision of how to deal with Sextus, who has been found guilty of the
palace conspiracy, Brutus and Manlius are mentioned as examples of
figures who have previously committed criminal acts in the name of
the state, thus separating the private sphere from the public-political
arena:

Принимать ли Титусу забытые меры?
Забыть друга Секстуса, были те примеры,
Забыли Брутус, Манлий всю ласку отцову,
Жалость и дружба молчи, теперь вы не к слову. (3.7, р. 43)

Should Titus take precautions long forgotten?
Should he forget his friend Sextus? There have been examples of that,
Brutus and Manlius have forgotten their father's kindness,
Pity and friendship be silent; you are out of place.

In the course of Sextus's interrogation, in which the guilty man does
not dare to reveal why he has offended their friendship, Titus makes
another implicit reference to Brutus, when he compares Sextus to the
guilty son and wonders whether his friend deserves to live or die.
Whereas Brutus, in punishing his sons, acts not like a father but like an

---

19 Koselleck, *Critique and Crisis*.

honest governor who respects the law, Titus demonstrates to Sextus his ability to separate the role of sovereign-judge from his role as friend: "Открой сердце Титусу, одни здесь надежно. / Не мни что Монарх с тобой повери, как другу, / Цесарь то не будет знать, почту за услугу" (Open your heart to Titus, it is safe with him / Do not think that I am here with you as a monarch; trust me as a friend, / Caesar will not know, and I will take it [your confession] as a favour) (3.6, p. 44). If before and during the interrogation, the emperor is uncertain which of the two dimensions – the public or the private – will gain the upper hand, at the close of the third act it is the private sphere that dominates and wins over Titus: "Полно Секст думать о том, будем друзьями паки, / Забудем прошедшия те преступки всяки, / С сердца Титус выкинул, я все забываю, / Тебя обнимаю я, и тебя прощаю" (Sextus, do not think about it, let us be friends, / let us forget about all that happened, / Titus does not hold it in his heart, I forget everything, / I embrace you and pardon you for everything) (3.11, p. 49).

Titus's exercise of clemency toward the conspirators thus contrasts with the actions of Brutus, who did not hesitate to condemn his own children to death. If Brutus embodies the model of government in which the two halves – public and private – stand in opposition to one another, Titus represents the possibility of a solution to the dualism between morality and state interests. In Stählin's version, clemency is an allegory of the reformist project of Enlightenment culture and an act of social harmony that serves to stabilize governing power without challenging the authority of the ruler. The performance of the Metastasian opera thus allowed Elizabeth, who had recently ascended the throne thanks to a coup d'état, to present her government as a reformist project, another criterion for the legitimacy of her power. Given the uncertainties regarding Elizabeth's succession, the *Clemenza*, therefore, constituted the central element of what Richard Wortman has defined as "scenarios of power" and assumed the task of establishing Elizabeth's lawful legitimacy, a task almost identical to that of her oath and manifestos issued after the coup d'état.[20]

The *Clemency* of Catherine

After the first production in 1742 and until the last one in 1746, Metastasio's opera was performed about nine times in Russia.[21] In 1746,

---

20 Anisimov, *Afrodita u vlasti. Tsarstvovanie Elizavety Petrovny*, 143–4. On the interpretation of Elizabeth's manifestos of 25 November 1741 and 22 January 1741, see Kiselev, "'Po pravam vsego sveta,'" 114.

21 Lutsker and Susidko, "'Miloserdie Tita' v Rossii," 11.

the successor to the throne, Catherine II, witnessed the last of these productions. The opera must have impressed the tsarina – who was notoriously unenthusiastic about the genre of tragedy – to the point of spurring her desire to see another adaptation of the *Clemenza* on the Russian stage. The commission for the work was given to the poet Iakov Kniazhnin, who wrote the *Titovo miloserdie* (*The Clemency of Titus*) in 1778; it was performed in St Petersburg at the theatre of the Winter Palace in 1779. Rather than writing another line-by-line translation for the purposes of understanding the plot, Kniazhnin wrote the first Russian tragedy in music with chorus and ballet. His adaptation of Metastasio's *Clemenza* is an important reference point for the genre of musical drama in Russia.

Neither the subject nor the theatrical poet entrusted with the commission were chosen at random. Since Catherine came to power in the wake of a palace revolution very similar to that of Elizabeth, the purpose of the opera remained steady: to buttress the legitimacy of the empress. Aware both of the opera's potential to portray scenarios of royal authority and of the need to re-enact them, the empress had explicitly demanded of the playwright а "изображеніе великаго Тита, какъ совершенное подобіе ангельской души Ея" (representation of the great Titus as a perfect image of his angelic soul): in other words, the political and moral portrait that she wished to display of herself.[22] As for the author, Kniazhnin was a playwright skilled in the creative translation of dramatic texts. Indeed, Kniazhnin was called the Russian Racine and Euripides after the success of his first tragedy *Dido* (1769), a free adaptation of Metastasio's *Didone abbandonata*. However, the playwright's political position and biography are still full of holes. Even today, critics disagree as to whether Kniazhnin should be considered a craftsman of Catherine's glory or a revolutionary who prepared the ideology of the Decembrist movement.[23] In fact, Kniazhnin was sentenced to death in 1773 after being formally charged with embezzling public funds. Even if the accusation could have been founded, Kniaznin did not deserve capital punishment as Catherine, inspired by *Del delitto e delle pene* (*On Crime and Punishment*, 1764) by Cesare Beccaria, had abolished it except in cases of *lèse-majesté*.[24] It is reasonable to assume that the harshness of the sentence was due

22 Kniazhnin, *Sobranie sochinenii*, 1: 9.
23 Veselovskii, "Ideinyi dramaturg ekaterininskoi epokhi"; Gudzii, "Ob ideologii Ia.B. Kniazhnina," 659–64.
24 Wortman, *The Development of a Russian Legal Consciousness*, 10.

to the fact that the ideas expressed in Kniazhnin's tragedies did not please Catherine because they contradicted the image of the state she wished to convey. It is therefore possible to link Kniazhnin's condemnation to the anti-tyrannical ideas contained in his tragedy *Olga* (1770). This opera was a rewriting of Voltaire's *Mérope* (1743) and contained a rebuke to a mother who wanted to usurp her son's throne.[25] It is no coincidence that the tragedy, composed for the eighteenth birthday of Prince Pavel Petrovich (r. 1796–1801), Catherine's son and heir, remained unpublished during the author's lifetime.[26] Since the *Titovo miloserdie* was written after Kniazhnin had been pardoned, the tragedy was, most likely, the precondition for pardon. Taking into account that the opera was commissioned by the empress to illustrate her power and that its author experienced Catherine's clemency firsthand, the *Titovo miloserdie* represents a work that allows us to better understand how images of sovereignty change as power passes from one ruler to another.

In particular, three scenes that Kniazhnin added to the Metastasian storyline, all of which show significant deviations from the version performed during Elizabeth's reign, can give us a first indication of how the function of the opera and the image of the sovereign changed. The first of these scenes is the *incipit* of the tragedy, in which the politicization of the plot and the description of the conspiracy reach a level that is of considerable importance to the economy of the opera.[27] Indeed, the tragedy no longer opens with the scene of the private meeting between the lovers Sextus and Vitellia, but rather with a public ceremony, during which the senate confers on Titus the title *pater patriae*, according to the will of the Roman people. The emperor rejects

25 See Marasinova, *Vlast' i lichnost'*, 310; Kulakova, "Zhizn' i tvorchestvo Ia.B. Kniazhnina," 10.

26 Kniazhnin is best known to posterity for the controversy that arose after his death over his tragedy *Vadim Novgorodskii* (*Vadim of Novgorod*, 1789), which reworks the theme already addressed by Catherine II in her tragedy *Iz zhizni Riurika* (*From the Life of Rurik*, 1786). Kniazhnin was aware that the challenge against the power of the monarchy by its hero, a defender of liberal republican institutions, might actually occur and withdrew the opera from publication. The tragedy was published in 1793, after the poet's death, by Princess Ekaterina Dashkova in an anthology dedicated to comedies in the series *Rossiiskii featr* (*Russian Theatre*), and it has been regarded as an attack on Catherine's monarchical ideology.

27 The emphasis on the political dimension of the plot is due to two factors. First, Kniazhnin's sources included, in addition to the work of the imperial poet, the tragedy *Titus* by Pierre-Laurent de Belloy (1727–75), a reworking of Metastasio and

the title and expresses his desire to be called "человек на троне" (a man on the throne) (1.1, p. 59).[28] The opening lines of the tragedy have an exact correspondence to historical reality: in 1767, the members of the legislative commission approached Catherine with a request to accept the titles "Catherine the Great, the Wise, Mother of the Fatherland" to thank her for "преприятый подвиг утвердить непреложными законами блаженство" (the heroic act she has undertaken to establish her benevolence with indispensable laws).[29] The tsarina expressed her gratitude, accepting the third but rejecting the first two titles as still premature.[30]

Kniazhnin's rewriting of the *incipit* was, therefore, a reference to the event that constituted an additional coronation for Catherine.[31] This ceremony allowed the empress to assume the title of "Mother of the Fatherland" inherited from Elizabeth, while reinforcing the function of family mythology that was part of her political agenda.[32] Referring to the work of the legislative commission appointed by Catherine, Kniazhnin created a new model of the ideal sovereign. Sextus, in fact, argues that "не Тит здесь царствует, здесь царствует закон" (it is not Titus who rules here, but the law) (2.6, p. 79). Throughout the tragedy, Titus, as Catherine's alter ego, is repeatedly defined as "податель" (lawgiver) (3.4, p. 98) and "хранитель закона" (protector of the law) (3.9, p. 108). These definitions have a counterpart in historical reality: Catherine was the first Russian sovereign who actually attempted to continue the reforms of Peter I by providing the country with legislative institutions capable of managing the vast empire. Aware that the Russian judicial system was so weak that, instead of being the sovereign's primary prerogative, it could barely enact her will, the empress was keen to

---

Voltaire's *Brutus*, which the playwright wrote in 1758 after working as an actor at the Russian court. De Belloy published the work in 1760 and sent a copy to Catherine II with a dedication in verse. Second, political importance was given to Kniazhnin's work as translator when, a few years before the *Titovo miloserdie*, he translated Corneille's *Cinna*, in which the political aspect is a genuine call to action, sparking debate on the monarchical and republican forms of government. See Joly, "Metastasio e l'ideologia del sovrano virtuoso," 91. It is also known that Kniazhnin was enthralled by his reading of Voltaire's *Mort de César*.

28 I cite from *Titovo Miloserdie*, in Kniazhnin, *Sobranie sochinenii*, 1: 56–114. Hereafter quoted by act, scene, and page numbers. English translations of the tragedy are mine.
29 Marasinova, *Vlast' i lichnost'*, 166.
30 Omel'chenko, "*Zakonnaia monarkhiia*," 115–16.
31 Wortman, "The Representation of Dynasty," 45.
32 Schierle, "Patriotism and Emotions," 74.

transform the law into a fundamental instrument of her government to strengthen the monarchy itself.[33]

The manual Catherine wrote to provide a basis for future legislation was printed in 1767 under the title *Nakaz kommissii o sostavlenii proekta novago ulozheniia* (Nakaz, or Instructions to the Commission for the Composition of a Plan of a New Code of Laws). The convocation of the legislative commission and the publication of the *Nakaz* represent, at least on paper, not only a pivotal moment in Catherine's reign, but also an invitation to public dialogue between the ruler and her subjects.[34] Catherine's reputation as an enlightened sovereign, both contemporary and posthumous, owes much to this document, which was reprinted more than twenty-five times in nine different languages during her reign and which, although never put into practice, was read and commented upon by many European intellectuals, including Voltaire, Frederick the Great, and Diderot.

It is clear, therefore, that the allusion to the acts of the legislative commission and the *Nakaz* in the opening scene of the tragedy had the function of updating the earlier representations of the mother of the fatherland. The author drew a portrait of an absolute monarch with self-limiting and clearly defined power; a reformer and ruler elevated to the throne with broad popular consent; an autocrat bowing before the law of the state; a legislator whose decrees benefited all social classes; and a propagator of civil liberties and equality before the law.

The image of the sovereign-legislator is better described in another episode that the poet added to the storyline of the Metastasian opera. In the tenth scene of the second act, Annius reports to Titus on the affairs of state. The senator claims that, under the emperor's rule, all his subjects are happy except for those who have broken the law and are now justly suffering. Titus openly disagrees with the senator's position and decides to change the existing laws so that he can also forgive criminals:

Не редко в строгости законы суть не правы.
О судии! Внемлите вы уставы,
Что человечество гласит.
Несчастных сих я узы разрешаю,
Убийцам лишь единым не прощаю.
В том благость мне сама претит.

---

33 Hosking, *Russia: People and Empire*, 98.
34 Whittaker, *Russian Monarchy*, 108.

Often the laws are unjust in their severity.
Judges! Listen to the laws
Of humanity!
I will break the chains of these unfortunate men,
And I will pardon all but the murderers.
The goodness of heart itself prevents me from doing this. (2.10, p. 88)

We should compare this scene with the *Slovo na den' koronovaniia Eia Velichestva Imperatritsy Ekateriny II* (*Address on the Coronation Day of Her Majesty Empress Catherine II*, 1762) by Aleksandr Sumarokov (1717–77), a court poet and the first Russian dramatist. This comparison is justified for three reasons. First, Sumarokov was Kniazhnin's father-in-law and a dramatic father figure.[35] Second, Sumarokov received the *Nakaz* in 1767 for his review and commentaries, which shows that the writer held the position of semi-official counsellor in the early years of Catherine's reign. Finally, a significant part of the *Slovo* was devoted to the issue of justice and the correct application of the law. By urging Catherine to be a mother and judge simultaneously, Sumarokov recalled the subject of Titus:

Плакал Тит, когда беззаконникам подписывал казни; плакал но подписывал; ибо без того, был бы он участником соделаннаго ими беззакония. Буди Государыня, буди всегда Материю любезному своему народу! Награждай добродетель, исправляй пороки наши и рази беззакония! [...] Злодеи ни малейшаго помилования не достойны: Политика определяет им казни, дабы отвратити других от подобнаго злодейства, а истина отомщения требует [...].

Titus wept when he assigned death sentences to the criminals; he wept, but he signed them, for otherwise he would have become an accomplice to their crimes. Be the governess, be always a mother to your obliging people! Reward virtue, correct our vices and strike down lawless acts! [...] Criminals should not be spared: Politics prescribes them the punishment to prevent others from committing similar crimes, and truth demands revenge [...].[36]

By reinterpreting history and making Titus execute the traitors according to the law, Sumarokov hoped to be able to guide the empress by

---

35 It is worth noting that both Kniazhnin and Sumarokov graduated from the Cadet corps, a special institution that prepared members of the Russian hereditary nobility for service in the army and life at court. Cf. Levitt, *Early Modern Russian Letters*, 7.
36 Sumarokov, *Slovo na den' koronovaniia Eia Velichestva Imperatritsy Ekateriny II*, 230–1. The translation is mine.

proposing a cautious plan of legislative policies. He advocated the death penalty because he believed that the monarch must limit his or her power through laws: "Самодержавию никто, кроме истинны, закона предписать не может; но колико мы подчинены Самодержавцам, толико они подчинены истинне" (No one, except truth, can prescribe laws for the autocracy; but to the extent that we are subject to autocrats, they are subject to truth), wrote Sumarokov in the *Slovo*.[37] The example of Titus, therefore, served to support the poet's argument that the ruler must impose punishment as the law prescribes, without making any changes. Indeed, the author added a few lines later: "Кажется мне что надлежит умягчати законы, ежели они излишно строги, а не казни законами определенныя" (I believe that the law must be mitigated if it is too severe, but not the punishments set by the law).[38] Sumarokov developed this argument even further in another essay, "O kazni" (On capital punishment, 1774), in which he insisted on the necessity of the systematic application of the death penalty both to prevent the repetition of unlawful acts and as revenge for the murdered.[39] The playwright saw his role as educating and enlightening the Russian nobility through theatre and literature; he considered it his duty to exhort the autocracy to rule justly according to the law.[40] The fact that Sumarokov's outspoken coronation speech remained unpublished was a sign that Catherine was irritated by the role of mentor that the dramatist had assumed and by the prominent position that the first professional writer had claimed for himself in creating a state discourse.

It is obvious that the recently pardoned Kniazhnin, although he shared Sumarokov's liberal views, had no choice but to include an episode that would make his own Titus the exact opposite of Sumarokov's character. Moreover, it is useful to read this passage of the tragedy in light of what Catherine herself wrote in paragraph 91 of chapter 8 of the *Nakaz*:

Часто законодавец, хотящий уврачевати зло, не мыслит более ни о чем, как о сем уврачевании; очи его взирают на сей только предлог; и не смотрят на худые оттуда следсвия. Когда зло единожды уврачевано, тогда мы не видим более ничего кроме суровости законодавца; но порок в общенародии остается от жестокости сей произрастший; умы народа испортились, они приобыкли к насильству.

---

37 Ibid., 232.
38 Ibid.
39 I thank Marcus Levitt for bringing Sumarokov's essay to my attention.
40 Zhivov, "Pervye russkie literaturnye biografafii kak sotsial'noe iavlenie," 54–65; Levitt, *Early Modern Russian Letters*, 16.

It often happens that a legislator who wants to eliminate an evil, thinks of nothing but the cure, that his eyes are fixed on, and he does not take into account the inconveniences that accompany it: As soon as the cure is accomplished, nothing is seen but the severity of the legislator; but the evil resulting from this severity remains among the people; their minds are corrupted, they are accustomed to violence.[41]

If, therefore, Sumarokov insisted on the necessity of limiting the sovereign's power through the law, Kniazhnin added the scene in which Titus modifies the law to show his genuine clemency, a scene that illustrated the positions expressed by Catherine in the *Nakaz*.

In the third scene added by Kniazhnin, which departs from the structure of the Metastasian opera, Annius, after discovering the conspiracy, tells Titus of the Senate's decision to punish the traitors to prevent another coup, confident that the emperor will approve:

Патриции стыдом, уныньем пораженны,
Кленя сей лютый день, тово лишь только ждут,
Чтоб были их тобой решенья подтверждены.
Уже на казнь преступников ведут,
И для внушения таким сердцам боязни,
Хотя их строги казни,
Но праведны они.
Потомки оными, узрев в грядущи дни,
Какую злобу Рим к твоим врагам имеет,
Измерят казнью их его к тебе любовь.
[…]
Чтобы злодеев сих пролита кровь,
Чтобы Секстовы свершились казни строги,
Законы требуют, вселенна, Рим и боги.
И если сих уже преступников простишь,
Ты милосердием к злодейству путь явишь.

The patricians, struck by shame and despair,
Cursing that terrible day, only wait
For their decisions to be confirmed by you.

---

41 Catherine II, *Nakaz kommissii o sostavlenii proekta novago ulozheniia*. Subsequent quotations are from this edition, henceforth parenthetically cited by chapter in Roman numerals and paragraph numbers. English translations are mine.

The criminals have already been sentenced to execution,
To strike fear into the hearts of those people,
And though the punishments are severe,
They are just.
Descendants, looking back from the future,
What wrath Rome had against your enemies,
Will measure their love for you by these executions.
[...]
To shed the blood of criminals,
And Sextus's severe execution,
Are demanded by law, and the universe, and Rome, and the gods.
But if you pardon these criminals,
You will show them with clemency the path to crime. (3.5, pp. 99–100)

Confronted with the dilemma of whether to punish or pardon the conspirators, Kniazhnin's Titus chooses the path of mercy and forgiveness, the path taken by his literary predecessors, from Augustus in Corneille's *Cinna* to Metastasio's protagonist. It seems, then, that, even in this passage, the playwright intended to paint a portrait of Catherine, the opera's patron, as a lenient judge and defender of civil liberties. However, when we read Titus's decision in light of two other paragraphs of the *Nakaz*, it becomes clear that the motivations guiding Titus, and, by extension, the empress, are anything but humanitarian. In paragraph 85 of chapter 8, Catherine asserts that "в тех странах, где кроткие наказания, сердце граждан оныни столько же поражается, как в других местах – жестокими" (in those countries where lenient punishments are applied, the hearts of the citizens are as influenced by them as by harsh punishments in other parts). According to the empress, the effect of clemency was based on the theatrical mechanism of manipulating the collective emotions of the audience, which move quickly from fear of the harshness of the condemnation to relief at the great humanity of the ruler. Indeed, in the following paragraph, the empress states that "Воображение в людях действует при сем великом наказании так же, как бы оно действовало при малом" (the imagination of the people is affected by this severe punishment to the same degree, as it would have been by a light one) (8, § 86). These paragraphs make it clear that, for Catherine, the execution of the sentence and the pardon were equally effective in their effect on the public. There was not much difference between the terror consummated by execution and the terror alleviated by pardon. In fact, Elena Marasinova's research confirms that, in this period, the sentence of death and the actual execution should be considered almost identical measures of punishment.[42] Thus, one could say that the theatre of prosecution, judgment, and sentencing follows the same logic as a tragic drama, in which "l'apparechio degli instrumenti di miserabile morte" (laying out the instruments of a miserable death) can move and heal us as much as the sight of an actual execution, which might provoke nothing but horror, and turn us to stone.[43]

"Refracted" Clemency

Returning to the initial question about the changing functions of the opera and images of sovereignty in the context of the transition of power from one monarch to another, we can note that the reception of Metastasio's *Clemenza* in eighteenth-century Russia is a representative case of how the imperial poet's libretto could be reappropriated to underscore the scenarios of power of a particular ruling sovereign. One could argue that the two Russian adaptations of the Metastasian opera are rewritings adapted to a particular ideology, texts in which political or ideological considerations dominate. These versions not only aim to influence the way audiences read them or hear them in the theatre, but they also reveal the extent to which the political agenda and power dynamics of the court are the true motivating factors for librettists, composers, and translators. What also seems to be characteristic of the Russian reception of Metastasio is that both works analyzed here, in addition to being rewritten to depict scenarios of power and function as manifestos for the monarchies of Elizabeth and Catherine, also confront – in different ways and with different solutions – the great dilemma of the Enlightenment, defined by Koselleck as the attempt to resolve and unify moral and political action.

In the version by Stählin, the artistic director of the celebrations of Elizabeth's coronation, the act of clemency juxtaposes Brutus and Titus, presenting the latter, and thus the empress, as the paradigm of the sovereign capable of realizing the ideal of the Enlightenment and overcoming the conflict between the political and the private, moral spheres. It is difficult to imagine, however, that Stählin was unaware of how little such a representation corresponded to reality. Although the prologue alluded to the coup d'état, allegorized in the "joyful chorus of singers," it contained no reference to the way in which the empress came to

---

42   Marasinova, "Smertnaia kazn' i politicheskaia smert' v Rossii serediny XVIII veka," 53–69.
43   Giacomini, *De la purgazione de la tragedia*, 370–1. See Hoxby, *What Was Tragedy?* 180–1.

power and even less to how she demonstrated her clemency. On 18 January 1741, the day after the coup d'état, Elizabeth sentenced to death the enemies of the State who had ruled the country just the day before.[44] Even though, as mentioned above, Elizabeth's opponents – Ostermann, Münnich, and Löwenwolde – were eventually pardoned, they were nevertheless exiled to Siberia. The tsarina who had preceded Elizabeth to the throne, Anna Leopol'dovna, was spared public punishment, but was nevertheless imprisoned. The death sentence for opponents of the empress was thus replaced with a political death. It is clear that Elizabeth was not particularly lenient, but for Stählin, who was well aware of the function of the court spectacle, the task of staging the opera was an opportunity to win the favour of the empress, who was notoriously averse to the presence of foreigners at her court.

Kniazhnin's adaptation presents us with yet another response to the Enlightenment's dilemma about the possibility of merging moral actions and State interests, the public and the private, expressed once again in Titus's implicit reference to Brutus: "Быть подданных судья, ты меньше ль их отец?" (Does the fact that you are the judge of your subjects make you less their father?) (3.9, p. 108). Given that Catherine's clemency was by no means a retraction of the death penalty, but a powerful instrument of government and a supreme act of sovereign authority, Titus ends up no different from Brutus.[45] When Kniazhnin updates Catherine's portrait by representing her as a reformer in the legislative arena, he simultaneously shows that the Enlightenment dream of resolving the dialectical tensions between morality and politics was never even considered by Catherine, any more than it was by her predecessor. Ultimately, the playwright expresses the fundamental disillusionment of the eighteenth-century liberal Russian aristocracy with Enlightenment absolutism.[46]

---

44 Anisimov, *Afrodita u vlasti*, 134.
45 For an in-depth analysis of manifestations of sovereignty in rituals of punishment, see Ospovat, "The Catharsis of Prosecution," in *Dramatic Experience*, 189–219.
46 My analysis refutes the reflections by Elise Kimerling Wirtschafter that "[i]n eighteenth-century Russia, [by contrast,] absolute monarchy effectively coopted morality into politics, so that morality could serve as an instrument of reconciliation." See Wirtschafter, *The Play of Ideas in The Russian Enlightenment Theater*, 176.

8 Recognition Scenes: Handel's *Oreste*, Audience Reception, and Competition at the London Opera

ROBERT C. KETTERER

George Frederick Handel's *Oreste* (London 1734), based on the events in Euripides's *Iphigenia among the Taurians*, is a fascinating and unusual attempt to reimagine an extant Greek tragedy in the form of a late baroque opera. *Oreste* is not in Handel's canon of most-noticed operas for the reason that it is a pasticcio: its arias are taken from music previously composed for Handel's other dramas. Although the creation of a *self*-pasticcio was one of Handel's innovations in this piece, pasticcio operas in general run afoul of our expectation – inherited from the Romantics – that works of genius will be unique, original, and organic.[1] In addition, the conditions of the first performances of *Oreste* have compromised its being taken seriously as a work in its own right. Beginning with the treatises of André Dacier and extending into the nineteenth century to the operas of Richard Wagner and the scholarship of Ulrich von Wilamowitz-Moellendorf, Greek tragedy has been treated as a form that is in essence ritual, solemn, communal, and instructive. The motivations for creating *Oreste* were commercial, partisan, and promotional. Handel had found himself hard-pressed by the creation of a new, rival opera company, the Opera of the Nobility; he had lost his place at the Haymarket Theatre; and most of his star singers had gone over to the competition. He needed to remind London's audiences of his past achievements as a composer while programming an entire season of operas and oratorios that would have box office appeal and bring his audience to the Covent Garden Theatre, where he had set up his new

---

1 On our notion of the autonomous musical work as an invention of the early nineteenth century, see Goehr, *Imaginary Museum*; DeSimone, *Power of Pastiche*, 56–7 discusses pasticcio as a challenge to scholarly analysis because of "the puzzle piece assembled to create even just one work." For a critique of Goehr's denial that the "work concept" applies to the baroque period, see White, "If It's Baroque."

operation. *Oreste* was written for a brief run in early December. Perhaps as a result of apparent haste, the libretto for *Oreste* is so condensed from its Italian original that it can seem allusive to the point of obscurity.

Given all this, discussion of *Oreste* requires us, even more than usual, to adjust our perceptions to those of the opera's original audience. We will observe how this particular combination of classical drama and familiar music fit into Handel's programming of the Covent Garden season of 1734–5, and more generally, into the evolving sense of what tragedy was and what it might be used for in the context of the contemporary London theatre scene. I will argue that the original audiences of *Oreste* could be counted on to amplify for themselves the attenuated libretto with previous knowledge of the story: this knowledge arose less from familiarity with Euripides's original Greek tragedy than from what they knew of the story from other kinds of reading – Roman literature, encyclopedias of antiquity, journalistic references – and from their experiences of the Orestes narrative in the contemporary London theatre. My approach here is pragmatic: I ask what there was about the story of Orestes and Iphigenia that people would recognize and like, and how Handel and his production team exploited that knowledge and pleasure to keep them coming to Covent Garden. In the creation of *Oreste*, Handel was experimenting with ways to present his own music and his singers' abilities as a way to carry his new company forward in its competition with the Opera of the Nobility through the summer of 1735.

Programming for a Difficult Season: London 1734–5

In the 1720s, George Frederick Handel's Royal Academy of Music at the King's Theatre in the Haymarket had had a virtual monopoly on the production of Italian opera in London under the royal charter and patronage of the king. Beginning in the fall of 1733, that monopoly was challenged by a rival company, the Opera of the Nobility, that began to produce operas at Lincoln's Inn Fields under the patronage of Prince Frederick, son of George II and heir to the throne. At the end of the spring season of 1733, all but one of Handel's important singers, including the castrato *primo uomo* Senesino, had already decamped to the new company; only the soprano Anna Maria Strada del Pò remained with Handel's company. In June of that same year, over at the Drury Lane Theatre, there was an actor's secession (or strike) due to labour disputes. The two upsets were unconnected, but the result was that the London theatre scene was very unsettled in this period and the companies struggled to keep financially afloat and performing. Handel had to produce his 1733–4 season with a new troupe of singers, and then, his contract being up at the King's Theatre in the summer of 1734, he moved them to the newly built Covent Garden Theatre. There he produced opera and oratorios until fall 1737, when he returned to composing for the Haymarket Theatre under a new company.

This chaos nevertheless stimulated Handel to create some of his most varied and interesting seasons, especially in 1734–5, as he fought to maintain his position as the principal opera composer in London.[2] (See Figure 8.1.)

> *Il pastor fido* (Opera: revival, November)
> *Arianna in Creta* (Opera: revival, November)
> *Oreste* (Opera: pasticcio, December)
> *Ariodante* (Opera: premiere, January–February)
> *Esther* (Oratorio after Racine: revival, March)
> *Deborah* (Oratorio: revival, March)
> *Athalia* (Oratorio after Racine: London premiere, March–April)
> *Alcina* (Opera: premiere, April–July)

Figure 8.1. Handel's 1734–5 Season[3]

He drew on work from the recent years to produce two revivals, *Il Pastor Fido* with the ballet *Terpsicore* as its prologue, and *Arianna in Creta* (*Ariadne on Crete*); a pasticcio opera, *Oreste* (*Orestes*, the subject of this enquiry); and three biblical oratorios, *Deborah*, *Esther*, and *Athalaia*, which included new organ concertos he performed at their interludes. He also composed two new operas on stories from Ariosto, *Ariodante*, mounted in January of 1735, and *Alcina* that rounded out the season that ended in July. The choice to include successful productions from previous seasons to open in the fall of 1734 made sense, in part because Covent Garden had as one of its major attractions the sensational dancer Marie Sallé, who performed the ballets in *Terpsicore* and afterwards in *Oreste*. In the early spring, the triad of biblical pieces could command attention in the Lent and Easter seasons. The new operas *Ariodante* and *Alcina* ran opposite the winter and spring seasons at Lincoln's Inn Fields.

---

2 "It was a period of great competition and rivalry, but also a period of great stimulation" (Harris, *Librettos of Handel's Operas*, 7: xi). "Handel's 1734–35 Covent Garden season [was] one of the most attractive programmes that he ever mounted in London" (Burrows, *Handel*, 2: 242).
3 Burrows, *Handel*, 239–40; 521–2.

What, then, of the *Oreste*, produced in mid-December just as the Opera of the Nobility was running a version of Handel's own opera *Ottone*? *Oreste* received three performances, sandwiched between the revival of *Arianna in Creta* in November and December, and the premiere of his newly composed *Ariodante* in January of 1735. We are told by the periodical *The Bee* that their majesties were present at *Oreste* on 21 December and that the opera was received with great applause.[4] Superficially at least, as a "Greek tragedy" and a pasticcio opera, *Oreste* is a different animal and an outlier. It looks like a stop-gap, essentially a concert of Handel's recent hits, constructed to fill out the pre-Christmas season. That is what it was, but it was also produced at a time when Handel and his company could ill afford to squander energy and resources that would alienate its audience. It was a strategic pivot between the fall and the all-out competition of the spring. It is worth asking, Why this libretto to that music? How could it expect to attract attention? And what did it aim to accomplish?

Pasticcio Opera: Remixing the Familiar

A baroque *pasticcio* opera normally had a libretto text that was set with arias by several different composers, reused from previous compositions, and arranged as needed for dramatic expressions of rage, jealousy, erotic passion, and so forth.[5] The arias were arranged by a production team that could include agents, singers, writers, and a composer, sometimes a significant composer such as Handel. The directing composer usually wrote the recitative and might add some new arias or dance music as needed. Singers brought in their own special arias, sometimes called "suitcase arias," meant to show them at their best and to please the audience with famous numbers. To cite an example of the usual practice, Handel arranged a pasticcio on Metastasio's libretto *Catone in Utica* (*Cato in Utica*) in 1732 that included arias by Vivaldi, Hasse, Leo, Porpora, and Vinci.

The practice of producing pasticcios was widespread in Europe and, specifically for our purposes, in London, where it was a vehicle for the audience to hear not only their favourite tunes and singers but the latest musical fashions in continental operatic style. Italian opera in eighteenth-century London (as distinct from Purcell's semi-operas in the late seventeenth century) began with the production of pasticcios,

---

4 "The Bee," 21 December 1734. In Deutsch, *Handel*, 377. See a similar notice at Burrows, *Handel: Collected Documents*, v. 3: 38.

5 Price, "London Pasticcio."

and only after Handel's arrival in London were new single-composer Italian works regularly produced by the opera companies in the 1720s and 1730s. Handel himself, as the director of opera companies, was involved in the production of at least nine pasticcios for London between 1725 and 1737.[6] After Handel's generation, pasticcio operas once again became as much the practice as the exception in London for the rest of the century.[7] They could be ramshackle and sloppy, but, as one commentator put it, they could be quite successful unitary dramas, if "prepar'd by a Person that is capable of uniting different Styles so artfully as to make 'em pass for one."[8] The pasticcio was a familiar and regular operatic form that deserves discussion for the ways it channelled and adapted established librettos and music. What is more, it might be a medium for introducing new kinds of music and experimentation in form.[9]

In Handel's *Oreste*, however, we have a pasticcio of an original kind. Rather than showcasing other composers' arias, Handel set *Oreste* with music entirely from his own operas, drawing from compositions as early as *Agrippina*, written for Venice in 1709, and including numbers from nine of his subsequent operas produced in London.[10] He made no effort to disguise, from regular opera-goers at least, that this was recycled music. His point, in fact, seems to have been to encourage audience recognition of music composed for earlier operas as an act of self-promotion that was part of his competition with the rival Opera of the Nobility. Carlo Lanfossi has shown that audience familiarity with the music was already part of the pasticcio culture and practice in London, deriving from attendance at productions by the competing opera companies and from widely circulating print copies of operatic song collections.[11] The libretto of Handel's *Oreste* does not call the opera a pasticcio; the notices referred to it as a "new opera" – this, too, was

---

6 Roberts, "Pasticcio," 491–3.
7 On pasticcios in the early eighteenth century, Roberts, "Pasticcio," 491–2; Strohm, "Handel's Pasticci"; Price, "London Pasticcio," 17: "[I]t was the prevailing form of Italian opera in London from 1705 until the early years of the nineteenth century."
8 The quotation is from an anonymous *A Critical Discourse on Opera and Musick in England* (1709), cited by Price, "London Pasticcio," 18.
9 This was its purpose from its beginning in London: DeSimone, *Power of Pastiche,* 93–5.
10 Handel, *Oreste*, xxii; Landgraf, "*Oreste*," 466–7.
11 Lanfossi, *Handel as Arranger*, 200; 216: "The pasticci, traditionally viewed as a mere filler in-between the performances of 'real' operas, were instead a key strategy on behalf of the producers to showcase their soundscape of choice [.]" I am most grateful to Dr Lanfossi for sharing his work with me.

usual in the print culture surrounding the production of pasticcios, since "pasticcio" was not yet a term in general use for this dramatic format.[12] Nevertheless, the final chorus was the same as that in *Arianna*, which had performance runs twice that calendar year, and which audience members might have heard as recently as the previous week.[13] Handel newly composed some of the dance music at the end of all three acts, but he also used music from *Terpsicore*, a ballet that served as a prologue to a revival of *Il Pastor Fido* earlier that season. (See Figure 8.1.) The *Terpsicore* music had already been heard the previous spring, as had several of the important arias taken from *Sosarme*. Three of the arias came from Handel's *Ottone*, the opera that was currently being played by his rivals at Lincoln's Inn Fields with Handel's former and now estranged *primo uomo* Senesino in the cast.[14]

The Libretto: *Oreste* and the Orestes myth

The Italian libretto of *Oreste* was adapted for Handel's production anonymously from Giangualberto Barlocci's *Oreste*, produced in Rome in 1723 with music by Benedetto Micheli.[15] It may have attracted Handel partly because his new *primo uomo* Carestini had sung the role of Pilade in the 1723 Roman production and was already familiar with the opera.[16] Like Gluck's later *Iphigénie en Tauride*, *Oreste* was nominally based on the story in Euripides's *Iphigenia among the Taurians*. It is one of only three texts Handel set with a plot suggested by an extant Greek tragedy.[17] The other two were the 1727 *Admeto*, with a libretto loosely based on the story in Euripides's *Alcestis*, and the secular oratorio *Hercules* of 1744–45, more directly adapted from Sophocles's *Women of Trachis*. At first glance, it might appear that Handel – who wrote forty-two operas altogether between 1705 and 1740 – was not particularly attracted to librettos based on the classical Greek tragedies. In this

---

12 DeSimone, *Power of Pastiche*, 56.

13 The last three performances of *Arianna* were 4, 7, and 11 December. *Oreste* opened 18 December.

14 Lanfossi, *Handel as Arranger*, 200.

15 The librettist was probably Giacomo Rossi or Angelo Cori, but Handel may have had a hand in the libretto's creation. See Handel, *Oreste*, xxiii and note 40.

16 Handel, *Oreste*, xviii.

17 *Extant* is an operative word here. Plots involving Perseus and Andromeda, Theseus and Medea, or Bellerophon that had originally appeared in Greek tragedies that no longer survive were popular from the start of opera. Their sources tended to be retellings in later Greek and Roman sources such as Hyginus, Ovid, Apollodorus,

he was not unusual. If one looks at Handel's most important contemporaries, one finds that opera's long-standing claim to roots in Greek tragedy did not actually involve adapting those originals.[18] Scarlatti did not write any operas with subjects taken from Greek drama; Vivaldi composed one, *Ipermestra*, based on the Danaïd myth originally told by Aeschylus, although the particular episode of Hypermenstra's wedding night came from later retellings of a now-lost play. Bononcini composed one, an *Astianatte* (*Astyanax*), adapted from Racine's *Andromaque*, itself derived from Euripides's *Andromache*, about which more will be said below. The fact was that there were not that many librettos to be had that were based on the extant Greek tragedies. Again, to pick a few examples of notable librettists who were contemporary with Handel, the prolific Florentine librettist Antonio Salvi wrote only two librettos from Greek tragedy, the *Astianatte* and *Ipermestra* mentioned above. Pietro Metastasio wrote a single example, also an *Ipermestra*, but not until 1744. The subject continued to find an adapter in Calzabigi's *Ipermestra*, a deliberate response to Metastasio's, with a setting by Salieri titled *Les Danaïdes*, as Tessing Schneider describes in this volume. Apostolo Zeno, who preceded Metastasio as court poet in Vienna wrote only two such librettos, *Ifigenia in Aulide* and *Andromaca*. Handel's Greek tragic pieces, actually five in number if we count secular oratorios and add *Teseo* and *Semele*, which had been the subjects of now-lost Greek tragedies, amount to something like an enthusiasm for Greek tragic subjects in comparison with contemporary taste and practice. This may reflect the classicizing interests of his librettists Haym (*Teseo*, and perhaps *Admeto*), Broughton (*Hercules*), and Congreve (*Semele*), but the fact remains that Handel chose to set them, and we may tentatively suggest that, in addition to the legitimization effected by an appeal to the Greek tragic tradition, Handel's own personal taste factored into the choice of *Oreste* for the year's programming at Covent Garden.

Bernd Baselt, in the introduction to his critical edition of the opera, observes that "the central figure in the drama is no longer Iphigenia, the heroine of the classical legend, but the title figure Orestes." He suggests that "Handel transforms Orestes into a hero ready to meet any challenge

---

or Plutarch. Handel's *Teseo* (London, 1713) is one such case. There were originally *Aigeus* plays by Sophocles and Euripides on the same story, the details of which were reported in Plutarch's "Life of Theseus," Apollodorus, and Ovid. The story was used in Quinault's *Thésée* which was adapted for Handel by Nicola Haym.

18 See also the survey in Strohm, "Ancient Tragedy in Opera," 165–70.

and whose strong words are accompanied by equally strong action." Iphigenia has "maiden-like grace," and Hermione, sung by Handel's loyal *prima donna*, Anna Maria Strada, is a figure who displays "heroic mastery of blows of fate."[19] In contrast, Gerard Jones, director of a 2016 production of *Oreste* in London said, "All these people are awful. That's the starting point."[20] An examination of the literary and dramatic background suggests that Handel was using his audience's understanding of the story received from a variety of different sources to play in the grey areas between these extremes of heroism and awfulness.

That their understanding was based on a knowledge of Euripides's *Iphigenia among the Taurians* is true only in a very general sense. The opera tells a variation of a story that Euripides himself may have invented: that Artemis rescued Iphigenia from being sacrificed at the hands of her father Agamemnon at the Bay of Aulis and transported her to the land of the Taurians on the Black Sea. There she became a priestess in a cult of human sacrifice overseen by the Taurian king Thoas. Iphigenia very nearly sent Orestes to be sacrificed on Artemis's altar; at the last moment, brother and sister recognize one another and the plot is turned from threatened sacrifice to a rescue-drama.[21] Through a ruse perpetrated by Iphigenia, she, Orestes, and Pylades successfully escape with the cult statue of Artemis and try to sail away. They are almost recaptured by Thoas and his troops, but everyone is rescued at last by Athena, who arrives as *dea ex machina* to make peace with all parties, and to declare that the three Greeks will return home, where Iphigenia will become the focus of several local cults. Euripides's play, performed around 414 BCE, is itself a kind of pastiche of events and motifs taken from epic and previous tragedies written on Agamemnon and his dysfunctional family, arranged to take the whole tale a step further. It is also unusual, not so much because it ends happily, but because no one even gets seriously hurt in the process, and the enemy king remains in power. Iphigenia in fact explicitly rejects a suggestion by Orestes that they kill Thoas (Euripides, *Iphigenia among the Taurians*, lines 1020–4).

The play received notice from Aristotle in the *Poetics* (1454a7, 55a18) for the effective way in which it blended its *anagnorisis* (recognition) with its *peripeteia* (reversal) in an unusually lengthy central scene. Iphigenia, still unaware of who the two captives in her power are, resolves to save

---

19   Handel, *Oreste*, xxiii.
20   Ashley, "Compelling and revolting."
21   One of the best modern appreciations of the scene is still Burnett, *Catastrophe Survived*, 47–75.

one of them so he can take a letter back to Greece to her family. Orestes and Pylades, also unaware of who Iphigenia is, each argues he should die for the other, but ultimately it is decided that Pylades will return home. When Iphigenia reveals that the letter is to go to Orestes, Pylades simply hands the letter to his friend, and brother and sister are reunited.

The bare bones of this narrative were very familiar in late seventeenth- and early eighteenth-century England, but not necessarily because people were reading Euripides. The popular translations of the complete Greek tragedies by Pierre Brumoy were the main source of knowledge of Greek tragedy in the eighteenth century, but they did not begin to appear until 1730, with an English translation in 1759.[22] Most educated people would have known the story via the more familiar Latin retellings that altered the focus of the story in important ways.[23] Passages in Cicero's *De Amicitia* and Ovid's elegiac *Tristia* and *Letters from Pontus* emphasize the profound and faithful affection of the two men.[24] Ovid's language borders on the romantic, calling their love beautiful (*pulcher*) and wondrous (*mirus*). But Ovid also points out the inherent difficulty of heroizing a matricide and at the outset expresses doubt if Orestes as a character is reverent or criminal (*dubium pius an sceleratus Orestes*), leaving the character open to interpretation in subsequent versions of the story. Hyginus's *Fabulae* (120–2) and Lucian's *Toxaris* (6) add a further twist, perhaps based on a lost tragedy by Sophocles.[25] According to Hyginus, Thoas changed his mind and pursued Iphigenia and Orestes after they had left his kingdom, leading Orestes to kill Thoas.

Consequently, when filtered through these Latin and later Greek sources, by the early modern period the story had changed in some important ways. Pierre Gautruche in his late seventeenth-century *Poetical History* gives this summary:

> According to [Apollo's] advice, [Orestes] went [to the land of the Taurians] with his dear friend Pylades, the son of king Strophius, who had always lived with him, and run the same dangers, ... Orestes and Pylades were [caught by the Taurians and] taken and presented to Thoas the high

---

22   Brumoy, *Le Théâtre des Grecs*.
23   For a full treatment of the Latin tradition see Hall, *Adventures*, ch. 5, 92–110. Hall observes the latent theatricality of Ovid's poetic versions of the story (105–6). She also discusses Lucian *Erotes* 47 and Augustine *Confessions* 4.6, which suggest a homoerotic relationship between the two men (107–10).
24   Cicero, *De Amicitia*, 24; Ovid, *Epistulae ex Ponto*, 3.2.43–96; Ovid, *Tristia* 4.4.69–80.
25   On Lucian's *Toxaris*, see Hall, *Adventures*, 106–7.

priest, who commanded there as a sovereign prince. He condemned but one of the two to death, which caused a hot dispute between Orestes and Pylades, for either of them was willing to lay down his life to save his friend's. The lot fell upon Orestes, therefore he was given to the keeping of Iphigenia, who was the priestess of Diana. But it happened that she quickly knew and acknowledged her brother. Afterwards they resolved both to run away, and to free themselves from the eminent peril, by killing the inhumane butcher Thoas; which they found an opportunity to accomplish. At the same time Pylades came to them and they all three together fled away with speed, with the statue of Diana.[26]

An "Additional note" by Gautruche (232–3) adds, "After [Orestes's] return he caused his friend to take his dear sister Electra to wife. He afterwards married Hermione, the daughter of Helena for whom he stabb'd Pyrrhus, the son of Achilles, who had taken her by force. He was afterwards a very happy prince, and succeeded his father in the government of the kingdom of Argos." As in the Ciceronian and Ovidian sources, the long recognition scene in Euripides's *Iphigenia in Tauris* and Iphigenia's subsequent ruse to remove the statue – that is, almost three-quarters of Euripides's play – have disappeared from the received myth by the end of the seventeenth century, as has the rejection of murder as a solution to the Atreid curse. Iphigenia's objections to killing Thoas in the original tragedy were overridden by the subsequent narratives, and the sunny reconciliations at the end of Euripides's *IT* were exchanged for one final murder. For those who received the story, the Euripidean version was somehow too nice for its own genre. The important elements of the story became the sufferings of Orestes and his self-sacrificing friendship with Pylades; the Greeks' escape by the murder of King Thoas; and the inclusion of a double marriage of Pylades to Electra and Orestes to Hermione, the daughter of Helen and Menelaus.

In England, letters and essays in the popular press that refer to the story emphasized the faithful and self-sacrificing friendship between Orestes and Pylades. The *Plain Dealer* of 20 April 1724, observed:

There is nothing more talked of in the world and less easily found than friendship; everyone pretends to it, and not one in a million really possesses this noble passion which is the most generous that can actuate and adorn the soul of man. ... For want of authentick and real examples of

---

26 Gautruche, *Poetical Histories*, 231–2. Throughout I have modernized capitalization in the early-modern texts but kept original spelling.

this noble quality in the mind of man, so conducive to his happiness and pleasure as well as profit, the antient poets have had recourse to fiction, and told us stories of their fabulous Pylades and Orestes.

Most of these journalistic references take an uncritical view of the friendship, but there were also naysayers who found the story of Orestes and his friendship with Pylades morally objectionable. In an essay on the nature and virtue of gratitude in the *British Journal* of 5 March 1726, the writer opines,

> I think the story of Pylades and Orestes an ill moral. The latter had perpetrated the most horrible villainy in nature [Orestes's murder of his mother Clytemnestra] for which the gods had fixed a curse on him, yet his friend [Pylades] took his part and became accessory to the crime, by the succor and comfort which he ministered to the committer of it. ... Nor is the warrant of heaven to Orestes for doing that horrid act any argument in favor of his friend, at least in our times. *We* can never suppose that a supreme being, all-good and all-just should command an action, and punish the performance of it; so that what I said already must be true, that it is a bad moral, or else its theology will make no moral at all, nor of any use to us.

It was thus possible to see this relationship as something other than an emblem of ideal friendship and to observe the darkness in what had, after all, been part of the original story of madness and family violence.

The English baroque theatre also explored the Iphigenia and Orestes narrative from various points of view. Hall and Macintosh have discussed Iphigenia plays on the London stage in the previous two generations. These included plays by Charles Davenant (*Circe*, 1677, revived 1719), Abel Boyer (*Achilles; or, Iphigenia in Aulis*, 1699 or 1700), John Dennis (*Iphigenia*, 1699/1700), Racine (*Iphigénie*, 1722, performed in French), and Lewis Theobald (*Orestes*, 1731). Racine's and Boyer's plays are based on the sacrifice at Aulis. Davenant, Dennis, and Theobald wrote versions of *Iphigenia among the Taurians*. An observation by Dennis in his Preface to his *Iphigenia* may represent all three versions: "The *subject* that I chose in order to [effect] my design has been handled by several; yet the *fable or plot* is intirely [*sic*] my own." The result is that by this time the Euripidean original is very far in the background.[27]

---

27 This is not in itself an unusual practice in adapting Euripidean tragic themes. See Hoxby, *What Was Tragedy?*, 176–9, and more generally his chapter 4, "Operatic Discoveries," 162–99.

Lewis Theobald's 1731 *Orestes* is most relevant for an examination of what Handel's audience may have thought about the plot and characters of the Taurian story, since it is closest chronologically to Handel's *Oreste*. It was a semi-opera, which was an English form of theatre such as one finds in Henry Purcell's *Dioclesian* or *King Arthur*. Theobald's *Orestes* had a spoken text interspersed with songs, music, and dancing, sometimes relevant to the plot, sometimes not, and was not an entirely serious entertainment. In that respect at least, as Hall and Macintosh observe, it picked up on the more cheerful aspects of the Euripidean *Iphigenia among the Taurians*.[28] Its premiere was anticipated with interest in the London *Daily Journal* (15 March 1731): "We hear that there is now in rehearsal at the Theatre Royal in Lincoln's-Inn Fields, a new dramatick opera, call'd ORESTES, which is design'd to be performed in a few Days. And that the necessary preparations are making with the utmost dispatch for it, as the musick, cloaths, scenes, machines, and other decorations, are to be all entirely new."

In Theobald's version of the tale, the land of the "Tauric Scythia" is controlled by King Thoas, who is about to marry the enchantress Circe, here the Queen of Sarmatia, who was exiled for misbehaviour. He is served by Iphigenia, a captive who oversees the sacrificial cult of Diana, and with whom Thoas is actually in love. Orestes and Pylades appear, devoted friends as always, and at the right moment quarrel over which of them is to die in place of the other (3.2). Orestes's beloved wife Hermione, sent by Athena, also appears, anxious about the welfare of her wandering husband. Romantic entanglements multiply to the maximum possible confusion; marital fidelity and sexual jealousy abound. The Greeks finally escape, Circe having caused general mayhem and life-endangerment in the meantime. But in the final scene Circe, rather than Thoas, dies – and by her own hand. Thoas closes the play with a moralizing closing speech over her body. Theobald's *Orestes* played only three times in the spring of 1731, but it made enough of an impression that a tag from the play was quoted in the 6 June *Daily Courant* of that year to introduce a stern essay calling for civility in public political disputes.

One other contemporary drama that could have significantly coloured the way an audience viewed the characters in Handel's opera was Ambrose Philips's *The Distrest Mother*. This was a highly successful English translation of Racine's *Andromaque* that premiered in 1712 and played in London throughout the eighteenth century. The original

---

28 Hall and Macintosh, *Greek Tragedy*, 54, 59–60.

story here was in Euripides's *Andromache*, an anti-Spartan tragedy written in the 420s BCE. But by Racine's own admission, reproduced by Philips in his preface, the greater influence on *Andromaque* and thus on *The Distrest Mother* comes from book 3 of Virgil's *Aeneid*, where Aeneas meets Andromache at her new home in Greece. Philips's play is set in Epirus, where Achilles's son Pyrrhus is king and betrothed to Hermione, daughter of Helen and Menelaus. Hermione loves Pyrrhus, but his eye has wandered to Andromache, the widow of Hector, who along with her son Astyanax are captives in his court after the fall of Troy. Orestes and Pylades have arrived in Epirus, Orestes still persecuted by his mother's Furies, and for a long time in love with Hermione. *The Distrest Mother* opens with a reunion of Orestes and Pylades, who express their devotion again in passionate terms:

> ORESTES: O *Pylades*! What's life without a friend!
>   At sight of thee my gloomy soul clears up;
>   My hopes revive, and gladness dawns within me.
>   After an absence of six tedious moons,
>   How could I hope to find my *Pylades*,
>   My joy, my comfort! on this fatal shore?
>   Even in the court of *Pyrrhus*? in these realms,
>   These hated realms, so cross to all my wishes:
>   Oh, my brave friend! may no blind stroke of fate
>   Divide us more, and tear me from my self.
> PYLADES: O prince! O, my *Orestes* ! O, my friend–!
>   Thus let me speak the welcome of my heart. *[Embracing.]*

In the course of the play, Pyrrhus rejects Hermione and succeeds in forcing Andromache to marry him through a combination of threats and promises connected with her son; she submits, but plans suicide right after the wedding. The jealous Hermione in the meantime persuades Orestes to murder Pyrrhus for her at the marriage altar. Subsequent to the murder, Hermione goes mad from grief and kills herself; Orestes flees with Pylades, tormented by Furies of his mother *and* Pyrrhus, which leaves Andromache, now queen of Epirus, to restore order. It is a tragedy, surely enough, and it leaves Orestes and Hermione, both characters in the Iphigenia story as the eighteenth century knew it, with their reputations for rational or ethical behaviour damaged.

The Distrest Mother had eighty-four performances between its premiere in 1712 and the opening of Handel's *Orestes* in 1734, with twenty-one performances at Drury Lane and Goodman's Fields in the years

1729–34.[29] These performances included one staged at Goodman's Fields on 12 December 1734, six days before the opening of *Orestes* on the 18th; and another three that took place at Covent Garden in early January 1735. The familiarity of *The Distrest Mother*, I suggest, made it a more significant point of reference for Handel's theatre-going audience than either John Dennis's *Iphigenia*, which closed in 1700 for lack of funds, or even Theobald's, which assuredly made an impression but played only the three times. If the audience thought of Orestes, Pylades, or Hermione as dramatic figures, it was Philips's presentation of them that had likely made the most vivid impression. I will argue that the Ovidian-style tension between the noble friendship of the two men and the criminal, not to say homicidal, behaviour of Orestes in Philips's play, as well as the erratic and maddened figure of Hermione, played a role in Handel's dependence on audience recognition of those characters and their situation.

Filling in the Blanks: Reception as Participation

The cast of Handel's *Oreste* includes the title role (Oreste), Hermione (Ermione), Iphigenia (Ifigenia), Pylades (Pilade), Thoas (Toante), and a Taurian captain called Philoctetes (Filotete, not the character in Sophocles's play by that name). The opera includes the standard eighteenth-century preoccupations that we identified from Gautruche. Orestes plays a central role, sung originally by Handel's new primo uomo, the castrato Carestini; Orestes begins in madness but is subsequently characterized by a vigorous set of defiant arias. The friendship with Pylades, premiered by the new tenor sensation John Beard, emphasizes with striking arias the central scenes in which Pylades is taken away from Orestes. In the finale, brother and sister enact the famous recognition of one another, after which Thoas is killed in an offstage battle by Orestes and Pylades. As in Theobald's *Orestes*, Hermione is included in the cast, sung in fact by the prima donna, Strada, making the role central to the opera. She arrives early in the first act, searching for Orestes, is reunited with him by the end of act 2, and plays a crucial role in the recognition of Iphigenia and Orestes in the final scenes.

Recent scholarship has praised the opera for its compactness and vigorous forward movement of action, achieved in part by drastically cutting Barlocci's original Italian recitative. Bernd Baselt asserts that in Handel's version of the libretto "the action was propelled toward

---

29 Schneider, *Index to the London Stage*, 658.

the climax of act 3 with an urgency seldom found in Handel's London opera libretti."[30] That compactness and brevity of expression on the libretto page can nevertheless create obscurity of action, motivation, and emotional response.[31] Of course, a libretto is not the same thing as a fully developed script for spoken drama, even less so if it was to be sung for an anglophone audience with limited understanding of Italian. Dramatic connections and motivations had to be filled in by Handel's music and its interpretation by the singer-actor. Moreover, Burrows suggests that Handel's public was most interested in the singers and dancers and cared less about dramatic coherence or even the music.[32] But here is where audience recognition of the opera's forebears comes into play. Handel and his anonymous librettist relied on their audience's familiarity with the immediate literary and theatrical background we have just been observing.

Evidence for compression that depends on audience recognition of the dramatic situation appears at once in the printed libretto. "The Argument" reads in its entirety as follows:

> The Grecians, after a ten years siege, having conquer'd and destroy'd Troy, with the loss also of Agamemnon, who was killed by Aegisthus, paramour of Clitemnestra his wife, who possess'd the throne, contrary to the right of her son Orestes: He now being grown up not only to revenge his father's death, but also to recover his lost crown, kill'd Aegisthus, and his mother Clitemnestra. Thence it happen'd that Orestes, troubled by his remorse of his crimes, (having committed others) became mad, and at one time every day was cruelly tormented by the Furies; and not being able to find any remedy for his madness, he had recourse to the oracle, by which being answered, that he should become free, after he had been at Tauris expos'd for a sacrifice to Diana; Thither he goes, followed by Pylades, his most faithful friend.
>
> What follow'd, this drama shows.

This is condensed from Barlocci's *Argomento* in such a way that it effectively obscures the action to come instead of clarifying it. Handel's

---

30 Handel, *Oreste*, xxii; see also appreciations at Burrows, *Handel*, 183; Landgraf, "*Oreste*," 467; Hicks, "Orestes ('Oreste')." On the issue of dramatic coherence see the incisive summary by Strohm in his 1992 *Notes* review of Baselt's critical edition of *Oreste*.

31 The libretto of *Oreste* is not unique in this regard. Similar gaps occur, for example, in librettos Handel had set recently, such as the pasticcio opera *Arbace*, adapted from Metastasio's *Artaxerxes*, and the oratorios *Deborah* and *Athalia*.

32 Burrows, *Handel*, 246–7.

Argument cuts sentences from the original that explained the sacrifice of Iphigenia, the murder of Pyrrhus, and the marriage of Orestes and Hermione, events on which the action of this opera depend.[33] The focus is on Orestes, with a nod at the end to the famous friendship with Pylades. It identifies the action of the first scene in which Orestes appears solo, and that is all. It makes no mention of Iphigenia and Hermione, although these are characters played on stage by the seconda and prima donna, respectively. It is even slightly misleading if we take the phrase "follow'd by Pylades" to mean that he is with Orestes at the outset. If this is not simply haste or carelessness on the part of the adapter of the Argument, then it is a choice only to explain the place and reason for Orestes's opening lyrics, and to throw the burden of interpretation on the audience – a process enabled by the story's many versions and the composer's ability to play on the expectations of the audience.

Two scenes in act 1 demonstrate the process. Orestes appears solo in the first scene, and the Argument has adequately set us up for it; it is evidently the time of day that he is tormented by the Furies for his past crimes. (All English texts are taken from the printed libretto, rather than a literal translation from the Italian, because this gives the clearest idea of how the producer intended an English audience with limited Italian to receive the piece.[34] Italian text is provided where a comparison is helpful.)

A wood, sacred to Diana, with a statue. Orestes alone.
[*Lyric*] Away my thoughts; [*Pensieri, voi mi tormentate*]
You cloud the fair sereneness of my mind.
[*Recitative:*] O, thou chaste daughter of immortal Jove,
Give to my troubled breast required peace,
That since the heav'ns have promised it,
Their promise, and my hope, may not be false.
But are you still deaf to my ardent pray'r?
[*Accompanied recit*] Alas! I feel within the vengeful Furies,
They rend my heart; here raging madness burns.
O cease these wild emotions,
If you desire revenge, see, see, you have it,
I plunge myself in Lethe's deep recess.
(*Wearied by the tormenting Furies, he throws himself on a stone.*)

---

33 For a comparison of the Italian and English Arguments, see Handel, *Oreste*, xix.
34 The text is from the facsimile of the original 1734 libretto reproduced in Handel, *Oreste*, xxx–xxxix.

The opening two lyric lines, *Pensieri, voi mi tormentate* in Italian (literally, "My thoughts, you torment me") have a jerky rhythm in the strings that, combined with the piercing oboe that intertwines with the vocal line, serves as shorthand for the cries of a tormented soul. This is followed by recitative, first *secco* then *accompagnato*, explaining why his thoughts torment him, after which he falls asleep, exhausted, on a rock, to be discovered by Iphigenia. The lyric passage is from Handel's *Agrippina*, a work written for Venice nearly twenty years before; the aria was sung by Agrippina (soprano), who, after devising convoluted stratagems to put Nero on the throne, finds that her schemes have gotten out of her control and comes close to a nervous breakdown with her arioso, *Pensieri, voi me tormentate*. Handel used the idea again for his *Teseo* in London in 1713, as Medea contemplated her own torments. The passage identifies Orestes through his emblematic madness and sets the scene. It is an effective opening musically, plunging *in medias res*, and the audience can fill in the details from their common knowledge of the story they might find in Ovid or Gautruche. If they have seen or read *The Distrest Mother*, they have themselves observed Orestes accrue some of those Furies as alluded to in the Argument (Orestes, troubled by his remorse of his Crimes [having committed others]). Memory of the spoken play can help fill in the blanks, but it may also, at least temporarily, raise doubts about whether we are seeing this Orestes as a hero or a villain – the Ovidian *dubium pius an sceleratus* – an Orestes who will redeem himself, or one whose story, as the essayist in the *British Journal* complained, "has no moral at all."

Four scenes later, in act 1, scene 5, Hermione and Pylades appear. The scene is a "port of the sea, with ships." The sum of their lines is as follows. The English of the libretto reads:

> HER. [recit]: At length I've gain'd
> The long, and much desir'd coast of Tauris.
> Where heav'n has promised end to all my griefs.
> But where, my dear Orestes, where art thou?
> [Aria] I hop'd, my dearest spouse to have been bless'd
> With sight of thee, but all my hopes are vain.
> That comfort is deny'd, and I'm depriv'd
> Of him in whom my joys were plac'd.
> (Meets *Pylades*)
> PYL. [recit] O sorrowing Hermione, will you
> Ne're cease your plaints?

Who is Hermione? Why is she there? Where did Pylades come from? Did he arrive with Orestes? Why does he tell her to stop weeping?

Barlocci's Italian audience had a complete explanation in its *Argomento* and a subsequent scene with an aria by Pylades to fill in these blanks. In Handel, that is all the dialogue we get, for immediately after Pylades's question to Hermione, Philoctetes enters to arrest the two as foreigners who are liable to sacrifice.[35] Some of these puzzles are never answered in Handel's version, and perhaps they do not need to be. Nevertheless, a regular theatregoer could recognize the situation and understand it. The tradition reported in Hyginus and Gautruche had it that Hermione finally married Orestes. If audience members knew Theobald's *Orestes*, they knew that the gods had sent Hermione to find her husband; Hermione's line about her dear Orestes identifies her as the gentler and finally happy Hermione of Gautruche and Theobald, not the vengeful, maddened Hermione of *The Distrest Mother*. As to the presence of Pylades in this scene, the opening scene of *The Distrest Mother* (as quoted above) had set up the expectation that Pylades and Orestes in their travels might indeed have become separated and reunited.

From this point, Handel and his librettist continue to play with audience expectations of the story. Pylades, taken from Hermione in chains by Philoctetes and the Taurians, sings a resolute "Vado intrepido alla morte" (The view of death intrepid I can bear, / But to here leave thee is my chiefest care). The aria was originally from Handel's *Sosarme,* which had played the previous spring at the Haymarket with nearly the same cast as *Oreste.* For the moment, at least, Pylades's legendary devoted friendship with Orestes is transferred to Hermione, Orestes's wife. It marks her as an important character, who in the third act will in fact overshadow the importance of Pylades and Iphigenia herself. It will be Hermione, not Pylades, who effects the recognition of Orestes and Iphigenia. In that important role, she ends act 1 with a vigorously defiant aria, "Dite pace, fulminate," (You promise peace, you dart your lightnings down [also from *Sosarme*]), in which she complains that the heavens who promised her peace have abandoned her to the cruel attentions of Thoas. Though she began as the gentler Hermione from Theobald, Handel's music at the end of act 1 reveals her potential to become the fierce, aggressive character from *The Distrest Mother*, a role she will continue in subsequent arias, notably her vigorous, third act denunciation of Thoas in "Mostro disumanato! Non sempre invendicato / Si resterà il mio cor." (Inhuman monster! My heart will find out some means of full revenge.)

---

35 Handel, *Oreste*. xx.

Act 2 of *Oreste* invokes the famous friendship of Orestes and Pylades with three striking arias as the friends are united and then immediately separated. In the first scene of the act, Orestes discovers the captured Pylades at the temple of Diana (where, in act 1, Iphigenia had sent him to hide). Orestes attempts to free his friend, but is himself captured and put in chains as a consequence. Pylades is once again taken away and sings a lament of sad farewell; Orestes responds with a rage aria (*Oreste*, 2.7–8 in the libretto; numbers 18 and 19 in the score). It will be helpful here to compare the full versions in Italian and English in the libretto.

PILADE. Partir si deve. Ahi fiera,
    Partenza, che si rende a me piu atroce
    Sul pensier, che tu sei
    Per mia sola cagion condotto a morte.
ORESTE. Di questo viver mio faccia a sorte.
PILADE. [Aria] Caro amico, a morte io vò,
    E ti lascio qui dolente.
    Ne mai più ti rivedrò. [*parte*]
ORESTE. Ingiusti Numi, ancora,
    Delle sventure mie sazi non siete?
    [Aria] Un interrotto affetto?
    Un misero sospetto,
    Un disperato sdegno
    M'impiono il dolor,
    M'infiamman di furor
    Moro d'affanno.
    È la vergogna ancor
    M'avvampa di rossor.
    Morte di sazierà
    Fato tiranno.

PYLADES: And must we part, my friend?
    Ah, cruel task, but harder still to me,
    As I reflect that I'm the only cause
    Of your appointed doom.
ORESTES: It is the will of fate.
PYLADES: [Aria] Dear friend, to death I go,
    And leave you here in grief.
    I ne're shall see you more.
ORESTES: Ye powers! Must I be longer wretched?
    Have not I prov'd enough to appease your wrath?
    [Aria] An interrupted love,

Tort'ring jealousy,
Desperate disdain
Fill me with torments,
Inflame me with fury:
I dye with grief.
And guilty shame still adds
Its torture to my soul.
O tyrant Fate,
My death shall appease thee.

Handel took the music for Pylades's "Caro amico, a morte io vò" from his *Tamerlano*; the original aria was "Mia figlia non pianger, no" (My daughter, do not weep, do not). The captive prince Bajazet takes leave of his daughter as he is being sent to his death by the tyrannical Tamerlane. The situations are parallel, as Pylades is being sent to his death by Thoas, and apparently the passage suggested to Handel a sad parting appropriate to a loving, but not romantic, pair. Orestes's following aria "Un interrotto affetto" (literally, "An interrupted passion") is a different matter, and the words, if not the music, misfire slightly. The aria was originally from *Ottone,* which Handel had revived the previous fall in 1733, and which was staged again by the Nobility without Handel's involvement the week before the opening of *Oreste* in December 1734. The aria began "Un disprezzato affetto" (A rejected passion) and expressed the jealousy of a lover who thinks he has been jilted.[36] The word change from "disprezzato" in *Ottone* to "interrotto" suits the situation of the separated men in *Oreste,* but does nothing to alter the erotic charge of the words.

As we saw, both Ovid and Racine/Philips had used the language of love to describe the relationship between the two men, and there was an ancient tradition of homoeroticism attached to their story (see note 23). Handel's treatment need not imply a physical relationship: George Haggerty and others have shown that it was usual for English male homosocial relationships to be expressed in terms that sound erotic, but that in the eighteenth century signified a profound friendship of the kind aspired to by the English nobility and bourgeoisie.[37] Nevertheless, the words of "Un interrotto affetto" are inappropriate to the situation, even if we should suppose that Orestes and Pylades are lovers as well as friends, for Pylades is being taken off to death, not someone else's bed. The point here is better made not by the words but by Handel's

---

36 *Ottone,* Act 3, no. 28; see Handel, *Oreste,* 158.
37 Summarized at Haggerty, *Men in Love,* 15.

suitably angry music for Orestes's aria, punctuated by staccato quarter notes and abrupt rests between phrases that illuminate both Orestes's anger and the suddenness with which the reunion of the two men had been broken off. It may be, too, that in commandeering the music to create new meaning here, Handel was also expecting his audience to recognize this rage aria and his move to repossess the music and meaning from the production of *Ottone* playing concurrently at Lincoln's Inn.

Three scenes later, Orestes himself has been rescued from captivity by Iphigenia, who does not as yet know who he is, and he has a quiet moment to rejoice at his own release while expressing anxiety for his apparently doomed friend ("Dopo l'orrore / Di un cielo turbato," no. 22):

> After the gloomy horrors
> Of a troubled sky,
> More fair and pleasing
> The sun again appears.
> But this my breast
> Can ne're be fully blest
> If fate will force
> My dearest friend from me.

This sequence of arias, therefore, suggests that the threat to heroic male bonding will become the centre of dramatic interest. But this is a bait and switch. As we observed, Hermione has been waiting in the wings since act 1. Just after Orestes's "Dopo l'orrore" (After the gloomy horrors), he and Hermione reunite briefly and then are separated again by an enraged Thoas. They sing a lamenting duet taken from a similar situation in Handel's *Floridante*, and act 2 closes with their heartbreak as the focus of attention.

In the final scenes of the opera, Orestes still has not revealed his identity to Iphigenia or Thoas. Thoas wants to sacrifice both Greeks; Pylades and Orestes each offer to die for the other. Iphigenia finally recognizes Orestes through the agency of Hermione rather than Orestes, and reveals her own identity to Thoas as the daughter of Agamemnon. Thoas is ready to execute them all, but Philoctetes, out of love for Iphigenia, leads a revolt of the people against Thoas, and there are choral cries of "Die, tyrant, die." Thoas is pursued offstage and killed, presumably by Pylades, who returns to sing the triumph of the Taurians and their Greek guests with the aria "Del fasto dì quell' alma" (no. 35):

> We have gained the glorious victory
> The tyrant's fallen from his throne:

Our fame calls us to triumph
And raises its flight to the skies.

Orestes follows with a recitative declaring that the Taurians are now free of Thoas's oppressive rule and are in full possession of their liberties, but his final aria is a lilting celebration of his love for Hermione. The opera thus ends not only with the safe reunion of Hermione, Orestes, and Iphigenia: husband and wife, brother and sister; but also as a celebration of the overthrow of tyranny, as expressed most vigorously by Pylades. What began in the first scenes with allusions to the darker aspects of Orestes's life and the tragedy of Hermione in *Andromaque* and *The Distrest Mother* has concluded as the triumphal reunion of Orestes and Hermione. Pylades gets his moment of glory and then must defer to the reunited couple. Iphigenia herself fades into the background, matched finally with Philoctetes.

Thus the opera ends with Thoas's violent death, not as in Euripides, but as reported in the later sources and summaries. One might have thought, given the propensity of Italian serious opera to provide a happy ending even in instances where the received story ends badly, that this was the time to return to the source-play and retrieve the built-in happy ending of Euripides's *Iphigenia among the Taurians*, in which family units are restored and the villain forgiven. The Euripidean original is in point of fact more decorous than Handel's opera. Barlocci/Handel preferred a battle to the death, albeit offstage, and a subsequent triumphal celebration of the overthrow of tyrannical power. It is what André Dacier called a double catastrophe, "hereuse pour les bons, & funeste pour les méchans" (one fortunate for the good and deadly for the wicked).[38] To the extent that any baroque opera can do so, Handel's *Oreste* flirts with the fierce, *in*decorous instincts of the wilder Greek tragedies. It begins in madness and shattered family relationships, goes on to threaten the execution of human sacrifices, ends in the violent death of the villain, and indeed opens the door to a perspective on the whole as an "ill moral" enacted by "awful" people.

In this respect, *Oreste* reproduces the dramatic structures of Handel's own *Giulio Cesare* (London 1724), in which the lustful and unscrupulous Tolomeo is defeated by Caesar and Cleopatra, or of the young

---

38 Dacier, *Le poétique d'Aristote* [1692], 187. See also Hoxby, *What Was Tragedy?*, 179–87 on the Taurian story as a tragedy of "anticipated woe," which extends the discussion of the operatic Iphigenia to Gluck's *Iphigénie en Tauride*. In *Oreste* the woe of Hermione surpasses that of Iphigenia.

Metastasio's experiment in tragic death by suicide *Il Catone in Utica* (Rome 1727). Handel's *Oreste* is, to be sure, an experiment in pasticcio. But it is also one of a comparatively small number of baroque operas that look forward to a more violent and tragic form of opera that would develop in the later eighteenth century and carry on into the nineteenth. The balance and politesse of mature Metastasian *opera seria* that was to dominate the next generation of operas reflected mid-century distaste for tragic excess. The more violent world view was to emerge in a more pronounced way in the later eighteenth century in works like Gluck's *Iphigénie en Tauride* or Calzabigi's libretto *Ipermestra*.[39]

The opera *Oreste* was, in consequence, a shrewd strategic choice in Handel's battle with the rival opera company, striking a balance between retrospectives of his music and avant-garde dramatic trends to create a link between the autumn and winter–spring seasons at Covent Garden. As the analysis above attempts to show, Handel and his librettist were demanding a lot from the audience, playing a wide-ranging intertextual game with them, and expecting them to recognize the shared cultural knowledge of the story, derived from Latin literary sources, handbook information, journalistic references, and, especially, English stage adaptations. Not everyone would come with the same knowledge, of course: audience response is always as varied as the number of attendees. But ideas, impressions, and versions of the story of Orestes and Iphigenia were widely disseminated in the culture. Audience recognition of the characters, enhanced by their simultaneous recognition of the music that characterized those familiar dramatic figures, allowed Handel to cut the recitative to the bone and let his auditors fill in the blanks in their individual ways with what they had previously read and seen.

As an attention-getter, the opera was striking for a couple of reasons that we have noted already. Producing an operatic version of an extant "Greek tragedy" was not unique, but it was unusual. The title *Oreste*, which appears to shift focus from the original heroine Iphigenia to the long-suffering Orestes, would have for its London audience resonances of faithful friendship, but also, potentially, a frisson of horror at the background of madness and matricide depicted in the original *Oresteia* of Aeschylus and the *Orestes* of Euripides. However, it is only a frisson: unlike the Aeschylean-style horror that Schneider describes in Calzabigi's *Ipermestra* in this volume, the emphasis shifts in the course of

---

39 See chapter 9 for the contrasts between Metastasio's *Ipermestra* and Calzabigi's more
Aeschylean version of the same story.

the opera from the male drama of Orestes and Pylades to the heroism of the Euripidean-Racinian Hermione more familiar from *The Distrest Mother*. In this way, the opera connected with an ongoing English interest in Racinian tragedy, and so with Handel's spring oratorios *Esther* and *Athalia*, both of them based on Racine's biblical tragedies written with the Greek model in mind.[40]

Three operas of November, December, and January of 1734–5 – *Ariadne in Crete*, *Orestes*, and *Ariodante* – also form a unit. All three present distressed maidens (Ariadne, Hermione, and Genevra) who are the victims of male tyrants (Minos, Thoas, The Scottish King) ruling at the wild edges of the world (Crete, the Crimea, and Ariosto's version of Scotland). The contemporary term for this kind of drama about suffering women was she-tragedies, a term perhaps invented by Nicholas Rowe as early as 1714; this was a kind of serious drama that overtook the theatres as their audiences were becoming increasingly female.[41] She-tragedy itself was transforming in the 1730s into a sentimental tragedy that cared less about coherence of plot than about the pathos of its suffering heroines and heroes. In a musical drama, such a plot allowed for concentration on the music of the arias rather than on subtleties of plot and theme. As Brett and Haggerty have shown, Handel also made use of this sentimental turn in tragedy in his oratorio *Athalia*, which had its London premiere in the spring of 1735.[42]

Dulce ut *utile*

Eighteenth-century theorists held Greek tragedy to a high moral standard, famously adapting Horace's dictum from the *Ars poetica* that art should be *dulce et utile* (*both* pleasurable *and* useful). While the received tradition, described above, suggests that an audience member might see a lesson in the power of friendship of Orestes and Pylades, or the steadfastness of marital love of Hermione, the moral grounding of our story about a recovering matricide is problematic – "a very ill moral" in the eighteenth-century essayist's terms; "all these people are awful," in the words of the modern director – and, as was suggested above,

---

40 On Racine on the early modern English stage, see Hall and Macintosh, *Greek Tragedy*, 33–6.
41 For English she-tragedy and Euripides, see Hall and McIntosh, *Greek Tragedy*, 64–98, especially the overview at 64–70, and 78–9 on the female audience.
42 Hall and McIntosh, *Greek Tragedy*, 88–92; Brett and Haggerty, "Handel and the Sentimental," 117–19.

Handel and his librettist used the dramatic tradition and musical memory of the audience to toy with those problems. I have tried here to trace an aesthetic for *Oreste* to suggest that Handel was thinking in terms of the sweet *as* the useful. He and his librettist were engaging with the practical mechanics of reception and recognition to put a Greek-like tragedy on an eighteenth-century stage for purposes of programming and audience building.

I do not mean by that to suggest that the product was empty display – quite the opposite. Handel's audience apparently could play sophisticated games with both music and text, and to please them, even for an entertainment that ran for only three performances, his company had to provide something that would challenge and interest them. The statement in *The Bee* that the opera received "great applause" suggests he succeeded, although such a statement is not unusual in public notices like this, and perhaps is not a reliable indicator of public approval. Nevertheless, the production of *Oreste* evidently did get the attention of the Opera of the Nobility. The following May, they too produced a Greek tragic opera, an *Iphigenia in Aulis* with music by Porpora and starring Handel's former singers, which suggests that they hoped to imitate or surpass something that had been a successful experience at Covent Garden earlier in the season. Despite the short run of *Oreste*, the competition recognized that something had worked. So did Handel: the experiment of the self-pasticcio was successful enough that he repeated it twice more after his return to the King's Theatre in the Haymarket with his quasi-historical *Alessandro Severo* in 1738, and in 1739 with the mythological pastoral *Giove in Argo*.[43]

---

43 On the self-pasticcios, see Burrows, *Handel*, 543; Roberts, "Pasticcio," 493.

9 Terror and Intoxication: Calzabigi's *Ipermestra o Le Danaidi* (1778–1784)

MAGNUS TESSING SCHNEIDER

Few eighteenth-century opera librettos elicited such strong reactions as Ranieri Calzabigi's *Ipermestra o Le Danaidi*. Shortly after its publication in 1784, an anonymous Neapolitan critic, F.D.S., dismissed Calzabigi's *tragedia per musica* as "un estrema caricatura di spettacolo e di tragico senza economia, senza misura, incapace d'interessarci e di muoverci" (an extreme caricature of theatre and of the tragic, without economy, without measure, incapable of interesting or moving us).[1] According to a Tuscan critic, it was not a tragedy at all, in fact, but rather a "festa teatrale" that placed Calzabigi among those who ventured to "ridur l'Opera a vero spettacolo" (reduce opera to pure spectacle).[2] A Bolognese critic, Giambattista Alessandro Moreschi, found the work *too* tragic, however, describing it as

[...] componimento pieno di squallore, e di spaventosa melanconìa, e degno di essere paragonato alla tragedia del vecchio Eschile, nel quale al primo aprirsi della scena raccapricciarono così gli Ateniesi, che i Magistrati si velarono gli occhi, i giovani gridarono, le donne abortirono, e tutti furono atterrite vieppiù dal tumulto, dalla confusione, dallo strepito che nacque improvviso per lo spettacolo rappresentato.[3]

[...] a piece full of wretchedness and fearful melancholy, and worthy of comparison with the tragedy by the aging Aeschylus, in which the

---

1 "Lettera di F.D.S. ad un amico contenente un giudizio sull'*Ipermestra,* tragedia per musica di Ranieri Calsabigi" (March 1784), in Tufano, *I viaggi di Orfeo,* 112–25 at 124–5. All translations are the author's unless otherwise stated. As for the spelling of the poet's name, I follow current standard by using the form "Ranieri Calzabigi," rather than the form widespread in the eighteenth century, "Ranieri (de') Calsabigi."
2 *Novelle letterarie pubblicate in Firenze,* 15.xxii (28 May 1784): 348–9.
3 Moreschi, "Osservazioni sopra l'*Ipermestra,*" 141.

opening scene so horrified the Athenians that the magistrates covered their eyes, the young people screamed, women miscarried, and everyone was increasingly terrified by the tumult, the confusion, and the clamour unexpectedly caused by the performance.

The Spanish Jesuit Esteban de Arteaga accused Calzabigi of abandoning himself to the maxim attributed to Voltaire, "frappez plutôt fort que juste" (strike hard rather than exactly), consequently denouncing him as "uno de' principali corruttori del moderno musicale teatro" (one of the main corruptors of modern musical theatre).[4] And the influential Neapolitan critic and historian Pietro Napoli-Signorelli never tired of rejoicing in the failure of Calzabigi's "sconnesse ed improprie" (incoherent and improper) *Danaidi* ever to reach the stage.[5]

Calzabigi's tragic libretto also had its defenders, however. Another Tuscan critic reproached the "freddi pedanti ragionatori" (cold, pedantic reasoners) for being too distracted by their poetic rules to appreciate the "mille situazioni spettacolose, tenere, terribili, tetre e tratte dalle viscere della favola" (thousand spectacular, tender, terrible, and sombre situations, drawn from the bowels of the fable), which "tengono in grandissima agitazione le anime sensibili" (keep sensitive souls in the greatest agitation).[6] The Venetian playwright Count Alessandro Pepoli, who credited Calzabigi with reinventing Greek tragedy, praised *Ipermestra* – this work of a "genio robusto" (sturdy genius) – for its "situazioni nuove e sublime" (novel and sublime situations); and in 1790, Calzabigi himself published a lengthy response to Arteaga's criticism.[7]

Common to those criticizing the tragic libretto was a faithful adherence to the dramaturgical principles of the late imperial court poet Pietro Metastasio, the century's most celebrated author of tragic librettos, whose hegemonic status Calzabigi had dared to challenge, first with his librettos for Christoph Willibald Gluck's three Viennese "reform" operas, and now with *Ipermestra*. They were especially repelled by the

---

4 Arteaga, *Le rivoluzioni del teatro musicale italiano*, 3 (1785): 123, 125.
5 Napoli-Signorelli, *Elementi di poesia drammatica*, 122. Other references to Calzabigi's *Ipermestra* by Napoli-Signorelli are found in *Storia critica de' teatri antichi e moderni*, 6 (1790): 287–8; "Discorso sopra varie tragedie di Agamennone," 121; *Addizioni alla Storia critica*, 343n1; *Vicende della coltura nelle due Sicilie*, 7 (1811): 279; "Ricerche sul sistema melodrammatico," 61; *Storia critica*, revised edition, 10.II: 172–3.
6 *Giornale de' letterati*, 53 (1784): 279–80.
7 Pepoli, "Lettera ad un uomo ragionevole," 21; "Risposta che ritrovò casualmente nella gran città di Napoli il Licenziato Don Santigliano di Gilblas y Guzman y Tormes y Alfarace" (1790), in Calzabigi, *Scritti teatrali e letterari*, 2: 360–550 at 420–40.

scenes of horror and violence, as forty-nine of King Danao's daughters massacre their bridegrooms on the wedding night, and are later shown suffering the torments of hell. Other points of contention, however, were the dependence on dance and stage machinery, the sexual allusions, the subversive political meanings, and the use of mythological rather than historical subject matter for a tragedy. To its critics, Calzabigi's *Ipermestra* marked a regression to the extravagant tastes of the seventeenth century, while its radical features were ignored or misunderstood. Hence, the libretto and its early reception offer rich insights into conflicting views of tragic opera during the late Enlightenment.

A Neapolitan tragedy

Calzabigi probably first got inspired to write an opera about Hypermnestra and the Danaids after attending the Viennese premiere of Jean-Georges Noverre's tragic ballet *Hypermnestre* in 1769. This innovative work, originally produced in Stuttgart in 1764 with music by Johann Joseph Rudolph, culminated with a massacre scene that the Italian poet would later emulate: the sons of Égyptus are heard screaming behind the curtain as the Danaïdes attack them, after which the audience beholds the horrifying tableau of the murdered bridegrooms.[8] Noverre later wrote of the performance in Vienna:

> Cette représentation fit une telle impression sur une partie du peuple, qu'en voyant les Danaïdes, les spectres, la mort et les parques, elle prit la fuite. Deux poëtes Italiens, au service de deux souverains, vinrent me complimenter; le coeur ému, et les yeux encore baignés de larmes; ils me dirent: vous êtes aujourd'hui le Schakespéar de votre art, vous êtes cruel, et pour sécher nos pleurs, vous auriez du terminer votre ballet par une jolie contredanse. Ce conseil bizarre donné par deux hommes spirituels mais vivement affectés me persuada que je ne pouvoir recevoir une éloge plus flatteur.[9]

That performance made such an impression on a part of the audience that they took flight at the sight of the Danaïdes, the Spectres, Death and the Fates. Two Italian poets in the two sovereigns' service came to compliment me. Their hearts moved and their eyes still bathed in tears, they said to me: "You are the Shakespeare of your art today! You are cruel – and to dry our

---

8 On Noverre's *Hypermnestre*, see Brandenburg, "Hypermnestra und die Danaiden," 150–7; Dotlačilová, *Costume in the Time of Reforms*, 262–71.

9 Noverre, *Lettres sur la danse, sur les ballets et les arts*, 2 (1803): 165.

tears you should have ended your ballet with a pretty contredanse." This bizarre advice given by two witty but deeply affected men persuaded me that I could not have received a more flattering eulogy.

No doubt the two Italian poets were Calzabigi and his fellow Livornian and former protégé Marco Coltellini, both of whom were in the service of Empress Maria Theresa and Emperor Joseph II in 1769, and both of whom were committed to reforming Italian tragic opera.[10]

Ipermestra o Le Danaidi did not materialize until several years later, however. Calzabigi wrote it in Pisa in 1778, not long after completing his *Semiramide*, which has not survived.[11] Like the earlier libretto, *Ipermestra* was written for Gluck who had found *Semiramide* ill-suited to the intended performers, after which Calzabigi returned to his old idea of a Hypermnestra tragedy, the manuscript of which he sent to the composer in November.[12] It is not known for which theatre the opera was conceived, but Marina Mayrhofer suggests that it may have been intended for Gluck's planned visit to Naples.[13] At some point before the fall of 1780, the composer had been invited to mount four of his operas – apparently all on librettos by Calzabigi – before the Neapolitan court, which the poet hoped might revolutionize tragic opera in Italy.[14] The plans were cancelled, however, after the death of Maria Theresa on 29 November 1780. It was probably then that Gluck, without consulting Calzabigi, had two of his French librettists, Baron Jean-Baptiste-Louis-Théodore de Tschudi and François-Louis Gand Le Bland Du Roullet, turn *Ipermestra* into a *tragédie lyrique*, which was offered to the Académie Royale de Musique. Fatigued by illness, however, the aging composer eventually gave up work on this opera, and turned the French libretto over to his pupil Antonio Salieri who completed the score under his

---

10   Noverre himself admitted that the offstage chorus in *Hypermnestre* was partly inspired by his work on Gluck's and Calzabigi's *Alceste* in 1767, for which he had choreographed the ballets; see ibid., 2: 161.

11   See Calzabigi's letter to Antonio Montefani of 31 July 1778, in Ricci, *I teatri di Bologna*, 640.

12   "Lettre au Rédacteur du *Mercure*" (25 June 1784), in Calzabigi, *Scritti teatrali e letterari*, 1: 257–67 at 258.

13   Mayrhofer, *Relazioni elettive*, 25–6. Brandenburg suggests, on the other hand, that the two librettos were originally intended for Paris; see "Hypermnestra und die Danaiden," 157–8. In that case, however, it would seem illogical for Gluck to commission an Italian libretto; Calzabigi should have been less surprised than he was by his decision to have it translated into French.

14   See Calzabigi's letter to Prince Wenzel Anton von Kaunitz-Rietberg of 9 September 1780, quoted in Croll, "Gluck, Wien und Neapel," 42–3.

supervision.[15] As *Les Danaïdes*, it was finally premiered on 26 April 1784 at the Paris Opéra where it became one of Salieri's most enduring successes.[16] Calzabigi, who had only heard of Salieri's opera in February of that year, wrote an angry letter to *Mercure de France*, in which he chided Du Roullet for downplaying its indebtedness to his *Ipermestra*. He also used the occasion to respond to a long review of Salieri's opera in the same journal, arguing that any dramaturgical weaknesses were attributable to the French adaptation and not to the Italian original.

In 1783, before hearing of *Les Danaïdes*, Calzabigi had persuaded the famous castrato singer Giuseppe Millico to set *Ipermestra* to music in accordance with his own principles of dramatic declamation, probably after realizing that Gluck was never going to do it.[17] A performer closely associated with the works of Gluck and Calzabigi, Millico may have been involved in the private Neapolitan productions of their operas *Paride ed Elena* (1770) and *Alceste* (1767) in 1777 and 1779, but it was probably his own opera, *La pietà d'amore*, which made Calzabigi ask him to set *Ipermestra*.[18] In his preface to that opera (signed 15 June 1782), Millico had declared allegiance to the principles of the Gluck-Calzabigi reform, referring to his own experience of singing the male lead in *Orfeo ed Euridice* (1762) in Parma in 1769 under Gluck's direction.[19] As Irene Brandenburg has observed, the financial independence of the star singer would also have allowed him to engage in musical experiments without caring too much about prevailing Neapolitan tastes.[20]

Millico's score for *Ipermestra*, which he finished toward the end of the year, was written in the style of the Viennese reform operas: the music enhances the passions expressed by the poetry and the dramatic situations, providing contrasts of light and shade; the overture sets the mood for the action of the drama; the difference between recitative and closed numbers is diminished; and dramatically superfluous repetitions

---

15 On the genesis of *Les Danaïdes*, see Mayrhofer, *Relazioni elettive*, 26–9.

16 According to Ewans, it was performed 127 times at the Paris Opéra between 1784 and 1828; see "Aeschylus and Opera," 207.

17 Calzabigi, "Lettre au Rédacteur du *Mercure*," 259, 266.

18 On Millico's appearance in *Paride ed Elena*, in which he created the role of Paride, see my article "The Judgement of Rousseau," 257–8, 263. On his possible involvement in the Neapolitan Gluck premieres, see my article "A Song of Other Times," 39, 46n60. As I show here, Millico had already come to Naples in the spring of 1777, not, as usually claimed, in 1780.

19 Millico's preface to *La pietà d'amore* is reproduced in Brandenburg, *Vito Giuseppe Millico*, 94–8. For a recent essay on Neapolitan opera reforms, with a special focus on *La pietà d'amore*, see DelDonna, "Tradition, Innovation, and Experimentation."

20 Brandenburg, *Vito Giuseppe Millico*, 109.

and ornaments are avoided.[21] After hearing some of the numbers around Naples, the Russian ambassador, Count Andrey Kirillovich Razumovsky, decided to have selected arias performed at his house in honour of Prince Charles of Taranto, the brother of King Ferdinand IV of Naples (and himself the future King Charles IV of Spain). When the court got news of this, the concert was repeated at the Royal Palace at Caserta.[22] According to a report from December, the work "ha avuto il più grande incontro e si spera, che questo introdurrà un nuovo gusto tanto ne' Drammi, che nella Musica Teatrale" (had the greatest success, and it is hoped that it will introduce a new taste in drama as well as in theatrical music).[23] On 7 January, the concert was given once more, at the Court Theatre in the city, before two of Queen Maria Carolina's visiting siblings: Joseph II and Duchess Maria Amalia of Parma.[24] All three of them would have known *Orfeo ed Euridice* and *Alceste* from their youth in Vienna. According to Calzabigi, the audience found Millico's music "admirable."[25] On 1 March, *Ipermestra* was finally performed "presque en entire" (almost in its entirety) before King Gustav III of Sweden at Razumovsky's house.[26] On this occasion, Calzabigi and Millico were asked to write a celebratory prologue for the opera in honour of the Swedish king: they complied and wrote the cantata *Gli Elisi o sia L'ombre degli eroi* (Elysium, or The Shades of the Heroes).[27] Both the poetry and the music of *Ipermestra* witnessed a "succes étonnant" (an astonishing

---

21   These are the principles outlined in the preface to the printed score of *Alceste* (1769), written by Calzabigi but signed by Gluck; see Howard, *Gluck*, 84–5. See also Hoxby's discussion of the *Alceste* preface in the introduction to this volume. Two copies of the score for Millico's *Ipermestra* survive: one is held by the Biblioteca del Conservatorio di musica Luigi Cherubini in Florence, and one by the Bibliothèque nationale de France in Paris. In addition, two separate copies of Ipermestra's grand solo scene in 2.3 survive: one is held by Musik- och teaterbiblioteket in Stockholm and one by the Music Library of Western University in London, Ontario, which also holds a copy of Linceo's and Ipermestra's recitative and duettino from 1.1.

22   See Calzabigi's letter to Kaunitz of 10 March 1784, quoted in Brandenburg, *Vito Giuseppe Millico*, 110.

23   Archivio di Stato di Modena, Cancelleria Ducale: Avvisi e notizie dall'estero, no. 89, quoted in Lattanzi, "Vita musicale a Napoli," 422.

24   Prota-Giurleo, "Breve storia del teatro di corte," 143.

25   Calzabigi, "Lettre au Rédacteur du *Mercure*," in *Scritti teatrali e letterari*, 1: 259.

26   Calzabigi's letter to Kaunitz of 10 March 1784, in Brandenburg, *Vito Giuseppe Millico*, 110.

27   For a study of this cantata and a modern edition of the libretto, see Tufano, *I viaggi di Orfeo*, 139–81. In 2016, I located the full score for *Gli Elisi*, which for a long time was considered lost, at Musik- och teaterbiblioteket in Stockholm where it received its modern premiere on 1 June 2018, at Ulriksdal Palace Theatre.

success) this time, the poet wrote.[28] This was confirmed by the king's private secretary, Gudmund Göran Adlerbeth, who left the following description in his travel journal:

> Jag fann den förträfflig och af en originell smak, som gjorde det djupaste intryck. Ouverturen var ett mästerstycke och beredda åhörarna genast till den häpenhet och sinnesrörelse, som i detta dystra, men högt stämda teaterstycke framgent underhöllos.[29]

> I found [the music] excellent and of an original taste, which made the deepest impression. The overture was a masterpiece and immediately prepared the listeners for that awe and commotion, which is constantly maintained in this gloomy but lofty play.

F.D.S. also found Millico's composition "eccellente," though he could not understand how it was possible to write beautiful music for such a horrific libretto.[30] It was for this occasion, furthermore, on which *Ipermestra* was sung by "les meilleures voix de notre grand opéra" (the best voices of our grand opera house), that Calzabigi had the libretto printed.[31] The Royal Theater Deputation now proposed to King Ferdinand that *Ipermestra* receive its premiere at the Teatro di San Carlo on 13 August 1785, since "uno Spettacolo totalmente diverso dai soliti" (a spectacle totally different from the usual ones) was bound to please both the court and the general public.[32] Due to the difficulty of finding choristers for the production, however, the premiere was postponed till 4 November, and eventually it was cancelled altogether. Millico had insisted that *Ipermestra* required a mixed chorus of forty adult professionals and three to four months of rehearsals, the expenses for which

---

28 Calzabigi's letter to Kaunitz of 10 March 1784, in Brandenburg, *Vito Giuseppe Millico*, 110.
29 Letter 44 (2 March 1784), in Adlerbeth, *Gustaf III:s resa i Italien*.
30 F.D.S., "Lettera ad un amico," in Tufano, *I viaggi di Orfeo*, 125.
31 Calzabigi, "Lettre au Rédacteur du *Mercure*," in *Scritti teatrali e letterari*, 1: 259. The leading singers of the San Carlo in the 1784 Carnival were the soprano Marina Balducci, the tenor Domenico Mombelli, and the soprano castrato Francesco Roncaglia, while Antonia Rubinacci, as the *terza donna*, always appeared in trouser roles; see Sartori, *I libretti italiani a stampa*, nos. 339, 9988. Probably, these were the singers who sang the roles of Ipermestra, Danao, Linceo and Pelasgo on 1 March. Very likely, the singers of Ipermestra and Linceo would also have sung the roles of Ombra di Cristina and Ombra di Gustavo Vasa in *Gli Elisi*, both of which are written for sopranos.
32 Quoted from Prota-Giurleo, *La grande orchestra*, 44.

the theatre management found excessive.[33] So far, the opera has never been performed on a public stage.

Aeschylean or Baroque?

If Calzabigi's tragic librettos *Semiramide* and *Ipermestra* were written for Naples, it may be no coincidence that they shared their titles with two librettos by Metastasio, from 1729 and 1744, respectively, both of which had been performed in new settings at the San Carlo in recent years: *Ipermestra* by Niccolò Piccinni, which had premiered in 1772, and *Semiramide riconosciuta* by Pietro Alessandro Guglielmi, which had premiered in 1776.[34] As Paolo D'Achille has argued in his recent comparison of librettos based on the Hypermnestra myth, Calzabigi seems to have deliberately sought a comparison with the older poet.[35] In both operas, he apparently aimed to expose the weaknesses of Metastasio's mythological dramas by treating the same subjects more in the manner of the Greeks. In doing so, he returned to the approach he had followed with his adaptation of Euripides's *Alcestis*: basing opera librettos directly on ancient Greek models rather than on Senecan or French adaptations or imitations, the standard approach of eighteenth-century librettists.[36]

In *Semiramide*, "terrore" was as prominent as "compassione" had been in *Alceste*, Calzabigi observed.[37] And whereas terror, which Aristotle highlights as a central aspect of tragedy, is basically absent from Metastasian drama, it is prominent in Calzabigi's *Ipermestra*. Although Calzabigi may have drawn inspiration from Hypermnestra's letter in Ovid's *Heroides*, as Sarah Brown Ferrario argues (the *Double Heroides* were the main source, indeed, for his *Paride ed Elena*), his tragic libretto specifically invokes the theatre of Aeschylus: the only one of the three Greek tragedians who

---

33 See Millico's letter to the Royal Theater Deputation of 22 June 1785, in Prota-Giurleo, *La grande orchestra*, 45–6. Napoli-Signorelli claimed that it would have cost no less than 15,000 *scudi*; see *Elementi di poesia drammatica*, 122.

34 Sartori, *I libretti italiani a stampa*, nos. 13604, 21589.

35 D'Achille, "Variazioni linguistiche," 244. Giovanni De Gamerra suggested, however, that *Semiramide* was modelled on Voltaire's tragedy *Sémiramis* (1748); see *La Corneide*, 7: 146n25.

36 Napolitano, "Greek Tragedy and Opera," 37. Apart from Calzabigi's *Alceste*, one of the few exceptions was Coltellini's Sophoclean *Antigona*, which premiered in St. Petersburg in 1772 with music by Tommaso Traetta. In his contribution to this volume, Ketterer discusses the complex relationship between Euripides's *Iphigenia among the Taurians* and George Frideric Handel's *Oreste* from 1734, which is not, strictly speaking, an adaptation of the Greek tragedy.

37 Letter to Montefani of 1 May 1778, in Ricci, *I teatri di Bologna*, 634.

had not yet been adapted for the operatic stage.[38] Aeschylus's *Suppliants* treats an earlier episode of the myth of the Danaids: the arrival of Danaus and his daughters to Argos. But he also wrote a lost tragedy, the *Danaids*, which was the final play of the trilogy, preceded by the *Suppliants* and the *Egyptians*. Notably, not until 1952 did scholars establish that these tragedies were sequential, with the *Egyptians* portraying the massacre and the *Danaids* revealing its aftermath.[39] Whether or not Calzabigi was aware of the titles of the lost tragedies, his *Ipermestra* functions as a sequel to the *Suppliants*, as pointed out by Michael Ewans who (albeit referring to the French adaptation of the libretto) argues that the manipulative and tyrannical character of the operatic king and the wild maenadic behaviour of his daughters are indebted to their portrayal in the Aeschylean tragedy.[40] It is noteworthy, too, that the latter features King Pelasgus of Argos, a character absent from later dramatic adaptations of the myth before Calzabigi's, in which he appears as Danao's officer, Pelasgo. But perhaps Calzabigi's most significant debt to Aeschylus is the emphasis on terror, a fact not lost on Moreschi who, in one of the quotations produced in the beginning, was reminded of the horrifying performance of the *Eumenides* described by the ancients.

Calzabigi's interest in Aeschylus was uncommon at the time. From the Renaissance until the nineteenth century, the oldest of the Greek tragedians was also the least popular: he was translated into the vernacular languages much later than the two others, and French playwrights nearly always turned to Sophocles, Euripides, and, especially, Seneca when writing tragedies on classical models.[41] It was only in the Romantic age that readers and playwrights generally began to appreciate the Aeschylean universe, which has been characterized as "a world at once remote and exotic, yet primal in its evocation of the struggle of male and female, its enactment of terror, cunning, and lust, its insistence on

---

38 Ferrario, "Aeschylus and Western Opera," 189–90. Susanna Phillippo suggests that Joseph de La Grange-Chancel's libretto *Cassandre* for Toussaint Bertin de la Doué and François Bouvard (Paris, 1706) might be an adaptation of Aeschylus' *Agamemnon*; see "Clytemnestra's Ghost," 77. However, according to Girdlestone, this libretto is heavily indebted to Seneca's *Agamemnon* and to Claude Boyer's 1666 tragedy *Agamemnon*; see *La tragédie en musique*, 161–2.

39 See Winnington-Ingram, "The Danaid Trilogy of Aeschylus."

40 Ewans, "Aeschylus and Opera," 206, 208–9n5–6.

41 While translations of Sophoclean and Euripidean tragedies were available in Spanish, French, English, and Italian by the end of the sixteenth century, there were no vernacular versions of Aeschylus before the seventeenth century; see Burian, "Tragedy Adapted for Stages and Screens," 229–30.

the presence of the sacred in the world," featuring "a skeletal but gripping drama of civic crisis, of ideologies in conflict and clashing forms of power."[42] With his lyric tragedy *Prometheus Unbound* (1820), for example, Percy Bysshe Shelley wrote a sequel to *Prometheus Bound*, corresponding to the lost second part of the pseudo-Aeschylean trilogy *Prometheia*, just as Calzabigi's libretto corresponds to the lost sequels to the *Suppliants*. Victor Hugo invoked the name of Aeschylus in the preface to his trilogy *Les Burgraves* (1843), later comparing his own position as the originator of a new form of theatre to that of Aeschylus.[43] And it was Richard Wagner's reading of the *Oresteia*, the only surviving Greek trilogy, in 1847 that inspired him to create a stage festival modelled on the ancient Dionysia. In Ewans's view, in fact, the most important operatic works with a relationship to Aeschylus before Sergey Taneyev's *Oresteia* (St. Petersburg, 1895) are Wagner's massive tetralogy *Der Ring des Nibelungen* (Bayreuth, 1876) and Salieri's *Les Danaïdes* – derived, of course, from Calzabigi's libretto.[44]

Like Hugo more than half a century later, Calzabigi was fascinated with Aeschylus as the original tragedian. Establishing the first permanent theatre, Calzabigi wrote, Aeschylus had introduced the practice of creating theatrical effects while leaving the refinement of the art to his successors. He was "assai meno perito" (much less skilled) than those who followed, but just as the rough and majestic Pierre Corneille "formò" (trained) the elegant Jean Racine who then trained Prosper Jolyot de Crébillon and Voltaire, Aeschylus had trained Sophocles who then trained Euripides.[45] In England, notably, a similar position was held by the crude and sublime William Shakespeare, "l'Eschilo inglese" (the English Aeschylus), though he lacked successors to rival his position:

ancora vi signoreggia, ancora spaventa, ancora fa arricciare i capelli agli spettatori, a dispetto d'essersi e ripuliti e istruiti, perché quando questo singolar Poeta intende di spaventare, distrugge colle sue fiere, strette, vibrate espressioni ogni prevenzione, ogni difesa.[46]

[Shakespeare] still commands [the English stage]; he still terrifies and still makes the hair of the spectators stand on end, although they have been

---

42 Burian in the introduction to Aeschylus, *The Suppliants*, xi–xii.
43 Dudouyt, "The Reception of Greek Theater in France since 1700," 245.
44 Ewans, "Aeschylus and Opera," 205–6.
45 Calzabigi, "Risposta che ritrovò casualmente," 476; and "Lettera al Signor Conte Vittorio Alfieri sulle quattro sue prime tragedie" (20 August 1783), in *Scritti teatrali e letterari*, 185–232 at 192.
46 Calzabigi, "Lettera al Signor Conte Vittorio Alfieri," in *Scritti teatrali e letterari*, 197–8.

both polished and educated: for when this singular poet wants to terrify, he destroys all inhibitions and defences with his fierce, keen, and vibrant expressions.

Italy, however, had always lacked an Aeschylus. Turning his back on the Arcadian reform, Calzabigi did not agree with those who compared Apostolo Zeno to Aeschylus and Metastasio to Sophocles and Euripides.[47] As a consequence, there was no hint "[d]ella forza tragica, dell'urto delle passioni, delle sorprendenti rivoluzioni teatrali" (of the force of tragedy, of the clash of passions, of the surprising theatrical reversals) on the Italian stage, without which the theatre can produce no terror.[48] It was this deficiency that Calzabigi wanted to correct, proposing a rebirth of Italian musical drama through a radical break with Metastasian dramaturgy. His verdicts on Shakespeare and on Noverre – also the founder of a new theatrical genre, the *ballet en action* – should be seen in this light, as should his privately communicated suggestion that Pepoli might aspire to become the Sophocles to his Aeschylus.[49] It is therefore inaccurate to describe *Ipermestra* as an example of anti-Shakespearean rationalism, just as the similarities with Metastasio's *Ipermestra* – which Calzabigi downplayed in his response to Arteaga – should be regarded less as imitations than as corrective rewritings.[50]

The most striking feature of Metastasio's treatment of the myth is his omission of Ipermestra's murderous sisters and their bridegrooms. No one is permitted to die in his drama lest the principle of the *lieto fine* be violated. Danao's demand that Ipermestra kill her bridegroom on the wedding night is motivated less by hatred than by fear because his death by Linceo's hand has been predicted by an oracle. Nevertheless, he is so moved by his daughter's loyal devotion that he eventually retracts the order – and indeed, the prediction never comes true. With the omission of Linceo's brothers, it remains unclear, however, why Danao could not simply kill his single son-in-law himself but insists on imposing the

---

47 See Blair Hoxby's discussion of this narrative in the introduction to this volume.

48 Calzabigi, "Lettera al Signor Conte Vittorio Alfieri," in *Scritti teatrali e letterari*, 187.

49 Pepoli, "Lettera ad un uomo ragionevole," 32. On Calzabigi's attempt to return to the primitive origins of theatre, see also Schneider, "A Song of Other Times," 27, 29–30.

50 On *Ipermestra* as an anti-Shakespearean work, see Parodi, "*Les Danaïdes* di Tschudi-Du Roullet e Salieri," 121–7. On echoes of Shakespeare's *Romeo and Juliet* and *Othello* in Calzabigi's last libretto, *Elvira*, see my article "Legacy of an Anti-Patriot," 49. For Calzabigi's comparison of his tragedy to Metastasio's, see "Risposta che ritrovò casualmente" in *Scritti teatrali e letterari*, 426–7. On reminiscences of Metastasio in *Ipermestra*, see especially Lazzeri, *La vita e l'opera letteraria di Ranieri Calzabigi*, 72–4.

atrocious task on his daughter, and later on his niece Elpinice whom he tries to marry off to Linceo when Ipermestra refuses to comply.

Apart from pointing to the obvious illogicalities of this dramatic construction, Calzabigi objected to the suppression of all hints of the primitive origins of the myth, including the raw emotionality of terror. By removing the Danaids and focusing exclusively on Ipermestra's conflict between filial obedience and marital affection, Metastasio had essentially turned the tragedy into a modern comedy. Danao reasons like a "politico di caffè" (coffeehouse politician), Calzabigi scoffs, and spies on the lovers among the trees in what resembles the "giardino di Versaglies" (Garden of Versailles) like some Pantalone de' Bisognosi out of the commedia dell'arte.[51]

Several contemporary critics noted that Calzabigi, while turning his back on Metastasio in his own *Ipermestra*, returned to the format of Philippe Quinault's librettos for Jean-Baptiste Lully from the 1670s and 1680s, with their mythological subjects and integration of dance, spectacle, and divine interventions.[52] Indeed, as Robert Ketterer points out in his contribution to this volume, which focuses on George Frideric Handel's pasticcio *Oreste* (London, 1734), scenes of terror and violence were much more common in operas from the seventeenth and early eighteenth centuries, before the Arcadian reform set in. But while Pepoli recognized Calzabigi's reappraisal of that period as an attempt to reconnect to a tradition more in touch with the primitive origins of European tragedy, others merely saw it as a relapse into a past less tasteful and enlightened.[53] Next to Metastasio's *Ipermestra*, Arteaga thought, Calzabigi's drama looked like a "stravagante quadro" (an extravagant picture) by Luca Giordano (a Baroque artist) next to a painting by Correggio (one of the Renaissance masters).[54] He objected, for example, to the dancing Amorini who lead the bridal couples to their chambers in act 3, scene 1. Carrying torches and flower garlands, the appearance of such fantastical creatures among the human characters offended Metastasian verisimilitude.[55] Both he and F.D.S. objected to

51 Calzabigi, "Risposta che ritrovò casualmente" in *Scritti teatrali e letterari*, 445–7, 452–4.

52 Arteaga, *Le rivoluzioni del teatro musicale italiano*, 3 (1785): 123; Moreschi, "Osservazioni sopra l'*Ipermestra*," 141; Napoli-Signorelli, *Storia critica de' teatri antichi e moderni*, 6 (1790): 286.

53 Pepoli, "Lettera ad un uomo ragionevole," 21, 32.

54 Arteaga, *Le rivoluzioni del teatro musicale italiano*, 3 (1785): 122.

55 Arteaga, *Le rivoluzioni del teatro musicale italiano*, 3 (1785): 123. References are to Calzabigi, *Ipermestra o Le Danaidi*. My warm thanks to Lucio Tufano for supplying me with a PDF of the libretto.

the appearance of the Danaidi dressed as bacchantes in act 5, scene 2, possessed with ritual madness and carrying thyrsi (staffs topped with pines cones and wreathed with ivy), torches, and blood-stained daggers (see Figure 9.1). Arteaga saw this as an unmotivated piece of spectacle, and F.D.S. dismissed it as a comic masquerade out of the popular theatre.[56] What scandalized Italian critics outright, however, was the infernal scene, in which the enchained Danaidi, "agitate da terrore, tormento, e disperazione" (shaken by terror, torment, and desperation), perform a "orribile, scomposto, e breve ballo" (horrible, discomposed, and brief dance), while an offstage chorus of Demoni conclude the opera with the following lines:

> Da que' tanti, ed eterni lor mali
> imparate, orgogliosi mortali
> la giustizia de' numi a temer. (5.ultima)

> Learn from their many and eternal pains, proud mortals, to fear the justice of the gods.

F.D.S., Arteaga, and Napoli-Signorelli all referred to the "demoni" (demons) as "diavoli" (devils), either mistaking the Christian for the pagan hell or conflating the two. F.D.S. compared the infernal spectacle and its alleged God-fearing moral to the scene that concludes *Il convitato di pietra* (The Stone Guest): a popular farce with roots in the religious theatre of seventeenth-century Spain, in which the seducer and perjurer Don Giovanni Tenorio ends up among the damned in hell.[57] To Arteaga, the devout moralizing was reminiscent of the ridiculous speeches of John the Apostle in Ludovico Ariosto's *Orlando Furioso* (1532), while Napoli-Signorelli simply saw the scene as backsliding to the mythological operas of the past century.[58]

---

56 Arteaga, *Le rivoluzioni del teatro musicale italiano*, 3 (1785): 124; F.D.S., "Lettera ad un amico," 123, and "Replica ad un amico o sia Appendice alle osservazioni fatte sull'Ipermestra, tragedia per musica del Sig. Consigliere de' Calsabigi" (April 1784), in Tufano, *I viaggi di Orfeo*, 125–37 at 133–4.

57 F.D.S., "Lettera ad un amico," 124. In fact, an operatic version of the farce, with music by Giacomo Tritta, had premiered at the Teatro de' Fiorentini in the Carnival of 1783. Here the infernal scene concludes with the following lines, sung by all the characters: "Ecco il fin di chi mal' opra: / Ecco il Cielo che sà far" (This is the end of evildoers! This is what heaven is capable of). Lorenzi, *Il convitato di pietra*, I.17.

58 Arteaga, *Le rivoluzioni del teatro musicale italiano*, 3 (1785): 123, 125; Napoli-Signorelli, "Discorso sopra varie tragedie di Agamennone," 121.

Figure 9.1. Costume design for one of the Danaïdes as a bacchante. *Les Danaïdes*, act 5 (Paris, 1784, Académie Royale de Musique). Arkivet på Kungliga Operan (Sweden).

In his response to these criticisms, Calzabigi consistently referred to classical models, stressing his fidelity to cultural characteristics. The Amorini, he pointed out, are not actual cupids but rather children in costume; and Greek, Etruscan, and Roman paintings and reliefs as well as the writings of Lucian and Catullus show that ancient wedding festivities involved masques of this type.[59] The appearance of the Danaïdi as bacchantes is indebted to Ovid's story of Pentheus's murder by his mother and her companions, all possessed by Dionysian madness, and it helps explain how Danao's daughters are induced to murder their bridegrooms.[60] The final scene depicts the pagan hell, the concluding lines imitating Phlegyas's lines in Virgil's depiction of the underworld.[61] Sung by pagan deities, he implied, the admonition is less a moral intended for the instruction of the audience than an evocation of the metaphysical terror characteristic of primitive religious beliefs. This impression might be enhanced by the poetic and musical echoes of the infernal scene in *Orfeo ed Euridice*, which also draws inspiration from Virgil.[62]

It is illuminating, furthermore, to compare the response of Italian and French critics since the three "classical" pantomimes were retained in *Les Danaïdes*.[63] The Hymens (rather than cupids) in act 3, scene 3 drew no comment from reviewers in Paris, but the *Mercure de France* described the appearance of the Danaïdes as bacchantes in act 5, scene 5 as "une idée hardie & très-poétique" (a bold and very poetic idea), while the union of stage design, pantomime, and music in the infernal scene formed "un des Spectacles les plus frappans qu'on ait encore présentés sur aucun Théâtre" (one of the most striking spectacles yet presented on any stage).[64] According to the otherwise skeptical Louis-François Metra, this "vraiment belle & magnifique" (truly beautiful and magnificent) tableau even led to "réflexions aussi morales qu'attendrissantes" (moral as well as tender reflections).[65] Tschudi and Du Roullet had suppressed the Virgilian admonition; but it is nevertheless remarkable

---

59 Calzabigi, "Risposta che ritrovò casualmente" in *Scritti teatrali e letterari*, 429–30.
60 Ibid., 435–8.
61 Ibid., 427–9, 438–40. Calzabigi clearly found it fit to make this clearer, however, in the revised version of the tragedy, by having the contested lines sung by "Numi infernali" (infernal deities) rather than the demons that critics took for devils; see the edition found in Calzabigi, *Poesie e prose diverse*.
62 See Brandenburg, *Vito Giuseppe Millico*, 142–3.
63 References are to [Du Roullet and Tschudi,] *Les Danaïdes*.
64 *Mercure de France*, 19 (8 May 1784): 76–7.
65 *Correspondance littéraire secrète*, 20 (12 May 1784).

that French critics in no way shared their Italian colleagues' contempt for visual spectacle. On the one hand, this reflects the extent to which machine operas continued to be held in esteem in France, Bruno Brizzi even describing the infernal scene in *Les Danaïdes* as a tribute to the conventions of the national theatre (notwithstanding its Italian origins).[66] On the other hand, it reflects the extent to which the oratorical Arcadian neoclassicism of the early eighteenth century – especially as represented by Metastasio – still dominated the poetic discourse among Italian critics in the 1780s. Even into the twentieth century, in fact, Italian scholars routinely compared Calzabigi's *Ipermestra* unfavourably to Metastasio's.[67]

The problem of the wicked character

Among the features of Calzabigi's *Ipermestra* to which F.D.S. objected were Danao's extreme wickedness and the willingness with which his daughters agree to murder their bridegrooms in act 2, scene 1, which he found implausible.[68] Tschudi and Du Roullet apparently agreed to some extent about the latter, for in their adaptation the Danaïdes recall the injustices committed against them by their uncle before consenting, and their immediate reaction to their father's order is a surprised exclamation: "Justes Dieux!" (Good heavens! 2.1). Nevertheless, Metra deplored the "odieuse complaisance" (odious complacency) with which they accept the order in the French opera, as well as the "sangfroid digne des scélérats les plus consommés" (cold-bloodedness worthy of the most consummate scoundrels) with which they execute it.[69] Jean-François de La Harpe also disapproved of the "multitude de furies dans toute leur horreur" (multitude of furies in all their horror), and of the barbarity that "soulève le cœur sans l'émouvoir un moment ni de pitié ni de terreur" (agitates the heart without moving it either to pity or to terror).[70]

Italian critics, too, objected to this perceived lack of emotional effect, though they tended to couch their protests in demands for greater verisimilitude. As Calzabigi went beyond "certi limiti prescritti al verisimile, al naturale, al decente" (certain limits prescribed by the

---

66 Brizzi, "Uno spunto polemico calzabigiano," 142.
67 See Pera, *Ricordi e biografie livornesi*, 271; Lazzeri, *La vita e l'opera letteraria di Ranieri Calzabigi*, 74.
68 F.D.S., "Lettera ad un amico," 115, 119, 123; "Replica ad un amico," 128–9.
69 *Correspondance littéraire secrète*, 20 (12 May 1784).
70 Letter 107, in La Harpe, *Correspondance littéraire*, 235.

verisimilar, the natural, and the decorous), wrote F.D.S., "l'effetto il più violento riducesi al nulla perché nulla ha più di comune col cuore umano" (the most violent effect is reduced to nothing, having nothing more in common with the human heart).[71] Not even Shakespeare, Calzabigi's favourite tragedian, or John Dryden, Shakespeare's Restoration heir, would have conceived of anything as strange and barbarous as the massacre scene (4.5), which Calzabigi might want to sacrifice "al costume, alla decenza, all'umanità" (to propriety, to decorum and humanity) in the next edition of his tragic libretto.[72] Moreschi, who praised Metastasio for removing "ogni orrore, ogni tragica tristezza" (all horror, all tragic gloom) from the musical theatre, also condemned Calzabigi for cultivating "quel meraviglioso ch'è fuori delle umane passioni" (the marvelous that lies beyond human passions).[73] While this led Moreschi to reject Aeschylus as a model for modern tragedy, Arteaga accused Calzabigi of not being sufficiently true to Aeschylus. The latter had not painted Danaus and his daughters in such "abborriti e tetri" (loathsome and sombre) colours, he declared; in the *Suppliants*, "altro non respirano fuorchè riconoscenza, umiltà, tenerezza e divozione verso gli Dei" (they breathed nothing but gratitude, humility, tenderness, and godliness).[74] It was Calzabigi, therefore, who had turned the Danaids into "energumene sanguinarie" (bloodthirsty women possessed by demons) and their father into "un perfido, uno spergiuro, un mostro" (a traitor, a perjurer, a monster).[75]

Calzabigi reacted differently to these criticisms. F.D.S.'s assertion that not even Shakespeare would have included the massacre scene seems to have struck a note with him, for the scene is indeed omitted in the revised version of the libretto he published in 1793.[76] However, he scornfully rejected what he saw as Arteaga's saccharine abatement of the ancient myth. "Danao è scellerato come ce lo descrivon tutti" (Danao is as wicked as everybody describes him), he wrote of his opera; "le Danaidi sue figlie sono quelle feroci sicarie che ognun sa, all'inferno condannate" (the Danaidi his daughters are those ferocious assassins who are condemned to hell, as we all know).[77] Their

---

71 F.D.S., "Lettera ad un amico," in Tufano, *I viaggi di Orfeo*, 112.

72 F.D.S., "Replica ad un amico," in Tufano, *I viaggi di Orfeo*, 133.

73 Moreschi, "Osservazioni sopra l'*Ipermestra*," 140.

74 Arteaga, *Le rivoluzioni del teatro musicale italiano*, 3 (1785): 123–4.

75 Ibid., 124.

76 As part of this change, he also rewrote Danao's opening soliloquy in 5.1; see Calzabigi, *Poesie e prose diverse*.

77 Calzabigi, "Risposta che ritrovò casualmente" in *Scritti teatrali e letterari*, 422.

humility and godliness in the *Suppliants* are feigned, he added, as they conceal their truly barbarous and ferocious nature to find protection and shelter in Argos.[78]

Though Calzabigi seems to have cherished Aeschylus above all for his emotional force, this does not mean that his libretto – the first one he wrote after the earthshaking event of the American Revolution – is apolitical. In fact, the wickedness of Calzabigi's Danao forces both Iper-mestra and Pelasgo to make moral choices with which the eponymous princess and Danao's confidant in Metastasio's drama are never con-fronted. Meekly accepting the authority of her essentially goodhearted father, Metastasio's Ipermestra never actually defies him but rather ap-peals to his conscience with moral arguments. In effect, the demands of patriarchy and kingship are never questioned, the obedient daughter and royal subject remaining loyally devoted to Danao till the end of the opera when she even offers to exchange her own life for his. In contrast, Calzabigi's Ipermestra protests vehemently against her father's abuse of power; and after he has threatened to kill her if she disobeys, she no longer feels bound by filial obligation to protect him. During the second half of the tragedy, she trembles only for Linceo, not for Danao, and her futile plea for her father's life in act 5, scene 6, uttered a moment before she faints in Linceo's arms, has the character of an emotional reflex.

The difference between the two poets' treatment of Danao's closest associate is no less emphatic. Metastasio's Adrasto gives expression to his unblinking loyalty in this aria after he and Danao have plotted Linceo's death and the king has clasped his servant in his arms:

> Più temer non posso ormai
> quel destin che ci minaccia;
> il coraggio io ritrovai
> fra le braccia del mio re. (1.7)[79]

> Now I can no longer fear that destiny which threatens us; I found courage in my king's embrace.

Calzabigi's Pelasgo, on the other hand, gives expression to his contempt for the king as soon as the latter has left the stage:

> Ho finor sofferto assai
> presso al trono, e fra' tiranni;

---

78   Ibid., 433.
79   Metastasio, *L'Ipermestra*.

ma svaniscano gl'inganni,
e si scopre alfin l'error. (3.7)

I have suffered much close to the throne and among tyrants till now; but deceptions will vanish, and error is eventually recognized.

Clearly, these arias represent two very different conceptions of the relation between monarch and subject. In fact, Pelasgo seems to detach himself from his alter ego Adrasto as an obsequious courtier duped by the royal propaganda of which he himself is a part. By implication, Calzabigi also detaches himself from the political thinking of Metastasio who, as Enrico Zucchi argues in another essay in this volume, emphasized the unconditional loyalty of royal subjects, rejecting the possibility of regicide as sacrilegious.[80] In this context, it is striking that the sympathetic critic of the *Giornale de' letterati* chose to quote Pelasgo's aria as a sample "dei pensieri e della facilità dello stile" (of the thinking and fluent style) characteristic of Calzabigi's tragedy, while the conservative F.D.S. wrote disparagingly of this "aria da repubblicano, da moralista e da filosofo" (republican, moralistic, and philosophical aria).[81]

The political resonances help explain why Calzabigi chose to retain the Aeschylean character of Pelasgus, though he gave him a different social status. According to Thalia Papadopoulou, Aeschylus portrays Pelasgus as a "proto-democratic" king, and he served as "the prototype for the presentations of Theseus as the 'democratic' king *par excellence*" in Sophocles's *Oedipus at Colonus* and in Euripides's *Suppliants*, and also of Demophon, who serves a similar function in Euripides's *Children of Heracles*.[82] Ferrario adds that while Aeschylean tragedy is pro-aristocratic, it is nonetheless anti-tyrannical, and it might therefore "have been interpretable by European readers and audiences, at least in certain contexts, as anti-monarchical."[83] By implication, Metastasio's departure from Aeschylus can be said to have marked a departure from the political principles of Athenian democracy.

---

80 Cf. Zucchi's discussion of the exchange between Massimo and Ezio on the topic of rebellion in Metastasio's *Ezio* (1728), which reflects a conflict similar to the one in his *Ipermestra* between Linceo and his friend Plistene on the one hand, and Ipermestra and Adrasto on the other. For an analysis of Mozart's comparable rejection of Metastasio's religious concept of kingship in *La clemenza di Tito* (Prague, 1791), see my article "From Metastasio to Mazzolà."

81 *Giornale de' letterati*, 53 (1784): 280; F.D.S., "Lettera ad un amico," 120.

82 Papadopoulou, *Aeschylus: Suppliants*, 105.

83 Ferrario, "Aeschylus and Western Opera," 197.

Whether or not Calzabigi meant his *Ipermestra* to be an anti-monarchical work, the effect is enhanced through the parallel he draws between Aeschylus and Shakespeare, already hinted at in his reported compliment to Noverre. Calzabigi was not the first one to draw such a parallel: in 1750, in his famous essay on ancient and modern tragedy, Voltaire had compared the Ghost of Hamlet's father to the Ghost of Darius in the *Persians*; and in 1765, Elizabeth Montagu had compared the Witches in *Macbeth* to the Furies in the *Eumenides* in her *Essay on the Writings and Genius of Shakespeare*.[84] But the parallel Calzabigi draws seems to extend beyond the two playwrights' evocation of supernatural terror. What connects them is also the image of the tyrant who both generates terror and is terrified of his own misdeeds.[85] Apart from the actions of Danao himself, Ipermestra's and Pelasgo's revolt against him indeed creates the image of a tyrant of Shakespearean dimensions whose power is undermined by his perjuries. Calzabigi drove the point home by basing Danao's soliloquy in act 5, scene 3 on the soliloquy of Richard III in act 5, scene 3, a translation of which he included in his open letter to Count Vittorio Alfieri of 1783.[86] In Calzabigi's rewriting of Shakespeare, the blood-stained Danaids take the place of the ghosts of Richard's victims in triggering the king's recognition of his own villainy and his resultant fear of himself:

> Son partite una volta! ... I lor funesti
> sguardi, gli atti feroci, i tetri volti
> m'hanno atterrito ... L'empie
> m'uccideran, se non le uccido! ... Io tremo ...
> Ma perchè? ... Son pur solo;
> e numeroso stuolo
> d'armati è in mia difesa ... E pur ... pavento ...
> Di chi? ... Pavento di me stesso ... Un mostro
> io sono ... È ver ... Lo sono ... E se il negassi;
> universale un grido,
> contro di me, reclamerebbe ... Ognuno
> m'abbomina, m'aborre, e mi vuol morto ...
> E se mai giunse al porto
> se si salvò Linceo? ... Seguaci, amici,

---

84 Voltaire, *La tragédie de Sémiramis*, 27–8; Hoxby, "Joanna Baillie, the Gothic Bard, and her Tragedies of Fear," 111–12.

85 For a recent comparison of the two playwrights along these lines, see Schein, "Tyranny and Fear in Aeschylus's *Oresteia* and Shakespeare's *Macbeth*."

86 Calzabigi, "Lettera al Signor Conte Vittorio Alfieri" in *Scritti teatrali e letterari*, 224–5.

complici troverà ... L'empia Ipermestra
mi tradì; mi deluse ... Ah! mora, e tutte
l'altre con lei ... Quella, perchè innocente ...
(Sì ... trasportato a forza
a dirlo sono, a confessarlo!) E queste
perché son scellerate! ... Ah! del rimorso
ostinato, crudel che a me fa guerra,
lasciar non voglio un testimonio in terra.
È un inferno quel fremito interno
Di terrore, di rabbia, d'orrore
Che rodendo, straziando mi va!
Da me stesso fuggire io vorrei ... (5.3)

Now they have left! ... Their sinister stares, their ferocious deeds and gloomy faces terrified me ... The villains will kill me if I don't kill them! ... I tremble ... But why? ... I am alone, and a large crowd of armed men defend me ... And yet ... I fear ... Whom? ... I fear myself ... I am a monster ... It is true ... I am ... And if I denied it, a universal cry would contradict me ... Everyone abominates me, abhors me, and wants me dead ... And what if Lynceus reached the port and was saved?... He will find followers, friends, accomplices ... The villainous Hypermnestra betrayed me, deceived me! ... Ah, let her die, and all the others with her ... She, because she is innocent ... (Yes ... I am forced to say it, to admit it!) And they, because they are evil! ... I do not want to leave behind on earth one witness of the relentless, cruel remorse that besieges me. That internal throbbing of terror, of rage and horror, which gnaws and mangles me, is hell! I would flee from myself ...

Notably, neither Pelasgo's nor Danao's soliloquies have any equivalents in *Les Danaïdes*; and since Danaüs is killed by Pélagus here (and not by a band of soldiers, like Calzabigi's Danao), the absence of a soliloquy for the captain is remarkable. Quite understandably, one critic complained that it is unclear why he kills the king, and the Paris audience judged the dénouement to be the most defective part of Salieri's opera for that reason.[87] Without his moment of Shakespearean self-reflection, furthermore, the king becomes a much less engaging character: in the equivalent scene in the French libretto (5.6), he simply gives expression to his thirst for vengeance, hoping that Lincée has been killed. His "vengeance insatiable fatigue sans intéresser" (insatiable vengefulness is tiring without being interesting), wrote Metra, the *Mercure de France* complaining

---

87 *Mercure de France*, 19 (8 May 1784): 77.

that Danaüs has "qu'un sentiment, &, pour ainsi dire, qu'une seule atti-tude" (but one sentiment and, as it were, but a single pose).[88]

These changes by Tschudi and Du Roullet, which reduced the effect of Salieri's opera, were probably motivated by political rather than dramaturgical concerns. In light of Pierre Beaumarchais's problems with the censors in connection with *Le Mariage de Figaro* (which pre-miered just three days after *Les Danaïdes*, at the Comédie-Française) and his libretto for *Tarare* (Salieri's third and last opera for Paris, from 1787), both of which depict the undermining of tyranny, it is perhaps no won-der that the "republican" aria of the disloyal officer and the breakdown of the paranoid tyrant, which we find in Calzabigi's libretto, were con-sidered too politically subversive for the stage of the Opéra.

Living through a nightmare

Although conservative Italian commentators seem to have disap-proved of Calzabigi's portrayal of a royal sovereign as a treacherous tyrant – something Metastasio had never attempted – the most fre-quent point of criticism on the peninsula was the reliance of his *Ip-ermestra* on visual spectacle, which was mostly rejected as shallow sensationalism.[89] This verdict was even repeated by his biographer, Ghino Lazzeri, who thought that Calzabigi merely focused on the "op-posizione di feste e di scene lugubri, di imenei e di stragi, di danze nuziali e di ridde infernali" (juxtaposition of festivities and lugubri-ous scenes, of weddings and massacres, of nuptial dances and infernal reels), whereas Metastasio had focused on Ipermestra's "terribile situ-azione."[90] Eighteenth-century French critics – though some of them ap-preciated the violent contrasts between the wedding celebrations and the horror scenes in *Les Danaïdes* – also found that the festive scenes, with their lack of dramatic variation and progression, diverted atten-tion too much from the principal action.[91]

---

88 *Correspondance littéraire secrète*, 20 (12 May 1784); *Mercure de France*, 20 (15 May 1784): 132.
89 See F.D.S., "Lettera ad un amico," 113; *Novelle letterarie*, 15.xxii (28 May 1784): 348–9; Arteaga, *Le rivoluzioni del teatro musicale italiano*, 3 (1785): 123; Moreschi, "Osservazioni sopra l'*Ipermestra*," 141.
90 Lazzeri, *La vita e l'opera letteraria di Ranieri Calzabigi*, 74.
91 See *Journal de Paris*, 118 (27 April 1784): 517; *Affiches, annonces, et avis divers, ou Journal général de France*, 53 (1 May 1784): 257–8; *Mercure de France*, 19 (8 May 1784): 75; *Mer-cure de France*, 20 (15 May 1784): 131–2; *Journal politique, ou Gazette des gazettes* (May 1784, second fortnight): 72; *Correspondance littéraire, philosophique et critique*, 2: 493–4.

A comparison of the two librettos suggests that this problem was more pronounced in the French adaptation, however, which lacks the sense of intoxication that gives unity to the drama and drives the action inexorably forward in the Italian original. In the opening scene of *Ipermestra*, Danao encourages his nephews to "inebriarvi il petto, / e di Bacco, e d'Amor" (intoxicate your breast with Bacchus as well as Cupid), while Linceo and Ipermestra sing: "T'abbraccio pur" (I'll embrace you) and "Ti stringo pure al seno" (I'll clasp you to my breast). In the banquet scene in act 3, scene 1, the sexual allusions become more explicit, the chorus singing of "in braccio a Venere / instancabile il piacer" (the inexhaustible pleasure in Venus's arms), of embraces that are tight "[p]iù del tralcio, e più dell'edera" ([tighter] than the vine and the ivy), and of kisses that are "avidi, e spessi" (avid and frequent). Danao urges the couples to enjoy the "di fumoso Lieo tazze spumante" (sparkling cups of heady Lyaeus) while preparing for a "più caro piacer" (dearer pleasure), and he encourages Ipermestra to abandon her "pudore importuno" (importunate modesty), while Linceo looks forward to the "dolce momento" (sweet moment) of the wedding night. In these scenes, sexual intoxication is blended with the alcoholic intoxication that later melds into the sanguinary intoxication of the Danaidi, which culminates in the shocking bacchanalian scene of act 5, scene 2. Calzabigi explained that Danao gets his daughters drunk so as not to give them space "alla riflessione, al pentimento" (for reflection and repentance).[92] But intoxication is an omnipresent mental state throughout the drama, even as Linceo returns at the end to avenge his brothers, "ebro di sdegno" (intoxicated with wrath) (5.4).

The problem was that the straightforward references to sexual pleasure offended scenic decorum in both Naples and Paris. F.D.S. objected to many of the quoted lines, which portrayed Danao as an "epicureo" (epicurean) and a "buon galante" (fine gallant), and to the sight of Ipermestra on her bed with loose hair in act 4, scene 1.[93] The French adapters agreed, Du Roullet claiming that the Italian libretto was full of thoughts and expressions, "dont la délicatesse & la chasteté de nos mœurs théâtrales seroient vivement blesses" (which would have deeply injured the delicacy and chastity of our theatrical manners).[94] Hence, in act 1, scene 2 of *Les Danaïdes*, Lincée presses Hypermnestre's hand instead of embracing her; in act 3, scene 1, the titillating references

---

92 Calzabigi, "Risposta che ritrovò casualmente" in *Scritti teatrali e letterari*, 437.
93 F.D.S., "Lettera ad un amico," 114, 119–20; see also "Replica ad un amico," 127–8, 130–2.
94 [Du Roullet,] "Réponse de l'Auteur du Poëme des *Danaïdes*," 87.

to the pleasures of the bridal bed as well as Danao's complaint about Ipermestra's modesty have been suppressed; and act 4 is set in a gallery and not in Hypermnestre's bedroom.

Without the sexual excitement, however, the blood frenzy of the Danaïdes becomes less visceral and terrifying. Despite the assertions of early commentators, Calzabigi's use of chiaroscuro in *Ipermestra* depends less on the contrast between festive and gloomy scenes than on the contrast between the title heroine's state of terror and the other characters' state of intoxication. The centrality of Ipermestra's terror to the play's dramaturgical conception appears from the motto Calzabigi gave his tragedy: an uncredited quotation from the *Epithalamium* of the fifth-century Gallic poet Sidonius Apollinaris, in which a robe is embroidered with images of faithful spouses from ancient myth (it is worth noting that the ones immediately preceding Hypermnestra are Orpheus and Alcestis, the title characters of Calzabigi's two previous tragedies for Gluck):

Solus, Hipermestrae servatus munere, Lynceus
Effugit: aspicies illam sibi parva paventem,
Et pro dimisso tantum pallere marito.[95]

Lynceus alone escapes, saved by the grace of Hypermestra; you could see her there, fearing little for herself and pale only with anxiety for the husband she has suffered to depart.[96]

The motto captures the basic emotional impetus of the opera. From the moment in act 2, scene 1 when Ipermestra learns of her father's murderous plot, she finds herself in a constant state of anxiety for her husband, culminating in her distracted soliloquy in act 4, scene 2. Her terror then dissolves in the following scene as she learns that Linceo has managed to escape: "Salvo è lo sposo; ho di tremar finito" (My husband is safe; I have finished trembling) (4.3). The terror does not, however, disappear from the opera. It is simply transferred to Danao who now fears the avenging Linceo, later fears his raving daughters, and finally fears himself, as conveyed in his Shakespearean soliloquy in act 5, scene 3. This turn of events was predicted by Ipermestra in act 2, scene 2, as she warned him – also echoing *Richard III* – that the ghosts of his

---

95 Calzabigi, *Ipermestra o Le Danaidi*, 3.
96 Translation taken from Sidonius, *Poems and Letters*, 1: 239. D'Achille was the first scholar to identify the source of the motto; see D'Achille, "Variazioni linguistiche," 253n35.

murdered nephews would eventually make him tremble with remorse and self-loathing. In *Les Danaïdes*, however, this transfer of terror from one character to another is missing, due to the suppression of Danao's soliloquy and the softening of the contrast between the title heroine's states of mind before and after she hears of her husband's escape. This explains why both the *Mercure de France* and Baron Friedrich Melchior von Grimm complained that Hypermnestre's situation remains unchanged from act 2 onwards.[97]

In Calzabigi's *Ipermestra*, the pervasive contrast between terror and intoxication, detached from the individual characters, creates the experience of living through a nightmare. In the opening scene, Linceo and Ipermestra compare their wedding to a "dolce sogno" (sweet dream) (1.2), Linceo adding that "parmi ancora di sognare" (I still seem to be dreaming); but the nature of the dream changes radically in act 2, scene 1, when Ipermestra learns that Danao wants to avenge himself on his nephews: "Sogno? Deliro?" (Am I dreaming? Am I delirious?). In a grisly reversal of the choral prayer to Juno and Hymen in act 1, scene 1, Danao and his daughters invoke Nemesis, announcing the transformation of the wedding dream into a delirious vision of hell. In act 1, scene 1 they prayed that anyone violating the sacred marriage vows would be devoured by sacred fire, feel the wrath of Erebus, and be shaken by the hatred and fury of the Eumenides; but in act 2, scene 1 these references to hell acquire new significance. Danao demands that his daughters pierce the hearts "ove albergan le Furie" (where the Furies harbour) when their bridegrooms are "d'impure voglie acceso" (kindled by impure desires), perverting the fire metaphor from act 1, scene 1 where he addressed his nephews as "voi, che amore accende, / infiamma gioventù" (you whom love kindles, whom youth ignites). While describing the bridegrooms as harbouring the Furies, he instructs his daughters as follows: "Accorto riso / vi sfavilli nel viso, / v'arda l'odio nel cor" (Let a cunning laughter flicker on your faces while hatred burns in your hearts). Ironically, the imagery suggests that it is really his daughters who are consumed by infernal flames, Ipermestra suggesting the same when describing how "ne' lor fieri volti io veddi accesa / sete di sangue" (I saw bloodthirstiness kindle their ferocious faces) (2.3). The perversion of the fire imagery adds a sinister subtext to the choreographic image of the torch-carrying Amorini who lead the bridal couples to their chambers in act 3, scene 1, which points back to

---

97 *Mercure de France*, 20 (15 May 1784): 132; *Correspondance littéraire, philosophique et critique*, 2: 493.

the choral praises of the "fausto lume" (auspicious light) of Hymen's "gioconde fiaccole" (joyful torches) in act 1, scene 1. These implications are still lost on Danao, however, who fears that Ipermestra's tears and silence will awake "mille sospetti, e mille furie" (a thousand suspicions and a thousand Furies) (3.3) in Linceo's breast. At the end of act 4, the flames and furies of hell then invade the earth, though still offstage, as Danao orders Linceo's ships to be destroyed with "mille faci ardenti" (a thousand burning torches) (4.4), while his dying nephews cry from the wings in act 4, scene 5: "Le furie trattieni" (Restrain the Furies), "Oh mostri d'Averno" (O monsters of Avernus), "Oh nozze d'inferno" (O infernal wedding). It is only when Danao encounters his daughters as bacchantes, however, some of them carrying torches in a fearsome reversal of the torches of Hymen and Cupid, that he realizes that they are the ones resembling "dell'Erebo le Furie" (the Furies of Erebus) (5.2). In his grand soliloquy in act 5, scene 3, acknowledging his responsibility for creating the infernal nightmare, he feels hell raging in himself yet remains committed to his hatred. "L'ultime furie mie sfrenar conviene" (I will release my last Furies) (5.4), he announces after summoning Ipermestra, and "[d]a mille furie / agitare mi sento" (I feel shaken by a thousand Furies) (5.5). The infernal scene that ends the opera, the palace having disappeared in a rain of fire, is the climax and ultimate visualization of the furious bloodthirsty intoxication that has built up during the opera. Though denounced by eighteenth-century Italian critics as a concession to popular superstition, it is, rather, a vision of the darkest recesses of the human mind.

Calzabigi stated himself that the presentation of the Danaidi as bacchantes took its cue from Ovid. But as Papadopoulou has pointed out, both the maenadic scene and the collapse of the royal palace at the end are reminiscent of Euripides's *Bacchae*,[98] a play that, with its vivid depiction of group violence and ritual madness, culminating with the horrific dismemberment of King Pentheus, is at least as incompatible with Metastasian poetics as the Aeschylean tragedies.[99]

---

98 Papadopoulou, *Aeschylus: Suppliants*, 149n58.

99 The *Bacchae* does not seem to have inspired opera librettos before Calzabigi's *Ipermestra*, though Simon Perris suggests that the libretto by Marquis Charles Auguste de La Fare for the 1703 opera *Penthée*, set by Duc Philippe II of Orléans, could be based on it; see "Bacchant Women," 524. According to Girdlestone, the source could just as well be Ovid; see *La tragédie en musique*, 165. The collapse of the palace in *Ipermestra* is also reminiscent of the end of Quinault's and Lully's *Armide* (1686), however, which helps explain why commentators found that the libretto harked back to French Baroque opera. For a reproduction of Jean Bérain's stage design for the finale in *Armide*, see fig. 2.1 in this book.

In fact, R.P. Winnington-Ingram proposed that Euripides deliberately used Aeschylus as a model in *Bacchae*, perhaps specifically his lost tragedy *Pentheus*, pointing out that *Bacchae* and Aeschylus's *Eumenides* and *Suppliants* are the Greek tragedies in which the chorus figures most prominently.[100] While the Euripidean *Bacchae* thus fit naturally into the terrifying Aeschylean universe, Calzabigi departs from Euripides in one significant respect: the murderous intoxication of his bacchantes is not induced by the god Dionysus but by their father Danao. Such a transformation of *Bacchae* is in line with the famous interpretation of the tragedy that Winnington-Ingram wrote, with the Nuremberg rallies fresh in memory.[101] To him, Dionysus was not a deity worthy of worship. When he "is manifested in the play as the purveyor of drugs of many kinds, as the source of ecstasies and disasters, as the enemy of intellect and individuality and the defence of man against his isolation, as a power that can make him feel like a god while acting like a beast, as a spirit that partakes of the beauty and the callousness of man's natural environment," observed the learned classicist in 1948, "this is a god whom all can recognize."[102] After the traumatic experience of the Second World War, it was hardly possible to see in Dionysus anything but a reflection of the manipulative, histrionic tyrant who had kindled the collective madness.

Did Calzabigi write under the impression of historical events as well, or did he simply sense the bloodthirsty madness lurking beneath the veneer of civilization? It was, after all, only a few years after the planned premiere of his and Millico's *Ipermestra* that the tragedy of Pentheus was acted out on the streets of Paris, initiating another reign of terror.

---

100 Winnington-Ingram, *Euripides and Dionysus*, 2–3.
101 See Easterling, "A Show for Dionysus" in Easterling, *The Cambridge Companion to Greek Tragedy*, 36.
102 Winnington-Ingram, *Euripides and Dionysus*, 9–10.

10 From *Serio* to Sentimental: The Legacy of Tragic Opera in Carlo Goldoni's *Drammi Giocosi per Musica*

PERVINCA RISTA

The Arcadian reform of Apostolo Zeno (1669–1750) and Pietro Metastasio (1698–1782) is often cited as the source of the definitive rift between the tragic and comic in opera. Master and pupil set out to salvage musical theatre from its lacklustre state by remodelling it on the blueprint of the ancient Hellenic tradition, ever the idealized embodiment of purity and power. In their wake, tragic opera was "purged" of all comic corruption.

Most histories of music narrate a perhaps unintended result of this Arcadian overhaul of tragedy: that comic opera, cast aside, was finally emancipated. Yet this linear theory of separation is just that – a theory, and one hardly upheld by the conciliatory vision later playwrights and composers searched for in their own output. This chapter explores how Arcadian principles of tragic opera gradually collided with the new rationalism and artistic demands of the Enlightenment, a tension that ultimately created the nuanced, realistic styles we have inherited as classical opera. Venetian playwright Carlo Goldoni (1707–93), who led a long and successful "double life" as a librettist, must be recognized as the driving force of this transformation.

While renowned as one of the greatest comic writers of his century, Goldoni made his first attempts at writing plays as an aspiring tragedian. He did so while studying law, and likely made tragedy his first choice in recognition of its status as a genre more for learned, cultured audiences. He structured his first play, *Amalasunta* (1732), "according to all the laws of Aristotle and Horace ... for which," he recounts, "avea spogliato bastantemente la *Didone* e l'*Issipile* di Metastasio" (I had sufficiently robbed the *Didone* and *Issipile* of Metastasio).[1] Yet, despite his best

---

1 Carlo Goldoni, *Memorie Italiane*, 10: 9.

intentions, Goldoni soon learned that even the purest models were not fail-proof. His trusted entourage pointed out that he had still violated some of the rules of good tragedy, and trying to fix such a malformed work was pointless. Such was the sting of defeat for the young ambitious author that *Amalasunta* ended its quest for success in Goldoni's fireplace.

This unhappy outcome did not deter Goldoni in the slightest from making other attempts in *opera seria*, however, not only in his youth but as an established comic author, too. Clearly, even during his most successful years, he was conscious of the public esteem that tragic opera continued to enjoy. His comedy *Terenzio* (1754), written over twenty years after *Amalasunta*, was still fulsome in its recognition of Metastasio's work:

> In tutti i teatri d'Europa non si rappresentano che i Drammi vostri. Si replicano nel teatro medesimo le dodici, le venti volte. Non vi è compositore di Musica, che non le abbia sperimentate. Non vi è casa, non vi è persona, che non ne sia provveduta. Sono numerosissime le edizioni, e fortunati coloro che le hanno stampate. I Comici ancora se le sono appropriate per molto tempo, e con profitto notabile le hanno senza musica rappresentate. Da moltissime genti si sanno per la maggior parte a memoria, e pure si gustano sempre, piacciono ogni ora di più, e qualunque Dramma espongasi sulle scene, ha sempre un massimo disavvantaggio, se non è della felicissima penna del Metastasio.[2]

> In all the theatres of Europe we find none but your plays. They are given in the same theatre twelve, even twenty times. There is no composer of music that has not tried them. There is no home, no person who does not possess them. Numerous are the editions, and fortunate those who have printed them. Even actors have made them their own, staging them without music to notable profit. The people know them by heart, and yet they are still loved, every day more, and any other drama that is given will suffer a major disadvantage unless it springs from the felicitous pen of Metastasio.

By this account and many others, Metastasio stands out as the true authority in opera theatre during the first half of the eighteenth century. A second-generation Arcadian (after his teacher Apostolo Zeno) who had surpassed his master, his name was – and in large part remains – almost synonymous with *melodramma* and *opera seria*. His texts provided the uncontested models of these forms. His was the standard, the golden rule, the blueprint for success.

---

2 Goldoni, foreword to *Terenzio*. All translations are by the author.

Clearly conscious of this, Goldoni himself opted into the Arcadian academy in the mid-1740s, a choice that might initially appear at odds with his lifelong investment in realism and comedy. The reality is likely more nuanced. Goldoni used his Arcadian name, Polisseno Fegejo, to sign many of his texts – including the *Terenzio* – as an act of homage (much like the aforementioned Preface), or more advantageously as a stamp of prestige, rather than as a true seal of fidelity to Arcadian poetic principle. Clearly, the quotidian reality and social critique of his comedies was at odds with the philo-classical, bucolic spirit of Metastasian theatre as it was expressed in works such as *Didone abbandonata* (1724), *L'Olimpiade* (1733), or *La Celemenza di Tito* (1734).

Goldoni's Arcadian affiliation appears even more rhetorical in light of the fact that comedy and comic opera, while first relegated to the accompaniment of tragic plays and *opera seria*, began to evolve into new genres once *ousted* by Zeno, Metastasio, and the "true" Arcadians. As we examine texts in the sections that follow, it will be useful to keep in mind how the divergence between the tragic and comic worlds spilled over into all aspects of musical structure as well. For example, Metastasian opera invested in arias as the elements of greatest effect, and it was made up entirely of these solo pieces in alternation with *versi sciolti*, free recitative unbound by obligations of rhyme or metre that could corrupt its "natural" quality. The *da capo* aria, in particular, which resumes previously heard text and music at its end to create a tripartite structure, catered perfectly to the philo-classical requirements of equilibrium and proportion, becoming a hallmark of this type of theatre. Yet the characteristics that made this musical form so desirable from an Arcadian perspective were the same ones that rendered it unusable for Goldoni, who ever more openly pursued the psychological dimension in his theatre (both recited and sung), with verisimilitude as the cardinal rule. The circular nature of the *da capo* aria hindered any progression of action, thought, or emotional state, making it completely unusable as a means of advancing the plot. Musical theatre and comic opera in particular needed different solutions, and Goldoni sensed an opportunity.

Goldoni's output from about 1748 onwards (right about the time he officially became an "Arcadian") reflects a clear shift from a desire to emulate tragic opera theatre to a search for new horizons. While the author never launched an explicit polemic on the constraints of inflexible *opera seria* (feeling the weight, no doubt, of that towering tradition), he did leave behind, in addition to his *Mémoires* and Prefaces, two meta-theatrical commentaries. These offer a useful window into his own, very different vision, which we will explore in the following sections for the insights they offer into our author's intent. That said, his strongest statement in favour of innovation is arguably his entire life's work, a long path of experimentation from statutory *opera seria* to comic *intermezzi* to an entirely new, complex, and versatile genre: the *dramma giocoso per musica*. Uniquely, Goldoni's new type of opera theatre did not require or seek an explicit divorce from his early models, quite unlike the Arcadian approach. Instead, he created complete novelty from an artful synthesis of every experience that had come before, in the name of coexistence, balance, and rationality. The sections that follow explore how elements of the *opera seria* tradition were assimilated and renewed, how the end result speaks to the legacy of tragic opera, and how it continued to enrich opera theatre, even in the realm of comedy.

The *Dramma Giocoso Per Musica*

Goldoni was a practical connoisseur of *opera seria*, the Venetian *intermezzo*, and the Neapolitan *commedia per musica* traditions. His contributions to comic opera, therefore, cannot be credited to any single influence, but to a novel reinterpretation and fusion of complementary trends. The variety of dramatic possibilities afforded by each genre would push him to experiment and progressively expand his own texts, enriching them with elements of the other forms, culminating in the consolidation of a new operatic genre, the *dramma giocoso per musica*.

The primacy of Goldoni's role in the creation of this new form of musical theatre is still little recognized, but it cannot be overstated. Before *La scuola moderna* (1748), his first text of this kind, we know of only two other such works performed in Venice: *La libertà nociva* (Perilous Freedom) and *L'ambizion delusa* (Thwarted Ambitions), 1744, with music written by Rinaldo di Capua on texts adapted by Giovanni Barlocci. Both works were imported from Naples. These titles, seen in the context of the density of playbills of the time, are scarcely discernible amid the myriad of concomitantly staged musical works, from Metastasian *drammi per musica* to the more popular *intermezzi, drammi eroi-comici, opere bernesche, commedie per musica, divertimenti giocosi, farse,* and other sundry forms.[3] It is noteworthy that Goldoni dabbled in a variety of these forms until his first *dramma giocoso* in 1748, after which he devoted himself almost exclusively to this new genre. Over the span of two decades (1748–68), during his mature and most prolific years, he created nearly fifty texts of this kind (and likely would have continued, except

---

3 See Selfridge-Field, *A New Chronology of Venetian Opera and Related Genres.*

that his transfer to Paris, where he found little openness to his new works, significantly blunted and eventually extinguished his output). If, before Goldoni, the *dramma giocoso* was hardly detectable against the backdrop of musical ferment of early eighteenth-century Venice, after Goldoni – who essentially formed the genre into what it is – the *dramma giocoso* became an international model, shaping musical traditions outside Italy and reaching later generations, all the way to the Mozart and Da Ponte operas.

What distinguished the *dramma giocoso* from the many other musical forms available at the time? And what role did the tragic tradition play in its formation? The answers to these questions were clear to Goldoni from the start, who, in the preface to his very first *dramma giocoso La Scuola Moderna* (1748), explained,

> Non avendo servito il tempo per mutar tutta l'opera, come erasi divisato, si è mutata tutta la materia buffa, la quale, se non parerà bene intrecciata colla seria, ciò è provenuto per la necessaria brevità; e vivi felice.[4]

> Not having had the time to rewrite the entire opera, as I had originally set out to do, I have changed all of the comic material, which, if it should not appear well interwoven with the tragic, this is the result of necessary brevity; and may you live happily.

The *dramma giocoso* is, therefore, "materia buffa … intrecciata colla seria," (comic material interwoven with tragic). It is this coexistence, this double dramatic extension, that would make the *dramma giocoso*, which was later to evolve into *opera buffa*, an emblem of the eighteenth-century European musical tradition, and one that is still very much alive in our contemporary classical music culture.[5]

---

4 Goldoni, preface to *La Scuola Moderna* (1748). A word must be spent on *La Scuola Moderna* to clarify that this work is a *pasticcio*; that is, Goldoni inserted portions of his own invention within a preexisting text (there is still debate in scholarship as to the exact source), as was quite common at the time. This is Goldoni's only *pasticcio*; all subsequent *drammi giocosi* were written entirely by him, in both their comic and tragic content. For more information on his sources, see Bellina, "La 'Maestra' esaminata"; and Selfridge-Field, *A New Chronology*, cit., 514.

5 For a partial chronology of studies in this area, though specific attention to the *drama giocoso* remains unfortunately rare, see (in alphabetical order) Crotti, *Libro, Mondo, e Teatro*; Emery, *Goldoni as Librettist*; Fido, "Riforma e controriforma del teatro; Gallarati, *Musica e Maschera*; Mangini, "Itinerari e approdi di Goldoni librettista"; Rista, *At the Origins of Classical Opera*; Weiss, *Opera, A History in Documents*.

La scuola moderna is an excellent example of how, in practical terms, *buffo* and *serio* were made to coexist in the early phases of Goldoni's work in the genre. In this work and others like it, *parti serie* and *parti buffe* ("serious roles" and "comic roles") are assigned to different sets of characters whose linguistic style differentiates them as illustrious persons worthy of appearing in a tragedy or lower- to middle-class figures better suited to a comedy. Goldoni would eventually move past this conventional association of tragedy with nobility and of comedy with the merchant and servant classes, but the association was a strong one that had been forged by Roman grammarians such as Diomedes and Donatus.[6]

The action of *La scuola moderna* involves two couples, one *buffa*, one *seria*, each troubled by an unwanted third party. Drusilla, the shrewd *maestra* of the "modern school," is coveted by an elderly aristocrat, ironically named Belfiore (Pretty Flower). She is planning to marry his nephew but pretends to accept Belfiore's advances to obtain lavish gifts and carve out a small dowry for herself. An uninhibited *parte buffa*, this peculiar teacher imparts lessons on the true nature of modern society, such as:

> Tutti fingono, tutti. I mercadanti,
> per mantener i vizi e le gran spese,
> fingon la roba di lontan paese;
> gli orefici, vendendo
> la tombacca per oro,
> guadagnano un tesoro. Gli avvocati
> fingono che il cliente abbia ragione
> sol per mangiargli il fegato e il polmone;
> e i medici, fingendo
> la malattia morale,
> traggon il proprio ben dall'altrui male;
> fingon gli uomini affetto, ed è interesse;
> fingon le donne anch'esse:
> vedrai un bel visin, ma quello è finto,
> con la biacca e il carmin coperto e tinto.[7]

> Everyone deceives, everyone. Merchants
> to support their vices and large expenses

---

6 See Hoxby, *What Was Tragedy?*, 58–61.
7 Goldoni, *La Scuola Moderna*, 1.7.339–53.

make believe that their goods come from distant lands;
Goldsmiths, selling copper for gold
rake up a fortune. Lawyers
pretend their clients are right
only to strip them of liver and lungs,
and doctors, feigning
the illness to be lethal
draw their gain from others' misfortunes;
men feign affection, but it is only interest,
and women deceive too:
you'll see a pretty face, but that's all fake
covered and tinted with flour paste and blush.

While clearly comic, Drusilla's commentary is imbued with Goldoni's characteristic critical stamp that uses humour as a vehicle for truth and anchors itself solidly in the present, in those quotidian individual affairs and affections that are universal. The academy is, after all, the "modern" school, and by Drusilla's account modernity would appear to be governed by the laws of falsehood and individual advantage (a lesson she imparts through her conduct, as well as through her more formal "lessons"). Of note on a formal level is the discursive, quotidian language Goldoni uses to characterize his *parti buffe*, and, in the case of the piece cited above, its position midway through the scene instead of at its end as a typical exit aria. Its placement within the text in particular, as well as the sketched rhyme scheme, suggests that this may have been Goldoni's first attempt at a form he would later use frequently, the *arietta*: a solo piece that can stand alone but is more concise and flowing than a full aria, able to maintain the flow of the action, rendering the plot less static and more lifelike. Unfortunately, the whereabouts of Ciampi's musical setting of *La scuola moderna* remain obscure, and therefore we cannot consult it to shed more light on this episode.

In contrast to the tone, pacing, and broader social commentary of Goldoni's comic roles, the *serio* material is a return to the realm of Metastasian opera, without any shadow of parody or satirical play. The comic couple, or trio, alternates scenes with a second pair of characters who set a very different tone. The young nobles Rosmira and Ergasto are deeply in love and wish to marry, but they cannot do so because Rosmira's aunt, her only remaining relative, covets the young man for herself. Rosmira, continually mistreated, and Ergasto, grieved by both his own suffering and hers, sing in measured, elevated, aristocratic verse, leagues away from the rapid dialogues, puns, and sarcasm of the comic pair. Their language carries echoes of classic, rather generic leitmotifs. Ergasto's first solo aria is representative:

L'alma gelar mi sento
sento mancarmi il cor,
oh che crudel momento!
che sfortunato amor![8]

I feel my soul freezing
my heart giving way
oh, what a cruel moment!
what luckless love!

His beloved's arias are much of a piece:

Troppo è crudel tormento
questo che in cor mi sento. Un giorno intero
senza veder l'amante,
è pena da morir. Ditelo voi,
anime innamorate,
se fia tormento e duolo
star lontano dal suo bene un giorno solo.
Fanciulle semplici
che molle e tenero
avete il cor,
quel duolo barbaro
che il sen mi lacera,
potrete dir,
se il fier tormento
che in sen mi sento
può far morir.[9]

Too cruel is the torture
that I feel in my heart. An entire day
without seeing my love
is a fatal pain. You be the judge
you souls who are in love
if it be torment and grief
to be away from one's beloved for a whole day.
Unaffected girls
whose heart
is sweet and tender

---

8 Goldoni, *La Scuola Moderna*, 1.6.311–18.
9 Ibid., 1.10.395–410.

that cruel pain
that tears my breast,
you can testify
if the fierce torment
I feel in my breast
can make us die.

The register and style of these exit arias, which contain no development within them but rather expound upon a single emotion, are a clear extraction from the tragic opera tradition. Goldoni would later modify *serio* parts as well, but in this first attempt, the decision to preserve the coexistence of comic and tragic – albeit with little homogeneity, stylistically speaking – is telling in its own right, and it lays the groundwork for a much broader spectrum of dramatic registers and plot complexity.

On Tragedy and Comedy

This is not to say that the coexistence of comic and tragic is a theatrical measure unique to Goldoni, or to the eighteenth century for that matter. The two were already intertwined in the much more ancient tradition of the *Commedia dell'arte*,[10] which preserved differences in language, gesture, and social circumstance in the interactions between *amorosi* (the term literally means "lovers," but was used figuratively to denote characters of higher rank, whose parts were completely scripted) and *maschere* (masks: comic, archetypal characters whose parts were improvised). The true novelty brought by Goldoni is the manner in which tragic and comic, traditionally kept separate stylistically even if within the same work, transition into a new, seamless, and decidedly modern coexistence, one that prioritizes balance, realism, and the intimate psychological dimension.

Something must be said, in this regard, on the broader ideological context that shaped the evolution of later eighteenth-century opera, sometimes called opera of the Enlightenment. Clearly the nascent criteria for balance and verisimilitude were dominant offsprings of the rational aesthetic that, while not unopposed, was ever more prevalent. As early as 1726, a telling prologue was given by the actors of the S. Samuele Theatre as part of the inauguration of the new performance

---

10 For detail on Goldoni's relationship with the *Commedia dell'arte* tradition, see Ferrone, *La vita e il Teatro di Carlo Goldoni*.

season. In the *Introduzione alle recite della truppa dei comici nel teatro Grimani a S. Samuele, per l'Autunno di quest'anno 1726, posta in musica dal Sig. Gio. Battista Pescetti* (the lengthy title on the frontispiece), the actors' entrance is preceded by a dialogue between Neptune and Adria, a local sea goddess, who summons them thus:

> Vanne, tutti gl'invia
> In questa spiaggia, e dille,
> Ch'io vo veder in questa prima impresa
> Misto al serio il giocoso,
> Il ridicolo al grave, e ogn'un s'adopri
> Che dall'alto mio Soglio,
> Il merito d'ognun pesar io voglio.[11]

> Go, and summon them
> Let them all gather on this shore, and tell them
> that I wish to see in their opening work comedy mixed with tragedy
> lightness mixed with gravity, and that everyone make an effort
> for I will be judging their merit
> from my high throne.

Though written at the apex of tragic opera's dominance, this peculiar text appears to foreshadow a looming change in the aesthetic of musical theatre, one that would seek reconciliation between tragedy and comedy in a new, calibrated dynamic.

Goldoni helped to bring this transition about beginning very early in his career. In fact, as a young author and librettist he too created a meta-theatrical commentary on the topic of tragedy and comedy for some of the very same actors who had performed the 1726 prologue. His 1736 *divertimento*, *La Fondazion di Venezia* (*The Founding of Venice*), bears too many affinities to be coincidental:[12] its prologue presents an allegorical dialogue between *Musica* and *Commedia* (intended more broadly as spoken drama, i.e., not song) that heralds, even more deliberately, the presence of *serio* elements in comic opera.

Personified Music, who hearkens from the depths of archaic opera, represents the noble sphere of tragedy, while Comedy draws her merits

---

11 *Introduzione alle recite della truppa dei comici nel teatro Grimani a S. Samuele, per l'Autunno di quest'anno 1726, posta in musica dal Sig. Gio. Battista Pescetti* (Venice: Alvise Valvasense, 1726), 3.

12 Vencato has written about the connection in her introduction to *Drammi musicali per i comici del S. Samuele.*

from her present glory in Venice.[13] Goldoni reaffirms that Comedy can be both useful and the pleasurable, as Horace says poetry should be; through the pleasure of laughter, she delivers the medicine of self-realization:

> La Commedia son io:
> Quella che sulle scene
> Dà lode alla virtù, biasmo agli errori,
> Mostrando in varie guise
> "Le donne, i cavalier, l'arme e gli amori;"
> Quella per cui sovente
> Di sé mirando il vergognoso esempio,
> Detesta il vizio, e divien giusto l'empio.[14]

> I am Comedy
> she who in the theatre
> gives praise to virtue, and reprimand to error
> showing, in different guises,
> "Ladies, knights, arms, and loves"
> I am she by whom often
> seeing in himself the shameful example
> the villain comes to detest his vice, and becomes righteous.

What follows is an aria in which Comedy expounds upon herself as a metaphorical mirror, implying that effective theatre should reflect the realities of both society and the individual, and that it has the capacity to fulfill the higher calling of moral redress and social commentary – the efficacy of which, we understand, hinges directly on the degree of realism achieved. Music's verses are more allusive, but no less clear: "Io sol posso tener gli animi intenti/ Al dolce suon dei miei canori accenti [...] Ora per la virtù risorto è il zelo,/ Ed io son virtù che vien dal cielo"[15] (I alone have the power to keep souls attentive/ With the sweet sound of my song [...] Now a zeal for virtue has risen again / And I am that virtue that comes from the heavens). In these words, we find an unmistakable reprise of the Platonic belief in Music's power to move the affections (a reference to the idealized Hellenic origins of opera),

---

13 "Quanto l'itala scena/ Di me si pregi, / e quanto in questi lidi" (How greatly I honor/the Italian stage/ and these very shores). Goldoni, prologue to *La Fondazion di Venezia*, 51–2.

14 Ibid., 9–16.

15 Ibid., 48–9.

coupled with an explicit evocation of the Arcadian reform ("Ora per la virtù risorto è il zelo" [Now a zeal for virtue has risen again]), which ideally aimed to reconnect tragic opera to that original purity and contemplative virtue.

Ultimately, the conflict for supremacy of one over the other is resolved by an illuminating sentence:

> Oggi l'una di voi non è bastante
> Senza l'altra piacer su queste scene.
> Se non ha la Commedia
> L'ornamento del canto,
> Spera invan riportar applauso e vanto.
> E la Musica stessa,
> Se non ha ne' suoi drammi oltre ragione
> Qualche comica azione,
> Se conserva il rigor della Tragedia,
> Anzi che dar piacer, suo canto attedia.
> Eugualmente ad entrambe
> La stessa sorte arride.[16] *etc.*

> Today, neither of you alone is enough
> to give pleasure without the other.
> If Comedy is without
> the ornament of song
> her hopes for applause and fame will be in vain.
> And Music,
> if her works are without some element of comedy,
> if she preserves only the rigor of Tragedy,
> will not please, but only tire.
> The same destiny
> smiles upon both.

Just as song cannot live without words, neither can comedy or tragedy live without taking on some aspect of the other.

It is also telling that Goldoni's principal theatre, that of his comedies, followed much the same principle of coexistence. In fact, the centrality of this principle to the author's dramatic voice is not only depicted through the plots and structures of his plays but explicitly declared in his *Il teatro comico* (*The Comic Theatre*), long considered (in accordance

---

16 Ibid., 105–16. Comedy recalls a famous line from Ariosto's *Orlando Furioso*.

with the author's own wishes) the *commedia-manifesto* of his realist "reform" of comic theatre. It is a work that documents a shift from the structures of the *Commedia dell'arte* – based on archetypal characters who largely improvised – to the Goldonian *commedia di carattere* – complex, full-bodied, scripted plays that his actors, accustomed to improvisation, initially struggled to commit to memory.

Il teatro comico premiered in 1750, two years after Goldoni began writing *drammi giocosi per musica*. That season, he entered into a famous (or infamous) wager with impresario and lead actor Girolamo Medebach, promising to produce sixteen new *commedie di carattere* for the *S. Angelo* theatre (a regular theatre season put half as many new works into production each year, at best, making Goldoni's plan quite the feat). In the service of this vast undertaking, print editions were instructed to list *Il teatro comico* as the first comedy of the series, being, as Goldoni put it, "prefazione ... alle mie Commedie ... nella quale ho inteso di palesemente notare ... tutti quei fondamenti su' quali il metodo mio ho stabilito" (a Preface to my comedies ... in which I resolved to openly make known all of the principles on which I have established my method of theatre).[17] Goldoni's reason for openly presenting the makeup of his "new method," by this point familiar enough to Venetian audiences, lies largely in his polemic with the neglected state of comic theatre, which he advocates should be rescued to restore Comedy to its higher potential: "rendere lo smarrito onore alle nostre scene con le buona Commedie, che sieno veramente Commedie, e non scene insieme accozzate senz'ordine e senza regola" (to restore the lost honour of our theatre with good Comedies, that be real Comedies, and not just a collection of scenes, thrown together without order or principle).[18] It is here, with *Il teatro comico* and the fifteen masterworks that followed, that Goldoni puts into practice his new cardinal rule: "Quanto si rappresenta sul Teatro non deve essere se non la copia di quanto accade nel Mondo" (What we represent on stage should be nothing else but a mirror of what truly happens in the real world). It is here, too, that he unveils his vision for a new equilibrium between, "Teatro," i.e., the traditions that became his foundation, and "Mondo," the complex, diverse, and compelling reality that was his inspiration.[19]

17 Goldoni, foreword to *Il teatro comico*.
18 Ibid.
19 Goldoni, "Prefazione dell'autore alla Prima Raccolta delle Commedie." See also Mario Baratto, *Tre saggi sul teatro: Ruzante, Aretino, Goldoni* (Vicenza: Neri-Pozza), 1964.

Nearly every scene of *Il teatro comico* reveals some aspect of the author's ideology, but the connections to opera are the purpose of its inclusion in the current chapter.[20] Before moving on to view how the *dramma giocoso* evolved in its fusion of tragic elements with comedy, it will be beneficial to review the following dialogue between Orazio, the *capocomico* (originally played by Medebach himself), and Placida, *prima donna* of the troupe (played by Medebach's wife Teodora, Goldoni's original *donna di garbo,* who, coincidentally, excelled in sentimental roles):[21]

EUGENIO: Sedici commedie in un anno?
ORAZIO: Si certamente, egli le ha fatte. Si è impegnato di farle, e le ha fatte.
[...]
PLACIDA: Perché dunque vogliamo fare una farsa, e non piuttosto una delle migliori commedie?
ORAZIO: Cara signora, sapete pure, che ci mancano due parti serie, un uomo, ed una donna. Questi si aspettano, e se non giungono, non si potranno fare commedie di carattere.
PLACIDA: Se facciamo le Commedie dell'Arte, vogliamo star bene. Il mondo si è annoiato di veder sempre le cose istesse, di sentir sempre le parole medesime, e gli uditori sanno cosa deve dir l'Arlecchino, prima ch'egli apra la bocca. Per me, vi protesto signor Orazio, che in pochissime commedie antiche reciterò; sono invaghita del nuovo stile, e questo sol mi piace, *etc.*[22]

EUGENIO: Sixteen comedies in a year? That's impossible.
ORAZIO: Yes, of course he wrote them. He promised that he would, and he did.
PLACIDA: Why then do you want to perform a farce, and not one of the best comedies?
ORAZIO: My dear lady, you already know that we are missing two *parti serie,* a man and a woman. We are waiting for them, but if they don't come, we won't be able to perform any *commedie di carattere.*

---

20 For further reading see Vescovo, "Guardando Verso la Scena."
21 See Herry, "Goldoni e la Marliani ossia l'impossibile romanzo."
22 Ibid., 1.2.91–4; 108–20.

PLACIDA: Well, if we want to keep performing Commedia dell'Arte, let's wish ourselves well. The world is tired of always seeing the same things, and hearing the same words, and the audience knows what Arlecchino is going to say before he even opens his mouth. I protest, signor Orazio, that I will take part in very few of the old comedies; I am taken with this new style, it is the only one I like.

This passage declares that Goldoni's *commedia di carattere* needs *parti serie* too in order to survive ("se non giungono, non si potranno fare commedie di carattere" [if they don't come, we won't be able to perform any *commedie di carattere*]). The author's cardinal criterion, as he states elsewhere repeatedly, is realism, and realism can only be achieved through the lifelike intermingling of tragic, *serio* elements with comedy. In this light, the *parti serie* of Goldoni's *drammi giocosi* can be understood not only as a heritage of Metastasian *melodramma*, but also as a heritage that Goldoni consciously confirms through his own aesthetic preference – a cardinal foundation of his own brand of theatre, recited or sung, that champions relevance to its audience as a beneficial mirror of universal human values and truths.

Evolution

The coexistence of *buffo* with *serio* becomes a quintessential trait of the *dramma giocoso per musica* in the wake of *Il teatro comico*. In fact, from 1751 onwards, Goldoni chose to write about thirty opera texts exclusively of this kind until he moved to Paris eleven years later. This body of work, still under-studied compared with Goldoni's earlier texts for music and later spoken drama, affords an unparalleled window onto the evolution of a genre that, by the end of the century, would take centre stage. It is worth enumerating some of its legacies: these include the creation of the ensemble finale[23] and the ever-increasing use of solo *ariette*[24] *and* small ensembles (duets and trios). Such new formal arrangements effectively dismantled the monotony of recitative and arias in standard

---

23 The practice of bringing several or all characters together at the end of each act, so as to amplify – with the union and interweaving of each individual musical voice – the dramatic effect of each ending.

24 The standard arias of tragic opera were expected to follow a tripartite "ABA" form, that is an exposition, a development, and a return to the opening material of the end of the piece. This structure, in particular in its return to opening material at the end, meant that a character's single emotion or state of mind necessarily dominated the whole piece. Repetitions were used to showcase vocal virtuosity and musical ornamentation. *Ariette*, literally "little arias," abandoned the practice of the "ABA"

alternation. Goldoni's legacy is nowhere more evident than in Mozart: of the twenty-eight closed pieces of *Le nozze di Figaro* (*The Marriage of Figaro*), for instance, a good half are ensembles. Yet by far the most important innovation we witness in the *drammi giocosi* is the progressive dismantling of the boundary between *buffo* and *serio*, a process of fusion that would ultimately give birth to new, organic dramatic solutions, such as the *mezzo carattere* (to which we will return).

The ways in which Goldoni departs from norms in his handling of the relationship between comic and tragic are manifold. One of these, for example, is by calling into question the automatic association of *buffo* and *serio* roles in conjunction with rank: nobility and populace, *amorosi* and *maschere*. As early as 1754 with *Il filosofo di campagna*, we come across an aristocrat who is, contrary to the other family members who act as *parti serie*, a *parte buffa*. The character is Don Tritemio, a corrupt nobleman spurred by avarice and a weak mind. He resolves to give his daughter Eugenia in marriage to the alleged "country philosopher," a man he in fact considers a *villano* but who is rich enough to obviate any other concern. The result is a strident divarication in style and decorum between the father, Tritemio, and his daughter Eugenia. The latter, faced with the prospect of a forced marriage and powerless against the rights of paternal authority, inspires pathos through her plight in the manner of a true tragic heroine. Eugenia has to rely completely on her maid, Lesbina, for deliverance from her unhappy sentence, entering into a *rovesciamento* (reversal) of traditional authority that presages Mozart's stricken Contessa Almaviva some decades later, who, in like manner, depends on Susanna to determine the outcome of her own story.

Goldoni takes a further step outside of the common practice with *Le nozze* (1755), a work that does not separate *serio* and *buffo* parts in the character list, a choice that others soon followed (though the divisions remain discernible through class difference and mode of expression). In this case, the central aristocratic couple show none of the measured composure of Eugenia's *parte seria*. Goldoni actually showcases them in the throes of a quotidian marital crisis, one that is on its way to a fullblown divorce. The tone is rather materialistic and curt as the two begin to divide their assets:

---

form entirely. These concise musical moments in free form emerge seamlessly and reconnect to the dialogue without interrupting its flow and logical development. Most important, therefore, the *ariette* were able to carry plot development (for example, transitioning a character from sadness to anger to forgiveness, within the same musical number), the reason Goldoni used them continuously.

CONTE. Come dissi,
   d'ogni effetto dotale
   che portò la Contessa in questa casa,
   preparatemi i conti.
   [...]
CONTESSA. Badate; nel contratto
   vi ha da essere un patto,
   per cui nel caso di restituzione
   s'han da considerare i frutti ancora.
   [...]
CONTE. Poi penseremo a sciorre il matrimonio.
CONTESSA. Liberata sarò io da un tal demonio.[25]

COUNT. As I said, prepare the accounts of everything the Countess
   brought as dowry to this house.
COUNTESS. Be mindful; in the contract there should be an agreement that, in
   the case of restitution, interest accrued must also be accounted for.
COUNT. Then we will see to ending this marriage.
COUNTESS. I will be freed from such a devil.

But when she is alone, the Countess's rage gives way to melancholy in an
aria that rings as a clear precedent to Mozart's "Dove sono i bei momenti"
(Where are the good times) aria of Le nozze di Figaro forty years later:

Per una serva
il marito di me fa poca stima?
Ah dove, dove andò l'amor di prima?
Ah dove è andato
quel primo affetto?
Ah che l'ingrato
mio sposo in petto
cangiato ha il cor.
Duran per poco
quei primi istanti;
si spegne il foco,
cessa l'ardor.[26]

My husband disrespects me
for a servant girl?

25   Goldoni, Le nozze, 2.3.512–23.
26   Ibid., 1.2.92–103.

Ah where, where is the love we first had?
Ah where
has that first love gone?
Ah, my ungrateful
husband has
changed his heart.
Those first moments
are fleeting;
then the flame burns out,
the ardour ceases.

The seamlessness with which Goldoni transitions his *parti serie* from introspection and nostalgia to bickering and anger is an important indicator of his progress in amalgamating *buffo* and *serio*.

The broadened expressive spectrum of these *parti serie*, and the flexibility with which they move from one end of the stylistic spectrum to the other, is the key to transitioning these characters from the more static styles of their Metastasian origins to a renewed role as vehicles of sentimental realism and deeper dramatic content. Goldoni's progress in his effort to moderate the discrepancies between *serio* and *buffo* eventually brought about the birth of an entirely new dramatic figure, ushering in a new age of modern opera: the *mezzo carattere*.

The *Mezzo Carattere*

The origins of the *mezzo carattere* are difficult to trace. Goldoni's first appears startlingly early, in 1751, and antecedents are difficult to confirm. Based on the consolidation of these roles through the chronology of his opera texts, in any case, the affirmation of the *mezzo carattere* as a dominant theatrical device – if not its creation altogether – must be credited to Goldoni.

His first pair of *mezzi caratteri* appears in *Il Conte Caramella* (1751), an opera text created in the thick of his efforts to stretch the governing laws of prose theatre and right on the heels of the "year of the sixteen comedies." The frontispiece bears witness to their functional flexibility, placing them clearly midway between the *serio* and comic characters.

SERI
LA CONTESSA OLIMPIA: moglie del [wife of] Conte Caramella
IL MARCHESE DI RIPOLI: di lei amante [enamoured of her]
MEZI CARATERI
DORINA: giardiniera della contessa [gardener of the countess]

IL CONTE CARAMELLA: Creduto morto, in abito da pellegrino [believed dead, dressed as a pilgrim]
BUFFI
GHITTA: serva rustica della contessa [rustic servant of the countess]
CECCO: contadino di lei amante [farmer enamoured of her]
BRUNORO: contadino e tamburino di truppe suburbane [farmer and drummer of the local militia]

This text, in the manner of Goldoni's more typical *drammi giocosi*, is built around a multiplicity of narrative threads (an amorous plot involving the comic characters, another concerning the aristocrats), which are ultimately interwoven in a final reconciliation by the end of the work. The dominant dramatic line, however, is that of the protagonist and his quest (which leads him to suspend his identity temporarily) to reclaim his rightful place in his home and in his marriage. False rumours report that he has died on the battlefield, but the Count returns home disguised as a necromancer to ascertain whether his wife has remained faithful to him; the work is a perfect eighteenth-century reprise of the Homeric *Odyssey*, were it not that Goldoni had actually adopted a much more recent model, Joseph Addison's 1714 play *The Drummer; or, The Haunted House*.[27]

In an opera governed by comic dramatic irony, and the excitement of disguise and revelation, Goldoni takes care to provide a counterweight to the humour in the fully formed *parte seria* of the grieving Contessa Olimpia where Addison does not.[28] Her role may appear to be secondary because her arias are few, but she marks a significant step forward in the direction of psychological realism in the conflicting emotions she experiences over the span of the plot, as illustrated by the excerpts below. In fact, the carefully crafted emotional intimacy of this character establishes an important precedent for the sentimentalism that would become increasingly prominent in opera theatre over the next half century. Goldoni derives the pathos that colours her part from the most tragic of plights – self-doubt:

---

27 Addison's title stems from an element of the play: a servant plays a war drum at night, which the other members of the household take to be the Count's ghost (therefore, confirming his death). Goldoni also chooses to preserve this characteristic. See Addison, *The Drummer*.
28 Addison's Mrs Trueman is often a vehicle for comic sarcasm or wry social commentary. When Sir George Trueman, returned in disguise, asks whether his wife has grieved him, his servant assures him: "Longer than I have known any widow's – at least three days ... she was drown'd in tears till such time as the Taylor had made her widow's weeds – indeed they became her" (Addison, *The Drummer*, 2.1).

Ah, ch'io d'errar pavento e non ho core
d'abbandonarmi a nuovi affetti in preda;
par ch'estinto il consorte ancor non creda.[29]

Ah, I am afraid of falling and haven't the heart
to give myself over to new affections;
it would seem I still can't believe my husband to be gone.

Torn between rumours of her husband's death and an enduring, irrational hope that he might somehow still be alive, she observes her own emotions almost as an outsider, conveying the depth of her turmoil and eliciting compassion.

The greater novelty of *Il Conte Caramella*, however, is Goldoni's first *mezzi caratteri*, who further erode the boundaries between *buffo* and *serio* styles. The role of the Count, for example, who typically would have been treated as a *parte seria* on the basis of his higher rank, becomes comedic in the scenes where he is disguised. In the garb of a necromancer, his tone becomes colloquial and direct, in stark contrast to the expression of the full male *parte seria* (his rival, the Marquis of Ripoli), who speaks as if he had dropped out of a historical tragedy: "se ardirai cotanto, ignorante, impostore, proverai tu il mio sdegno e il mio furore. Cessa di provocarmi, trema dall'ira mia," *etc.* (If you dare as much, ignorant impostor, you will feel my wrath and fury. Don't provoke me, tremble at my rage, etc.).[30] In Galuppi's score, this translates into a reduction in the number of the set arias given to the Count (in comparison to those for the Marquis, for example), and more space for novel, free-form pieces that flow in and out of recitative. These new liberties are apparent in the following trio in which the disguised Count proves his worth as a diviner to the Countess and her maid, Dorina (the second *mezzo carattere* of the work, whose role is one of dominance among her peers):

CONTE: Orsù perché crediate
   ch'esser possa il futuro a me svelato
   qualche cosa dirovvi del passato.
   Pria d'essere sposata,
   il conte capitano
   vi prese per la mano una mattina.
   Fuggiste modestina,
   vi vergognaste un poco

29 Goldoni, *Il Conte Caramella*, 2.2.568–70.
30 Ibid., 3.2.1077–81.

ma vi ridusse in loco solitario.
Diceste: "Temerario,
andate via di qui,"
movendo in dir così la bocca al riso.
Ed ei con un sorriso
amante pronto e scaltro...
CONTESSA: Basta così, non voglio sentir altro.
DORINA: (Com'è venuta rossa). *(da sé)*
CONTESSA: (Io non so come ei possa
queste cose sapere per minuto). *(da sé)*
[...]
DORINA: Non gli badate, ch'egli è un ciarlatano.
CONTE: Io sono un ciarlatano? Sfacciatella,
io ti farò cambiar sensi e favella.
Rammenta quella borsa
che tu dal conte avesti
allora che facesti la mezzana.
E cosa non è strana,
se tu procuri adesso
di fare ancor lo stesso col marchese.
Il tutto mi è palese
e so che un regaletto ...
DORINA: Basta così ... (Che tu sia maledetto). *(da sé)*[31]

COUNT: So that you believe
that I can truly see the future,
let me tell you something of the past.
Before you were married,
The Count, Captain,
took you by the hand, one morning.
You fled him shyly,
you were a bit ashamed,
but he led you to a solitary place.
You told him: "Rogue,
go, leave me at once,"
but in saying so moved your lips to laughter.
And he, with a smile,
a quick and ready lover ...
CONTESSA: That's enough, let us hear no more.

---

31 Ibid., 2.4.608–41.

DORINA: (Look, she's blushing) *(aside)*
COUNTESS. (I wonder how he can know these things
in such detail.) *(aside)*.
[...]
DORINA: Pay him no mind, he's just a charlatan.
COUNT: Me, a charlatan? Insolent woman,
I'll make you change your mind and your words.
Remember that fine purse
you were given by the Count
when you acted as his go-between.
And now is no marvel
if you try do the same
for the Marquis.
I see it all,
and I know that a little gift ...
DORINA: That's enough ... (may you be damned) *(aside)*.

As even the position of the text indicates, the Count's sung portions are embedded within recitative that creates different dialogical levels; the characters interact as a trio, the women speak among themselves, and each has lines *a sé* (aside), creating dramatic irony for the spectator. This short excerpt is an early example of the dynamism and flexibility afforded by the *mezzo carattere*, as a hybrid between a solo aria and an ensemble piece that is placed in the midst of a scene rather than at its close. It also demonstrates how the *mezzo carattere* became a driving force for new musical forms.

A final innovative element of *Il Conte Caramella* is found in its resolution. The Count, rid of his disguise and restored to his rightful place in his home and his marriage, banishes the Marquis with the authority of his original stature and shows noble magnanimity at the same time:

Vattene, scellerato,
il piacere di trovare
una sposa fedele a questo segno
tutta mi fa depor l'ira e lo sdegno.[32]

Go, infamous one,
the joy of reuniting with
such a faithful wife
is enough to extinguish my outrage.

---

32 Ibid., 3.ultima.1321–4.

Clearly, his role transforms with ease into a full *parte seria*, while language and demeanour shift accordingly. Goldoni searches for a new dramatic figure with the ability to transcend character types, and further breaks down the separation of dramatic categories.

Later *mezzi caratteri* have more to say on the changing balance of tragic and comic in Goldoni's *drammi giocosi*, and in this regard perhaps none speaks more eloquently than *La Checchina* or *La Buona Figliuola* (1758/60), one of the most successful operas of the century in Niccolò Piccinni's musical rendering. Goldoni derived this *dramma giocoso* from one of the more celebrated products from the "year of the sixteen comedies," his 1750 *La Pamela*. This text for recited comedy was in turn inspired by Samuel Richardson's epistolary novel *Pamela; or Virtue Rewarded*.[33] The rising influence of the European novel tradition was clearly palpable by mid-century given not only Goldoni's choice of subject, but also the impressive number of spin-offs by other authors prompted by Richardson's original. This was without doubt a contributing factor to the rising sentimentality of predominantly comic opera and the interpolation of *romanzesco* (romance) elements in prose theatre as well.

Pamela had already enjoyed huge success in 1750, achieving a record of eighteen consecutive performances at its Venetian premiere. *La Cecchina* too was acclaimed internationally, especially once it received its second musical setting by Niccolò Piccinni in 1760 (the 1758 score by Domenico Fischietti is lost). Goldoni's translation of the work from comedy to opera prompted quite a few structural changes, but he maintained and even greatly enhanced the psychological characterization of the two protagonists in the opera, which is ideally suited to the flexible boundaries of the *mezzo carattere*. As in previous practice, Goldoni places Cecchina and her Marquis centrally within the character list, midway between *seri* and *buffi*. Stylistically, the two have little in common linguistically with the *parti serie*, who express themselves in the habitual Metastasian vein. Behaviourally, they are equally distant from the *parti buffe*, as the depiction of their unattainable love and interior conflict is imbued with compassion, never comedy.

In forming the two sentimental *mezzi caratteri*, Goldoni further pursues the linguistic simplification he first essayed in *Il Conte Caramella*. Cecchina's verses are concise and her terms measured, reflecting her unaffected simplicity:

---

33 For more on this chain of transmission, see Gallarati, *Musica e Maschera* and Crotti, introduction to Goldoni, *Pamela fanciulla- Pamela maritata*.

Vo cercando e non ritrovo
la mia pace e il mio contento
che per tutto meco porto
una spina in mezzo al cor.[34]

I search but cannot find
either peace or comfort;
the thorn in my heart
follows me everywhere.

Even when invoking death, her lines are tender and remain under-stated. Her style of expression differs substantially from what a *parte seria* might employ in the same circumstances:

Almen fra queste piante
avrò un po' di riposo.
Ah son sì stanca di sofferir
gl'insulti della nemica sorte
che son costretta a desiar la morte.[35]

Perhaps in this garden
I may find some respite.
I am so weary of bearing
fate's insults
that I must wish for death.

At the triumphant resolution of the *dramma*, Cecchina is revealed to be of aristocratic heritage, thereby ennobling her in the eyes of her de-tractors and permitting her, finally, to wed the man she loves. Yet her reaction is one of realistic confusion and interior conflict:

Ah, signori, vorrei
far i doveri miei; ma ho ancora il cuore
fra la gioia confuso e fra il timore.[36]

Ah sirs forgive me,
I would like to do my duty; but my heart is still confused,
divided between joy and fear.

34 Goldoni, *La Cecchina*, 1.16.417–20.
35 Ibid., 2.12.812–16.
36 Ibid., 3.11.1252–4.

Instead of pride or triumph, hesitation marks this critical turn of events for the heroine, once more emphasizing her modesty and sensitivity. *La Buona Figliuola* is, from beginning to end, an exercise in sentimentalism. For Daniel Heartz, it was the Goldoni libretto "destined to surpass all his other librettos in the influence it yielded,"[37] and some scholars have gone so far as to designate it as the very cradle of romanticism in opera.[38] This *dramma giocoso* also bears witness to Goldoni's progressive attraction to the psychology of the individual, an attraction equally plain in his prose theatre. His mature *commedie di carattere* and opera texts alike demonstrate a search for dramatic content within the psyche and its universal struggles, making external events progressively less central to the tension of his works. Goldoni's theatre is less about escape or abstraction and more about introspection. The drama in his works is psychological and sentimental, and his choice of contemporary, realistic settings seamlessly translates the emotional experiences of his stage characters to an audience of real individuals. His consistent choice of subject matter – the intimate yet universal facets of human nature and vice – aimed to let his audiences identify with what they saw and heard, perhaps gaining greater insights into their own lives and behaviours. These principles lie at the very core of Goldoni's essence as an author, and appear quite radical if we consider the success of some of his fiercest competitors (i.e., Carlo Gozzi), who in the same years were producing fantasy works, set in distant lands and times.[39] Without a doubt, the new moderation of the *mezzo carattere*, and above all its tendency toward the pathetic and the sentimental, are products of Goldoni's assimilation of the tragic opera tradition and his redirection of it toward modern realism and rationality.

Legacy

The effect that Goldoni's new measure of *materia buffa* and *seria* had in the arc of opera history is not easy to quantify. In addition to the circulation of the texts themselves, which we know to have been extensive, many of Goldoni's collaborators (both actors and musicians) became conduits for his texts, and, in the thriving network of cultural exchange that characterized the second half of the eighteenth century

---

37 Heartz, "Goldoni, Don Giovanni and the dramma giocoso."
38 Finetto, "La Pamela e La Buona Figliuola."
39 Many of Gozzi's works, such as *Turandot* (1762), or *The Love of Three Oranges* (1761), would go on to greater success a century or more later, in the throes of Romanticism and even (with Prokofiev) post-Romanticism.

in particular, brought them far and wide. A comprehensive tally of the period's performances of Goldoni's musical works, based on surviving documents (the total counts, therefore, could easily be higher) was issued recently in an appendix to the newest critical edition of his complete works.[40] Based on these statistics, a very clear picture emerges even from what still may be partial counts: of the sixty-nine new comic operas premiered in Venice between 1749 and 1761 (after which Goldoni accepted a new charge at the Parisian *Comédie Italienne*, and his output became less regular), forty-four used texts by Goldoni. Broadening to the entire Italian peninsula, of an estimated 2,000 operas given through the entire arc of the 1700s, nearly 300 used libretti by Goldoni. Most important, his *drammi giocosi* began to circulate outside of Italy as early as 1749, resulting in hundreds of documented performances not only throughout the whole of Europe but as far as Moscow, St Petersburg, and even young Philadelphia in the nascent United States, all before the turn of the century. The incredible reach of Goldoni's operas, and therefore the structures and styles they transmitted, is indeed humbling, and a true testament to the rich fabric of the cultural exchange of the Enlightenment and the dawning modern era. The assiduous export and transmission of these works unmistakably accounts for their power to influence nascent national schools and later traditions, in which affinities abound, as we have seen.

Indeed, the list of composers who set Goldoni's works to music is almost as endless as the chronology of their performances.[41] A few of the "foreign" names alone (the first setting of Goldoni's operas was carried out by Italian composers, many by "Il Buranello" Baldassarre Galuppi and others by celebrated exponents of the Neapolitan school) include Florian Gassmann (1729–74) in Presburg, Pedro Avondano (1714–82) in Lisbon, Carl Dittersdorf (1739–99) and Franz Joseph Haydn (1732–1809) in Esterhaza, Antonio Salieri (1750–1825) in Vienna, and the young W.A. Mozart (1756–91), among others, whose *Finta Giardiniera* has been called "a clumsy offspring of *La Buona Figliuola*."[42] The great variety of musical adaptations created, which put into practice Goldoni's novel dramatic structures, implies the gradual assimilation of his theatrical innovations by the generations that immediately followed. And the reappearance of features such as *parti buffe, parti serie, mezzi caratteri,*

---

40 Goldoni, *Drammi Comici per Musica*, ed. Urbani and Vencato.
41 Again, the comprehensive catalogue is found in the new Marislio edition, previously cited.
42 Heartz, *Mozart's Operas*, 199.

psychological elaboration, and the ever more assiduous employment of lifelike, flowing musical structures (*ariette*, ensemble pieces, ensemble finales) in, for example, the Mozart/Da Ponte "Italian" operas, is anything but coincidental. It is a direct inheritance.

We can even find direct textual echoes from Goldoni's librettos in other dramatists' works, testifying to the minute level on which his texts had become part of the public repertoire. Cimarosa's *Il maestro di cappella* uses verses taken directly from Goldoni's 1757 *dramma giocoso, Il viaggiatore ridicolo*.[43] The same opera, known throughout Europe by 1770, contains a prototypical catalogue aria that – while more punning – resonates strikingly with Leporello's analogous feature in Da Ponte's *Don Giovanni*:

> A Lion la Contessa la Cru.
> A Paris la Madama la Gru.
> A Madrid la Duchessa del Bos.
> In Inghilterra Mileda la Stos.
> In Germania ho le mie Baronesse.
> In Moscovia le mie Principesse.[44] *etc.*

> In Lyon the Countess la Cru.
> In Paris Madame la Gru.
> In Madrid the Duchess of Bos.
> In England Mylady of Stoss.
> In Germany I have my baronesses.
> In Moscow I have my princesses. *etc.*

The famous verses "vorrei e non vorrei … son fra il si e il no" (I'd like to but I don't want to … I'm between yes and no), Zerlina's celebrated opening in "La ci darem la mano" (*Don Giovanni*) (1.3), first appear in Goldoni's *Arcifanfano re dei matti* (2.8. 806), and the list of citations and imitations (not only by Da Ponte) could continue further.

---

43 "Ci sposeremo fra suoni e canti / Sposi brillanti, pieni d'amor. Voglio i violini, voglio i violoni / Voglio il fagotto, con l'oboè [*suonano corni da caccia*] / questo strumento non fa per me" (We shall wed amidst music and song / Beautiful spouses, full of love. I want violins and cellos / I want the bassoon with the oboe [*hunting horns are played*] / this instrument doesn't suit me) (Carlo Goldoni, *Il viaggiatore ridicolo* 3.3.1030–4). Note the allusive use of hunting horns to signify "cornuto" (cuckold), a comic device Mozart reuses in Figaro's "Aprite un po' quegli occhi" aria (*Nozze di Figaro*, 4.8).

44 Ibid., 2.4.605–10.

Later librettists Marco Coltellini and Giovan Battista Casti also took after Goldoni in various aspects of their own theatre, though an analysis of their works exceeds the scope of this study.

We can conclude, however, by noting just how much darkness and tragedy the *dramma giocoso per musica*, now a mature genre, can support. Mozart's *Don Giovanni* (1787) furnishes an ideal example. The delicate balance of this work, with its interweaving of *parti buffe*, *serie*, and *mezzi caratteri* – and the profound psychological depth that results from this admixture – could not have been achieved without the groundwork laid by Goldoni.

Mozart's operas are just one witness to Goldoni's continued influence in opera theatre well beyond his time, though it can be argued that it (particularly in the humanizing psychological depiction of his characters and the realism of the highs and lows they traverse) travels well into the nineteenth century. Goldoni's greatest legacy in music can therefore be defined as the renewal of both tragic and comic opera traditions through a new, modern fusion of the two: one that erased centuries of division between *serio* and *buffo*, uniting these once opposed modes into a new, homogeneous, organic style of theatre able to reflect and respond to its own times, and to our own.

Bibliography

Ackerman, Robert. *The Myth and Ritual School: J.G. Frazer and the Cambridge Ritualists*. New York: Garland, 1991.

Addante, Luca. *Repubblica e controrivoluzione. Il 1799 nella Calabria cosentina*. Naples: Vivarium, 2005.

Addison, Joseph. *The Drummer; or, The Haunted House*. London: Dodsley, 1715.

Adlerbeth, Gudmund Göran. *Gustaf III's resa i Italien: Anteckningar*. Edited by Henrik Schück. Stockholm: Albert Bonniers förlag, 1902.

Aeschylus. *The Suppliants*. Translated by Peter Burian. Princeton: Princeton University Press, 1991.

Affiches, annonces, et avis divers, ou Journal général de France 53 (May 1, 1784).

Ago, Renata. "Hegemony over the Social Scene and Zealous Popes (1676–1700)." In *Court and Politics in Papal Rome, 1492–1700*, edited by Gianvittorio Signorotto and Maria Antonietta Visceglia, 229–46. Cambridge: Cambridge University Press, 2002.

Aigaliers, Pierre Laudun d'. *Art poétique françois*. Paris: Antoine Du Brueil, 1597.

Ajello, Raffaele. *Arcana Juris. Diritto e politica nel Settecento italiano*. Napoli: Jovene, 1976.

Åkerman, Susanna. *Queen Christina of Sweden and Her Circle: The Transformation of a Seventeenth-Century Philosophical Libertine*. Brill Studies in Intellectual History, vol. 21. Leiden: E.J. Brill, 1991.

Alfieri, Vittorio. *Opere*. Edited by Francesco Maggini. 5 vols. Florence: Le Monnier, 1926–.

– *Vita scritta da esso*. Edited by Luigi Fassò. Asti: Casa d'Alfieri, 1951.

Andrews, Richard. "The Cinquecento Theatre." In *The Cambridge History of Italian Literature*, edited by Peter Brand and Lino Pertile, 277–98. Cambridge: Cambridge University Press, 1996.

Anisimov, Evgenii. *Afrodita u vlasti. Tsarstvovanie Elisavety Petrovny*. Moscow: Ast, 2010.

Anthony, James R. "Jean-Baptiste Lully." In *The New Grove French Baroque Masters*, edited by James R. Anthony, 1–70. New York: Norton, 1986.

Ariani, Marco. *Tra classicismo e manierismo: il teatro tragico del cinquecento*. Florence: L.S. Olschki, 1974.

Aristotle. *On Rhetoric: A Theory of Civil Discourse*. Translated and edited by George Kennedy. 2nd ed. New York: Oxford University Press, 2007.

Aristotle. *Poetics*. Translated by Anthony Kenny. Oxford: Oxford University Press, 2013.

– *"Art" of Rhetoric*. Translated by J.H. Freese. Loeb Classical Library. Cambridge: Harvard University Press, 1926.

Aristotle's Art of Poetry. Translated from the Original Greek, According to Mr. Theodore Goulston's Edition. Together with Mr. D'Acier's Notes Translated from the French. London: Dan. Browne and Will. Turner, 1705.

Arlen, Shelley. *The Cambridge Ritualists: An Annotated Bibliography of the Works by and about Jane Ellen Harrison, Gilbert Murray, Francis M. Cornford, and Arthur Bernard Cook*. Metuchen, NJ: Scarecrow Press, 1990.

Arnaud, Antoine. *The Art of Speaking, Written in French by Messieurs du Port Royal. Rendered into English*. London, 1676.

Arteaga, Stefano. *Le rivoluzioni del teatro musicale italiano dalla sua origine fino al presente*. 3 vols. Bologna: Trenti, 1783–85.

– *Le rivoluzioni del teatro musicale italiano dalla sua origine fino al presente*. 2nd ed. 2 vols. Venice: Carlo Palese, 1785.

Ashley, Tim. "Oreste review – compelling and revolting; whether it serves Handel is another matter." *Guardian*. Nov. 9, 2016.

Aubignac, François Hédelin, abbé d'. *La Pratique du théâtre* [1657]. Edited by Hélène Baby. Paris: Honoré Champion, 2001.

– *The Whole Art of the Stage. Containing not only the Rules of Drammatick Art, But Many Curious Observations about It*. London: printed for the author, 1684.

Auld, Louis E. *The "Lyric Art" of Pierre Perrin, Founder of French Opera*. 3 vols. Institute of Medieval Music, Henryville, 1986.

Baillet, Adrien. *Jugemens des sçavans sur les principaux ouvrages des auteurs*. 4 tomes in 9 vols. Paris: Antoine Dezallier, 1686.

Baratto, Mario. *Tre saggi sul teatro: Ruzante, Aretino, Goldoni*. Vicenza: Neri-Pozza, 1964.

Barnett, Dene. *The Art of Gesture: The Practices and Principles of 18th Century Acting*. Heidelberg: Carl Winter, 1987.

Batteux, Charles. *Les Beaux arts réduits à un même principe* [1773]. Geneva: Slatkine, 1969.

Bayard, Marc. "Le roi au cœur du théâtre: Richelieu met en scène l'Autorité." In *L'Image du roi, de François Ier à Louis XIV*, edited by T.W. Gaehtgens and Nicole Hochner, 191–208. Paris: Éditions de la Maison des sciences de l'homme, 2006.

– "Les faiseurs d'artifice: Georges Buffequin et les artistes de l'éphémère à l'époque de Richelieu." *XVIIe Siècle* 230 (2006): 151–64.

– ed. *Rome-Paris, 1640. Transferts culturels et renaissance d'un centre artistique.* Rome and Paris: Académie de France à Rome-Villa Médicis and Somogy Editions d'Art, 2010.

Beaussant, Philippe. *Lully, ou Le musicien du Soleil.* Paris: Gallimard, 1992.

Beijer, Anne. "Une maquette de décor récemment retrouvée pour le 'Ballet de la Prospérité des armes de France' dansé à Paris, le 7 février 1641. Étude sur la mise en scène au Grand Théâtre du Palais-Cardinal avant l'arrivée de Torelli." In *Le Lieu théâtral à la Renaissance,* edited by Jean Jacquot, 377–404. Paris: CNRS, 1964.

Bellina, Anna Laura. "La 'Maestra' esaminata." Introduction to Gioacchino Cocchi, *La maestra.* Milan: Ricordi, 1987.

Beni, Paolo. *Pauli Benii Eugubini In Aristotelis Poeticam commentarii: in quibus ad obscura quaeque decreta planius adhuc dilucidanda, centum poeticae controuersiae interponuntur & copiosissime explicatur.* [Padua]: F. Bolzettam, 1613.

Beniscelli, Alberto. *Felicità sognate. Il teatro di Metastasio.* Genova: Il melangolo, 2000.

Bergalli, Luisa. *Agide re di Sparta, dramma per musica.* Venice: Marino Rossetti, 1725.

– *Eleazaro, azione sacra.* Vienna: G.P. Van Ghelen, 1739.

– *Farnace. Dramma per musica da rappresentarsi nel teatro di S.A.S.E di Baviera nel Carnevale del'anno 1740.* Munich: Vötter, 1740.

– *Le avventure del poeta, commedia.* Venice: Cristoforo Zane, 1730.

– *Le commedie di Terenzio, tradotte in verso sciolto da Luisa Bergalli.* 6 vols. Venice: Cristoforo Zane, 1735–9.

– *L'Elenia, dramma per musica.* Venice: Alvise Valvasense, 1730.

– *Teba, tragedia.* Venice: Cristoforo Zane, 1728.

– ed. *Componimenti poetici delle più illustri rimatrici d'ogni secolo.* 2 vols. Venice: Antonio Mora, 1726.

– trans. *Opere di Racine tradotte.* Venice: Domenico Loise, 1736.

– trans. *Teatro ebraico ovvero Scelta di tragedie tratte d'argomenti ebraici.* Venice: Pietro Valvasense, 1751.

Bertola de' Giorgi, Aurelio. *Osservazioni sopra Metastasio. Con alcuni versi.* Bassano: Remondini, 1784.

Bettinelli, Giuseppe, ed., *Opere drammatiche del Sig. Abbate Metastasio.* 4 vols. Venice: Giuseppe Bettinelli, 1733.

Biagi, Guido. "Lettere inedite di Lodovico Antonio Muratori ad Apostolo Zeno e di questo a lui." *Rivista delle biblioteche e degli archive* 7 (1896): 38–54.

Bjurström, Per. *Giacomo Torelli and Baroque Stage Design.* Stockholm: Nationalmuseum Stockholm, 1961.

Blocker, Déborah. *Instituer un "art": Politiques du théâtre dans la France du premier XVIIe siècle.* Paris: Honoré Champion, 2009.

Bloechl, Olivia Ashley. *Opera and the Political Imaginary in Old Regime France.* Chicago: University of Chicago Press, 2017.

Bodin, Jean. *Les six livres de la République.* Paris: Cartier, 1599.

Bohnert, Cécile. "La poétique des paroles de musique selon Pierre Perrin: l'exemple de *La Mort d'Adonis.*" Edited by Anne-Marie Goulet and Laura Naudeix. Brussels: Mardaga, 2010.

Boileau-Despréaux, Nicolas. *Satires.* Edited by Albert Cahen. Paris: Librarie E. Droz, 1932.

Bolduc, Benoît. *Andromède au rocher. Fortune théâtrale d'une image en France et en Italie (1587–1712).* Florence: Leo Olschki, 2002.

– *La Fête imprimée. Spectacles et cérémonies politiques (1549–1662).* Paris: Classiques Garnier, 2016.

Borchmeyer, Dieter. "Wagner and Nietzsche." In *Wagner Handbook,* edited by Ulrich Müller and Peter Wapnewski, 327–42. Cambridge: Harvard University Press, 1992.

Boyer, Claude. *Dessein de la tragédie des* Amours de Jupiter et de Sémélé, *représentée sur le Théâtre Royal du Marais, inventé par le Sieur Buffequin, Machiniste.* Paris: Pierre Promé, 1666.

Brandenburg, Irene. "Hypermnestra und die Danaiden: Ein 'sujet véritablement terrible' in Glucks Werk und Vita." In *Symposiumsbericht: Gluck und Prag: Nürnberg, 20. –22. Juli 2012,* edited by Thomas Betzwieser and Daniel Brandenburg, 147–61. Gluck-Studien 7. Kassel: Bärenreiter, 2016.

– *Vito Giuseppe Millico: Studien zu Leben und Werk eines komponierenden Kastraten im 18. Jahrhundert.* PhD thesis, Universität Salzburg, 1995.

Bray, René. *La Formation de la doctrine classique en France.* Paris: Librairie Nizet, 1963.

Brett, Philip, and George Haggerty. "Handel and the Sentimental: The Case of 'Athalia.'" *Music & Letters.* 68, no. 2 (1987): 112–27.

Brewer, Daniel. "Stages of the Enlightened Sublime: Narrating Sublimation." *Theatre Journal* 38, no. 1 (1986): 5–18.

Brizzi, Bruno. "Uno spunto polemico calzabigiano: *Ipermestra o Le Danaidi.*" In *La figura e l'opera di Ranieri de' Calzabigi: Atti del convegno di studi (Livorno, 14–15 dicembre 1987),* edited by Federico Marri, 119–45. Florence: Leo S. Olsckhi editore, 1989.

Brosses, Charles de. *Lettres familières écrites d'Italie à quelques amis en 1739 et 1740.* Edited by Hippolyte Babou. 2 vols. Paris, 1858.

Brumoy, Pierre. *Le Théâtre des Grecs.* 3 vols. Paris: Rollin père, Coignard fils & Rollin fils, 1730.

Brunetière, Ferdinand. *Manuel de l'histoire de la littérature française.* Paris: Librairie Ch. Delagrave, 1898.

Bucciarelli, Melania. *Italian Opera and European Theatre, 1680–1720: Plots, Performers, Dramaturgies.* Turhout: Brepols, 2000.

Bulwer, John. *Chirologia: or the Natural Language of the Hand... Whereunto Is Added, Chironomia: Or, the Art of Manuall Rhetoricke.* London, 1644.

Burian, Peter. "Tragedy Adapted for Stages and Screens: The Renaissance to the Present." In *The Cambridge Companion to Greek Tragedy*, edited by P.E. Easterling, 228–83. Cambridge: Cambridge University Press, 1997.

Burnett, Anne Pippin. *Catastrophe Survived: Euripides' Plays of Mixed Reversal.* Oxford: Clarendon Press, 1971.

Burney, Charles. *Memoirs of the life and writings of the Abate Metastasio. In which are incorporated, translations of his principal letters.* 3 vols. London: G.G. and J. Robinson, 1796.

Burrows, Donald, Helen Coffey, John Greenacombe, and Anthony Hicks, eds. *George Frederick Handel: Collected Documents.* Cambridge: Cambridge University Press, 2014.

Bywater, Ingram. *Aristotle on the Art of Poetry.* Oxford: Clarendon, 1909.

Cahusac, Louis de. *La Danse ancienne et moderne.* 3 vols. The Hague, 1754.

– *La danse ancienne et moderne: ou, traité historique de la danse.* Edited by Nathalie Lecomte, Laura Naudeix, Jean-Noël Laurenti. Paris: Desjonquères; Paris: Centre national de la danse, c. 2004.

Calder, William M. III, ed. *The Cambridge Ritualists Reconsidered.* Atlanta: Scholars Press, 1991.

Calhoun, Alison. "Corneille's *Andromède* and Opera: Practice Before Theory." *Cahiers du Dix-Septième* 16, no. 1 (2015): 1–17.

Calzabigi, Ranieri. "Dissertazione su le Poesie Drammatiche del Signore Abate Pietro Metastasio." In Pietro Metastasio, *Poesie*, 1: 19–204. Paris: Quillau, 1755; Genova: Olzati, 1766.

– *Ipermestra o Le Danaidi, tragedia per musica.* In *Poesie e prose diverse* I. Naples: Onofrio Zambraja, 1793.

– *Poesie e prose diverse.* 2 vols. Naples: Onofrio Zambraja, 1793.

– *Scritti teatrali e letterari.* Edited by Anna Laura Bellina. 2 vols. Rome: Salerno Editrice, 1994.

Carter, Tim. "Mask and illusion." In *The Cambridge History of Seventeenth-Century Music*, edited by Tim Carter and John Butt, 241–82. Cambridge: Cambridge University Press, 2005.

– Carter, Tim. "Stile rappresentativo." *Grove Music Online.* 2001. Accessed 14 Jun. 2022. https://www.oxfordmusiconline.com/grovemusic/view/10.1093/gmo/9781561592630.001.0001/omo-9781561592630-e-0000026774.

Castelvetro, Ludovico. *Poetica d'Aristotele vulgarizzata e sposta.* Edited by Werther Romani. 2 vols. Bari: G. Laterza, 1978–9.

Catherine II. *Nakaz kommissii o sostavlenii proekta novago ulozheniia.* Moscow: pri Senate, 1767.

Cauthen, Paul. "Merope (libretto)." *Grove Music Online.* 2002. Accessed 14 Jun. 2022. https://www.oxfordmusiconline.com/grovemusic/view/10.1093 /gmo/9781561592630.001.0001/omo-9781561592630-e-5000005902.

Cessac, Catherine. *Marc-Antoine Charpentier.* Translated by E. Thomas Glasow. Portland: Amadeus Press, 1995.

Charpentier, Marc-Antoine. *Médée. Tragédie en musique. Livret de Thomas Corneille.* Edited by Edmond Lemaître. Paris: Editions du Centre National de la Recherche Scientifique, 1987.

– *Médée.* Les Arts Florissants. Dir. William Christie. Erato 4509-96558-2, 1995. 3 CD.

– *Médée.* Le Concert Spirituel. Mus. dir. Hervé Niquet. Film dir. Vincent Boussard. Aller Retour Production EDV 1507, 2004. DVD.

Charron, Pierre. *De la sagesse. Trois livres.* Paris: Feugé, 1621.

Chemello, Andriana. "Le ricerche erudite di Luisa Bergalli." In *Geografie e genealogie letterarie. Erudite, biografe, croniste, narratrici, épistolières, utopiste fra Settecento e Ottocento*, edited by Adriana Chemello and Luisa Ricaldone, 49–88. Padua: Il Poligrafo, 2000.

– "Luisa Bergalli letterata di chiara fama." In *Luisa Bergalli. Poetessa drammaturga traduttrice critica letteraria. Atti del convegn*, edited by Adriana Chemello, 20–2. Mirano, VCE: Eidos, 2007.

Cherbuliez, Juliette. *In the Wake of Medea: Neoclassical Theater and the Arts of Destruction.* New York: Fordham University Press, 2020.

Chiabò, M., and F. Doglio, eds. *Origini del dramma pastorale in Europa.* Viterbo: Centro Studi sul Teatro Medioevale e Rinascimentale, 1984.

Cicero. *De Oratore.* Translated by E.W. Sutton and H. Rackham. 2 vols. Loeb Classical Library. Cambridge: Harvard University Press, 1942.

Civardi, Jean-Marc. *La querelle du Cid: (1637–1638): édition critique intégrale.* Paris: Champion, 2004.

Coeffeteau, Nicholas. *Tableau des passions humaines, de leurs causes et leurs effets.* Paris, 1630.

Cohen, Mitchell. *The Politics of Opera. A History from Monteverdi to Mozart.* Princeton: Princeton University Press, 2017.

Cook, Harold J., and Sven Dupré. "Introduction." In *Translating Knowledge in the Early Modern Low Countries*, edited by Harold J. Cook and Sven Dupré, 3–17. Berlin: LIT-Verlag, 2013.

Corneille, Pierre. *Andromède.* In Corneille, *Théâtre.* Vol. 4, edited by Hélène Visentin, directed by Liliane Picciola. Paris: Classiques Garnier, 2024.

– *Théâtre complet.* Edited by Alain Niderst. 3 vols. Rouen: Publications de l'Université de Rouen, 1984.

– *Trois discours sur le poème dramatique* [1660]. Edited by Bénédicte Louvat and Marc Escola. Paris: Garnier-Flammarion, 1999.

Correspondance littéraire, philosophique et critique, adressée à un souverain d'Allemagne, pendant une partie des années 1775–1776, et pendant les années 1782 à 1790 inclusivement, par le Baron de Grimm et par Diderot. 3 vols. Paris: F. Buirson libraire, 1813.

Couvreur, Manuel. *Jean-Baptiste Lully: musique et dramaturgie au service du prince.* Brussels: M. Vokar, 1992.

Cox, Virginia. *The Prodigious Muse: Women's Writing in Counter-Reformation Italy.* Baltimore: Johns Hopkins University Press, 2011.

Cox, Virginia, and Lisa Sampson. "Volume Editors' Introduction." In *Flori, A Pastoral Drama by Maddalena Campiglia*, edited and translated by Virginia Cox and Lisa Sampson, 1–35. Chicago: University of Chicago Press, 2004.

Crescimbeni, Giovan Mario. *Commentarii alla sua istoria della volgar poesia.* 5 vols. Rome, 1702–11.

– *La bellezza della volgar poesia.* Rome: Buagni, 1700.

– *L'Arcadia del Canonico Gio. Mario Crescimbeni.* Rome: de'Rossi, 1708.

– *L'istoria della volgar poesia.* Rome: Chracas, 1698.

Cristiani, Chiara. "L'idea di impero: dalla tradizione classica all'*Astrea placata* di Metastasio." *La Rassegna della letteratura italiana*, 112, no. 1 (2008): 93–105.

Croll, Gerhard. "Gluck, Wien und Neapel." In *Napoli e il teatro musicale in Europa tra sette e ottocento: Studi in onore di Friedrich Lippmann*, edited by Bianca Maria Antolini and Wolfgang Witzenmann, 37–43. Florence: Leo S. Olschki, 1993.

Crotti, Ilaria. Introduction to Carlo Goldoni, *Pamela fanciulla, Pamela maritata.* Venice: Marsilio, 1995.

– *Libro, Mondo, e Teatro.* Venice: Marsilio, 1999.

Cureau de la Chambre, Marin. *The Characters of the Passions.* Translated by J. Holden. London, 1650.

Curran, Stuart. "Recollecting the Renaissance: Luisa Bergalli's *Componimenti Poetici* (1726)." In *Strong Voices, Weak History. Early Women Writers & Canons in England, France, & Italy*, edited by Pamela Joseph Benson and Victoria Kirkham, 263–86. Ann Arbor: The University of Michigan Press, 2005.

D'Achille, Paolo. "Variazioni linguistiche e drammaturgiche sul mito di Ipermestra nel melodramma italiano tra Sette e Ottocento." In *Spazi e contesti teatrali: Antico e moderno*, edited by Stefano Novelli and Massimo Giuseppetti, 243–62. Amsterdam: Adolf M. Hakkert Publishing, 2017.

Dacier, André. *Le poétique d'Aristote, traduit e français, avec des remarques.* Paris: Claude Barbin, 1692.

– *La poétique d'Aristote contenant les règles les plus exactes pour juger du poëme heroïque, & des pieces de theater, la tragedie & la comedie. Traduite en françois, avec des remarques critiques sur tout l'ouvrage, par Mr. Dacier.* Amsterdam: Chez J. Covens & C. Mortier, 1733.

Daolmi, Davide. "La Drammaturgia al servizio della scenotechnica. Le 'volubili scene' dell'opera barberiniana." *Il Saggiatore musicale* 18, no. 1 (2006): 5–62.

Darlow, Mark. "Eighteenth-Century French Musical Theatre." *French Studies* 66, no. 1 (2012): 68–77.

Davenant, Sir William. The Authors Preface [1650], *Gondibert*. Edited by David F. Gladish. Oxford: Clarendon Press, 1971.

De Benedetto, Renato. "Poetics and Polemics." In *Opera in Theory and in Practice*. Part II, vol. 6 of *The History of Italian Opera*, 1–71, edited by Lorenzo Bianconi and Giorgio Pestelli. Chicago: The University of Chicago Press, 2003.

De Gamerra. Giovanni. *La Corneide: Poema eroi-comico.* 7 vols. [Livorno: Lapi, 1781.]

Degauque, Isabelle. *Les tragédies de Voltaire au miroir de leurs parodies dramatiques: d'*Oedipe *(1718) à* Tancrède *(1760).* Paris: Honoré Champion, 2007.

DeJean, Joan. *Ancients Against Moderns: Culture Wars and the Making of a Fin de Siècle.* Chicago: University of Chicago Press, 1997.

DelDonna, Anthony R. "Tradition, Innovation, and Experimentation: The Dramatic Stage and New Modes of Performance in Late Eighteenth-Century Naples." In *Quaderni d'italianistica* 36, no. 1 (2015): 139–72.

Delmas, Christian. *La Tragédie de l'âge classique (1553–1770).* Paris: Éditions du Seuil, 1994.

– "L'unité du genre tragique au XVIIᵉ siècle." *Littératures classiques* 16 (1992): 103–23; reprinted in *Mythe et Histoire dans le Théâtre classique. Hommage à Christian Delmas,* edited by Fanny Népote-Desmarres and Jean-Philippe Grosperrin, 33–54. Toulouse: Société de Littératures Classiques, 2002.

– *Mythologie et mythe dans le théâtre français (1650–1676).* Genève: Droz, 1985.

Demuth, Norman. *French Opera: Its Development to the Revolution* [1969]. New York: Da Capo Press, 1978.

Dennis, John. *The Critical Works of John Dennis.* Edited by Edward Niles Hooker. 2 vols. Baltimore: Johns Hopkins University Press, 1939.

De Sanctis, Francesco. *Opere.* Edited by Niccolò Gallo. Milan: Ricciardi, 1961.

DeSimone, Alison. *The Power of Pastiche. Musical Miscellany and Cultural Identity in Early Eighteenth-Century England.* Clemson, SC: Clemson Univeresty Press, 2021.

Descartes, René, *Œuvres philosophiques de Descartes.* Edited by Ferdinand Alquié. 3 vols. Paris: Classiques Garnier, 1989.

– *The Passions of the Soul* [1649]. Translated by Stephen H. Voss. Indianapolis: Hackett, 1989.

Desmarets de Saint-Sorlin, Jean. *Mirame, Tragi-comédie.* Edited by Catherine Guillot and Colette Scherer. Rennes: Presses Universitaires des Rennes, 2010.

Deutsch, Otto. *Handel: A Documentary Biography*. New York: W.W. Norton, 1955.

Dill, Charles. *Monstrous Opera: Rameau and the Tragic Tradition*. Princeton: Princeton University Press, 1998.

– "Pellegrin, Opera and Tragedy." *Cambridge Opera Journal* 10, no. 3 (1998): 247–57.

– "Rameau Reading Lully: Meaning and System in Rameau's Recitative Tradition." *Cambridge Opera Journal* 6 (1994): 1–17.

Dixon, Susan M. *Between the Real and Ideal: The Accademia Degli Arcadi and Its Garden in Eighteenth-century Rome*. Newark, NJ: University of Delaware Press, 2006.

Dominguez, Véronique. "Les machines du théâtre français: de la technique à l'illusion (XIVᵉ–XVIIᵉ s.)." In *Engins et machines: l'imaginaire mécanique dans les textes médiévaux*, edited by Fabienne Pomel, 105–29. Rennes: Presses Universitaires de Rennes, 2015.

Doni, Gio Battista. *Annotazioni sopra il Compendio de' generi e de' modi della musica*. Rome: A. Fei, 1640.

Dotlačilová, Petra. *Costume in the Time of Reforms: Louis-René Boquet Designing Eighteenth-Century Ballet and Opera*. PhD thesis, Stockholm University, 2020.

Dotoli, Giovanni. *Temps de préfaces: le débat théâtral en France de Hardy à la Querelle du "Cid."* Paris: Klincksieck, 1996.

Dryden, John. *The Works of John Dryden*. Edited by Edward Niles Hooker and H.T. Swedenberg, Jr. 20 vols. Berkeley: University of California Press, 1956–89.

Dubos, Jean-Baptiste. *Réflexions critiques sur la poésie et sur la peinture*. Paris, 1719. Translated by Thomas Nugent as *Critical Reflections on Poetry, Painting, and Music, with an Inquiry into the Rise and Progress of the Theatrical Entertainments of the Ancients*. London, 1748.

Dudouyt, Cécile. "Phantom Chorus: Missing Chorality on the French Eighteenth-Century Stage." In *Choruses, Ancient and Modern*, edited by Joshua Billings, Felix Budelmann, and Fiona Macintosh, 203–24. Oxford: Oxford University Press, 2013.

– "The Reception of Greek Theater in France since 1700." In *A Handbook to the Reception of Greek Drama*, edited by Betine van Zyl Smit, 238–56. Malden, MA and Oxford: Wiley-Blackwell, 2016.

– "Voltaire's Subliminal Enlightenment: Sophoclean 'Simplicity' and the Purpose of Tragedy." In *Shadows of the Enlightenment: Tragic Drama during Europe's Age of Reason*, 153–72. Columbus: The Ohio State University Press, 2022.

Duncan, David Allen. "Persuading the Affections: Rhetorical Theory and Mersenne's Advice to Harmonic Orators." In *French Musical thought, 1600–1800*, 149–75. Ann Arbor: UMI Research Press, 1989.

Duron, Jean. "Commentaire littéraire et musical." *Marc-Antoine Charpentier: Médée. L'Avant-scène opéra* no. 68 (1984): 59–97.

– Booklet. *Atys*. By Jean-Baptiste Lully. Les Arts Florissants. Dir. William Christie. Harmonia Muni 401257.59, 1987. 3 CD.

[Du Roullet, François-Louis Gand Le Bland.] "Réponse de l'Auteur du Poëme des *Danaïdes* à la Lettre de M. Cassabiggi [*sic*], imprimée dans le *Mercure de France*, N°· 34." *Mercure de France* 41 (October 9, 1784), 86–90.

[Du Roullet, François-Louis Gand Le Bland and Tschudi, Jean-Baptiste-Louis-Théodore de.] *Les Danaïdes: Tragédie-lyrique en cinq actes*. Paris: P. de Lormel, 1784.

Duso, Giuseppe, ed. *Il contratto sociale nella filosofia politica moderna*. Bologna: Il Mulino, 1987.

Dyzenhaus, David. "Hobbes and the Legitimacy of Law." *Law and Philosophy* 20 (2001): 461–98.

Dzelzainis, Martin. "The Ciceronian Theory of Tyrannicide from Buchanan to Milton." In *George Buchanan: Political Thought in Early Modern Britain and Europe*, edited by Caroline Erskine and Roger A. Mason, 173–87. Farnham: Ashgate, 2012.

Easterling, P.E., ed. *The Cambridge Companion to Greek Tragedy*. Cambridge: Cambridge University Press, 1997.

Eitner, Robert, ed. *Publikation älterer praktischer und theorestischer Musik-Werke*. Bd. 15 *Die Oper von ihren ersten Anfängen bis zur Mitte des 18. Jahrhunderts*. Vol. 3. Leipzig: Breitkopf und Härtel, 1885.

Else, Gerard F. *Aristotle's Poetics: The Argument*. Cambridge: Harvard University Press, 1967.

Emery, Ted. *Goldoni as Librettist, Theatrical Reform and the Dramma Giocoso per Musica*. Bern: Peter Lang, 1995.

Euripides. Vol. 1. Translated by David Kovacs. Loeb Classical Library. Cambridge: Harvard University Press, 1994.

Ewans, Michael. "Aeschylus and Opera." In *Brill's Companion to the Reception of Aeschylus*, edited by Rebecca Futo Kennedy, 203–24. Leiden: Brill, 2018.

Fabrizi, Angelo, Laura Ghidetti, and Francesca Mecatti, eds. *Alfieri e Calzabigi con un scritto inedito di Giuseppe Pelli*. Florence: Le Lettere, 2011.

Feldman, Martha. *Opera and Sovereignty: Transforming Myths in Eighteenth-Century Italy*. Chicago: The University of Chicago Press, 2007.

Felice, Elena Sala Di. "Zeno, Apostolo." *Grove Music Online*. 2001; accessed 14 Jun. 2022. https://www.oxfordmusiconline.com/grovemusic/view/10.1093/gmo/9781561592630.001.0001/omo-9781561592630-e-0000030928.

Fénelon, François de Pons de Salignac de la Mothe-. *Correspondance de Fénelon*. Edited by Jean Orcibal et al. 17 vols. Paris: Klincksieck, 1972–99.

Ferrari, Luigi. *Le traduzioni italiane del Teatro tragico francese nei secoli XVII e XVIII.* Paris: éduard Champion, 1925.

Ferrario, Sarah Brown. "Aeschylus and Western Opera." In *The Reception of Aeschylus' Plays through Shifting Models and Frontiers,* edited by Stratos E. Constantinidis, 176–212. Leiden: Brill, 2016.

Ferrone, Siro. *La vita e il Teatro di Carlo Goldoni.* Venice: Marsilio, 2011.

Fido, Franco. "Riforma e controriforma del teatro. I libretti per musica di Goldoni dal 1748 al 1753." *Studi Goldoniani.* 1985.

Finetto, Anna Maria. *"La Pamela* e *La Buona Figliuola*: Il Linguaggio Patetico di Goldoni." *Studi Goldoniani.* 1988.

Folina, Goldin. "Le 'tragiche miniature' di Metastasio." In *Il melodramma di Pietro Metastasio: la poesia, la musica, la messa in scena e l'opera italiana del Settecento: [atti del convegno internazionale di studi, Roma, 2-5 dicembre 1998],* edited by Elena Sala Di Felice and Rossana Caira Lumetti, 47–72. Roma: Aracne, 2001.

Forestier, Georges. "De la modernité anti-classique au classicisme moderne. Le modèle théâtral (1628–1634)." *Littératures Classiques* 19 (1993): 87–128.

– *"Iphigénie*: Notice." *Œvres complètes de Jean Racine.* Edited by Georges Forestier. 2 vols. Paris: Gallimard, 1999. 1: 1555–79.

– *Passions tragiques et règles classiques.* Paris: PUF, 2003.

Franchi, Saverio. *Drammaturgia Romana.* I. Rome: Edizioni di Storia e Letteratura, 1988.

Freeman, Robert. *Opera Without Drama: Currents of Change in Italian Opera, 1675–1725.* Ann Arbor, MI: UMI Research Press, 1981.

Fubini, Enrico. *Music and Culture in Eighteenth-Century Europe: A Source Book.* Translated from the original sources by Wolfgan Freis, Lisa Gasbarrone, and Michael Louis Leone. Translation edited by Bonnie J, Blackburn. Chicago: University of Chicago Press, 1994.

Fumaroli, Marc. "Les abeilles et les araignées." Introduction to *La Querelle des Anciens et des Moderns,* edited by A.M. Lecoq, 2–218. Paris: Gallimard, 2001.

Furetière, Antoine. *Dictionnaire universel.* The Hague: Arnoud and Reinier Leers, 1690.

Gallarati, Paolo. *Musica e Maschera.* Turin: EDT, 1984.

Garzonio, Stefano. "Metastasio e la poesia russa tra classicismo e romanticismo: la fortuna di un motivo." *Museum Patavinum* (1985): 313–26.

Gasté, Armand. *La querelle du Cid: pieces et pamphlets publiés d'après les originaux avec une introduction.* Geneva: Slatkine, 1970.

Gautruche, Pierre. *The Poetical Histories.* London: Pitt, 1671.

Gerbino, Giuseppe. *Music and the Myth of Arcadia in Renaissance Italy.* Cambridge: Cambridge University Press, 2009.

Giacomini Tebalducci Malespini, Lorenzo. *De la purgazione de la tragedia* [1586]. In *Trattati di poetica e retorica del cinquecento,* vol. 3, edited by Bernard Weinberg, 345–71. 4 vols. Bari: Gius. Laterza & Fifli, 1972.

Giazotto, Remo. *Poesia melodrammatica e pensiero critico nel settecento*. Milan: Fratelli Bocca, 1954.

Giraldi, Giovanni Battista. *Discorsi di m. Giovanbattista Giraldi Cinzio […] intorno al comporre dei Romanzi, delle Comedie, delle Tragedie, e di altre maniere di Poesia*. Venice: Gabriel Giolito de Ferrari et fratelli, 1554.

– *Raccolta di novellieri italiani. Gli Ecatommiti, ovvero cento novelle di Gio. Battista Giraldi Cintio*. 3 vols. Torino: Cugini Pomba e Comp. Editori, 1853.

Girdlestone, Cuthbert. *La tragédie en musique (1673–1750) considérée comme genre littéraire*. Geneva: Librairie Droz, 1972.

Goehr, Lydia. *The Imaginary Museum of Musical Works: An Essay in the Philosophy of Music*. Oxford: Oxford University Press, 1992. Rev. ed. 2007.

Giroud, Vincent. *French Opera: A Short History*. New Haven: Yale University Press, 2010.

Gluck, Christoph Willibald, Ritter von. *Alceste: tragedia*. Vienna: Nella stamparia aulica di Giovanni Tomaso de Trattnern, 1769.

Goldhill, Simon. *Victorian Culture and Classical Antiquity: Art, Opera, Fiction and the Proclamation of Modernity*. Princeton: Princeton University Press, 2011.

Goldin Folena, Daniela. "Le 'tragiche miniature' di Metastasio: poesia e dramma nei recitativi metastasiani." In *Il melodramma di Pietro Metastasio. La poesia, la musica, la messa in scena e l'opera italiana nel Settecento*, edited by Elena Sala di Felice and Rossana Caira Lumetti, 47–72. Rome: Aracne, 2001.

Golding, Alfred Siemon. *Classicist Acting: Two Centuries of Performance Tradition at the Amsterdam Schouwburg, to Which Is Appended an Annotated Translation of the "Lessons in the Principles of Gesticulation and Mimic Expression" of Johannes Jelgerhuis*. Lanham, MD: University Press of America, 1984.

Goldoni, Carlo. *Drammi Comici per Musica*. Edited by Silvia Urbani and Anna Vencato. 4 vols. Venice: Marsilio, 2007–20.

– *Il Conte Caramella*. Venice: Teatro S. Samuele, 1751.

– *Il teatro comico*. Milan: C. Signorelli, [1926].

– *Il viaggiatore ridicolo*. Parma, 1777.

– *La Buona Figliuola (La Cecchina)*. Parma: Teatro Regio Ducale, 1757.

– *La Fondazion di Venezia*. Venice: Teatro S. Samuele, 1736.

– *La Scuola Moderna*. Venice, 1748.

– *Le Nozze*. Bologna: Teatro Formagliari, 1755.

– *Memorie Italiane (Prefazioni ai Diciassette Tomi delle Commedie edite a Venezia da G.B. Pasquali [1761–1778])*. Edited by Roberta Turchi. Venice: Marsilio, 2008.

– "Prefazione dell'autore alla Prima Raccolta delle Commedie." Venice: Bettinelli, 1750.

– *Terenzio*. Vol. 5 of *"Tutte le opere" di Carlo Goldoni*. Edited by Giuseppe Ortolani. 2nd ed. N.p.: Mondadori Classics, 1955.

– *Tutte le opere*. Edited by Giuseppe Ortolani. 14 vols. Milan: A. Mondadori, 1935–56.

Goulbourne, Russell. "Voltaire's Masks: Theatre and Theatricality." In *Cambridge Companion to Voltaire*, edited by Nicholas Cronk, 93–108. Cambridge: Cambridge University Press, 2009.

Gravina, Gian Vincenzo. *Della ragione poetica*. 2 vols. Rome: Francesco Gonzaga, 1708.

– *Della tragedia libri uno*. Naples: Nicolò Naso, 1715.

– *De ortu et progressu juris civilis libri tres*. Rome: Perego Salvioni, 1835.

– *Scritti critici e teorici*. Edited by Amedeo Quondam. Bari: Laterza, 1973.

Greenberg, Mitchell. *Corneille, Classicism, and the Ruses of Symmetry*. Cambridge: Cambridge University Press, 1986.

Greer, Margaret Rich. *The Play of Power: Mythological Court Dramas of Calderón de la Barca*. Princeton: Princeton University Press, 1991.

Greg, Walter W. *Pastoral Poetry and Pastoral Drama: A Literary Inquiry, with Special Reference to the Pre-Restoration Stage in England*. New York: Russell and Russell, 1959.

Grey, T.S., ed. *Richard Wagner and His World*. Princeton: Princeton University Press, 2010.

Gros, Étienne. "Les origines de la tragédie lyrique et la place des tragédies en machines dans l'évolution du théâtre vers l'opéra." *Revue d'Histoire Littéraire de la France* 35 (1928): 161–93.

Guaita, Camilla. *Per una nuova estetica del teatro: L'Arcadia di Gravina e Crescimbeni*. Rome: Bulzoni Editore, 2009.

Guarini, Battista. *Il Verrato ovvera difessa de qvanto ha scritto M. Gioason Denores. Contra le tragidocomedie et le pastorili, in vn svo discorso di poesia*. Ferrara: Vincenzo Galdura, 1588.

Gudzii, Nikolai. "Ob ideologii Ia.B. Kniazhnina." *Literaturnoe nasledstvo* 19–21 (1935): 659–64.

Guyon-Lecoq, Camille. *La Vertu des passions: l'esthétique et la morale au miroir de la tragédie lyrique*. Paris: Honoré Champion, 2002.

Haggerty, George E. *Men in Love: Masculinity and Sexuality in the Eighteenth Century*. New York: Columbia University Press, 1999.

Hall, Edith. *Adventures with Iphigenia in Tauris*. Oxford: Oxford University Press, 2013.

Hall, Edith, and Fiona Macintosh. *Greek Tragedy and the British Theatre 1660–1914*. Oxford: Oxford University Press, 2005.

Händel, Georg Frideric. *Oreste: Opera in tre atti. HWV A^{11}*. Edited by Bernd Baselt. Bärenreiter: Kassel, New York, 1991.

Hanning, Barbara Russano. *Of Poetry and Music's Power: Humanism and the Creation of Opera*. Ann Arbor, MI: UMI Research Press, 1980.

Harris, Ellen. *The Librettos of Handel's Operas*. New York: Garland, 1989.

Harrison, Jane. *Themis*. Cambridge: Cambridge University Press, 1912.

Harris-Warrick, Rebecca. *Dance and Drama in French Baroque Opera: A History*. Cambridge: Cambridge University Press, 2016.

Hathaway, Baxter. *The Age of Criticism: The Late Renaissance in Italy*. Ithaca: Cornell University Press, 1962.

Heinsius, Daniel. *De Tragoediae Constitutione: On Plot in Tragedy* [1611]. Translated by Paul R. Sellin and John J. McManmon. Northridge, CA: San Fernando Valley Stage College, 1971.

Heartz, Daniel. "Goldoni, Don Giovanni and the dramma giocoso." *The Musical Times* 120, no. 1642 (Dec. 1979): 993–5 + 997–8.

Heartz, Daniel. *Mozart's Operas*. Berkeley: University of California Press, 1990.

Heller, Wendy. "Opera Between the Ancients and the Moderns." In *The Oxford Handbook of Opera*, edited by Helen M. Greenwald, 275–95. New York: Oxford University Press, 2014.

Henke, Robert. *Pastoral Transformations: Italian Tragicomedy and Shakespeare's Late Plays*. Newark: University of Delaware Press, 1997.

Henrichs, Albert. "Loss of Self, Suffering, Violence: The Modern View of Dionysus from Nietzsche to Girard." *Harvard Studies in Classical Philology* 88 (1984): 205–40.

– "The Last of the Detractors: Friedrich Nietzsche's Condemnation of Euripides." *Greek Roman and Byzantine Studies* 27 (1986): 369–97.

Herrero Sánchez, Manuel. "El padre Mariana y el tiranicidio." *Torre de los Lujanes* 65 (2009): 103–21.

Herrick, Marvin T. *Tragicomedy: Its Origin and Development in Italy, France, and England*. Urbana, IL: University of Illinois Press, 1962.

Herry, Ginette. " Goldoni e la Marliani ossia l'impossibile romanzo." *Studi Goldoniani* 8, 1988.

Hernandez, Alex Eric. "Medaea in Petticoats: She-Tragedy and the Domestication of Passion." In *Shadows of Enlightenment: Tragic Drama in Europe's Age of Reason*, edited by Blair Hoxby, 29–57. Columbus: The Ohio State University Press, 2022.

Hewitt, Barnard, ed. *The Renaissance Stage: Documents of Serlio, Sabbattini and Furtenbach*. Translated by Allaryce Nicoll, John H. McDowell, and George R. Kernodle. Coral Gables, FL: University of Miami Press, 1958.

Hicks, Anthony. "Oreste ('Orestes')." *Grove Music Online*. Oxford Music Online. (Accessed Dec. 1, 1992.)

Hitchcock, H. Wiley. *Marc-Antoine Charpentier*. Oxford: Oxford University Press, 1990.

Hobbes, Thomas. *Leviathan*. Edited by Noel Malcolm. Oxford: Clarendon Press, 2012.

Horace, *Satires, Epistles, and Ars Poetica*. Translated by H. Rushton Fairclough. Loeb Classical Library. Rev. ed. Cambridge: Harvard University Press, 1929.

Hosking, Geoffrey. *Russia: People and Empire*. Cambridge: Harvard University Press, 1997.

Howard, Patricia. *Gluck: An Eighteenth-Century Portrait in Letters and Documents*. Oxford: Oxford University Press, 1995.

Hoxby, Blair. "All Passion Spent: the Means and Ends of a *Tragédie en musique*." *Comparative Literature* 59, no. 1 (2007): 33–62.

– "Joanna Baillie, the Gothic Bard, and her Tragedies of Fear." In *Shadows of the Enlightenment: Tragic Drama during Europe's Age of Reason*, edited by Blair Hoxby, 99–122. Columbus: The Ohio State University Press, 2022.

– "Technologies of Performance: From Mystery Plays to the Italian Order." In *A Cultural History of Theatre in the Early Modern Age*, vol. 3, 161–82. Edited by Robert Henke. London: Bloomsbury Academic, 2017.

– "The Doleful Airs of Euripides: The Origins of Opera and the Spirit of Tragedy Reconsidered." *Cambridge Opera Journal* 17 (2005): 253–69.

– *What Was Tragedy? Theory and the Early Modern Canon*. Oxford: Oxford University Press, 2015.

– ed. *Shadows of the Enlightenment: Tragic Drama during Europe's Age of Reason*. Columbus: The Ohio State University Press, 2022.

Introduzione alle recite della truppa dei comici nel teatro Grimani a S. Samuele, per l'Autunno di quest'anno 1726, posta in musica dal Sig. Gio. Battista Pescetti. Venice: Valvasense, 1726.

Irwin, T.H. "Euripides and Socrates." *Classical Philology* 78 (1983): 183–97.

Jafee, Jay. *Medea among the Ancients and Moderns: Morality and Magic in French Musical Theatre of the Seventeenth Century*. PhD diss., New York University, 2001.

James, Susan. *Passion and Action: The Emotions in Seventeenth-Century Philosophy*. Oxford: Clarendon Press, 1997.

Johnson, James H. *Listening in Paris: A Cultural History*. Berkeley: University of California Press, 1995.

Joly, Jacque. "Metastasio e l'ideologia del sovrano virtuoso." In *Istituzioni culturali e sceniche nell'età delle riforme*, edited by Guido Nicastro, 9–40. Milan: Angeli, 1986.

Jouanna, Arlette. "I monarcomachi protestanti francesi e il dovere di rivolta." *Rivista di storia della filosofia* 50 (1995): 499–521.

Kambouchner, Denis. "Descartes and the Passions." In *The Oxford Handbook of Dexcartes and Cartesianism*, edited by Steven Nadler, Tad M. Schmaltz, Delphine Antoine-Mahut, 193–208. Oxford: Oxford University Press, 2019.

Kapp, Volker. "Corneille et la dramaturgie du théâtre à machines italien." In *Pierre Corneille*, edited by Alain Niderst, 407–12. Paris: PUF, 1985.

Kaufmann, Walter. *Tragedy and Philosophy*. Garden City, NY: Doubleday, 1968.

Kintzler, Catherine. *Poétique de l'opéra français de Corneille à Rousseau* [1991]. 2nd ed. Paris: Minerve, 2006.

– *Théâtre et opéra à l'âge classique: Une familière étrangeté*. Paris: Fayard, 2004.

Kiselev, Mikhail. "'Po pravam vsego sveta'. Legitimatsiia dvortsovogo perevorota 1741 g. i problema zakonnosti votsareniia Elizavety Petrovny." *Rossiia* 21 (2017): 98–116.

Kitto. H.D.F. *Greek Tragedy, A Literary Study.* Garden City, NY: Doubleday, 1954.

Kniazhnin, Iakov B. *Sobranie sochinenii.* 5 vols. Moscow: V Gubernskoj Tipografii u A. Reshetnikova, 1802.

Knox, Bernard. "The *Medea* of Euripides." *Yale Classical Studies* 25 (1977): 193–225.

Korndorf, Anna. *Dvortsy Khimery. Illuzornaia arkhitektura i politicheskie alluzii pridvornoi stseny.* Moscow: Progress-Traditsiia, 2011.

Korneeva, Tatiana, ed. *Le voci arcane. Palcoscenici del potere nel teatro e nell'opera.* Roma: Carocci, 2018.

Koselleck, Reinhart. *Critique and Crisis: Enlightenment and the Pathogenesis of Modern Society.* Cambridge, MA: MIT Press, 1988.

Kulakova, Liudmila. "Zhizn' i tvorchestvo Ia.B. Kniazhnina." In Iakov Knaizhnin, *Izbrannye proizvedenia,* 5–57. Leningrad: Sovetskii pisatel', 1961.

Lagarde, André, and Laurent Michard. *XVIIIe Siècle.* Paris: Bordas, 1962.

La Gorce, Jérôme de. *Berain, Dessinateur du Roi Soleil.* Paris: Herscher, 1986.

– *L'Opéra à Paris au temps de Louis XIV, histoire d'un théâtre.* Paris: Desjonquères, 1992.

– *Jean-Baptiste Lully.* Paris: Fayard, 2002.

La Harpe, Jean-François de. *Correspondance littéraire, adressée à son Altesse Impériale M.gr le Grand-Duc, aujourd'hui Empereur de Russie, et à M. le Comte André Schowalow, Chamberlain de l'Impératrice Catherine II, depuis 1774 jusqu'à 1789.* 6 vols. Paris: Migneret, 1801–7.

– *Lycée; ou Cours de littérature ancienne et moderne.* 18 vols. Dijon: V. Lagier, 1820–6.

La Motte, Antoine Houdar de. "Discours préliminaire." In *Textes critiques: les raison du sentiment,* edited by Françoise Gevrey and Béatrice Guion. Paris: Honoré Champion, 2002.

– "Second discours à l'occasion de la tragédie de *Romulus.*" In *Oeuvres.* 11 tomes in 2 vols., 4:155–6 [1754]; Geneva: Slatkine, 1970.

Lamy, Guillaume. *Explication mécanique et physique des fonctions de l'âme sensitive, des sens, des passions, et du movement volontaire.* Paris, 1678.

Landgraf, Annette. "*Oreste.*" In *The Cambridge Handel Encyclopedia,* edited by Annette Landgraf and David Vickers, 465–7. Cambridge: Cambridge University Press, 2009.

Lanfossi, Carlo. "*Handel as Arranger and Producer: Listening to Pasticci in Eighteenth Century London.*" PhD diss. University of Pennsylvania, 2018.

Lattanzi, Alessandro. "Vita musicale a Napoli nei dispacci del corrispondente della Cancelleria modenese (1779–1784)." In *Fonti d'archivio per la storia della musica e dello spettacolo a Napoli tra XVI e XVIII secolo,* edited by Paologiovanni Maione, 387–425. Naples: Editoriale scientifica, 2001.

Laudun d'Aigaliers, Pierre. *Art poétique François*. Paris: Anthoine Du Brueil, 1597.

Launay, Denise, ed. *La Querelle des Bouffons*. 3 vols. Geneva: Minkoff, 1973.

Laurain-Portemer, Madeleine. *Études mazarines*, I. Paris: De Boccard, 1981.

Lazardzig, Jan. "The Machine as Spectacle." In *Instruments in Art and Science. On the Architectonics of Cultural Boundaries in the 17th Century*, edited by Helmar Schramm, Ludger Schwarte, and Jan Lazardzig, 152–75. Berlin: Walter de Gruyter, 2008.

Lazzeri, Ghino. *La vita e l'opera letteraria di Ranieri Calzabigi: Saggio critico con appendice di documenti inediti o rari*. Città di Castello: Casa tipografico-editrice S. Lapi, 1907.

Le Brun, Charles. *Conférence sur l'expression des passions*. Presented to the Royal Academy of Painting and Sculpture, 1668.

Lecoq, Anne-Marie, ed. *La Querelle des Anciens et des Modernes*. Paris: Gallimard, 2001.

Lee, Daniel. *Popular Sovereignty in Early Modern Constitutional Thought*. Oxford: Oxford University Press, 2016.

Lefèvre, Wolfgang, ed. *Picturing Machines, 1400–1700*. Cambridge, MA: The MIT Press, 2004.

Le Pas de Sécheval, Anne. "Le Cardinal de Richelieu, le théâtre et les décorateurs italiens: nouveaux documents sur *Mirame* et le ballet de *La Prospérité des Armes de France* (1641)." *XVIIe Siècle* 186 (1995): 135–45.

Lesure, François. *Querelle des Gluckistes et des Piccinistes: texte des pamphlets avec introduction, commentaires, et index*. 2 vols. Geneva: Minkoff, 1984.

Levitt, Marcus. *Early Modern Russian Letters. Texts and Contexts*. Boston: Academic Studies Press, 2009.

Levy, Anthony. *French Moralists: The Theory of the Passions, 1585 to 1649*. Oxford: Clarendon Press, 1964.

Liechtenhan, Francine-Dominique. "Jacob von Stählin, académicien et courtesan." *Cahiers du monde russe* 43.2–3 (2002): 321–32.

Loewenstein, Joseph. "Guarini and the Presence of Genre." In *Renaissance Tragicomedy: Explorations in Genre and Politics*, edited by Nancy Klein Maguire, 33–55. New York: AMS Press, 1987.

Lomonaco, Fabrizio. "Diritto naturale e storia. Note su Gravina e Vico" *Archivio di storia della cultura* 12 (2000): 27–51.

Longpierre, Hilaire Bernard de Requeleyne, baron de. *Médée. Tragédie (1694)*. Edited by T. Tobari. Paris: Editions A.G. Nizet, 1967.

– *Médée. Tragédie*. Suivie du *Parallèle de Monsieur Corneille et de Monsieur Racine* (1986) et de la *Dissertation sur le tragédie de Médée par l'abbé Pellegrin (1729)*. Edited by Emmanuel Minel. Paris: Honoré Champion, 2000.

Lorenzi, Giambattista. *Il convitato di pietra, commedia di un atto per musica*. Naples, 1783.

Lounsbury, Thomas R. *Shakespeare and Voltaire*. New York: C. Scribner's, 1902.

Louvat-Molozay, Bénédicte. *Théâtre et musique. Dramaturgie de l'insertion musicale dans le théâtre français (1550–1680)*. Paris: Honoré Champion, 2002.

Luciani, Paola. "Aporie del modello tragico: Gravina e Metastasio." In *Sacro e/o profane nel teatro fra Rinascimento ed età dei Lumi*, edited by Stella Castellaneta and Francesco S. Minervini, 375–85. Bari: Cacucci, 2009.

Lutsker, Pavel, and Irina Susidko. "'Miloserdie Tita' v Rossii." *Starinnaia muzyka* 3 (1999): 8–11.

Lyons, John D. *Kingdom of Disorder. The Theory of Tragedy in Classical France*. Lafayette, IN: Purdue University Press, 1999.

Mace, Dean T. "Dryden's Dialogue on Drama." *Journal of the Warburg and Courtauld Institute* 5 (1962): 87–112.

Maffei, Scipione. *Teatro italiano o sia scelta di tragedie per uso della scena*. 3 vols. Verona: Jacopo Vallarsi, 1723–5.

Maffi, Alberto, ed. *Princeps legibus solutus*. Torino: Giappichelli, 2016.

Malebranche, Nicholas. *The Search After Truth*. Translated by Thomas M. Lenon and Paul J. Olscamp. *Elucidations of the Search After Truth*. Translated by Thomas M. Lennon. Cambridge: Cambridge University Press, 1997.

Malinovskii, Konstantin, ed. *Zapiski Jakoba Shtelina ob iziashchnykh iskusstvakh v Rossii*, 2 vols. Moscow: Iskusstvo, 1990.

Mamczarz, Irène. *Le théâtre Barberini et les fastes de l'opéra romain, 1632–1656*. Paris: Société internationale d'histoire comparée du théâtre, de l'opéra et du ballet, 2011.

– "Quelques aspects de l'interaction dans les théâtres italien, français et polonais des XVIe et XVIIe siècles: drame humaniste, comédie dell'arte, théâtre musical." In *Le théâtre italien et l'Europe xve-xviie siècles*, edited by Christian Bec and Irène Mamczarz, 171–217. Paris: PUF, 1983.

Marasinova, Elena. "Smertnaia kazn' i politicheskaia smert' v Rossii serediny XVIII veka." *Rossiiskaia istoriia* 4 (2014): 53–69.

– *Vlast' i lichnost': ocherki russkoi istorii XVIII veka*. Moscow: Nauka, 2008.

Marinelli, David N. *Carlo Goldoni as Experimental Librettist: The "Drammi Giocosi" of 1750*. PhD thesis. Rutgers University, 1988.

Marino, John A. "Introduction: On the Grand Tour." In *Early Modern Italy 1550–1796*, edited by John A. Marino, 1–8. Oxford: Oxford University Press, 2002.

Martello. Piero Jacopo. *Scritti critici e satirici*. Edited by Hannibal S. Noce. Bari: Laterra, 1963.

Matrimonium inter Magnates. I-Ras, *Archivio Cartari-Febei*, Busta 102, fol. 255r–v.

Mattheson, Johann. *Critica Musica*. Hamburg: Auf unkosten des autoris, 1722–5.

Maylender, Michele. *Storie delle Accademie D'Italia*, vol. 2 [1926]. Reprinted Bologna: Arnaldo Forni, 1976.

Mayrhofer, Marina. *Relazioni elettive: Studi sul teatro musicale classico*. Naples: Pagano editore, 1996.

Mazzuchelli, Gian Maria. *Gli scrittori d'Italia cioé notizie storiche, e critiche intorno alle vite, e agli scritti dei letterati italiani*. Brescia: Presso a G. Bossini, 1753–63.

McGeary, Thomas. "Fredrick, Prince of Wales." In *The Cambridge Handel Encyclopedia*, edited by Annette Landgraf and David Vickers, 245–6. Cambridge: Cambridge University Press, 2009.

Mellace, Raffaele. *Johann Adolph Hasse*. Palermo: EPOS, 2004.

Ménestrier, Claude-François. *Traité des tournois, joustes, carrousels, et autres spectacles publics*. Lyon: Jean Muguet, 1669.

Mersenne, Marin. *Harmonie universelle*. Paris, 1635–6.

Mesnardière, Jules de la. *La Poétique*. Paris, 1639.

Messberger, Rebecca. "The Italian Enlightened Reform of the *Querelle des Femmes*." In *The Contest for Knowledge: Debates over Women's Learning in Eighteenth-Century Italy*, edited and translated by Rebecca Messberger and Paula Findlen, 1–22. Chicago: The University of Chicago Press, 2005.

Messineo, Sacco. "I finali dei drammi metastasiani." In *I finali. Letteratura e teatro*, edited by Beatrice Alfonzetti and Giulio Ferroni, 93–110. Rome: Bulzoni, 2003.

Metastasio, Pietro. *Estratto dell'arte poetica d'Aristotile*. Edited by Elisabetta Selmi. Palermo: Novecento, 1998.

– *L'Ipermestra, dramma per musica*. Vienna: Giovanni Pietro van Ghelen, 1744.

– *Massime, similitudine e descrizioni estratte dalle poesie e disposte per ordine d'Alfabeto*. Genova: Olziati, 1785.

– *Tutte le opere*. Edited by Bruno Brunelli. Milan: Mondadori, 1943.

[Metastasio, Pietro, Jacob von Stählin, and Ivan Merkur'ev], *Miloserdie Titovo: Opera s prologom predstavlennaia vo vremia vysokotorzhestvennago dnia koronatsii eia imperatorskogo velichestva Elizavety Petrovny samoderzhitsy vserossiiskoi*. Moscow: Tipografia Akademii nauk, 1742.

Michelini, Ann N. *Euripides and the Tragic Tradition*. Madison: University of Wisconsin Press, 1987.

Milesi, Francesco, ed. *Giacomo Torelli. L'invenzione scenica nell'Europa barocca*. Fano: Fondazione Cassa di Risparmio di Fano, 2000.

Minor, Vernon Hyde. *The Death of the Baroque and the Rhetoric of Good Taste*. Cambridge University Press, 2006.

Mitchell, J. B. "Trevisan and Soranzo: Some Canonici Manuscripts from Two Eighteenth-Century Venetian Collections." *Bodleian Library Record* 8 (1969): 125–35.

Moles, J. "Notes on Aristotle, *Poetics* 13 and 14." *Classical Quarterly* 29 (1979): 77–94.

Montagu, Jennifer. *The Expression of the Passions: The Origin and Influence of Charles Le Brun's "Conférence sur l'expression générale et particulière."* New Haven: Yale University Press, 1994.

Montesquieu, Charles-Louis de Secondat de. *De l'esprit des lois.* Edited by Robert Derathé. Paris: Garnier, 1973.

Moreschi, Giambattista Alessandro. "Osservazioni sopra l'*Ipermestra.*" In *Osservazioni di vari letterati sopra i drammi dell'Abbate Pietro Metastasio.* Nice: Società tipografica, 1785.

Murata, Margareta, ed. *Strunk's Source Readings in Music History,* vol. 4: *The Baroque Era.* New York: Norton, 1998.

Muratori, Ludovico Antonio. *Della perfetta poesia italiana.* 2 vols. Modena: Bartolomeo Soliani, 1706.

– *Della pubblica felicità oggetto de' buoni principi.* Edited by Matteo Al Kalak. Rome: Donzelli, 2016.

Murray, Timothy C. "Richelieu's Theater: The Mirror of a Prince." *Renaissance Drama* 8 (1977): 275–98.

Mutini, Claudio. "Bergalli, Luisa." *Dizionario Biografico degli Italiani* 9 (1967): 63–8.

Napoli-Signorelli, Pietro. *Addizioni alla Storia critica de' teatri antichi e moderni.* Naples: Michele Migliaccio, 1798.

– "Discorso sopra varie tragedie di Agamennone." In *Opuscoli vari* 4: 97–123. Naples: Stamperia Orsiniana, 1795.

– *Elementi di poesia drammatica.* Milan, 1801.

– "Ricerche sul sistema melodrammatico lette a' Soci Pontaniani nelle adunanze de' mesi di Novembre, e Dicembre 1812." In *Atti della Società Pontaniana di Napoli* 4: 1–125. Naples, 1847.

– *Storia critica de' teatri antichi e moderni.* 6 vols. Naples: Vincenzo Orsino, 1787–90.

– *Storia critica de' teatri antichi e moderni divisa in dieci tomi.* Revised edition. 10 vols. Naples: Vincenzo Orsino, 1813.

– *Vicende della coltura nelle due Sicilie dalla venuta delle colonie straniere sino a' nostri giorni.* 8 vols. Naples, 1810–11.

Napolitano, Michele. "Greek Tragedy and Opera: Notes on a Marriage Manqué." In *Ancient Drama in Music for the Modern Stage,* edited by Peter Brown and Suzana Ograjenšek, 31–46. Oxford: Oxford University Press, 2010.

Naudeix, Laura. *Dramaturgie de la tragédie en musique (1673–1764).* Paris: Honoré Champion, 2004.

– Introduction to *La Premiére Querelle de la musiqe italienne, 1702–1706.* Edited by Laura Naudeix. Paris: Claissiques Garnier, 2018.

Nicole, Pierre. "De la comédie," in *Essais de morale.* 4 vols. Paris, 1672.

Nietzsche, Friedrich. *The Birth of Tragedy and The Case of Wagner.* Translated by Walter Kaufmann. New York: Vintage, 1967.

Norman, Buford. "Ancients and Moderns, Tragedy and Opera: The Quarrel over *Alceste*." In *French Musical Thought 1600–1800*, edited by Georgia Coward, 177–96. Ann Arbor: University of Michigan Press, 1989.

– *Touched by the Graces: The Libretti of Philippe Quinault in the Context of French Classicism*. Birmingham, AL: Summa Publications, 2001.

Norman, Larry F. *The Shock of the Ancient: Literature and History in Early Modern France*. Chicago: University of Chicago Press, 2011.

Nougaret, Pierre-Jean-Baptiste. *De l'Art du théâtre*. Paris, 1769.

Noverre, Jean-Georges. *Lettres sur la danse, sur les ballets et les arts*. 4 vols. St. Petersburg: Jean Charles Schnoor, 1803–4.

Ogarkova, Natalia. *Tseremonii, prazdnestva, musyka russkogo dvora. XVIII– nachalo XIX veka*. Saint Petersburg: Bulanin, 2004.

Olszewski, Edward J. *Cardinal Pietro Ottoboni (1667–1740) and the Vatican Tomb of Pope Alexander VIII*. Philadelphia: American Philosophical Society, 2004.

Omel'chenko, Oleg. *"Zakonnaia monarkhiia" Ekateriny II. Prosveshchennyi absolutism v Rossii*. Moscow: Jurist, 1993.

Oporto, Pablo Font. "Suárez, Mariana y el tiranicidio: convergencias, divergencias y silencios estratégicos," *Cuadernos Salamantinos de Filosofía* 44 (2017): 11–34.

Ospovat, Kirill. "The Catharsis of Prosecution: Royal Violence, Poetic Justice, and Public Emotion in the Russian *Hamlet* (1748)." In *Dramatic Experience: The Poetics of Drama and the Early Modern Public Sphere(s)*, edited by Katja Gvozdeva, Tatiana Korneeva, and Kirill Ospovat, 189–219. Leiden: Brill, 2016.

Palisca, Claude V. "The Alterati of Florence, Pioneers in the Theory of Dramatic Music." In *New Looks at Italian Opera: Essays in Honor of Donald J. Grout*, edited by William W. Austin, 9–38. Ithaca: Cornell University Press, 1968.

– *Baroque Music*. 2nd. ed. Englewood Cliffs, New Jersey: Prentice-Hall, 1981.

Papadopoulou, Thalia. *Aeschylus: Suppliants*. Companions to Greek and Roman Tragedy. London: Bloomsbury, 2011.

Parodi, Elena Biggi. "*Les Danaïdes di Tschudi-Du Roullet e Salieri e i suoi debiti nei confronti di Ipermestra o le Danaidi di Calzabigi*." In *Ranieri Calzabigi tra Vienna e Napoli: Atti del convegno di studi (Livorno, 23–24 settembre 1996)*, edited by Federico Marri and Francesco Paolo Russo, 101–27. Lucca: Libreria musicale italiana, 1997.

Pasquier, Pierre, ed. *Le Mémoire de Mahelot*. Paris: Honoré Champion, 2005.

Pennington, Kenneth. *The Prince and the Law 1200–1600. Sovereignty and Rights in the Western Legal Tradition*. Berkeley: University of California Press, 1993.

Pepoli, Alessandro. "Lettera ad un uomo ragionevole sul melodramma detto serio." In *Meleagro, tragedia per musica in tre atti*, 3–52. 2nd. ed. Venice: Stamperia Curti Q. Giacomo, 1790.

Pera, Francesco. *Ricordi e biografie livornesi.* Livorno: Francesco Vigo editore, 1867.

Perdichizzi, Vincenza. "Metastasio e Alfieri: note per un confronto." In *Drammi per musica di Pietro Metastasio,* edited by Pérette-Cécile Buffaria and Paolo Grossi, 115–37. Paris: Istituto Italiano di Cultura, 2008.

Perrault, Charles. *Critique de l'Opéra ou examen de la tragédie intitulée Alceste.* Paris, 1674.

C. *Parallèle des anciens et des modernes en ce qui regarde les arts et les sciences.* 4 vols. Paris, 1688–97.

Perrin, Pierre. *Les oevvres de poesie, de Mr Perrin, contenant les Ievx de poesie, diverses poesies galantes, des Paroles de musique, airs de cour, airs a boire, chansons, noels et motets, vne Comedie en musique, l'Entrée de la reyne, et La Chartreuse, ou La sainte solitude.* Paris: E. Loyson, 1661.

Perris, Simon. "Bacchant Women." In *Brill's Companion to the Reception of Euripides,* edited by Rosanna Lauriola and Kyriakos N. Demetriou, 505–48. Leiden: Brill, 2015.

Petrovska, Marija. *Merope: The Dramatic Impact of a Myth.* New York: Peter Lang, 1984.

Philips, Ambrose. *The Distrest Mother.* London, 1712.

Phillippo, Susanna. "Clytemnestra's Ghost: The Aeschylean Legacy in Gluck's Iphigenia Operas." In *Agamemnon in Performance 458 BC to AD 2004,* edited by Fiona Macintosh, Pantelis Michelakis, Edith Hall, and Oliver Taplin, 77–104. Oxford: Oxford University Press, 2005.

Piccolomini, Alessandro. *Annotationi Di M. Allesandro Piccolomini, nel libro della poetica d'Aristotele.* Venice: Giouanni Guarisco, & Compagni, 1575.

Pirrotta, Nino. "Temperaments and Tendencies in the Florentine Camerata." In *Music and Culture in Italy from the Middle Ages to the Baroque: A Collection of Essays,* 217–34. Cambridge: Harvard University Press, 1984.

Plutarch. *Moralia,* Vol, 1. Translated by Frank Cole Babbit. Loeb Classical Library. Cambridge: Harvard University Press, 1927.

– *Plutarch's Morals. Translated from the Greek by Several Hands.* Corrected and revised by William W. Goodwin. Introduction by Ralph Waldo Emerson. 5 vols. Boston: Little, Brown and Co., 1878.

Pocock, Gordon. *Corneille and Racine: Problems of Tragic Form.* Cambridge: Cambridge University Press, 1973.

Pocock, J.G.A. *Political Thought and History.* Cambridge: Cambridge University Press, 2009.

Powell, John S. "Music and Corneille's *Andromède.*" In *"L'Esprit français" et la musique en Europe. Émergence, influence et limites d'une doctrine esthétique,* edited by Michelle Biget-Mainfroy and Rainer Schmusch, 191–207. Hildesheim: Georg Ulms Verlag, 2007.

– *Music and Theatre in France 1600–1680*. Oxford: Clarendon Press, 2000.

Price, Curtis. "Pasticcio." *Grove Music Online*. 2001; Accessed 14 Jun. 2022. https://www.oxfordmusiconline.com/grovemusic/view/10.1093/gmo/9781561592630.001.0001/omo-9781561592630-e-0000021051.

– "Unity, Originality and the London Pasticcio." *Harvard Library Bulletin*, new ser. 2.4 (Winter 1991): 17–30.

Prota-Giurleo, Ulisse. "Breve storia del teatro di corte e della musica a Napoli nei sec. XVII-XVIII." In *Il teatro di corte del palazzo reale di Napoli*, edited by Felice de Filippis, 19–160. Naples: L'Arte tipografica, 1952.

Prota-Giurleo, Ulisse. *La grande orchestra del R. Teatro San Carlo nel Settecento (da documenti inediti)*. Naples: Largo S. Domenico 12, 1927.

Prunières, Henry. *La Vie Illustre et Libertine de Jean-Baptiste Lully*. Paris: Librarie Plon, 1929.

– *L'Opéra italien en France avant Lulli* [1913]. Paris: Honoré Champion, 1975.

Quintilian. *Institutio Oratoria*. Translated by H.E. Butler. 4 vols. Loeb Classical Library. Cambridge: Harvard University Press, 1920–2.

Racine, Jean. *Iphigenia/Phaedra/Athaliah*. Translated by John Cairncross. Harmondsworth: Penguin Classics, 1970.

– *Œuvres Complètes*. Edited by Raymond Picard. 2 vols. Paris: Bibliothèque de la Pléiade, 1950.

– *Œuvres complètes I: Théâtre-Poésie*. Edited by G. Forestier. Bibliothèque de la Pléiade. Paris: Gallimard, 1989.

– *Œuvres de J. Racine*. Edited by M. Paul Mesnard, 8 vols. 2nd. ed. rev. Paris: Hachette, 1885–90.

Ragunet, François. *A Comparison between the French and Italian Musick and Operas*. London, 1709.

Raguenet, François and Jean-Laurent Le Cerf de la Viéville. *La Première Querelle de la musique italienne, 1702–1706*. Edited by Laura Naudeix. Paris: Classiques Garnier, 2018.

Rameau, Jean-Philippe. *Observations sur notre instinct pour la musique*. Paris, 1754.

Ranum, Patricia M. *The Harmonic Orator: The Phrasing and Rhetoric of the Melody in French Baroque Airs*. [Hillsdale, New York?]: Pendragon, [2001].

Rapin, René. *Les Réflexions sur la poétique et sur les ouvrages des poètes anciens et modernes (1684)*. Edited by Pascale Thouvenin. Paris: Champion Classiques, 2011.

– *Réflexions sur la Poétique d'Aristote et sur les ouvrages des Poètes anciens et modernes* [1674]. Translated by Thomas Rymer as *Monsieur Rapin's Reflections on Aristotle's Treatise of Poesie: Containing the Necessary, Rational, and Universal Rules for Epick, Dramatick, and the Other Sorts of Poetry. With Reflections on the Works of the Ancient and Modern Poets, and their Faults Noted* [1674]. London: T. Warren, for H. Herringman, and sold by Francis Saunders, 1694.

Recueil général des opéras representez par l'Académie royale de musique, depuis son etablissement. 16 vols. Paris, 1703–45.

Ricci, Corrado. *I teatri di Bologna nei secoli XVII e XVIII: Storia aneddotica.* Bologna: Successori Monti editori, 1888.

Ridgway, R. S. "Voltaire's Operas." *Studies on Voltaire and the Eighteenth Century* 189 (1980): 119–51.

Riggs, David. "The Artificial Day and the Infinite Universe." *Journal of Medieval and Renaissance Studies* 5 (1975): 155–85.

Rista, Pervinca. *At the Origins of Classical Opera: Carlo Goldoni and the dramma giocoso per musica.* Bern: Peter Lang, 2018.

Roberts, John H. "Pasticcio." In *The Cambridge Handel Encyclopedia*, edited by Annette Landgraf and David Vickers, 491–3. Cambridge: Cambridge University Press, 2009.

Roach, Joseph R. *The Player's Passion: Studies in the Science of Acting.* Newark: University of Deleware Press, 1985.

Robortello, Francesco. *Francisci Robertelli Vtinensis in librum Aristotelis De Arte Poetica Explicationes.* Florence: In Officina Laurentii Torrentini Dvcalis Typographi, 1548.

Robuschi, Giuseppina Romagnoli. "Il Gravina tra Tito Livio e Vittorio Alfieri." *Aevum* 44 (1970): 116–51.

Rocco, Patricia. *The Devout Hand: Women, Virtue, and Visual Culture in Early Modern Italy.* Montreal: McGill-Queen's University Press, 2017.

Rorty, Amélie Oksenberg. "Descartes on Thinking with the Body." In *The Cambridge Companion to Descartes*, edited by John Cottingham, 371–92. Cambridge: Cambridge University Press, 1992.

Rosand, Ellen. *Opera in Seventeenth-Century Venice: The Creation of a Genre.* Berkeley: University of California Press, 1991.

Rosow, Lois. "French Baroque Recitative as an Expression of Tragic Declamation." *Early Music* 11 (1985): 469–79.

Rossi, Niccolo. *Discorsi intorno alla tragedia* [1590]. In *Trattati di poetica e retorica del cinquecento*, edited by Bernard Weinberg, 4: 59–120. Bari: Gius. Laterza & Figli, 1974.

Rubbi, Andrea. *Elogio di Pietro Metastasio.* Venice: Marcuzzi, 1782.

Russo, Francesco Paolo. "'Nitteti' e 'Demetrio' alla corte di Caterina II. Su alcuni adattamenti di testi metastasiani in Russia nella seconda metà del XVIII secolo." In *Il melodramma di Pietro Metastasio. La poesia, la musica, la messa in scena e l'opera italiana nel Settecento*, edited by Elena Sala Di Felice and Rossana Caira Lumetti, 511–36. Rome: Aracne, 2001.

Sacco Messineo, Michela. "I finali dei drammi metastasiani." In *I finali. Letteratura e teatro*, edited by Beatrice Alfonzetti and Giulio Ferroni, 93–110. Rome: Bulzoni, 2003.

Sadler, Graham. "Jean-Philippe Rameau." *The New Grove French Baroque Masters*. Edited by James R. Anthony. New York: Norton, 1986.

Saint-Évremond. *Œuvres en prose de Saint-Évremond*. Edited by René Ternois. 4 vols. Paris: Librarie Marcel Didier, 1969.

– *Works of Monsieur de St. Evremond, Made English from the French Original*. 3 vols. London: Printed for J. Churchill, et. al., 1714.

Saint-Mard, Rémond de. *Réflexions sur l'Opéra*. Paris, 1749.

Sala Di Felice, Elena, and Laura Sannia Nowé. *La cultura fra Sei e Settecento: primi risultati di una indagine*. Modena: Mucchi, 1994.

Sama, Catherine M. "'On Canvas and on the Page': Women Shaping Culture in Eighteenth-Century Venice." In *Italy's Eighteenth Century: Gender and Culture in the Age of the Grand Tour*, edited by Paula Findlen, Wendy Roworth, and Catherine M. Sama, 125–50. Stanford: Stanford University Press, 2009.

Sampson, Lisa. *Pastoral Drama in Early Modern Italy: The Making of a New Genre*. London, Legenda, 2006.

Sannia Nowé, Laura. "Epifanie e metamorfosi della clemenza nella letteratura drammaturgica del Settecento." In *La cultura fra Sei e Settecento*, edited by Elena Sala di Felice and Laura Sannia Nowé, 171–96. Modena: Mucchi, 1994.

Santangelo, Giovanni Saverio, and Claudio Vinti. *Le traduzioni italiane del Teatro comico francese nei secoli XVII e XVIII*. Rome: Edizioni di Storia e Letteratura, 1981.

Santovetti, Francesca. "Arcadia a Roma Anno Domini 1690: academia e vizi di forma." *Modern Language Notes* 112, no. 1 (1997): 21–37.

Sartori, Claudio. *I libretti italiani a stampa dalle origini al 1800: Catalogo analitico con 16 indici*. 7 vols. Cuneo: Bertola & Locatelli editori, 1990–4.

Sauval, Henri. *Histoire et recherches des antiquités de la ville de Paris*. Tome II, Livre Septième. Paris: Charles Moette and Jacques Chardon, 1724.

Savoia, Francesca. "Una storia tutta da raccontare: Luisa Bergalli Gozzi." In *Essays In Honor of Marga Cottino-Jones*, edited by Laura Sanguineti White, 109-22. Fiesole: Edizioni Cadmo, 2003.

Schein, Seth L. "Tyranny and Fear in Aeschylus's *Oresteia* and Shakespeare's *Macbeth*." In *Comparative Drama* 52, no. 1 (Spring 2018): 85–102.

Schelling, F.W.J. *The Unconditional in Human Knowledge: Four Early Essays (1794–1796)*. Translated by Fritz Marti. Lewisburg: Bucknell University Press, 1980.

– *The Philosophy of Art*. Edited and translated by Douglas W. Scott. Foreword by David Simpson. Minneapolis: University of Minnesota Press, 1989.

Schierle, Ingrid. "Patriotism and Emotions: Love of the Fatherland in Catherinian Russia." *Ab Imperio* 3 (2009): 65–93.

Schiller, Friedrich. "Theatre Considered as a Moral Institution." In *Friedrich Schiller: Poet of Freedom*, translated by William F. Wertz, 209–20. New York: Benjamin Franklin House, 1985.

– *Werke*, Vol. 20. *Unter Mitwirkung von Helmut Koopmann; herausgegeben von Benno von Wiese*. Weimar: Bohlaus, 2001.

Schlegel, August Wilhelm von. *Vorlesungen über dramatische Kunst und Literatur*. Edited by Eduard Böcking. Hildesheim: Olms, 1971.

Schneider, Ben Ross. *The London Stage, 1660–1800*. Carbondale: Southern Illinois University Press, 1979.

Schneider, Federico. *Pastoral Drama and Healing in Early Modern Italy*. Farnham: Ashgate, 2010.

Schneider, Magnus Tessing. "A Song of Other Times: The Transformation of Ossian in Calzabigi's and Morandi's *Comala* (1774/1780)." *LIR.journal* 11 (2019): 24–47.

– "From Metastasio to Mazzolà: Clemency and Pity in *La clemenza di Tito*." In *Mozart's* La clemenza di Tito: *A Reappraisal*, edited by Magnus Tessing Schneider and Ruth Tatlow, 56–96. Stockholm: Stockholm University Press, 2018.

– "Legacy of an Anti-Patriot: Calzabigi's *Elvira* in Naples, 1794." In *Stage / Page / Play: Interdisciplinary Approaches to Theatre and Theatricality*, edited by Anna Lawaetz and Ulla Kallenbach, 37–54. Copenhagen: Multivers, 2016.

– "The Judgement of Rousseau: *Paride ed Elena* by Gluck and Calzabigi (Vienna, 1770)." In *Rousseau on Stage: Playwright, Musician, Spectator*, edited by Maria Gullstam and Michael O'Dea, 255–84. Oxford: Voltaire Foundation, 2017.

Sébastiani, Florence. "La musique dans l'*Andromède* de Pierre Corneille (1650): L'usage, le goût et la raison." *Littératures classiques* 21 (1994): 195–205.

Selfridge-Field, Eleanor. *A New Chronology of Venetian Opera and Related Genres 1660-1760*. Stanford: Stanford University Press, 2007.

Selmi, Elisabetta. *"Classici e Moderni" nel'officina del* Pastor Fido. Turin: Edizioni dell'Orso 2001.

Seneca. *Tragedies*. Translated by Frank Justus Miller. Loeb Classical Library. Cambridge: Harvard University Press, 1979.

Shakespeare, William. *Hamlet*. Edited by Ann Thompson and Neil Taylor. The Arden Shakespeare. Third series. London: Bloomsbury, 2016.

Shuger, Debora. *Habits of Thought in the Renaissance: Religion, Politics, and the Dominant Culture*. Berkeley: University of California Press, 1990.

Sidonius. *Poems and Letters*. Vol. 1, edited and translated by W.B. Anderson. Cambridge MA: Harvard University Press, 1963.

Silk, M.S., and J.P. Stern. *Nietzsche on Tragedy*. Cambridge: Cambridge University Press, 1981.

Skinner, Quentin. *From Humanism to Hobbes: Studies in Rhetoric and Politics*. Cambridge: Cambridge University Press, 2018.

– "The Origins of the Calvinist Theory of Revolution." In *After the Reformation: Essays in Honour of J. H. Hexter*, edited by Barbara Malament, 309–30. Manchester: Manchester University Press, 1980.

Smith, Ayana. *Dreaming with Open Eyes: Opera, Aesthetics, and Perception in Arcadian Rome*. Berkeley: University of California Press, 2019.

Smith, D. Nichol, ed. *Eighteenth-Century Essays on Shakespeare*. 2nd ed. Oxford: Clarendon Press, 1963.

Snell, Bruno. "Aristophanes und die Ästhetik." In *Die Entdeckung des Geistes: Studien zur Entstehung des europäischen Denkens bei den Griechen*, 11–26. Hamburg: Claassen & Goverts, 1946.

Sozzi, Lionello. *Da Metastasio a Leopardi: Armonie e dissonanze letterarie italofrancesi*. Florence: Olschki, 2007.

Spagna, Arcangelo. "Discorso intorni a gli'oratorii." In *Oratorii, overo Melodrammi sacri*, Vol 1. Rome: Gio. Francesco Buagni, 1706; reprinted by Johann Herczog, *Musurgiana* 25, Lucca: Libreria Musicale Italiana, 1993.

Stackhous, Thomas. *The English Particles rendered into Classical Latin, according to their various significations for the use of the schools*. London: Cornish, 1772.

Staël, Anne Louise Germaine de. *Corinne ou l'Italie*. Edited by Simone Balayé. Paris: Gallimard, 1985.

Staffieri, Gloria. *Colligite fragmenta: la vita musicale romana negli "Avvisi Marescotti" (1683–1707)*. Lucca: Libreria Musicale Italiana Editrice, 1990.

Stählin, Jacob von. "Izvestiia o muzyke v Rossii." In *Muzyka i balet v Rossii*, translated by B.I. Zagurskii, 49–143. Leningrad: Muzykal'noe izdatel'stvo, 1935.

Stanford, W.B. *Greek Tragedy and the Emotions: An Introductory Study*. London: Routledge and Kegan Paul, 1983.

Stanton, Domna C. "The Ideal of 'repos' in Seventeenth-Century French Literature." *L'Esprit Créateur* 15 (1975): 79–104.

Stein, Louise K. *Songs of Mortals, Dialogues of the Gods: Music and Theatre in Seventeenth-Century Spain*. Oxford: Oxford University Press, 1993.

Stephen, Ruth. "A Note on Christina and her Academies." In *Queen Christina of Sweden: Documents and Studies*, edited by M. von Platen, 365–71. Stockholm: P.A. Norstedf and Söner, 1966.

Stewart, Pamela D. "Eroine della dissimulazione. Il Teatro di Luisa Bergalli." *Quaderni Veneti* 19 (1994): 73–92.

– "Luisa Bergalli." In *Italian Women Writers: A Bio-biliographical Sourcebook*, edited by Rinaldina Russell. Westport: Greenwood Press, 1994.

Strachey, Lytton. *Books and Characters, French and English*. New York: Harcourt, Brace and Company, 1922.

Strohm, Reinhard. "Ancient Tragedy in Opera, and the Operatic Debut of *Oedipus the King*." In *Ancient Drama in Music for the Modern Stage*, edited by Peter Brown and Suzana Ograjenšek, 165–70. Oxford: Oxford University Press, 2010.

– *Dramma per musica. Italian Opera Seria of the Eighteenth Century*. New Haven: Yale University Press, 1997.

– "Handel's Pasticci." In *Essays on Handel & Italian Opera*, 164–211. Cambridge: Cambridge University Press, 1985.

– [Untitled review of] *Oreste: Opera in tre atti*, by Georg Friedrich Händel, Bernd Baselt. *Notes* 49, no. 2 (1992): 788–90.

Strunk, Oliver, ed. *Source Readings in Music History*. Rev. ed. Gen. ed. Leo Treitler. New York: W.W. Norton, 1998.

Sumarokov, Aleksandr. *Slovo na den koronovaniia Eia Velichestva Imperatritsy Ekateriny II*. In *Polnoe sobranie vsekh sochinenii, v stihakh i proze*, 2: 229–38. Moscow: Universitetskaia tipografiia u N. Novikova, 1787.

Summo, Faustino. *Discorsi poetici*. Padua: Bolzetta, Francesco, 1600.

Talbot, Michael. "Girò [Tessieri], Anna." *Grove Music Online*. 2001; Accessed 14 Jun. 2022. https://www.oxfordmusiconline.com /grovemusic/view/10.1093/gmo/9781561592630.001.0001 /omo-9781561592630-e-0000040662.

Tamburini, Elena. *Due teatri per il Principe. Studi sulla committenza teatrale di Lorenzo Onofrio Colonna (1659–1689)*. Rome: Bulzoni, 1997.

– *Gian Lorenzo Bernini e il teatro dell'arte*. Florence: Le Lettere, 2012.

– "Guitti, Buonamici, Mariani, les Vigarani: Scénographes italiens en voyage à travers l'Europe." In *Les Lieux du spectacle dans l'Europe du XVIIe siècle*, edited by Charles Mazouer, 189–206. Tübingen: Gunter Narr, "Biblio 17," 2006.

Tcharos, Stefanie. *Opera's Orbit: Musical Drama and the Influence of Opera in Arcadian Rome*. Cambridge: Cambridge University Press, 2011.

The Tatler. 4 vols. London, 1789.

Thomas, Downing A. *Aesthetics of Opera in the Ancien Régime, 1647–1785*. Cambridge: Cambridge University Press, 2002.

– "Baroque Opera." In *Oxford Handbook of the Baroque*, edited by John D. Lyons, 370–85. Oxford: Oxford University Press, 2018.

– "Lyric Heroes." In *Héroïsme et Lumières*, edited by Sylvain Menant and Robert Morrissey, 65–85. Paris: Champion, 2010.

Tiedge, Faun Tanenbaum. "Porta, Giovanni." *Grove Music Online*. 2001; Accessed 14 Jun. 2022. https://www.oxfordmusiconline.com/grovemusic /view/10.1093/gmo/9781561592630.001.0001/omo-9781561592630 -e-0000041168.

Tiersot, Julien. "Gluck and the Encyclopædists." Translated by Theodore Baker. *Musical Quarterly* 16 (1930): 336–57.

Tilg, Stefan. "Jesuit Tragedy. An Underestimated Stage of Enlightenment Discourse." In *Shadows of the Enlightenment. Tragic Drama during Europe's Age of Reason*, edited by Blair Hoxby, 192–212. Colombus: The Ohio State University Press, 2022.

Timms, Colin. "Orlandi, Chiara." *Grove Music Online. Oxford Music Online. December 1, 1992*.

Trousson, Raymond. Introduction to *Œuvres Complètes de Voltaire*. Vol. 18C. Oxford: Voltaire Foundation, 2008.

Trousson, Raymond, and Jeroom Vercruysse, ed. *Dictionnaire général de Voltaire*. Paris: Honoré Champion, 2003.

Tufano, Lucio. *I viaggi di Orfeo: Musiche e musicisti intorno a Ranieri Calzabigi*. Rome: Edicampus, 2012.

Turchetti, Mario. *Tyrannie et tyrannicide de l'Antiquité à nos jours*. Paris: Garnier, 2013.

Van Nifterik, Gustaaf. "Lex princeps legibus solutus abrogata." *Fundamina* 20 (2014): 973–81.

Vencato, Anna. *Drammi musicali per i comici del S. Samuele*. Curated by Anna Vencato. Venice: Marsilio, 2009.

Vernant, Jean-Pierre and Pierre Vidal-Naquet. *Myth and Tragedy in Ancient Greece*. Translated by Janet Lloyd. New York: Zone Books, 1990.

Vescovo, PierMario. "Guardando Verso la Scena. Il Teatro Comico: Una Lettura." *Studi Goldoniani*, 2012.

Veselovskii, Iurii. "Ideinyi dramaturg ekaterininskoi epokhi: Kniazhnin i ego tragedii." In *Literaturnie ocherki*, 394–79. Moscow: Typo-litografia A.V. Vasil'eva, 1900.

Vettori, Piero. *Petri Victorii Commentarii, In primvum librvm Aristotelis de arte poetarum*. Florence: In officina Iuntarv, Bernardi Filiorum, 1576.

Visé, Donneau de. *Sujet des Amours de Vénus et d'Adonis, tragédie en machines, représentée sur le Théâtre Royal du Marais le 2 mars 1670*. Paris: Pierre Promé, 1670.

Visentin, Hélène. "Au cœur d'une mutation socio-politique et esthétique de l'art dramatique en France: le théâtre à machines à la Cour et à la Ville (1630–1650)." In *Rome-Paris, 1640: Transferts culturels et renaissance d'une centre artistique*, edited by Marc Bayard, 509–20. Rome and Paris: Académie de France à Rome-Villa Médicis and Somogy Editions d'Art, 2010.

– "Le 'dessein' de la pièce à machines: un cas particulier d'inscription du texte spectaculaire." *Texte* 33/34 (2003): 139–65.

– "Le théâtre à machines: succès majeur pour un genre mineur." *Littératures Classiques* 51 (2004): 20–2.

– "Machine Plays." In *The Oxford Handbook of the Baroque*, edited by John D. Lyons, 386–408. Oxford: Oxford University Press, 2019.

Voltaire, François Marie Arouet de. *Correspondance. Janvier 1749–Décembre 1757*. Edited by Theodore Besterman. Paris: Gallimard, 1975.

– *Œuvres Complètes de Voltaire*. Edited by Theodore Besterman et. al. 102 vols. Geneva: Institut et Musée Voltaire; Oxford: Voltaire Foundation, 1968–2020.

– *Sémiramis*. Amsterdam: Ledet, 1750.

Wagner, Richard. *Richard Wagner's Prose Works*. Translated by William Ashton Ellis. 2nd ed. 8 vols. London: Kegan Paul, Trench, Trübner & Co., 1895–9.

Wasserman, Earl. "The Pleasures of Tragedy," *ELH* 14 (1947): 283–307.

Webb, Daniel. *Observations on the Correspondence Between Poetry and Music.* London, 1769.

Weinberg, Bernard. *A History of Literary Criticism in the Italian Renaissance.* 2 vols. Chicago: University of Chicago Press, 1963.

– ed. *Trattati di poetica e retorica del cinquecento.* 4 vols. Bari: Gius. Laterzi & Figli, 1970–4.

Weiss, Piero. *Opera: A History in Documents.* New York: Oxford University Press, 2002.

– "Teorie drammatiche a 'infranciosamento'. Motivi della 'riforma' melodrammatica nel primo Settecento." In *Antonio Vivaldi. Teatro musicale, cultura e società.* Vol. 2, edited by Lorenzo Bianconi and Giovanni Morelli. Florence: Olschki, 1982.

Weiss, Piero, and Piero Jacopo Martello. "Pier Martello on Opera (1715): An Annotated Translation." *The Musical Quarterly* 66 (1980): 378–403.

White, Harry. "If It's Baroque, Don't Fix It: Reflections on Lydia Goehr's 'Work-Concept' and the Historical Integrity of Musical Composition." *Acta Musicologica* 69, no. 1 (1997): 94–104.

Whittaker, Cynthia Hyla. "Chosen by 'All the Russian People': The Idea of an Elected Monarch in Eighteenth-Century Russia." *Acta Slavica Iaponica* 18 (2001): 1–18.

– *Russian Monarchy: Eighteenth-Century Rulers and Writers in Political Dialogue.* DeKalb, IL: Northern Illinois University Press, 2003.

Wilamowitz-Moellendorff, Ulrich von. *Zukunftsphilologie!: eine Erwidrung auf Friedrich Nietzsches "Geburt der Tragödie."* Berlin: Borntraeger, 1872.

Williston, Byron, and André Gombay, eds. *Passion and Virtue in Descartes.* New York: Humanity Books, 2003.

Winnington-Ingram, R.P. *Euripides and Dionysus: An Interpretation of the Bacchae.* Cambridge: Cambridge University Press, 1948.

– "The Danaid Trilogy of Aeschylus." *Journal of Hellenic Studies* 81 (1961): 141–52.

Wirtschaftler, Elise Kimerling. *The Play of Ideas in The Russian Enlightenment Theater.* DeKalb, IL: Northern Illinois University Press, 2003.

Wood, Caroline. *Music and drama in the tragédie en musique, 1673–1715: Jean-Baptiste Lully and His Successors.* New York: Garland Pub., 1996.

Wood, Caroline, and Graham Sadler. *French Baroque Opera: A Reader.* Aldershot, Hants, U.K.: Ashgate, 2000.

Wortman, Richard. *The Development of a Russian Legal Consciousness.* Chicago: University of Chicago Press, 2010.

Wortman, Richard. "The Representation of Dynasty and 'Fundamental Laws' in the Evolution of Russian Monarchy." In *Russian Monarchy: Representation and Rule. Collected Articles,* 33–73. Boston: Academic Studies Press, 2013.

Wright, Thomas. *The Passions of the Minde in General* [1601]. Edited by William Webster Newbold. New York: Garland, 1986.

Wyduckel, Dieter. *Princeps legibus solutus. Eine Untersuchung zur frühmodernen Rechts-und Staatslehre.* Berlin: Dunker & Humboldt, 1979.

Zeno, Apostolo. *Alessandro Severo drama per musica.* Venice: Marino Rossetti, 1717.

– *Ifigenia in Aulide. Dramma per musica.* Venice: Domenico Lovisa, 1718.

– *La Merope drama per musica.* Bologna: Rossi e compagni, 1717.

– *Lettere di Apostolo Zeno Cittadino veneziano istorico e poeta cesareo.* 5 vols. Venice: Pietro Valvasense, 1752.

– *Statira drama per musica.* Venice: Marino Rossetti, 1705.

Zhivov, Viktor. "Pervye russkie literaturnye biograrafii kak sotsial'noe iavlenie: Trediakovskii, Lomonosov, Sumarokov." *Novoe literaturnoe obozrenie* 25 (1997): 24–83.

Zinar, Ruth. "The Use of Greek Tragedy in the History of Opera." *Current Musicology* 12 (1971): 80–94.

Zorzi, Marino. "La stampa, la circolazione del libro." In *Storia di Venezia, dalle origini alla caduta della Serenissima*, 8: 801–60. Rome: Istituto dell'Enciclopedia Italiana, 1991–8.

Zucchi, Enrico. "Metastasio e Calzabigi all'origine dei cori alfieriani. Note su Alfieri lettore della tradizione corale italiana." *Testo* 66 (2013): 77–91.

– "Sovrani temperanti e tiranni lascivi: allegorie della felicità pubblica e privata da Gravina a Metastasio." In *Allegoria e teatro tra Cinque e Settecento: da principio compositivo a strumento esegetico*, edited by Elisabetta Selmi and Enrico Zucchi, 295–313. Bologna: I Libri di Emil, 2016.

– "Suddito o giudice? Il contributo della tragedia italiana del Settecento alla definizione del concetto di 'popolo'." *Intersezioni. Rivista di storia delle idee* 36, no. 3 (2016): 343–62.

– "Tirannide e stato di natura. Sul rifiuto dell'assolutismo giusnaturalista nelle *Tragedie Cinque* di Gian Vincenzo Gravina." In *Prima e dopo il Leviatano*, edited by Merio Scattola and Paolo Scotton, 193–226. Padua: Cleup, 2014.

Contributors

Blair Hoxby is Professor of English at Stanford University. He is the author of *Mammon's Music: Literature and Economics in the Age of Milton* (2002) and *What Was Tragedy? Theory and the Early Modern Canon* (2015). He is the co-editor of *Milton in the Long Restoration* (2016) and the editor of *Shadows of the Enlightenment: Tragic Drama during Europe's Age of Reason* (2022).

Robert C. Ketterer is Professor of Classics at University of Iowa. He is the author of *Ancient Rome in Early Opera* (2009) as well as articles on classical drama and early opera. Recent titles include "Helpings from the Great Banquets of Epic: Handel's *Teseo* and *Arianna in Creta*" (in B. Forment, *(Dis)embodying Myths*, 2012) and "*Skene*, Image and Altar in Euripides's *Iphigenia in Tauris*" (in Liapis and Harrison, *Brill Companion to the Greek and Roman Theater*, 2013). Ketterer has served as Vice President of the American Handel Society and has received grants and fellowships from the Newberry Library and the Delmas Foundation.

Tatiana Korneeva, PhD (2008) in Classics, Scuola Normale Superiore di Pisa, has published extensively on seventeenth- and eighteenth-century Italian theatre and its cultural and comparative contexts. She is the author of *The Dramaturgy of the Spectator: Italian Theatre and the Public Sphere, 1600–1800* (2019) and *To the Court of the Tsarinas and Back Again: Italian Performers' Itineraries, Careers, and Networks across Europe* (2023). She currently holds an appointment at the Norwegian University of Science and Technology. Her interests include early modern political thought, the reception of classical tradition, the history of theatre in comparative perspective, and opera studies.

Pervinca Rista holds a PhD in Comparative Literature from the Johns Hopkins University, as well as four post-graduate degrees in violin performance from the Peabody Conservatory of Music and the Conservatorio Benedetto Marcello di Venezia. In 2016 she was awarded a prestigious Marie Sklodowlska Curie Individual Fellowship from the European Commission for her project "GoldOPERA," a study of the connections between theatre and music in the works of Carlo Goldoni. Pervinca has published articles in both Italian and English class-A journals, and her monograph, *At the Origins of Classical Opera*, was published by Peter Lang in 2018. Pervinca has shared her research results through public outreach in partnership with the Musei Civici Veneziani (Goldoni all'Opera). She has also led a "double life" as a professional musician, and continues to perform throughout Italy, where she now resides, as concertmaster and principal section leader.

Francesca Savoia is Professor of Italian at the University of Pittsburgh. Her areas of research and personal interest are: seventeenth-, eighteenth-, and early-nineteenth-century Italian literature and cultural history, theatre, and opera. Most recently, she edited a volume of essays on Italian letter writing (*Favellar ai lontani: Tipologie epistolari fra Sette e Ottocento*, 2015), published a collection of previously unknown letters of Giuseppe Baretti (*Il Baretti vostro*, 2013), and wrote a monograph on the same author: *Fra letterati e galantuomini* (2010).

Magnus Tessing Schneider, a theatre scholar specializing in Shakespeare and Italian opera, is currently a postdoctoral fellow within the research project Artistic Exchanges: The Royal Danish Theatre and Europe at Aarhus University. His monograph, *The Original Portrayal of Don Giovanni: An Original Mozart Performer and His Role*, was published by Routledge in 2021. He has published on Mozart, Monteverdi, and Calzabigi, including articles on the latter's librettos for Gluck's *Paride ed Elena*, Paisiello's *Elvira*, and Morandi's *Comala*.

Stefanie Tcharos is an Associate Professor of Musicology at University of California, Santa Barbara, whose research focuses on the critical history of opera and related vocal traditions, theories of genre, historiography, and cultural history. She has published articles, reviews, and book chapters on seventeenth- and eighteenth-century opera and the serenata, and is the author of *Opera's Orbit: Musical Drama and the Influence of Opera in Arcadian Rome* (Cambridge, 2011). She has co-directed the Center for the Interdisciplinary Study of Music at UCSB, and is currently co-editor of *Cambridge Opera Journal*.

Downing A. Thomas is Professor of French and Associate Provost and Dean of International Programs at the University of Iowa. In 2005, Thomas was named Chevalier dans l'Ordre des Palmes académiques (Knight in the Order of Academic Palms) by the French government. In 2007, Thomas was elected President of the Association of Departments of Foreign Language. In 2013, he was named Honorary Professor at Hebei Normal University. He has published *Music and the Origins of Language* and *Aesthetics of Opera in the Ancien Régime: 1647–1785*, and numerous articles and chapters in edited volumes.

Hélène Visentin is Professor of French Studies at Smith College. Her research specializes in early modern literature and culture, with a focus on the history and the aesthetics of the performing arts, and the relationships between art and power. She is the author of two critical editions of seventeenth-century plays: Chapoton, *La Descente d'Orphée aux Enfers, tragédie* (1640) (Rennes: Presses Universitaires de Rennes, 2004) and Rotrou, *Les Sosies, comédie* (1638) (Paris: S.T.F.M., 2005). She is also the co-author of two edited volumes: *L'Invraisemblance du Pouvoir. Mises en scène de la souveraineté au XVIIe siècle en France* (Paris: Presses de l'Université Paris-Sorbonne/Schena Editore, 2005) and *French Ceremonial Entries in the Sixteenth-Century: Event, Image, Text* (Toronto: C.R.S.S., 2007). She is currently involved in a digital humanities project on the seventeenth-century novel *La Princesse de Clèves* by Lafayette.

Enrico Zucchi obtained his PhD from the University of Padova in 2017. His research interests focus on seventeenth- and eighteenth-century European theatre. Recently he published editions of Giovan Mario Crescimbeni's *La bellezza della volgar poesia* (2018), and Pietro Calepio's *Paragone della poesia tragica d'Italia con quella di Francia* (2017). He also contributes to the research project Historiographie théâtrale comparée à l'époque moderne, directed by the Université Sorbonne – Paris IV, where he was Visiting Junior Scholar in 2016.

Index